THE TWO HORIZONS NEW TESTAMENT COMMENTARY

JOEL B. GREEN and MAX TURNER, *General Editors*

Two features distinguish THE TWO HORIZONS NEW TESTAMENT COMMENTARY series: theological exegesis and theological reflection.

Exegesis since the Reformation era and especially in the past two hundred years emphasized careful attention to philology, grammar, syntax, and concerns of a historical nature. More recently, commentary has expanded to include social-scientific, political, or canonical questions and more.

Without slighting the significance of those sorts of questions, scholars in THE TWO HORIZONS NEW TESTAMENT COMMENTARY locate their primary interests on theological readings of texts, past and present. The result is a paragraph-by-paragraph engagement with the text that is deliberately theological in focus.

Theological reflection in THE TWO HORIZONS NEW TESTAMENT COMMENTARY takes many forms, including locating each New Testament book in relation to the whole of Scripture — asking what the biblical book contributes to biblical theology — and in conversation with constructive theology of today. How commentators engage in the work of theological reflection will differ from book to book, depending on their particular theological tradition and how they perceive the work of biblical theology and theological hermeneutics. This heterogeneity derives as well from the relative infancy of the project of theological interpretation of Scripture in modern times and from the challenge of grappling with a book's message in Greco-Roman antiquity, in the canon of Scripture and history of interpretation, and for life in the admittedly diverse Western world at the beginning of the twenty-first century.

THE TWO HORIZONS NEW TESTAMENT COMMENTARY is written primarily for students, pastors, and other Christian leaders .... ige in theological interpretation of Scriptui

Colossians and Philemon

Marianne Meye Thompson

WILLIAM B. EERDMANS PUBLISHING COMPANY
GRAND RAPIDS, MICHIGAN / CAMBRIDGE, U.K.

© 2005 Wm. B. Eerdmans Publishing Co.

Wm. B. Eerdmans Publishing Co.
255 Jefferson Ave. S.E., Grand Rapids, Michigan 49503 /
P.O. Box 163, Cambridge CB3 9PU U.K.

Printed in the United States of America

10 09 08 07 06 05   7 6 5 4 3 2 1

Library of Congress Cataloging-in-Publication Data

Thompson, Marianne Meye.
    Colossians and Philemon / Marianne Meye Thompson.
        p.   cm.   — (The two horizons New Testament commentary)
    Includes bibliographical references (p.   ).
    ISBN-10 0-8028-2715-2 / ISBN-13 978-0-8028-2715-9 (pbk.: alk. paper)
        1. Bible. N.T. Colossians — Commentaries.
    2. Bible. N.T. Philemon — Commentaries.   I. Title.   II. Series.

BS2715.53.T46   2005
227'.7077 — dc22

                                                2005044587

www.eerdmans.com

To Richard J. Mouw
and in memory of
Robert A. Guelich
and
Donald H. Juel
friends, colleagues, and mentors

Contents

Abbreviations

ABD	*Anchor Bible Dictionary*
ACCSNT	*Ancient Christian Commentary on Scripture: New Testament*
Adv. Haer.	Irenaeus, *Adversus Haereses*
Ag. Ap.	Josephus, *Against Apion*
Ant.	Josephus, *Antiquities of the Jews*
CBQ	*Catholic Biblical Quarterly*
CCSL	Corpus Christianorum: Series Latina
CSEL	*Corpus Scriptorum Ecclesiasticorum Latinorum*
HTR	*Harvard Theological Review*
IJST	*International Journal of Systematic Theology*
JSNTSup	Journal for the Study of the New Testament Supplement Series
JTS	*Journal of Theological Studies*
KJV	King James Version
LCC	Library of Christian Classics
LXX	Septuagint
MT	Masoretic Text
NICNT	New International Commentary on the New Testament
NIGTC	New International Greek Testament Commentary
NIV	New International Version
NPNF	Nicene and Post-Nicene Fathers
NRSV	New Revised Standard Version
NT	New Testament
NTS	*New Testament Studies*
OT	Old Testament
RSV	Revised Standard Version
SBLDS	Society of Biblical Literature Dissertation Series
SNTSMS	Society for New Testament Studies Monograph Series

TEV	Today's English Version
WMANT	Wissenschaftliche Monographien zum Alten und Neuen Testament
WUNT	Wissenschaftliche Untersuchungen zum Neuen Testament
ZNW	*Zeitschrift für die neutestamentliche Wissenschaft*

Introduction to Colossians

Colossians has traditionally been grouped with the so-called "prison" or "captivity" epistles of Paul — Ephesians, Philippians, Colossians, and Philemon — because, like these other epistles, it refers specifically to Paul's chains or imprisonment or his status as a prisoner (Eph 3:1; 4:1; 6:20; Phil 1:7, 13, 14, 17; Col 4:3, 10, 18; Phlm 1, 9, 10, 13, 23). In some ways Colossians has been overshadowed by these other letters. Ephesians, for example, overlaps with Colossians at a number of points but tends to offer more fully developed versions of similar themes, and appears initially to be directed less to a specific occasion. Dubbed "the crown of Paulinism" (C. H. Dodd) and "the quintessence of Paulinism" (F. F. Bruce),[1] Ephesians sums up a number of Pauline themes, but Colossians lacks the same epitomizing style and pithy theological formulation. As one of the undisputed Pauline epistles, Philippians, with its famous hymn (2:5-11), autobiographical account of Paul's early days "in Judaism" (3:3-9), and references to righteousness under the law (3:6-14), has played an important role in discussions of Paul's life and theology. Even Philemon, the shortest of Paul's letters, has evoked two full-length monographs purporting to use this brief letter as an entree to Paul's world or theology.[2]

But if less ink has been spilled over Colossians, it is certainly not because it contains less material of value for understanding the development of early Christian theology or for a glimpse of some of the troubles besetting a first-century Christian congregation. In terms of theological substance, the "Christ-hymn" (1:15-20) rivals that of Philippians in its vision of the

1. C. H. Dodd, "Ephesians," in *The Abingdon Bible Commentary* (ed. F. C. Eiselen, E. Lewis, and D. G. Downey; New York: Doubleday, 1929), 1224-25. Bruce, *Paul: Apostle of the Heart Set Free*, 424, quoting A. S. Peake.

2. Burtchaell, *Philemon's Problem*, and Peterson, *Rediscovering Paul*, are two such monographs. See now, however, Walsh and Keesmat, *Colossians Remixed*.

preexistent Christ; there is rich material on the Christian life, particularly as it relates growth and maturity to knowledge and Christian conduct; the significance of the cross of Christ is developed with striking metaphors; and there is subtle probing of Christian spirituality as located in a (physical) body. As John Barclay puts it, Colossians offers a "comprehensive vision of truth — cosmic and human, spiritual and material, divine and mundane."[3] Therein lies the fundamental contribution of this letter. Yet a number of questions concerning basic introductory matters, such as the authorship, date, and occasion of the letter, continue to be explored.

Colossians as a Pauline Epistle

Many of the issues regarding the place of Paul's imprisonment and the date of the letter to the Colossians are relevant also to Philemon, for it has often been assumed that both were written about the same time, to the same Christian congregation, and in the course of the same imprisonment. But for many scholars, the prior question is whether Paul should be considered the author of this letter at all and, hence, whether the assumption that Philemon and Colossians were written under the same circumstances can hold.

In a nutshell, the kinds of challenges to Pauline authorship of letters such as 1 Timothy and Ephesians are brought to bear on Colossians as well, and we may rehearse them briefly. First, or so it is alleged, the vocabulary and style are not typical of the "undisputed Paulines" (e.g., Romans, 1 and 2 Corinthians, Galatians, and Philippians). But distinctive vocabulary cannot rule definitively against Pauline authorship, especially since the situation addressed in any letter to some degree determines the vocabulary used in that letter.[4]

Colossians also differs from certain undisputed Paulines in other ways. Gone are the sharp polemics, the rapid-fire series of biting questions (Rom 3:27–4:1; 6:1-3; 7:7; 8:31-35; 1 Cor 3:3-5; Gal 3:1-5), and the direct and pointed appeals to the readers such as "O foolish Galatians!" (3:1), "Already you are filled! Already you have become rich! Without us you have become kings!" (1 Cor 4:8), and "We have spoken freely to you Corinthians!" (2 Cor 6:11). In Colossians Paul's ire is not aroused as it is in these other epistles, and the tone

---

3. Barclay, *Colossians*, 77.

4. Beker's proposal that Paul's theology has a "coherent center" with "contingent" expression in various letters might suggest that differences in vocabulary in the various Pauline letters are a weak argument against Pauline authorship. Beker, *Paul the Apostle*, 11-19.

and style he adopts here pale in fervor when compared to Galatians or Corinthians. Such differences might be explained if the issues treated in the other epistles were of greater magnitude in Paul's eyes than those dealt with in Colossians. And yet, that is scarcely the case. In Colossians, the significance of the person of Christ and the sufficiency of his death on the cross for Christian faith and conduct are at stake. It is hard to imagine that Paul thought the issues were of lesser importance than those troubling the Galatians or other churches founded in the course of his mission.

In part, differences in style and tone can be explained by Paul's closer personal connections to the congregations of Galatia and Corinth: he had personally labored to establish the congregations there, as he had not at Colossae. The gospel was first proclaimed to the Colossians by Epaphras, whom Paul labels "our beloved fellow servant" and characterizes as one who "faithfully serves Christ on our behalf" (Col 1:7). While Paul understands his authority as apostle to the Gentiles to extend to this church, which one of his coworkers labored to found, his lack of personal familiarity with the Colossians may account for at least some of the softened rhetoric when compared, for example, with Galatians or Corinthians. Still, Paul had never visited the Roman congregation either, and yet his rhetorical strategies there are more like those of Galatians and the Corinthian correspondence than like Colossians.

There are also curious theological differences between Colossians and some of Paul's other letters. Lacking are treatments of justification or the Law, the role of the Spirit, and the overarching eschatological framework that is foundational to Pauline thought. Some of these absences can and should be explained by the simple observation that these issues were not problematic among the Christians of Colossae. But certain issues which have arisen in these congregations have indeed been treated by Paul — and very differently — in other places. Colossians spends a fair amount of space on the shape of Christian conduct, noting the virtues that are to characterize the believer in Christ. But whereas Romans, 1 and 2 Corinthians, and Galatians place Christian life squarely under the rubric of "the Spirit" or "fruits of the Spirit," Colossians devotes virtually no space to the role of the Spirit. The problem is not that Colossians fails to treat a typically Pauline theme, but that Colossians fails to treat this theme in a typically Pauline manner. It is simply impossible to imagine the Paul of Romans or Galatians offering a portrait of the Christian life without recourse to the agency of the Spirit; and yet that seems to be precisely what happens in Colossians.

These are some of the reasons for doubting that Colossians represents the spirit and substance of Paul's thought as Galatians and 1 Corinthians are taken to do. But in spite of the difficulties, there are scholars who continue to hold that Colossians was written by Paul, and I have tried to indicate briefly why some of the main objections cannot carry the weight sometimes assigned to them. In order to further account for the differences in style and tone, some interpreters appeal to coauthorship (with Timothy; see 1:1) in order to explain the differences, while still others assign the letter to a later student of Paul's or to someone who wrote in the Pauline tradition.[5] The question of authorship matters little to those interested first and foremost in interpreting the letter as it stands, without recourse to theoretical reconstructions of its origins and context. Such an approach has the advantage of allowing interpreters to focus on thematic, literary, or theological matters, and to steer clear of hypothetical accounts of the readers or their situation. But such an approach also unnecessarily severs this ancient communication from its historical moorings. Whatever we know — or don't know — of Paul or the Colossians, they were persons in specific contexts, struggling to understand, articulate, and live their faith in the diverse contexts of the first-century world. It matters, minimally, that we remember and encounter Paul and this congregation as brothers and sisters in Christ and not simply as literary constructs.

Who wrote this letter also matters a great deal to those interested in characterizing Pauline theology, the development of christological and theological thinking in the early church, the character of early controversies, and so on. In the present commentary, I will refer to the author of the letter as Paul because I believe that, in spite of the difficulties, the letter can still best be explained as written or authorized by Paul during his own lifetime. The decision for Pauline authorship has ramifications for a project such as this, which focuses its attention at the intersection of historical, exegetical, and theological concerns. Were the letter not by Paul, and could we confidently date it to the post-Pauline period, then we might also be able to sketch the development of the Pauline tradition. If the letter is assumed to be written by Paul, then it is easy to want to solve exegetical problems by appeal to other Pauline letters, or to treatments of similar themes elsewhere. While in interpreting any letter within the context of Paul's thought there will always be movement between the whole (Pauline theology) and the part (Colossians), we will endeavor to hear Paul's distinctive voice in Colossians before rushing in to fill the silences and close the gaps by too facile an appeal to other letters.

---

5. Inasmuch as I have nothing particularly new to add to the discussion of authorship, I refer the reader to the discussions in the commentaries. For Pauline authorship, see O'Brien, *Colossians, Philemon*, xli-xlix; for Timothy as coauthor, see Wall, *Colossians and Philemon*, 15-16, and Dunn, *Colossians*, 35-39; and for the case for pseudonymity, see Lincoln, "The Letter to the Colossians," and Lohse, *Colossians*, 84-91.

Moreover, we must be wary of over-confidently assuming that the letter is — or is not — written by Paul, as if we can simply gloss over any challenges in interpretation on that basis. At the same time, it can be useful to draw connections to other Pauline letters to show the continuity of thought between them and Colossians.

The Setting of the Letter in Paul's Circumstances

One of the reasons for accepting the authenticity of Colossians is that it overlaps at crucial points with the letter to Philemon. Both come from Paul and Timothy (1:1). The circumstances of imprisonment are similar (Col 4:3; Phlm 1, 13). The letters close with almost identical lists of personal greetings (Col 4:10-14, Aristarchus, Mark, Epaphras, Luke, and Demas; Philemon 23-24). If Colossians is pseudonymous, one must assume that the author has taken these details from Philemon and woven them into the fabric of the letter.[6]

Two things in particular provide the occasion for writing Colossians: First, Paul had received reports about the church, probably from Epaphras (1:7; but see Phlm 23), and wished to respond to them. Second, Paul is sending Onesimus to Philemon (Col 4:8-9; Phlm 12-13) in the hope of effecting reconciliation between them. Both letters may have been carried by Tychicus (Col 4:7-8), although the lack of reference to Tychicus in Philemon has raised some questions against this hypothesis. Given the greeting to Philemon, Apphia, and Archippus and "the church that meets in your house" in Philemon (Phlm 1-2), we may imagine that Philemon was also an important member, or leader, of the congregation of Christians in Colossae. Paul thus uses the occasion to send Onesimus and two letters to fellow Christians at Colossae.

The location of Paul's imprisonment remains equally difficult to determine. Three suggestions have been advanced. (1) Traditionally, the "prison epistles" have been located in Paul's imprisonment in Rome in the early 60s. However, some have argued that the distances involved, especially between Colossae and Ephesus on the one hand and Rome on the other hand, would render slow and difficult the kind of communication and travel suggested by these letters. Yet the various letters in the NT, as well as from other early Christian authors, suggest that such communication was both desirable and possible. Outside the NT, for example, we have the lengthy late-first-century letter

---

6. On the significance of such details for placing the letter in Paul's own lifetime, see the pointed questions in Dunn, *Colossians,* 37, who concludes that Paul gave Timothy a fair degree of license to formulate the letter as he saw fit.

usually called *1 Clement,* written by the church at Rome to the church at Corinth regarding problems that had arisen in the Corinthian congregation. Ignatius similarly wrote multiple letters to various Christian congregations in the early second century. Clearly letters carried by personal messenger were the primary means by which Christians maintained contact with each other in this period. (2) Some interpreters have proposed a date of composition in the mid-50s, during an assumed imprisonment in Ephesus. Such an imprisonment would have to be inferred from oblique allusions in Paul's letters to struggles during his time in Ephesus (1 Cor 15:32; 2 Cor 1:8-9; 6:5; 11:23-24). (3) A third possibility puts the writing of Colossians in the late 50s, during Paul's imprisonment at Caesarea Maritime (Acts 23:35; 24:26-27). One might note here the interesting, but not complete, overlap between the names of co-workers in Colossians and those who accompanied Paul, particularly as he journeyed towards Jerusalem and subsequent detention in Caesarea (Aristarchus, Acts 19:29; 20:4; 27:2; Timothy and Tychicus, 20:4; see also Acts 12:12, 25; 15:37, 39 for references to Mark; 4:36; 9:27–15:39 *passim* for Barnabas).

Not all the letters in which Paul speaks of himself as a prisoner need to have been written at the same time and from the same place although, as mentioned above, all are traditionally placed during Paul's Roman imprisonment toward the end of his life. It has been proposed that Paul's changed circumstances and age can account for the theological and stylistic differences from the undisputed letters — although Philippians belongs among the captivity epistles as well, and there have been few if any challenges to the authenticity of this letter based on its theological and stylistic differences from the "undisputed" Paulines. Undoubtedly we must allow for personal circumstances to have shaped the Apostle's thought and style; but such matters are indeed tricky to investigate, and we are reduced to speculation and conjecture about how Paul had "changed" in his outlook, theology, style, or general demeanor to account for the differences of Colossians from other letters attributed to Paul.

The Situation at Colossae

What, then, of the specific circumstances that caused Paul to write to the Colossian Christians? It is not easy to reconstruct the situation of the church that Paul addresses, since Paul does not specifically spell it out. Furthermore, since he had received his reports secondhand and had never visited the church, it is difficult to know how detailed and exact Paul's knowledge of the situation in Colossae was and to what extent his comments and exhortations are directed toward specific problems or issues. The key passage for determining the situation in the church at Colossae is 2:8-23, where Paul attacks a set of practices and rules that he deems inappropriate and wrong-headed. Sometimes called the "Colossian philosophy" or "teaching," this set of beliefs placed an emphasis on following certain rules and regulations, apparently promising new and greater depths of spiritual experience and insight. These rules and regulations demanded the observation of certain feasts and holy days ("festivals, new moons, or sabbaths," v. 16), recommended certain ecstatic spiritual experiences (v. 18), and urged fasting, self-denial, abstention from certain foods, and even abuse ("harsh treatment") of one's body and promised some greater "wisdom" (vv. 21-23).

The position taken in this commentary is that the Colossians are being influenced by Jews or, perhaps better, Jewish Christians, who advocated certain ascetic practices and ecstatic spiritual experiences in order to attain to "higher levels" of understanding the mysteries of God.[7] References to "festivals, new moons, or Sabbaths" appear in OT summaries of some of Israel's distinctive practices (1 Chr 23:31; Hos 2:11; Ezek 45:17). The warnings, "Do not handle! do not taste! do not touch!" could be taken as summaries of various food and purity laws of the OT. Similarly, for example, the *Letter of Aristeas,* typically dated in the second century BCE, contains the following explanation of the strictures of Torah: "Therefore lest we should be corrupted by any abomination, or our lives be perverted by evil communications, [God] hedged us round on all sides by rules of purity, affecting alike what we eat, or drink, or touch, or hear, or see" (142).

There is also ample evidence from early Judaism and Christianity of a strong interest in angels. For example, some scholars think that the Melchizedek of the Dead Sea Scrolls is the archangel Michael, and that the Songs of the Sabbath Sacrifice refer to participation in angelic worship of God. There are traditions of first-century Judaism that developed the statement in Exod 23:21 regarding the angel of the presence of God, who bore the name of God. Taking that statement quite literally, *3 Enoch* 12:5 speaks of the angel Metatron as "the lesser Yahweh." According to various Jewish texts, the Law was thought to have been mediated through angels (see Philo, *On Dreams* 1.141-43; Gal 3:19; Heb 2:2; Hermas, *Similitudes* 8.3.3). The book of Hebrews takes pains to show that Jesus is not an angel and, indeed, is set above the angels and so is worthy of worship (1:5-14). In Revelation, John the seer is caught up to heaven to witness the worship of the heavenly beings

---

7. For the view that the primary source of the teaching Paul combats is Judaism, see especially Dunn, *Colossians,* 29-35; Wright, *Colossians,* 24-29; Bockmuehl, *Revelation and Mystery,* 178-81.

around the throne of God and is warned against worshiping angels (Rev 19:10; 22:9). Justin Martyr, a second-century Christian author, does call Jesus an angel (*Dialogue* 34.2) and speaks of the OT appearances of the "angel of the Lord" as the appearances of the Logos of God. One need not look far beyond the seedbed of Judaism, or Jewish Christianity, to find parallels to the practices and beliefs against which Paul warns in Colossians.[8]

Furthermore, the pagan religious and cultural soil, with its belief in the hidden mysteries and the possibility of multiple initiations into them, proved fertile for the growth of views regarding the attainment of greater wisdom and knowledge. One can find in pagan literature of the time expectations that a religious adherent of the "mysteries" might well be expected to fast and engage in rigorous practices of self-denial, as well as observing festivals, as part of attaining to various religious experiences. For example, the *Metamorphoses,* also called *The Golden Ass,* written by Apuleius, portrays the trials of a would-be devotee of Isis, named Lucius. As he approaches initiation into the cult, Lucius is required to fast, abstain from certain foods and strong drink, engage in multiple ritual washings, and purchase new garments. Not long after his first initiation, a second initiation into the cult of Osiris and then yet a third initiatory rite are required of him.

One might well suppose that the Colossians found it difficult to grasp that the promise of the gospel lay precisely in the sufficiency of Christ and what he had done on their behalf and that while growth in knowledge and wisdom was desirable and possible, such growth did not entail probing further the hidden "mysteries" of God. By emphasizing the completion of God's plan in Christ and the fullness of revelation in him, Paul reminds the Colossians that these sorts of religious practices, superficially evidence of sincerity and devotion, are based on the mistaken premise that God has yet more to offer than has already been granted in Christ. Paul borrows language from both synagogue and pagan culture to underscore the revelation of the mystery that in Christ, "the fullness of deity dwelled bodily."

In making this point, Paul further counters one of the key aspects of this Colossian "philosophy" that, at the same time, remains most elusive to precise delineation. He refers to thrones, dominions, rulers, and authorities that are "seen and unseen" (1:13, 16; 2:10, 15), to angels (2:18), and to "elements" (2:8, 20), sometimes translated "elemental spirits," and speaks cryptically of "angelic worship" (2:18). From such references it has been concluded that this "Colossian philosophy" assumed the existence of intermediary be-

---

8. So Bockmuehl, *Revelation and Mystery,* 180, speaks of the "hodge-podge of practices (some conventional, some heterodox, some mystical) encountered in the local synagogue."

ings who were hostile to humans. These various spirits had to be placated, and the ascetic practices were intended to ward off their powers and influence. But on virtually every point, this reconstruction goes beyond what the letter actually says.[9] The data in Colossians can also be explained by reference to the interest in angels evident in Jewish and early Christian texts, and by Paul's desire to underscore the revelatory and redemptive significance and cosmic scope of Christ's work (2:12-15). And the "principalities and powers" are probably not to be equated with the "angels" referred to in 2:18.

Paul reminds the Colossians that in light of Christ's role in creation and his reconciling death on the cross the powers of the world are ultimately impotent. Nothing further need be done to secure the longed-for knowledge of God and understanding of the mystery of God. But the Colossians may have simply misinterpreted the Christian vocabulary of knowledge, maturity, and growth, succumbing to the belief — still popular today! — that there is some gimmick, some experience, some secret that will unlock greater depths of insight than have heretofore been attained. Paul reminds his readers that all wisdom and knowledge are hidden in Christ and that the treasures that are in him are theirs. God's gracious initiative has provided what they need. Their task is not to look elsewhere for this hidden wisdom but to look to what they have been taught already and to sink their roots deep into their very ground of being, Christ himself.

The Theological Contribution of Colossians

Colossians gives us a taste of Paul's gospel precisely when it is *not* being formulated in terms of justification by faith, in direct relationship to Torah and Judaism, or in the categories seen in Galatians and Romans. I do not mean to imply that the Colossians had received no instruction in such fundamental matters or that these concerns were no longer of significance to Paul, but simply that in this epistle Paul articulates his understanding of the gracious work of God in Christ in different terms. Because these terms are not those most typically thought to characterize Pauline thought, such as justification by faith, some commentators not only doubt Pauline authorship but also regard Colossians as an attenuation of the "purer" Pauline formulation of the gospel.[10]

9. For a fuller discussion of the issues surrounding the "principalities and powers" in Colossians, see the excursus following the discussion of 1:15-20 (pp. 36-39).

10. Ernst Käsemann is most notably associated with the critique of any formulation of the gospel that does not give pride of place to justification by faith. Where NT documents emphasize the role of the authoritative teachers, the importance of guarding doctrine, or the

It has sometimes been claimed that in Colossians "protology" has usurped the place of "eschatology," that is, the "first things" of creation have taken over the role assigned to the "final things" of the ultimate redemption of the cosmos. The tension between the "already" and "not yet" so characteristic of Paul's thought elsewhere has allegedly disappeared in Colossians, being replaced by a duality of what is "above," in the heavenly realms, which those in Christ now enjoy, and what is "below." This would suggest a movement in the direction of a theology of the created order, and such theology generally derives its impulse less from the future redemption and more from the present order of the world. In short, the eschatological framework of Paul's thought, articulated with such power in other letters and providing the ultimate hope for salvation, has been supplanted by a dualism of the heavenly and earthly realms. And to a large extent believers enjoy the blessings of the heavenly realm. Since they are "raised with Christ," believers are therefore to "seek the things above, where Christ is, seated at the right hand of God" (3:1). There is no straining for what lies ahead, no groaning of creation for redemption: God's blessings are available in the present time.

Two things may be said in response to these observations. First, while a case for the loss of future hope in Colossians can be made, it fails to persuade. Like other Pauline epistles, the triad of faith, hope, and love shapes the way in which Paul articulates Christian belief and conduct (1:4-6). Hope for what is yet to come plays an important role in Colossians, functioning to undergird a number of Paul's admonitions to the Colossians. Early on Paul speaks of "the hope laid up for you in heaven" (1:5), of "the hope of the gospel" (1:23), equating that hope with "the hope of glory" (1:27). Paul further reinterprets this "hope of glory" with a promise that when Christ "appears" then believers will be found with him "in glory." While Paul can certainly speak of the present glory of God revealed in Christ (2 Cor 4:6) and even state that believers have been "glorified" (Rom 8:30), he also refers glory to future hope (Rom 8:20-21; 2 Cor 4:17). To speak of a dissipation of future hope in Colossians surely misses a fundamental emphasis of the letter.

Second, Colossians lacks the explicit contrast between "this age" and the "age to come." The eschatological framework has been reformulated into a cosmic framework with a concomitant contrast between creation and renewal in Christ. "*All things* are made through him and for him" (1:16); "*all things* hold together in him" (1:17); and by his death he has reconciled *all*

---

church as the guardian of truth, Käsemann (and others) have argued that the early church's sense of the gracious initiative of God in Christ has given way to dogmatic formulation and church structure. These trends have been pejoratively labeled "early catholicism."

things (1:20). Christ is God's agent in creating, sustaining, and redeeming the cosmos. Alluding to the creation of human beings in the image of God (Gen 1:26-27), Paul speaks of a "renewal" of creation in the image of the creator (3:10-11). The renewal of all things will be marked by the "appearing" of Christ, whom Paul speaks of as "our life." That is, even as in Christ God gave life to the world, so also God now gives life to the world and will renew the world in Christ. The individual believer's life belongs within the cosmic work of God for all the world. What God will do for the world on a cosmic scale, God does for the church corporately and for the believer individually. Colossians frames the Christian hope in different terms: but it remains the same hope for the transformation of all created life.

In his discussion of the theology of Colossians, John Barclay notes that it is "at every point Christological, and it is the success of the author in disclosing Christ as the centre of all reality that integrates and energizes the letter."[11] One can scarcely allege that Christ is any less the center of reality in Romans, Galatians, or Philippians. But in part because of the brevity of Colossians and its resolute focus on the person and work of Christ, its christological center is all the more apparent. Of course the great "hymn" of 1:15-20 advances the claims of the christological center of Colossians. As we have already pointed out, and will do so repeatedly in the commentary and discussion of the epistle, Christ is the agent of God's work of creating, sustaining, and redeeming the world. Christ is the head of the cosmos, of every created thing (1:15-16), and of his own body, the church (1:18), and the ground of faith, hope, and love for the believer (1:27; 2:6-8). If Paul speaks in Galatians of Christ "who lives in me" (Gal 2:20), in Colossians he formulates the claim to encompass the entire universe. Christ is the life not only of the believer and of the church (3:1-4), but of the whole world.

Colossians underscores the supremacy and preeminence of Christ in that the one who died on the cross to reconcile all things is none other than the one through whom God created and sustains the world. As the title of one recent book has it, it is "not the cross, but the crucified" who accomplishes our salvation.[12] Although Christians talk, sing, and theologize about the cross, that is always only a shorthand way of referring to Jesus' death on the cross — and no epistle makes it more clear than Colossians that it is not the cross itself but the death of the one who is the head of all power and authority that effects the purposes of God. The cross is the locus of Christ's triumph over the powers (2:13-15). It is, therefore, no surprise that the argument of

---

11. Barclay, *Colossians*, 77.
12. Mertens, *Not the Cross, but the Crucified.*

Colossians moves from the Christ-hymn with its celebration of Christ's pre-eminence over the powers to an explication of the significance of the death of Jesus, in whom "the fullness of God was pleased to dwell," "making peace through the blood of his cross" (1:19-20).

In keeping with the emphases of the epistle on creation and reconciliation, Paul unpacks the meaning of Christ's death in primarily non-juridical categories. The death of Jesus brings redemption and forgiveness (1:13-14; 2:13-14), the pacification of those hostile to God (1:20-22), inclusion of all people in the family of God (1:12, 21-22; 2:11-13), and the granting of new life (2:12-13; 3:1-3). In the cross, one is "transferred" from the realm of darkness to the kingdom of God's beloved son, so that one participates in the reality of life, in Christ himself. "Participationist" terminology includes such aspects of Paul's thought as dying and rising with Christ, incorporation into the body of Christ, and union with Christ. These features of the argument of Colossians provide an entrée as well into Paul's understanding of the cross. Through the cross and resurrection of Christ, one participates in Christ in such a way that one receives the life that is his.

Finally, the epistle spends a good deal of space unpacking the implications of Christ's death for Christian conduct. Paul does not appeal here so much to the example of Christ as to the life expected of those who serve Christ the Lord and the realities of growth and maturity experienced in Christ. While as Lord Christ may command or expect particular sorts of conduct, nevertheless, the primary motivation for Christian behavior is not external regulations but identification with Christ in his self-giving death and resurrection to new life. So, for example, Paul speaks of being "buried with [Christ]" and "raised with him" (2:12; cf. vv. 13, 20), so that one currently lives a life "hidden with Christ" (3:3), anticipating the day when one appears with him in glory (3:4). Because one participates in the death and resurrection of Jesus, one is therefore to "put to death" the old way of life that is out of step with the new reality lived by and in Christ. In Christ, appropriate conduct is self-giving, directed toward the other, and colored by humility, graciousness, truth, and love. Christian behavior arises not from sheer human exertion but from allowing Christ's peace to govern conduct, and Christ's word to dwell within (3:15-16). The life of faithfulness is marked from beginning to end by its dependence upon Christ. Ultimately, such a way of life issues in gratitude, recognition of the gracious reality in which life is lived (3:17). Faith, hope, love, gratitude, humility, and graciousness: such are the measures of true spirituality.

Commentary on Colossians

1:1-2

1 Paul, by God's will an apostle of Christ Jesus, and Timothy, my dear brother:
2 To the saints in Colossae, those who are faithful, brothers and sisters in Christ:
May God our Father grant you grace and peace.

The openings of ancient letters were typically short and spare, identifying the author and recipients and including a single word of greeting. Greetings were sometimes elaborated by further descriptions of the recipient or the author. For example, in Acts the leaders of the early church send out a letter opening with rather full descriptions of author and recipients: "The brothers, both the apostles and elders, to the believers of Gentile origin in Antioch and Syria and Cilicia, greetings" (15:23). James identifies himself as a "servant of God and of the Lord Jesus Christ," writing to "the twelve tribes in the Dispersion" (Jas 1:1). Often such identifications of author or recipient provide clues to the purpose or content of the letter or to the relationship between author and reader. In this greeting, each description — of Paul, Timothy, and the Colossians — identifies these persons in some telling and important way.

Paul identifies himself as an apostle of Christ through God's will, indicating the origin of his apostleship. For Paul, to be an apostle — quite literally, one who is sent — meant that the risen Lord had encountered him and commissioned him to proclaim the Gospel. As his letters show, when his apostolic identity and commission were challenged, Paul insisted passionately on his commission to proclaim Christ as risen Lord (e.g., 1 Cor 9:1; Gal 1:12-16). Specifically, Paul was sent to the Gentiles (Rom 15:16; Gal. 1:16). Paul was commissioned *by* Christ to preach the news *about* Christ to those to whom Christ had not himself preached: the Gentiles (see Rom 15:8-9, 16; Matt 15:24). Paul's identification of himself as Christ's apostle sent particularly to the Gentiles permeates his letters. As we shall note later, this is part of what makes Paul Paul. The letter to the Colossians is itself an exercise of Paul's apostolic commission, for in it he reminds the Colossians of the content of the Gospel, and for Paul "apostle" and "Gospel" were simply two sides of one coin. For Paul, the apostolic commission *was* to proclaim the Gospel. The Pauline letters collected in the canon are part of the apostolic testimony to the Risen Christ.

Although Timothy is not designated as an apostle, he is at least the "cosender," if not in some way also the coauthor, of this letter, although this does not mean that we can simply explain all the distinctive aspects of this letter by assigning them to Timothy. Paul identifies Timothy both as "my dear brother," or fellow believer in Christ, and "fellow worker," referring to Timothy's labors alongside Paul. Paul's work was aided in myriads of ways by many coworkers, including Epaphras (1:7) and Tychicus (4:7) at Colossae. Elsewhere in the epistle, Paul describes them also as fellow workers, servants, or ministers (1:7; 4:7, 12-13). Paul often emphasizes his distinctive commission as an apostle, but the designation here lacks the polemical overtones it carries in other letters. But in all cases, Paul's reference to himself as apostle underscores the divine obligation laid upon him: "woe to me if I do not proclaim the gospel!" (1 Cor. 9:16).

There are three designations — "saints in Colossae," "those who are faithful," "brothers and sisters in Christ" — for the Colossian Christians. "Saints" marks them out as "set apart" for or dedicated to God, who transferred them into the divine realm of the "holy," where they belong to God in Christ (3:1-4) and consequently are to live lives worthy of that calling (3:5-10).[1] "Faithful" may indicate that some in the church have been *un*faithful, failing to walk firmly and resolutely in "the faith" (1:4, 23; 2:5, 7, 12). This would foreshadow the epistle's emphasis on the need for the Colossians to continue and be strengthened in the faith which they had been taught. Finally, the recipients are "brothers and sisters in Christ," a common familial designation in Paul and other early Christian literature for those who belong to the fellowship of Jesus' followers. In Christ they become brothers and sisters to each other, because through Christ they belong to God, "our Father," Paul's designation here for God.

Throughout the Old Testament, as well as in later Jewish literature, the ideal of harmony among brothers and the evil of sibling strife and rivalry are amply attested. One need only think of the pairs of brothers — Cain and

---

1. Moule, *Colossians and Philemon*, 4-5, takes "holy" as an adjective, which suggests the translation "holy and faithful brothers." See also 3:12, where "holy" is an adjective modifying "chosen ones."

Abel, Isaac and Ishmael, Jacob and Esau — or larger brotherhoods — Jacob's twelve sons — which are held up as tragic perversions of the ideal of brotherly affection and mutual obligation. By contrast, Ps 133:1 celebrates the goodness of brothers and sisters living together in harmony. A later Jewish document known as the *Testaments of the Twelve Patriarchs* purports to be the last words of the twelve sons of Jacob, and many of them warn of the dangers of competition, division and rivalry. Since the twelve sons of Jacob represent the twelve tribes of Israel, the message is clear: there are to be unity, mutual honoring, affection, and love among Israelites, as even among a family (e.g., *Testament of Joseph* 17:12; *Testament of Gad* 6:1-7), for all Jews are ultimately "brothers" (Tob 2:2; 2 Macc 1:1).[2] The early Christian letter called *1 Clement*, which was written about AD 95 by the church at Rome to the church at Corinth, notes the evils of schism — a problem of the church of Corinth in Paul's day that has apparently resurfaced — by recounting the biblical narratives of the conflicts between Cain and Abel, Jacob and Esau, Joseph and his brothers, Aaron, Miriam, and Moses, and so on (*1 Clement* 4:1-13).

One can find the ideal of brotherly affection documented in classical Greek literature and later Greco-Roman sources. As representative, one may cite the following statement of Plutarch, a first-century moralist:

> It is . . . of no slight importance to resist the spirit of contentiousness and jealousy among brothers when it first creeps in over trivial matters, practicing the art of making mutual concessions, of learning to take defeat, and of taking pleasure in indulging brothers rather than in winning victories over them.[3]

Not surprisingly, then, obligations to one's brothers and sisters, one's family in Christ, were primary also for early Christians. Their nuclear family was that of the family of Christ, and in their family they not only modeled the widely accepted virtues of "fraternal affection" and harmony, but did so because Jesus himself had called them to such self-giving love and modeled it in his life and death. More than once Jesus spoke of the ties of blood-relations being superseded by commitment to him. Jesus' "family" did not consist of his siblings and parents, but rather of all those who hear and do the word of God (Matt 12:46-50; Mark 3:31-35; Luke 8:19-21). Early Christians used terms

---

2. In an effort to avoid gender-specific language, modern translations often lose the family language, translating "Jews" instead of "brothers" or, in the New Testament, "believers" instead of "brothers."

3. *On Fraternal Affection* 17 = *Moralia* 488A. For a fuller discussion, with ample quotations, see deSilva, *Honor, Patronage, Kinship and Purity,* 157-97.

such as "brotherhood" (e.g., *adelphotēs*, 1 *Clement* 2:4; *philadelphia*, 1 *Clement* 47:5; 48:1) to indicate the unity and love of those who were "brothers and sisters."[4]

Not only did Jesus speak of his disciples as his "brothers and sisters," but he also noted that those in this family must be committed to it and to him more than to natural parents (Matt 10:37-38; Luke 14:25-33). Indeed God was now the common and one Father of all those who were Jesus' disciples (Matt 23:9). The idea that one's religious allegiances determined and even overrode all other allegiances can be found in various Jewish authors, such as Philo of Alexandria (20 BCE–50 CE), who wrote:

> But as for these kinships, as we call them, which have come down from our ancestors and are based on blood-relationship, or those derived from intermarriage or other similar causes, let them all be cast aside if they do not seek earnestly the same goal, namely, the honor of God, which is the indissoluble bond of all the affection which makes us one.[5]

In Philo, as in early Christian thinking, common religious allegiance bound its adherents not only to one and the same God but to each other. So also the community at Qumran, with its ideals for adherence to the sect, suggests a similar subordination of family and household ties for the sake of religious commitment, including commitment to a particular community. Among pagans, one may cite the Cynics, who held that the ideal philosopher was free from all worldly distractions brought about by the duties of family and home so that he could be "wholly devoted to the service of God" and to the universal family.[6] In other words, religious commitments entailed the subordination of family ties, but brought with them identification with and membership in a new community. Therefore, the idea that Christians are a new family in Christ with a different set of kin and new relationships was not novel in the ancient world. It matters all the more, therefore, how one names the particular family or community to which one belongs — what values, relationships, and commitments are part of this particular community? From whom does this community draw its identity? Whose character determines the shape of these relationships?

For Paul, it is God, as he is known in and through Christ, whose charac-

---

4. There is unfortunately no apt "inclusive" English translation for "brotherhood"; the term includes men and women.

5. *De Specialibus Legibus* 1.316. For a fuller discussion of similar passages in ancient literature and comparison to the Gospels, see Barton, *Discipleship and Family Ties.*

6. Epictetus, *Discourses* 3.22.69-72, quoting 69.

ter identifies and shapes the community of those who are brothers and sisters in Christ. Using the language of family, which is language that speaks of one's origins and identity, Paul speaks of God as "our Father." "Father" is a designation for God drawn from the OT, where God is said to be a father to Israel (e.g., Jer 3:4, 19; 31:9; cf. Hos 11:1). As Father, God calls Israel into existence, continues to care for it with mercy and compassion, and will redeem it from exile.[7] God is also father to the Davidic king (e.g., 2 Sam 7:14; Ps 2:7). This twofold usage continues in the NT, where God is said to be the Father of believers as well as of Jesus Christ. We see both in Colossians, where God is said to be "our Father" (1:2) and also "the Father of our Lord Jesus Christ (= the Messiah)" (1:3). Particularly in Romans and Galatians, Paul explains explicitly that it is by virtue of belonging to the Son and through the power of the Spirit that believers have been adopted into God's family and so may call upon God as "Abba, Father" (Rom 8:15-17; Gal 4:7). They now belong to God, and they do so because God has reconciled them and brought them into relationship with him and into the family that identifies itself in relationship to Christ (1:20-22). They also therefore belong to one another and have familial obligations to each other that cannot be set aside any more than a genetic relationship to another could somehow be abrogated.

Both the Nicene and Apostles' creeds speak of God as "the Father Almighty, Maker of heaven and earth." The English "Almighty" here renders the Greek *pantokratōr*[8] and the Latin *omnipotens*. The nuance of these two terms differs a bit, with the English being closer to the Latin, suggesting that God can do anything, that God has unlimited power. The Greek tends to have the sense of ruler, sovereign or governor, not so much the one who can do anything as the one who sovereignly governs the world. Thus it is closely related to the idea of God as Creator and is actually closer to the overall biblical picture of God as Father. The emphasis does not fall on God's capacity or power, but on God's faithfulness and sovereignty, thus echoing both the OT and NT pictures of God as a compassionate and trustworthy Father of his people. God's faithfulness is demonstrated above all in the gift of his beloved Son, through whom believers share in the inheritance that God grants (Col 1:12-13).

Paul further characterizes God as one who can be trusted to give grace and peace. The Greek word for grace *(charis)* adapts the typical Hellenistic "greeting" *(chairein)*, recasting it into a theologically freighted term that

---

7. For a fuller discussion see Thompson, *Promise of the Father.*

8. In the Pauline epistles, see 2 Cor 6:18; and then also the various references in Revelation (1:8; 4:8; 11:17; 15:3; 16:7, 14; 19:6, 15; 21:22).

points to God's gracious initiative in Christ. Paul not only greets the Colossians; he prays for them God's generous blessings. "Peace" reflects the typical Jewish greeting, "peace to you" or *shalom,* reflecting the words of the risen Christ to his disciples (Luke 24:36; John 20:21, 26). Through Christ, God has granted the Colossians both grace and peace.

In the first three verses of this letter, Paul refers to Jesus as "Christ Jesus" (1:1), "Christ" (1:2), and "Lord Jesus Christ" (1:3). Although Paul will use other designations for Jesus in this epistle, such as Lord (2:6; 3:17, 24), he most often simply refers to Jesus as *Christos,* the Greek translation of "Messiah." Although Paul does not mention Israel or the Jews specifically in this letter, it is doubtful that "Messiah" has lost all connotation for Paul of its original reference to God's anointed deliverer of Israel. Through Jesus the Messiah, God has now again brought deliverance from the enemies of his people, the powers that enslave them, so that they may be freed to serve the Lord and live together as reconciled people. The great mystery in which Paul rejoices is that the Gentiles, who were once estranged from God and his people, have now become part of the one people of God (1:21-23, 27). The Gentile Colossians have become "brothers and sisters" of a Jewish preacher — and they have done so by being united as followers of the Messiah of Israel, through whom God offers "grace and peace" to "every creature under heaven" (1:23). What God has done for Israel, God does for all the world.

1:3-8

3 We always give thanks to God, the Father of our Lord Jesus Christ, whenever we pray for you, 4 for we have heard of your steadfast faith in Christ Jesus and of the love that you have for all the saints. 5 Your faith and love come from the hope that is kept for you in heaven. You heard about this hope in the message of truth, the gospel, 6 that has come to you. Just as the gospel is bearing fruit and growing in all the world, so it is doing among you — and has been doing from the day you heard the gospel and came to know the grace of God in all its truth. 7 This is how you learned it from Epaphras, our beloved fellow servant, who faithfully serves Christ on our behalf. 8 He has told us of the love that the Spirit brings about in you.

Paul's report of his prayer for the Colossians presents Christian discipleship in terms of faith, hope, and love, a triad found elsewhere in Paul's letters (cf. 1 Cor 13:13; Gal 5:5-6; 1 Thess 1:3; 5:8; Rom 5:1-5). In Colossians, the emphasis falls on the hope which comes through Christ and which comprises the heart of the gospel. The gospel is conceived of both as a trustworthy message that the Colossians have heard and as the power to bring about and strengthen faith in Christ, love for others, and growth within individual Christians and the church. The Christian virtues of "faith" and "love" are not only responses to but also effects of the grace and power of the gospel of Christ. From the very beginning, Paul reminds his readers that their hope lies in what God has done for them in Christ and not in their own capacities or abilities — and certainly not in any other ceremonies, spiritual experiences, or other would-be powers or gods, features that are part of the "Colossian heresy" which has exerted its influence on the church. Their lives have now become part of the story of the gospel, God's gracious deliverance in Christ. Therefore, although they anticipate God's final consummation, they do not need something further or different to complete the gospel which they had received in faith.

Paul's letters typically begin with a thanksgiving, as was customary in ancient letters generally, but the use of a conventional form gives no reason to doubt his sincerity when he speaks of his thankfulness for the Colossians. Paul both models and urges the posture of thanksgiving (1:12; 3:15, 16), a posture of responsiveness and gratitude to God. In directing his prayer to "God, the Father of our Lord Jesus Christ," Paul acknowledges God as the source of the good gifts for which he is thankful. From God come the gospel, the truth, and the grace manifested in Jesus Christ and received by the Colossians. By speaking in the previous verse of God as the Father of those who are in Christ, and here as the Father of the Lord Jesus Christ, Paul makes it plain that there are both similarity and difference in the relationships between Jesus and God and between Jesus' followers and God. Both Jesus and believers belong to and find their identity in relationship to God. But that believers find themselves in relationship to God as Father *in Christ* means that it is through Christ and through his life, death, and resurrection that they find themselves related to God as Father. Jesus' relationship to God is, however, unmediated. God is the Father of "our Lord Jesus Christ," but believers know God as Father *in* Jesus Christ.

Paul's prayer begins with the recognition of the faith or faithfulness of the Colossians, a note that will be repeated throughout the letter as Paul urges his readers to remember the substance of the faith as they first heard it from Epaphras and not to fall prey to those who wish to add to or alter it (1:23; 2:5, 7, 19). "In Christ Jesus" designates the "sphere" in which believers live. The translation of πίστις/*pistis* ("faith") as "faithfulness" points to the steadfastness that ought to characterize Jesus' followers, and includes within it the nuance of trust or commitment as well. Paul alludes to the faithfulness that has characterized the discipleship of the Colossians, precisely because of the threat to the church posed by its misunderstanding of the gospel. He encour-

19

ages them to stay the course. For the present they need steadfast faith; such faith is produced by the sure hope they have in and for the future. Those who have no hope find perseverance difficult if not impossible, but hope makes the life of faith possible.

Hope can have either a subjective sense, referring to the act of hoping, to expectation, yearning, or desire, or it can have an objective sense, referring to what one hopes for (1 Thess 5:8; Gal 5:5; Rom 8:24-25). The descriptive phrase "kept for you in heaven" makes it clear that the second or objective sense is in view here. But otherwise the content of that hope is left unspecified. Later Paul writes of "the hope of the gospel which you heard, which has been preached to every creature under heaven" (1:23), qualifying that a few verses later as "Christ in you, the hope of glory" (1:27). In each case, "hope" has a forward-looking sense: it is what the gospel promises, what belongs to the reality of "glory," what is "kept for you in heaven." Such language easily leads to belief that all God's good gifts are to be gained someday, in the future. To be sure, Paul's language here and elsewhere suggests that the coming redeemed world cannot be fully fathomed in the present. But there is nevertheless continuity between what believers hope for and what they receive and enjoy in Christ in the present time.

At this point, Leander Keck helpfully speaks of *anticipation* and *participation* as two facets of Paul's understanding of salvation: those in Christ anticipate in hope the future blessings of salvation, but participate now through faith in the present blessings of salvation.[1] One of the particular concerns of this letter is to strengthen the believers' understanding of what is theirs by virtue of their belonging to Christ, and to connect that with all that they have been promised in the gospel. In Colossians, Paul draws the lines between the future hope and present faith as tautly as possible — which has led some commentators to argue that Paul lodges all God's blessings in the present and has abandoned or at least played down the hope for future transformation or realization of those blessings. But in this letter Paul combats the view that there is some greater hope to be experienced through visionary experiences and observance of certain regulations than that which is offered through and in Christ Jesus. Hence, the emphasis falls on present participation in the blessings offered through Christ. While "the "hope of glory" and what is

---

1. Keck, *Paul and His Letters,* 75-78. "Salvation" (σωτηρία/ *sōtēria*) and its various cognates are not actually used in Colossians. A variety of words, including words translated "rescue," "deliver," "forgive," "reconcile," and "make alive" are used to speak of what God has done in Christ. However, because "salvation" is both a common and general term in Christian vocabulary, it will serve us well in discussions of Colossians, so long as we do not presume to know its content before studying Colossians itself.

"kept for you in heaven" are future realities, what believers now have is a true foretaste of what will be theirs in fullness. What they participate in is an authentic foretaste of what they anticipate: the fulfillment of the promises of God's blessings and salvation.

Hope is the cause of the Colossian Christians' faith and love (1:4-5). Hope gives rise to faith; faith looks forward in hope. We see here some of the suppleness of Paul's thinking. Perhaps the most memorable instance of his use of "faith, hope, and love" is in 1 Corinthians 13, where he writes that, while faith, hope, and love abide, the greatest of them is love (v. 13). That is echoed when Paul exhorts the Colossians: "Above all, clothe yourselves with love" (3:14). He further characterizes Christian love as "love in the Spirit" or the "love that the Spirit brings about in you." Love expresses itself, as Paul says later in the letter, as "compassion, kindness, humility, meekness, and patience" (3:12). These traits, so contrary to the natural, grasping, self-seeking way of human beings (see 3:5-9), come about as the fruit of God's Spirit in the believer and the church.

But in Colossians hope takes center stage because the false teaching seems to hold out the promise of hope other than that lodged in God's work in Christ. Hope is also resolutely oriented toward the future, not because it denigrates the present but because in the present it experiences the foretaste of what is "kept for you in heaven." The hope of the Christian is not simply to "go to heaven" but to participate in the coming new world, the redeemed cosmos, which in some way already exists "in the heavens" (see also the new Jerusalem in Revelation 21). In the present, and in the sphere of Christ into which believers have been transferred and in which they and their relationships with others have been made new, they have a foretaste of that redeemed cosmos itself.

Although there is then continuity between present and future, eschatological hope can never be equated with progress, as though the world were simply running unimpeded on its course to ultimate perfection.[2] It is often said that the events of the twentieth century, especially the two cataclysmic world wars, sounded the death knell to a theology of "progress," to a belief that the situation of human beings is improving or can, through study, technology, and time, be expected to change steadily for the better, and that such change lies within human capacities and human control. But there is still ample evidence of belief in human ability to bring about utopia on earth. When such hopes fail to materialize, as they inevitably do, despair, nihilism, or simple resignation can easily take the place of optimistic aspirations of human

2. On the decline of modern secular hope, see Bauckham and Hart, *Hope against Hope*, 37.

progress. Perhaps ironically, Christian hope is utterly realistic about the human capacity for evil and the doubtful march of human progress, well aware that there is no guarantee that "things will get better." The book of Revelation, for example, testifies to the opposite expectation, and hope is aware of that possibility. Therefore, Christian hope has at its heart a trust in God's action for the salvation of the world. Put differently, progress focuses on what happens *in* this world, while hope focuses on what comes *to* this world from the transcendent realm where Christ now is.[3] This does not mean that there is no hope for this world, but rather that hope for this world does not come from within this world itself, but from the Creator who fashioned it, who sustains it, and who will re-create it.

In Paul's eschatological thought, the future — God's action for our salvation — has reached into the present, and it is this inbreaking of the revelation of God's glory, of the promises "kept for you in heaven," that gives hope in the present, hope that the situation of the world will be transformed, and that God has not abandoned the world to its own devices. To be sure, such hopes are finally justified only at the end of all things, when God's transforming work will ultimately be brought to fruition. Not without reason, "hope" typically falls under the rubric of eschatology, having to do with what one can hope for at the "end" of all things. But for Paul hope does not simply have to do with the end. It has also to do with the beginning of life in Christ, for such life always lives in and with the hope that the world does not determine its own course and that the death-dealing ways of the world are not the final word written over it.

1:9-14

9 So then from the day we first heard about you, we have not stopped praying for you, asking God to fill you with the knowledge of his will, by giving you all spiritual wisdom and understanding, 10 so that you may live in a manner worthy of the Lord, pleasing to him in every way: by bearing fruit in all kinds of good deeds, by increasing in your knowledge of God, 11 by being greatly strengthened by his glorious power for patience and endurance, and by joyfully 12 giving thanks to the Father who makes you fit to share in the inheritance that all the saints have in the light. 13 Indeed, the Father rescued us from the power of darkness and transferred us to the kingdom of his beloved Son, 14 through whom we have redemption, that is, the forgiveness of our sins.

3. Lincoln, "Colossians," 594.

In the previous section of the letter, Paul mentioned a number of things for which he was thankful, most notably that the gospel which the Colossians had heard and received had been bearing fruit and growing, producing among them faith, love, and hope. Now Paul turns from thanksgiving to petition, asking that the same power (v. 11) that had initially brought them out of the darkness of ignorance into the light of truth (vv. 13-14) would continue to strengthen them both to know and to do the will of God. What Paul had originally offered up in celebration and thanksgiving with respect to the Colossians, he now offers as a prayer on their behalf. And no doubt he anticipates being able to offer up continued prayers of thanksgiving and rejoicing that the gospel is continuing to work among the Colossians, strengthening and deepening their faith, love, and hope. In Paul's movement from thanksgiving to petition, as well as in the actual content of his prayer, we see also the integral connection between the gracious initiative and work of God among and through believers and the call to live in a manner that is "worthy of the Lord." Paul prays that God would fill the Colossians with knowledge of his will (v. 9) so that they might lead lives worthy of the Lord (v. 10) and thus grow in the knowledge of God (v. 10). Paul has not yet spoken directly about the troubles at Colossae, which clearly have to do with knowledge of the revealed mysteries of God. That is to say, there are in the congregation at Colossae some troubling ideas that there are yet further divine mysteries to be revealed or depths of esoteric knowledge to be plumbed. Paul reminds the Colossians of the knowledge and wisdom they have and, while he assumes that this knowledge can and must be deepened, this is not done by turning to some new revelation but by receiving the gift of God's wisdom and by faithful obedience to God's will.

Paul's prayer begins with the request that God would fill the Colossians with a "knowledge of his will by giving you all spiritual wisdom and understanding." In this formulation, there are clear echoes of virtues sought and lauded by Greco-Roman philosophers and moralists. In a discussion that influenced subsequent philosophical and moral discussions, Aristotle spoke of "wisdom, understanding, and prudence" (*sophia, synesis,* and *phronēsis*) as the highest virtues.[1] In this passage, Paul speaks of "wisdom" (σοφία/*sophia*) and "understanding" (σύνεσις/*synesis*), but his use of these words owes more to the OT and his heritage in Judaism, as two qualifying phrases make particularly clear. First, the knowledge that is desired is knowledge of God's will, and leads therefore to faithful conduct. Because the Colossian Christians are filled with wisdom, they are instructed to conduct themselves wisely (4:5).

---

1. *Nicomachean Ethics* 1.13.20.

Wisdom and insight issue in "all kinds of good deeds" (1:10). Second, the desired knowledge comes as a gift of God. This is indicated both by the passive verb (literally, "that you be filled with knowledge of his will"), and also by the adjective *spiritual (pneumatikos)*. Although Colossians seldom refers directly or explicitly to the work of the Holy Spirit, making it rather atypical of the Pauline correspondence, it is quite likely that the work of the divine Spirit is in view here.

There are striking parallels in, for example, the Dead Sea Scrolls, which, in dependence on the thought of the OT, stress that God grants all understanding (1QS 11.17-18; 3.15), reveals what is hidden, and makes his mysteries known, particularly to the community of the faithful at Qumran (those who preserved and produced the literature now known as the Dead Sea Scrolls). In the book of Wisdom, human understanding, wisdom, and knowledge come from the divine Spirit and lead to human conduct obedient to God's will. For example, "Who has learned your counsel unless you have given wisdom and sent your Holy Spirit from on high?" (Wis 9:17); "If the great Lord is willing, [the student of the Law] will be filled with the spirit of understanding; he will pour forth words of wisdom and give thanks to the Lord in prayer. He will direct his counsel and knowledge aright, and meditate on his secrets" (Sir 39:6-7). In Paul's letters we see the link between "Spirit" and "wisdom" most clearly in 1 Corinthians, where Paul contrasts human wisdom with the wisdom given by the Spirit of God (2:1-16).

The same point, though somewhat muted, is made here as well. God-given wisdom and insight grant a perspective from which one may grasp "a comprehensive vision of truth — cosmic and human, spiritual and material, divine and mundane — whose focal point is Christology."[2] Only the Spirit of God grants the insight to see in Christ the center of such a comprehensive vision of truth, for without the aid of the Spirit, one surely sees only a figure of the past, a teacher, a prophet — a failed one at that, for he was disowned by his own people and put to death by the real power of the time, Rome. But the Spirit of God removes the log in one's eye, that which impedes one from seeing God's truth. Without the aid of the Spirit, no one would dream up a comprehensive vision of truth whose "focal point" is Christ, crucified on a cross and raised to new life by God. Such a divinely given comprehensive vision of truth enables one to see, at least in part, the world from God's perspective, and so to live in harmony with the purposes of God. That such a vision of the world inevitably jars with the world's own understanding of truth and reality comes to its sharpest expression in the contrast of "darkness" and "light," rad-

2. Barclay, *Colossians,* 77.

ical opposites that speak of the Colossians' mode and sphere of existence before and after their conversion to Christ. For what they had once thought of as dark and incomprehensible was now to be seen as light; and what they had once thought of as light was now to be rejected as the path of darkness and death. This new perspective on one's past can be attained only once one has been transferred to the light: it is the light that enables one to see clearly.

And Paul does think of the Colossians as walking on a new and different path, using an idiom common to the Scriptures when he exhorts the Colossians to "live in a way worthy of the Lord." The Law is given, for example, so that God's people may "know the way in which they must walk and what they must do" (Exod 18:20). Elsewhere Paul speaks of living a life worthy of the gospel (Phil 1:27), of God (1 Thess 2:12), and of one's calling (Eph 4:1). But here — although not exclusively in Paul — the standard of conduct is the life, death, and resurrection of Jesus, whose authority is designated by the title "Lord" (cf. 3:24) but whose path is marked by humility and suffering (1:24). Because he is Lord, both the pattern of Jesus' life and his person serve as the measure of truth (2:6-8; 3:11), the pattern of conduct (3:1-3, 17), and, ultimately, the goal into which Christians grow in maturity (1:28). The particular shape of conduct that is "worthy of the Lord" is spelled out in four participial phrases which define the character of life that is pleasing to the Lord: (1) bearing fruit in good deeds, (2) growing in knowledge of God, (3) being strengthened for patience and endurance, and (4) joyfully giving thanks to the Father.

There is, first, a description of the concrete shape of Christian life as marked by "good deeds." The participle translated "bearing fruit" was applied earlier to the gospel itself (1:6), as was also the participle "growing" (or "increasing"), and both are now applied to Christian living. The power of the gospel encourages Christian discipleship and growth in the knowledge and understanding of God. The English translation of the third participial phrase, "being greatly strengthened by his glorious power," does not quite reproduce the nuance of the Greek, which quite literally would run "being empowered by the power of the might of God's glory." The piling up of synonyms for power, strength, and might again emphasizes the initiative of God, described in an abundance of phrases that underscore God's powerful work. Tellingly, this powerful work produces patience and endurance — virtues that are sometimes thought of as displaying an absence of power but are needed for facing trials, opposition, suffering, and even ordinary, day-to-day living.

The Christian life is to be characterized by joy and thanksgiving. Indeed, the thanksgiving is offered to "the Father who makes you fit to share in the inheritance that all the saints have in the light." It is thanksgiving for a divine gift, not a human achievement, a gift spoken of in terms of an "inheri-

25

tance" granted by the one whom the Colossians have now come to name as "Father." In Romans 8 and Galatians 4, Paul speaks of the adoption of Christians by God as heirs together with Jesus, the Son who inherits the promises of God. While in the OT "share" (also translated as "lot" or "portion") often refers to the inheritance of Israel in the promised land (Josh 19:9), the word also referred to one's participation in the salvation accomplished by God (e.g., LXX Ps 15:5). Here the thought is similar, for Paul speaks of the "inheritance" of the saints. Joined to the family that names the God of Israel as "Father," the Colossians are no longer a dispossessed people, but a people who belong to God and so share in the promises made to Israel. Their inheritance is the new kingdom of God's "beloved Son" (see also 1 Cor. 6:9-10; 15:50; Gal 5:21). In Christ, their past and their future have both been rewritten, and therefore their present can be marked by joy and thanksgiving.

This entire passage is brimming with terms for power and authority. Paul describes salvation as being delivered or rescued from "the power of darkness" to the "kingdom of [God's] beloved Son." The kingdom of God — here, the kingdom of God's Son — is not one of many competing kingdoms, as though it were one of several options one might elect. Indeed, in Daniel, the kingdom of God's people replaces all others and endures eternally (7:27); so also the "kingdom of our God and of his Christ" lasts forever (Rev. 11:15; 12:10; 19:6). The kingdom of God is different not only in duration but also in kind from human kingdoms. In Paul's writing, the "kingdom" can refer to the present reality of life in the Spirit (Col 1:13; Rom 14:17; 1 Cor 4:20) as well as to God's future act of salvation (1 Thess 2:12; 2 Tim 4:1, 18). In the present passage, God's kingdom or sovereign rule stands over against "the power of darkness." Paul writes here that in Christ God has "transferred" people from the oppressive power of darkness and evil to the liberating power, or kingdom, of the love and life offered through Christ.

Through the use of this powerful metaphor, Paul indicates what is at stake in God's granting of forgiveness: this is redemption, release from captivity, indicating that in Christ God has brought people out of the captivity and out from under the authority of sin, into freedom and the authority of Christ's reign. "Redemption" occurs several times in the Pauline literature (Rom 8:23; 1 Cor 1:30; Eph 4:30) and refers to liberation from imprisonment and bondage.[3] Augustine saw such deliverance prefigured in the exodus from Egypt: "Israel's own story illustrates this figure, when they were delivered from the

---

3. The idea, if not the word, is found in the OT (LXX) and in Jewish literature. In the Dead Sea Scrolls the community refers to itself as "the people whom God redeemed" (1QM 1.12; cf. 1QM 13.9).

power of the Egyptians and translated into the kingdom of the land of promise flowing with milk and honey, which signifies the sweetness of grace." In Christ, we "pass over" "from this tottering world to [Christ's] most solidly established kingdom."[4] As God delivered Israel from powers they could not overcome, so God delivers those in Christ from powers beyond their strength. Indeed, the Septuagint, the Greek translation of the Old Testament read by Greek-speaking Christians, uses the verb *errusato* ("he saved, rescued, delivered") to speak of God's rescuing Israel from the plague of the firstborn (Exod 12:27) and from the Egyptian soldiers at the shores of the sea (14:30). In Egypt and the exodus, God rescued his people from powers greater than they through the display of his own power. Through Christ, God has rescued people by overcoming the powers, not with a visible display of strength and destruction, but through the cross. Even as the Israelites were delivered from one master so that they might belong to and serve God alone, so the Colossians have been set free from the powers manifested in and as sin, estrangement, hostility, and alienation from God and others. The Colossians have been transferred to Christ's "most solidly established kingdom," to belong to and serve the one true God and to live in fellowship with the reconciled people of God.

1:15-20

15 He is the image of the unseen God, the firstborn of all creation; 16 for in him all things were created, in heaven and on earth, seen and unseen, whether thrones or dominions or rulers or authorities — all things have been created through him and for him. 17 He existed before all things, and in him all things hold together. 18 He is the head of the body, the church; he is the beginning, the firstborn of the dead, that in everything he might be preeminent. 19 For in him all the fullness of God was pleased to dwell, 20 and through him to reconcile to himself all things, whether on earth or in heaven, making peace by the blood of his cross.

Without doubt, this is one of the most memorable and influential passages in Colossians. It delineates the identity of Jesus Christ in relationship to God, creation, and the church, describing the way in which God's purposes for the world and humankind are brought to fruition through Christ. Densely packed with confessional language about the person and work of Christ, the passage is sometimes thought to be a hymn, or at least adapted from a hymn

---

4. Augustine, *On the Psalms* 77.30 (*NPNF* I, 8:377) and *Tractates on John* 55.1 (cited in *ACCSNT* 9:8).

in praise of Christ. Later in the letter Paul urges the Colossians to sing "psalms, hymns, and spiritual songs to God," and the present passage may be an example of an early Christian hymn. A letter from Pliny, governor of Bithynia in Asia Minor, to the emperor Trajan about the year 110 speaks of Christians singing hymns "to Christ as to a god" (*Letters* 10.96, 97), providing a glimpse into early Roman understanding of the Christian fellowship that stands in intriguing continuity with the NT. Whatever the source or form of the present passage, it contains a number of affirmations about Christ that lay the theological foundation for challenging the Colossian heresy. Specifically, the passage asserts the complete adequacy of God's revelation and salvation in Christ in order to show the futility of trying to gain a deeper understanding of or relationship to God through any other means. The hymn moves from creation through redemption, speaking of them separately but offering praise for God's work that begins in creation and anticipates the final reconciliation of all things. In its structure, it sets creation and redemption parallel to each other. Each has its focal point in Christ, who is the firstborn, agent, and goal of both creation and new creation.[1] Because Christ is the agent of creation, he is also the agent of the re-creation of the world. Here, then, in confessional terms and the language of praise we find testimony to the great drama of God's creation of the world and the promise of its final redemption. The God who made the world in Christ will redeem it through Christ, for God has not abandoned the cosmos and its inhabitants.

Of primary importance in this hymn and for understanding God's actions in the world is an understanding of who Jesus is in relationship to God. He is described as "the image of the unseen God" (v. 15) "in whom all the fullness of God was pleased to dwell" (v. 19). The Greek word for "image" (εἰκών/ *eikōn*) has the sense of something visible, and thus presents something of a puzzle to interpreters: how can that which is invisible be represented as or in an image?[2] But to say that Christ is the *image* of God means that, in some way, the unseen or invisible God becomes visible, moves into our sphere of sense perception, in the life of this human being.

Two strands of the biblical use of "image of God" are interwoven in this statement. First, it clearly echoes the assertion in Gen 1:27 that God created humankind "in the image of God" (LXX κατ᾽ εἰκόνα θεοῦ). Even as the image of God in Genesis is a human being, so too the image of God in Christ is a hu-

---

1. Lincoln, "Colossians," 570.

2. The church Fathers disagreed whether the "image" of the invisible God was itself invisible or visible and, hence, also whether it referred to the eternal relationship of the Father and Son or to the incarnate Son as the visible image of the invisible God. See *ACCSNT* 9:10-12 for selected quotations and the summary in Lightfoot, *Colossians*, 143-50.

man image, a human being. Later Paul writes that Christ is also the source of the renewal of humankind in that image (Col 3:10). Human beings, who are in biblical thought created in God's image, are now also re-created in Christ, who is the perfect image of God. Colin Gunton asks what it means to speak of Jesus as the image of God and answers: "First, that Jesus represents God to the creation in the way that the first human beings were called, but failed, to do; and second that he enables other human beings to achieve the directedness to God of which their fallenness has deprived them."[3] In other words, "Christ is not only *eikōn tou theou,* as was Adam, but also king over creation in a way vastly different from the first man."[4] This implies, in part, that Paul does not picture the re-creation of the world as a simple return to the way it was in Eden, but rather as the perfection of the world.

A second strand of the biblical background woven into the description of Christ as the "image of God" is ancient Israelite and Jewish speculation on the figure of "Wisdom," who emerges in the biblical book of Proverbs and later in the Apocryphal books of Sirach and Wisdom. Wisdom has a heavenly origin and dwelling (Proverbs 8; Sirach 24:1, 4; Wis 7:25) and a role in the creation of the world, subsequently descended to earth (Wisdom 9; Sir 24:3-17) and is uniquely embodied in the Torah given to Israel (Sir 24:7-12; Baruch 3:36-37; Wis 9:10; 4Q185 1.4, 10). As the mediator of God's instruction, Wisdom is the mediator of life and God's salvation. Furthermore, it is the reflection, mirror, and image of the working of God (Wis 7:25-26), a description which Colossians echoes in its description of Jesus Christ as "the image of the invisible God." But here the role of reflecting and imaging God and of bringing God the Creator to the world he has created is lodged in Christ. Hence to identify Christ as the "image" of God portrays the unique relationship of Christ to God. Through Christ, God can truly be known, inasmuch as Christ is the "image" of God.

Moreover, God can be known because his wisdom is *fully* embodied in Christ: "all the fullness of God dwells in him" (v. 19; "of God" is supplied to the present context from a similar assertion in 2:9). "All the fullness" echoes various biblical statements such as "The earth is the Lord and its fullness [all that is in it]" (Ps 24:1 [LXX 23:1]), thus asserting God's sovereignty over all the world, for "all its fullness" belongs to God. In Jeremiah, God asks, "Do I not fill heaven and earth?" (Jer 23:24). No part of the world is devoid of God's presence. Such language is echoed in Eph 1:23, which refers to the body of the church as "the fullness of the one who fills all in all." Somewhat more terse is

---

3. Gunton, *Christ and Creation,* 100.
4. Scroggs, *The Last Adam,* 97.

Paul's statement here: "all the fullness of God dwells in him." Here "the fullness of God" refers to the presence of God in Christ. In light of the situation at Colossae, that all the fullness of God dwells in Christ will serve to underscore the completeness of the knowledge that is made available through Christ. "To say that this fullness of God dwells in Christ, then, is most likely to mean that just as there is nothing in heaven or earth that is outside the divine presence and power, so also there is nothing outside the scope of Christ's presence and power, because Christ now sums up all that God is in interaction with the cosmos."[5]

Other statements in this passage focus on Christ's identity with respect to creation. These are not unrelated, of course, to the statements about Christ's identity with respect to God, since God is the one who "created the heaven and earth," and the affirmation of God as creator of the world plays a central role in both biblical and later Jewish conceptions of God.[6] E. P. Sanders suggested that "Judaism's most important single contribution to civilization"[7] was the conviction that the one God (εἷς ὁ θεός; Rom 3:30) is the Creator of the world. Colossians asserts that God's creation of the world was achieved through the agency of Christ and that he is, therefore, supreme over all the world, for all things are created through him (so also 1 Cor 8:6). Again, Paul — and other early Christians — borrow from Jewish wisdom traditions which spoke of God's wisdom as the means through which God created the world (Proverbs 8; Wisdom 7). By assigning to Jesus the role previously assigned to God's Wisdom, equated in some places with God's Torah or Law (e.g., Sirach 24:23), Paul has attributed to Jesus Christ the place in God's purposes elsewhere delegated to Wisdom or the Law. Paul has shifted the focus from God's creation through God's word or Wisdom to God's creation through Christ.

Not only did God create the world through Christ, but all things are continually sustained or held together in him as well. This statement also reflects certain wisdom traditions, and the wording is particularly close to Sir 43:26: ἐν λόγῳ αὐτοῦ σύγκειται τὰ πάντα (*en logō autou synkeitai ta panta*, "By his word all things hold together"). But here again the agent through which God holds the world together is not the Torah but Christ. The world is not part of God nor is God part of the world, but neither does the world exist independently of the sustaining power of God.

5. Lincoln, "Colossians," 599.

6. In his recent comprehensive study of devotion to Jesus in earliest Christianity, Hurtado notes two major themes in the monotheistic rhetoric of ancient Jews; one of these is "God's universal sovereignty as creator and ruler over all, even over the evil forces that oppose God" (*Lord Jesus Christ*, 36). On this point, see also Bauckham, *God Crucified*, 11.

7. Sanders, *Judaism: Practice and Belief*, 247.

To underscore that Christ is the integrating center of reality, Paul writes that all things were created *through him* and *for him.* Indeed, the three prepositional phrases — *through* him, *in* him, and *for* him — capture in three short strokes the totality of God's work in creating and redeeming the world.[8] A similar statement is found in the writings of Josephus, the first-century Jewish historian and apologist, who writes that God is "the beginning and middle and end of all things." But unlike Paul, Josephus notes that God had no agents, since he created the world "not with hands, not with toil, not with assistants, of whom he had no need" (*Ag. Ap.* 2.190-192; cf. *Ant.* 8.280). God alone caused the existence of all things — and there is no mediating agent. Employing the Greek philosophical categories of causation, another first-century Jewish author, Philo, wrote as follows about the various causes of creation: "That which comes into being is brought into being *through* an instrument, but *by* a cause. For to bring anything into being needs all these: the by which (τὸ ὑφ' οὗ), the from which (τὸ ἐξ οὗ), the through which (τὸ δι' οὗ), and the for which (τὸ δι' ὅ; *De Cherubim* 125-26). Such distinctions are echoed in the ways in which Paul speaks of God's work in creating the world in, through, and for Christ: not without Christ, and in organic unity with Christ. Later Irenaeus (ca. 180) would write that God created and re-created the world with "his own hands," namely, the Word and the Spirit. With this image, Irenaeus underscores both the unity of the Word and Spirit with the Father as well as their agency in creation and redemption: they are "the hands of the Father."[9]

That the world and everything in it were created in and through Christ and are held together in him means that there are no power structures, no rulers or authorities, which are independent of Christ's creating work and purposes. As the agent of God's creating work Christ has supremacy over all that is created, be they heavenly powers or the earthly rulers which seemed to triumph over him in the cross. Christ's supremacy is expressed in the epithet

---

8. In a famous article ("Christ as the Archē of Creation"), Burney offered the ingenious proposal that the so-called hymn in Col 1:15-20 reads the figure of Wisdom in Prov 8:22 in light of the opening statement of Gen 1:1, "In the beginning God created." Hebrew *rē'šît* can mean "beginning," "sum total," "head," and "firstfruits," and these meanings occur, he says, throughout Col 1:15-20. Similarly, the prepositions "through" *(dia)*, "in" *(en)*, and "for" *(eis)* develop three possible meanings of the Hebrew preposition *bᵉ* in the opening word of Genesis, *bᵉrē'šît*. For an accessible and concise summary of Burney's argument, see Lincoln, "Colossians," 604-5.

9. I am indebted to the late Colin Gunton for first calling this image to my attention and to Brian E. Daley, S.J., for supplying me with references (*Adv. Haer.* 4.7.4; 4.20.1; 5.1.3; 5.6.1; 5.28.4). For Irenaeus, however, God's wisdom is God's Spirit; hence, he speaks of "Word and Wisdom, Son and Spirit" (see *Adv. Haer.* 4.20.1).

firstborn of all creation (1:15), which is echoed later in the statement that he *was before all things* (v. 17). Although *firstborn* can refer to the order of birth, it also connotes the special status which was enjoyed by the firstborn son. Israel is spoken of as God's firstborn (Exod 4:22; Jer 31:9), meaning that Israel enjoys a special status as God's chosen and beloved people. In Psalm 89 the king of Israel cries out to God as Father, who establishes the king as "firstborn, the highest of the kings of the earth" (89:26-27). In other words, the designation of *firstborn* has as much to do with priority, status, and rank as it does with birth order, and that is the sense here, where Christ's supremacy as *firstborn* connotes his sovereignty over all the powers and authorities. Later Paul will speak of Jesus as the *firstborn* from the dead, meaning that he is the first to be raised in the resurrection of the dead expected at the end time. However, precisely because he is the first to be raised by God, he also holds supreme rank among all those who will be raised to life.

Thus this passage outlines the relationship of Christ to God and to creation, underscoring the cosmic scope of God's work in Christ. This text played an important role in the development of christological thought. Arius argued that "firstborn" (in both Proverbs and the New Testament) was strictly temporal and meant that Christ was created or born first. But the great orthodox church Father Athanasius, quoting Col 1:16 ("for in him all things were created"), wrote, "But if all the creatures were created in him, he is other than the creatures, and is not a creature, but the Creator of the creatures."[10] Such a statement is the outworking of the scriptural view that God alone is the Creator of all things. To identify Christ with the creation of the world is, therefore, to assign to him a unique divine prerogative and to identify him with — although not as — the Creator God of Israel.

The image of the church as the *body* of Christ (1:18; 3:15) is drawn from a picture for unity common in ancient literature.[11] The state was sometimes envisioned as a body in which all parts worked together for the common good. So the Roman historian Livy (59 BC–AD 17) records an appeal of the consul Menenius Agrippa, who used an elaborate metaphor of the Roman people as members of a body who gain nothing if they do not count the contributions of each part of the body to the good of the whole.[12] Paul adapts such thought to speak of Christ's relationship to the church in order to assert to whom the church, this particular earthly "body," ultimately belongs. The church is the body of which Christ, rather than any other lord or deity, is the

---

10. Athanasius, *Orations against the Arians* 2.62.
11. Mitchell, *Paul and the Rhetoric of Reconciliation,* 161.
12. Livy, *Historia* 2.32.9-12; there is a similar analogy in Epictetus, *Discourses* 2.10.4-5.

head; in him the church has its origins, and hence it also finds its identity and unity in Christ. It is "held together" in him (2:19; cf. 3:15).[13] According to the fourth-century Latin Christian writer called Ambrosiaster, this means that "if the whole body is ever deprived of its head, that is, separated from its Creator, there would be an insane and empty chaos."[14]

By including the church in a confessional passage that celebrates the cosmic dimension of God's work through Christ, the significance of the claims made for the role and identity of the church is graphically emphasized. The church is a body drawn from every people and social class (3:11), because the head of the church is one whose work is universal and cosmic in its scope, not only in redemption, but already in creation. Moreover, it is precisely this people that is being "renewed according to the image of its Creator" (3:10). In other words, the church of which Christ is the head is humanity as it was created to be.[15] Paul thus draws a parallel between Christ's role in creation and his role as *head* of the church. As the head of his body, the church, Christ is its source or beginning and its life and therefore rightfully has preeminence in it.

Having delineated the relationship of Christ to God, creation, and the church in some of the most exalted language in the NT, Paul locates the cross on a wide cosmic canvas. Not only has God created the world and continued to sustain it through Christ, but through Christ God also "reconciles all things to himself, by making peace through the blood of the cross." The language of reconciliation comes not from the sacrificial cult but from the discourse of political negotiation.[16] Parties engaged in hostile conflict have been reconciled to each other. So, for example, in narrating the wars between Antony and Caesar and between Herod and the Arabians, Josephus speaks of the work of the ambassadors as "making peace" so as to reconcile enemies to each other. Josephus even speaks of the power of an ambassador to "bring God's presence to human beings and reconcile enemies to one another" (*Ant.* 15.136; see also 15.124-38). Paul envisions a cosmic conflict, in which "principalities and powers" are arrayed against God. Moreover, human beings are estranged from and hostile toward both God and each other (Col 1:20-21). Through the death of Jesus, God has made peace, overcoming the alienation, and bringing an end to hostility. And yet we do not now see the

13. As Ridderbos, *Paul,* 376, aptly puts it: "Believers do not together constitute one body because they are members of one another, but because they are members *of Christ,* and thus are one body in Him" (emphasis added).

14. Ambrosiaster, *Commentary on the Letter to the Colossians* (CSEL 81/3:173), ACCSNT 9.

15. Barclay, *Colossians*, 88-89.

16. So Breytenbach, *Versöhnung.*

reconciliation of all things in its fulness. As Wolfhart Pannenberg phrased it, "the reconciliation of the world has been accomplished, but by anticipation."[17] Paul anticipates a time when the "very structures of reality themselves will be made right," but he also points to the full restitution of all things as yet in the future.[18]

Christ's unique agency in creation and redemption elevates him above all the principalities and powers. The various terms for "the powers" in this passage, including thrones, dominions, principalities and authorities, likely have in view both human rulers and non-human powers.[19] Unfortunately, Paul never goes into detail about the precise identity of any of these groups, for he seems to assume that his readers will understand the sorts of figures to which he is referring. The evidence from the Bible and Jewish literature suggests that the powers in view can be heavenly or spiritual beings, good or evil; the evidence from pagan literature points in much the same direction. Both Jews and Gentiles believed in the existence of a variety of cosmological spirits. In Jewish thought these included angels, various heavenly beings such as the cherubim and seraphim, and evil spirits such as demons and fallen angels. Pagans likewise believed in a variety of spirits and beings, including various gods, astral deities, and cult figures worthy of veneration; while some of these could be hostile to human beings, they were not necessarily so. To complicate matters further, some of the terms used here by Paul refer regularly in his letters to human institutions of authority, particularly the authority of government. While the "principalities" may exert their power in and through human institutions and human authority figures, they cannot simply be equated with or collapsed into those structures, but are "spiritual realities deeper than human power structures."[20] The comment of Lesslie Newbigin is worth quoting at length:

> The principalities and powers are real. They are invisible and we cannot locate them in space. They do not exist as disembodied entities floating above this world, or lurking within it. They meet us as embodied in visible and tangible realities — people, nations, and institutions. And they are powerful. What is Christ's relation to them? To recapitulate briefly: they are created in Christ and for Christ; their true end is to serve him. . . . they become powers for evil when they attempt to usurp the place which

---

17. Pannenberg, "Can Christianity Do without an Eschatology?" 29.

18. Wink, *Naming the Powers,* 54-55.

19. For a more detailed discussion of the identity of the "principalities and powers," see the excursus at the end of this section.

20. Barclay, *Colossians,* 84.

belongs to Christ alone. In his death Christ has disarmed them; he has put them under his feet; they must now serve him; and the Church is the agency through which his victory over them is made manifest and is effected as the Church puts on the whole armor of God to meet and master them. The language is pictorial, mythological if you like, because we have no other language. But the things described are real and are contemporary. They are at the heart of our business as Christians.[21]

In concentrating his attention on Christ's supremacy rather than on the identity or nature of the powers, Paul achieves three goals. First, he dispels the notion that there is viable access to God through other cult figures, deities, spirits, or angels, whoever or whatever they are; indeed, Christ is supreme over all of them because all were created through him. Hence, true faith is faith that is rooted in Christ and in the gospel preached about him (2:6-7). Second, by stressing Christ's supremacy over all visible and invisible powers, Paul reiterates the sufficiency of God's revelation and redemption in Christ. No powers operate in the world autonomously, and none can thwart God's purposes in Christ. None is more powerful than Christ; none can threaten the one joined to Christ. Third, Paul lays the groundwork for his understanding of Christian life as united with, centered in, and obedient to Christ. Nowhere does Paul offer instructions to the Colossians to either launch an assault on the powers or to protect themselves from the powers. Quite the contrary, for Christ has triumphed over them in the cross. Hence, in participating in Christ's death and resurrection, believers die to old loyalties and rise to a new life that is centered in Christ and that acknowledges his supreme lordship. The powers who now exercise authority in the world may in part shape the structures of the world in which human beings presently live. But the cross, not the powers, determines the shape of Christian existence. Christian discipleship, therefore, seeks to live in keeping with the power of Christ, a power that challenges and overthrows the ungodly powers of the world. Christians therefore refuse to take up the role of Messiah, but follow in the footsteps of the Messiah who liberates from the oppressive powers of the world.

21. Newbigin, *Gospel in a Pluralist Society,* 207-8. See also Wall, *Colossians,* 118-19, and Wright, *Colossians,* 72.

Excursus: The Principalities and Powers

The identity of the "principalities and powers" in Colossians has sparked no little debate. There are two references to them in the epistle, first in the statement that "in him all things were created, in heaven and on earth, seen and unseen, whether thrones or dominions or rulers or authorities" (1:16) and next in the assertion that on the cross Jesus "stripped the rulers and authorities" (2:15).

Who or what are these principalities and powers? On the one hand, they are understood to be spiritual beings, typically hostile to God and human beings, and are also then equated with demons or evil angels.[22] The "Colossian heresy" is then understood to include the belief that human beings need to use certain rituals or practices in order to placate and ward off these powers. On the other hand, the powers are often "demythologized" by modern interpreters to refer not to spirit-beings of some sort, but rather to institutionalized and corporate human evil. Walter Wink, in his four-part work on the "powers," argues that the "powers" do not have a separate spiritual existence, but are encountered primarily through the material reality of which they are the innermost essence. Wink writes, "The spirituality of an institution exists as a real aspect of the institution even when it is not perceived as such." For example, Wink speaks of the "spirit of a nation," which endures beyond its actual rule, in the lasting effects of its policies, contributions to culture, and additions to the sheer weight of human suffering.[23] For Wink, this is not just a way in which we might think about the powers today but what the terms actually denote in their NT contexts. By contrast, Clinton Arnold argues that the various references in Colossians to powers or authorities (1:13, 16; 2:10, 15), angels (2:18), and "elements" (2:8, 20) all have in view hostile angelic powers.[24]

One of the problems in determining the referent of these terms is that the Bible gives little clue to the reality which they designate. "Thrones" (*thronoi*/θρόνοι) is used in the OT and NT of thrones or seats of power occupied by human monarchs or authorities (Matt 19:28, Rev 4:4; 20:24). Dominions (*kyriotētos*/κυριότητος) occurs here and in Eph 1:21, as well as in 2 Pet 2:10 and Jude 8; in the latter two instances, the meaning is somewhat more

22. For example, O'Brien, *Colossians,* 46; Dunn, *Colossians,* 93; Arnold, *Powers of Darkness,* 90. This reading depends in part on taking 2:15 as referring to Christ's overcoming of these powers, implying that they had been hostile forces.

23. Wink, *Naming the Powers,* 105.

24. Arnold, *Colossian Syncretism,* 159.

obscure, but the reference may be to angels. Whatever the term means in Colossians, it will likely have the same meaning in Ephesians. "Rulers" (*archai*/ἀρχαὶ) can refer to non-human beings (Eph 3:10; 6:12), but also to human rulers (Titus 3:1). Similarly, "authorities" in the NT apparently has both referents as well. In Rom 13:1-3 the governing authorities in question are surely human governments of one sort or another (so also Tit 3:1); but in other cases "authorities" may designate spiritual or non-human figures of power (1 Cor 15:24; 1 Pet 3:22). One of the conclusions which we may draw from this evidence is that the terms in themselves are not used in technical ways, as if their referent could be deduced merely from the word itself.

Occurrences of these terms in Jewish apocalyptic literature include *1 Enoch* 61:10 (first century BC–first century AD) and *2 Enoch* 20:1 (late first century AD): "And he [God] will summon all the forces *(dynameis)* of the heavens, and all the holy ones above, and the forces of the Lord — the cherubim, seraphim, ophanim, all the angels of governance *(archai)*, the Elect One, and the other forces *(exousiai)* on earth and over the water." "And I saw there [in the seventh heaven] an exceptionally great light, and all the fiery armies of the great archangels, and the incorporeal forces *(dynameis)* and the dominions *(kyriotētes)* and the origins *(archai)* and the authorities *(exousiai)*, the cherubim and the seraphim and the many-eyed thrones *(thronoi)*."

Such an angelic hierarchy surrounding God's throne is also pictured in Revelation where, however, the throne is surrounded by other thrones on which the elders are seated (4:4; 20:4), as well by the seven spirits (4:5) and four living creatures (4:6, 8, 9). The heavenly host is also reflected in the OT, particularly in the Greek renditions of the Hebrew. Thus, for example, in Ps 148:2 (MT), "Praise him, all his angels, praise him, all his hosts" becomes "Praise him, all his angels, praise him, all his powers" (δυνάμεις/*dynameis;* see also Ps 103:21 [MT; 102:21 LXX]). Similarly, the phrase "YHWH, Lord of hosts" ("Lord Sabaoth") is rendered in the Greek as "Lord of the powers," which may well have influenced Paul's description of the supremacy of the Lord Jesus Christ over all the principalities and powers. In the prophets, "Lord of hosts" is rendered ὁ παντοκράτωρ (*pantokratōr;* "ruler of all" or "the Omnipotent"). One point to be gleaned from these references in Revelation and the OT is simply that not all so-called "powers" are viewed as demonic or hostile to human beings or God. That God is the Lord of all the powers demonstrates his superiority and supremacy over them but does not necessarily imply their hostility.[25]

The Greeks identified the planets with the five principal gods (Hermes =

---

25. Indeed, Arnold argues that the Colossians were invoking the protection of good angels against hostile or demonic powers.

Mercury; Aphrodite = Venus; Ares = Mars; Zeus = Jupiter; Kronos = Saturn). These astral gods were known to their worshipers as ἄρχοντες (*archontes*, "rulers").[26] A number of other terms are found in non-Jewish writings as well, including powers, dominions, thrones, and so on. Clearly these terms refer to independent beings, sometimes to astral deities, or to other sorts of spirits or powers. They may be hostile to human beings, but they need not be.

In determining the identity of the "principalities and powers" in Colossians, the following items in the book itself need to be considered, in addition to the background material.

1. Although no passage explicitly says that the authorities and powers are hostile to humankind, this inference has been drawn from the statements that all things, including all powers, have been reconciled in Christ (1:20), that on the cross Christ has stripped them of their armor and weapons (2:15), and that God rescues people from the power of darkness (1:13). Hence the powers refer to those entities overcome by Christ.

2. No passage equates these figures either with demons or fallen or good angels. Nor does Colossians speak of their destiny in terms of punishment or destruction (as is typical of Jewish apocalyptic writings that deal with evil spirits or fallen angels). Paul's descriptions may intend to include such figures, but the principalities and powers cannot be limited to demons or fallen angels.

3. No instructions are given regarding placating these powers, and the Colossians are never told they need not fear them (although this might be implicit). Nor are these powers ever said to *do* anything in particular. They are not, for example, assigned responsibility for human sin or for the "old person" that is to be cast off (3:9), nor are they spoken of as tempting human beings or inducing them to commit evil deeds. It is not clear, if these are hostile angelic forces, why the Colossians fear them or what these powers are alleged to be able to do. Paul's silence on how the Colossians are to respond to the powers is coupled with his insistence that the powers have been dealt with in Christ.

4. Paul apparently assumes that his readers will understand who or what he has in view in speaking of these powers; there is no explicit instruction about them, except with respect to the ways in which the powers were created in Christ and have been reconciled and shamed through the cross.

26. See Caird, *Principalities and Powers*, 14.

The way in which Paul treats these figures as known, rather than unknown, suggests that they are part of the Colossians' pagan past, much as Paul speaks of the "so-called gods" (1 Cor 8:5) to whom some still think they offer sacrifice in eating idol meat. The Colossians need instruction in the relationship of these powers to Christ, who otherwise might easily be mistaken for another of the powers.

In sum Paul understands the world to be a world in which "powers" threaten human life and well-being. One does not have to imagine a universe full of demons, evil spirits, and fallen angels to picture a world where there are powerful, hostile, destructive forces at work for evil and not for good. It is far too easy to list individual, corporate and cosmic forces of tradition, consumerism, illness, sin, nationalism, militarism, and so on, to show that there are anti-God powers at work in the world. At the same time, it is doubtful that Paul would have excluded from his worldview spirits of various sorts with which human beings had to contend. He never, however, gives us a detailed map of his cosmic universe. He rather paints a picture of the cosmic Christ through whom all principalities and powers will ultimately be subdued.

1:21-29

21 And you who were once estranged and hostile in mind, doing evil deeds, 22 he has now reconciled in [or by] his fleshly body through death, so as to present you holy and blameless and without fault before him — 23 provided that you continue securely established and steadfast in the faith, without shifting from the hope that is in the gospel that you heard and that has been proclaimed to every creature under heaven. I, Paul, became a servant of this gospel.

24 I am now rejoicing even as I suffer for your sake, and in my own flesh I am filling up the full measure of the afflictions of Christ for the sake of his body, that is, the church. 25 I became a servant of the church according to God's commission given to me for you. My commission was to make the word of God fully known, 26 that is, to make fully known the mystery that has been hidden throughout the ages and generations but has now been revealed to his saints. 27 To them God has chosen to make known the glorious richness of this mystery, given to the Gentiles, which is that Christ, the hope of glory, is among you. 28 We proclaim him, admonishing everyone and teaching everyone in all wisdom, so that we may present everyone perfect in Christ. 29 For this goal I labor, struggling with all the might with which he so mightily empowers me.

In the previous passage, Paul presented the full picture of God's work in and through Christ by portraying him as the agent of God's purposes in creating, sustaining, and reconciling the world. Now the Colossian Christians themselves are held up as a concrete example of God's reconciling work, for, though they were once estranged from God, in Christ they too have been reconciled to God and have become recipients of and participants in the great mystery of salvation. Paul reminds his readers that the mystery of God's purposes, hidden for generations and now revealed in Christ, has been made known even to the Gentiles. It is no accident that in the passage in which we first encounter the term "mystery," a term that focuses attention on God's revelation, there is a concomitant emphasis on faithful adherence to that which has already been proclaimed and made known to the Colossians. If the Colossians are itching for new revelations of "mysteries" and new elite experiences, Paul pulls them up short: he has exercised his apostolic commission to proclaim the gospel, and to make it fully known (vv. 25-26). Paul calls the Colossian Christians to a fuller grasp of the gospel, but it is the same gospel that they have already heard. It is the gospel of Jesus Christ, the one crucified on the cross, and Paul reminds them of the shape of that gospel when he speaks of the suffering which has been his lot as he fulfills his apostolic commission. Perhaps there is a subtle reminder to the Colossians that if they wish to probe the mysteries of Christ, they will do so by sharing in Christ's suffering, as Paul himself has done.

Paul describes the Colossians in their former life as "estranged and hostile in mind, doing evil deeds." Curiously, the verb "estranged" has no object: were the Colossians estranged from God or from others? A similar passage in Ephesians is illuminating, for there we read that the Gentiles were "separated from Christ, alienated from the commonwealth of Israel" (2:12). The human predicament is therefore spelled out as alienation from both God the Creator and his people. Paul's cryptic statement here reflects Jewish and Christian belief in a strong connection between proper relationship to God and relationship to one's fellow human beings. There is — or ought to be — an inseparable link between whom human beings worship and how they live. The theme runs throughout the OT, where the prophets excoriate the people for thinking that their acts of piety and worship can serve as a cloak for injustice done to the poor and needy (Amos 5:21-24; Isa 58:1-8; Jer 7:1-12). Similarly joining together love of God and neighbor, Jesus summed up the law with the twofold command to love (Matt 22:37-40).

Paul locates the estrangement and hostility in the disposition and actions of the Colossians prior to their reception of the gospel, contrasting what they "once" were with what they "now" are. In spite of human hostility, God is disposed to seek reconciliation with humankind and does so as an ambassa-dor who negotiates peace with an enemy at war.[1] God's work of reconciliation aims to present the Colossians — and all of God's people — as "holy and blameless and without fault before him" (v. 22; cf. Phil 1:10; Jude 24). Paul thus contrasts the hostile disposition of the Colossians with God's disposition to reconcile and make peace, and the evil deeds of the Colossians with God's in-tention to present them holy, blameless, and without fault, perfect in Christ (v. 28). Paul's gospel speaks of the transformation of the world and of human beings within it, so that God's creation might fulfill the purposes for which it was created.

Paul has greeted the Colossians as "saints" (1:2; cf. 3:12) — the same word here translated "holy" — and now he refers to God's work in them as a work that ultimately presents them as holy, thus making it possible for them to come into the presence of God, who is holy. When the Psalmist asks who shall stand in the "holy place of God," he answers his question: "Those who have clean hands and pure hearts" (Ps 24:3-6). To stand in God's holy place re-quires appropriate and commensurate purity. Yet typically "holy" refers to that which God is and human beings are not. Isaiah's vision of the holy God leads him to confess and bewail his own uncleanness (Isa 6:1-7), even as Pe-ter's confrontation with the power of Jesus drives him to his knees in a con-fession of his sinfulness (Luke 5:1-8). The hope to appear before God "holy, blameless, and without fault" clearly requires God's work of transformation. Similarly, "blameless" or "without blemish" is used especially in the OT of perfect sacrificial animals, but can also take on the moral connotation of hu-man blamelessness before God in word and deed (Num 6:14; Ps 15:2). "With-out fault" is judicial terminology, indicating that a person has no charged filed against him (cf. Col. 2:14).

The gospel that holds out the hope of reconciliation and transforma-tion for all human beings is proclaimed in the word of God (v. 25), described by Paul as "the mystery that has been hidden throughout the ages and genera-tions but has now been revealed to his saints" (v. 26) and further explicated by the statement "that Christ, the hope of glory, is among you" (cf. 4:3: "the mys-tery of Christ"). The so-called "mystery religions" had elaborate rites of prep-aration and initiation, but the actual realities into which people were initiated could not be reported to outsiders; hence their designation as "mysteries." But in the first-century Jewish context, "mystery" refers to something that is hid-den with God, stored up in heaven, until such time as God chooses to disclose

---

1. See the comments on 1:20, where it was noted that the language of reconciliation comes from the realm of political negotiation for peace in the context of war.

it.[2] In the literature of Jewish apocalyptic, such disclosure is typically made to seers and prophets by means of visions, dreams, or journeys into heaven, but in other Jewish texts, "mysteries" could refer to what was hidden in the Torah and to its interpretation by "inspired, skilled, and ethically qualified exegetes."[3] While the term "mystery" may have surfaced in the Colossian situation because of acquaintance with the "mystery religions," Paul's understanding of "mystery" clearly falls in line with its Jewish definition as that which has been hidden with God and is now disclosed, by the prerogative and in the purposes of God. Specifically, what was hidden for generations, namely, a plan to bring salvation to all the world, is now disclosed and made known in Christ.

Although Paul speaks of the manifestation of these mysteries "to his saints" (v. 26), he also underscores the universal scope of God's purpose when he speaks of the gospel's proclamation to "every creature under heaven." This rhetorical hyperbole describes the universal scope of the gospel and its open proclamation to all humankind. "All" signifies that there has been no exclusion among the recipients of the proclamation of the gospel, a point that is further underscored in 3:11 in Paul's description of the new humanity as encompassing in a unified whole in Christ the dualities — Greek and Jew, slave and free — that characterize human identity apart from Christ. Understanding of "the mystery that has been hidden throughout the ages and generations" (1:26) is not attained by the religiously or philosophically elite or through additional spiritual experiences or the acquisition of knowledge, but is disclosed through the word of God, which is to be fully proclaimed (1:25) to every person (1:28).[4]

Paul counts himself among those "saints" peculiarly entrusted with the charge to proclaim this mystery that has now been disclosed. Indeed, Paul not only proclaims God's redemptive plan; his ministry also epitomizes it, for as a Jew he proclaims God's salvation to the Gentiles. Paul's apostolic commission and labors are thus an integral part of God's uncovering of his purposes, which are pithily summarized in the statement, "Christ, the hope of glory, is among you." As the firstborn from the dead (1:18), the promised Messiah of *Israel,* crucified on the cross, is now living, present with and among the Gentiles, and this is the reality that Paul proclaims. God's purposes, no longer hidden, are to bring together one people comprised of Jew and Gentile. The

2. See the studies by Brown, *Semitic Background of the Term "Mystery,"* and especially by Bockmuehl, *Revelation and Mystery,* 124-26, 178-93.

3. See Bockmuehl, *Revelation and Mystery,* 125.

4. Hultgren, *Christ and His Benefits,* 99.

incorporation of the Gentile Colossians and Jewish believers into one people of God reveals how God's intention to reconcile all the world is presently being worked out. The reconciled people of God, in their multinational and multiethnic diversity, are a foretaste and promise of the reconciliation of all God's world to himself. God does not reconcile some people or part of the creation. In Christ, God has reconciled "all things . . . making peace by the blood of his cross" (1:20).

Here, then, is one meaning of the cross. Through it, God overcomes the barriers and boundaries set up by human beings, reconciling those estranged to himself and to each other "in his body" (1:21). Body refers to both the fleshly or physical body of Jesus and the church. Strikingly, Paul does not say that the church is *like* the body of Christ; it *is* the body of Christ, but not, however, the "fleshly body" of Christ. Paul thus asserts that it is through the death of Jesus' physical body that Jews and Gentiles are united in the one body of Jesus. It is through participation in the death of Jesus that one is joined to him, and thus becomes part of the one body.

Indeed, there is a striking emphasis in Colossians on Christ's body and, particularly, his physical (fleshly) body, surely because some in Colossae advocated practices of self-denial and deprecation of the body as the means to a deeper knowledge of God (2:20-23). Such an emphasis would be entirely in keeping with Hellenistic culture, where the physical body was regarded as inferior to the rational soul precisely because it belonged to the material world, or at least to the lower-status heavy material, the realm of σάρξ (*sarx*, "flesh"), rather than to the light, airy material of which the soul was supposedly made. Hence, discipline of the body, control of the baser physical and sexual impulses, even to the point of abstaining from sexual intercourse altogether, was seen as a sign of spiritual power, deeper insight, superior self-control, and participation in or access to the higher realms.[5]

But in Jewish and Christian thought, the body is integral to human personal identity.[6] Indeed, the physical body is integral to the identity of Christ, and it is precisely through his fleshly body that Christ effected salvation. Salvation cannot and does not consist in the liberation of the soul from the body, as the pun σῶμα σῆμα (*sōma sēma*, "the body is a tomb") suggested. Rather, salvation is conceived of wholistically, as the deliverance of the whole person from death to life, as the understanding of the resurrection of the body presupposes, to live in a cosmos redeemed from decay, destruction, and death. Hence, one theologian imagines our redemption in these words, "[I]n

5. See Hays, *Moral Vision*, 48-49. See also the discussion on 2:16-23 below.
6. Bauckham and Hart, *Hope against Hope*, 124.

raising our mortal body, God will redeem not just that body, the locus of our existence, but the entirety of our embodied life: the whole of our relationships, our experiences and our encounters, all that makes up our identity."[7] That is, of course, speculative to some degree, imagining what it must mean that our selves, and not just some aspect of our selves, are redeemed by God. But we are not who we are apart from our bodies; the body is not simply the case that holds the real self. Thus attempts to humiliate and subdue the body through denial (2:16-23), as though the body were the problem for believers, simply miss the mark, for they do not properly grasp the significance of either the resurrection of Christ's body or the future resurrection of believers for understanding life in the present order.

Moreover, it was through Christ's own death in his fleshly body that God brought about reconciliation and constituted the church as Christ's body. There is also then an intimate and intrinsic connection between the mode of Christ's death and the character of the church, so that one may rightly speak of the cruciform character of the church. Its identity is found in Christ, and that identity is shaped by the cross of Christ. So although Paul surely expected each individual believer to embody the story of Christ and in that way to manifest a cruciform spirituality, Paul's "spirituality of cruciformity is fundamentally *communal* in character. . . . [Paul's] mission was to announce the gospel of Jesus Christ as the true Lord of all — in continuity with the God of Israel and in contrast to the counterfeit lord, the Roman emperor — and to form visible alternative communities of cruciformity animated and governed by this true Lord."[8] In other words, Jesus' suffering and death on the cross determine the shape and character of the Christian community's mission in the world, because the church is Christ's body. And his body was given in death, as the words of the institution of the Lord's Supper remind those who partake (1 Cor 11:24). To say that Jesus' body was given "for you" emphasizes the reality of his death and the role of his body in effecting salvation. Since Christ gave his body in death for the salvation of the world, how can Christians imagine the body to be evil or not part of that which is redeemed by God?

In speaking of the revelation of the mysteries of God in Christ and the death of Jesus on the cross, Paul turns also to speak of his own suffering "as filling up the full measure of the afflictions of Christ, for the sake of his body, that is, the church" (v. 24). Exactly what Paul means here has occasioned no little debate. It is clear that as an apostle of the crucified Lord, Paul assumes that

7. Dabney, "Justified by the Spirit," 61-62.
8. Gorman, *Cruciformity,* 349.

it is simply part of the lot of an apostle to follow in the footsteps of his Lord. Even as Jesus manifested a costly obedience to God in the face of the world's hostility — an obedience that led to suffering and death — so the apostle who follows such a Lord can scarcely expect a different fate. But Paul also speaks of his suffering as "filling up the full measure of the afflictions of Christ," that is, somehow adding to or completing the very sufferings of Christ himself. Here Paul seems to envision not simply an imitation of Christ's suffering, but a participation in that very suffering (see also Gal 4:19; 2 Cor 1:5; 4:10-11; Phil 3:10). Paul likely has in mind a participation in the so-called "Messianic birth-pangs" (especially in Gal 4:19), the afflictions that would usher in the messianic age, since "afflictions" is typically used for the tribulations connected with the end times. Paul's participation in these afflictions signals that as a messenger of God's decisive salvation in Christ, he suffers the afflictions that are associated with the decisive eschatological or end-time events.

In the present context, the afflictions of which Paul speaks are not, then, the sufferings that are the lot of all human beings, including Christians, in the present world, but rather particularly the afflictions that beset Paul as he bears testimony to Christ and to the gospel. Here, then, "a suffering church is not the point; rather, it is the apostle suffering for the church."[9]

More particularly, Paul's afflictions are for the sake of the Gentiles. Paul thus "fills up the full measure of afflictions" by participating in the same reality of suffering as Christ did and for the same purposes, namely, the creation and ultimate redemption of the world. But there are at least three differences. First, Paul's suffering always points to and completes the suffering of Jesus. Second, as Paul puts it in Romans, Christ "became a servant of the circumcised" (15:8), whereas Paul has become a servant of Christ Jesus among and on behalf of the Gentiles (15:16). Paul's sufferings are an inevitable part of his commission as an apostle of Christ and a servant of the gospel and the church. The mystery that is now revealed to God's saints is that Christ is among the Gentiles, giving even them the hope of glory, and compelling Paul to minister in the same way and for the same ends as Christ did (cf. Phil 3:10-11).

And, third, the sufferings that Paul endures are genuinely the sufferings of Christ himself, because Paul — like the Colossians — has become a member of the body of Christ. It is the suffering, death, and resurrection of Christ in which Paul participates (Phil 3:10) — and because Paul is thus joined to Christ, Christ suffers in and through him. Paul writes elsewhere that when one member of the body suffers, all suffer together (1 Cor 12:26). As a member of Christ, part of Christ's body, Paul suffers as did Jesus in his physical body

9. Lincoln, "Colossians," 617.

45

(1:22). But the implication here is also that Jesus still suffers in the person of the apostle Paul. In the sufferings of the body of Christ, Christ himself suffers.

Here one may well be reminded of the narrative of Paul's encounter on the road to Damascus. As one persecuting the church, he has a vision of the risen Christ, who identifies himself with that church when he names himself "Jesus, whom you are persecuting." In his accounts of the martyrdom of the saints at Lyons, the church historian Eusebius wrote that in the torture and death of Sanctus, Christ was "suffering in that body" and so "accomplished most glorious things" (*Historia Ecclesiastica* 5.1.23). Similarly, in Blandina's sufferings, others saw "in the person of their sister the One who was crucified for them" (5.1.41). The sufferings of the martyrs are the very sufferings of Jesus himself. There are both imitation and participation in the sufferings of Christ; and in turn, Christ suffers in and as the members of his body suffer.

Paul suffers and labors to "present everyone perfect in Christ," a clause that recapitulates the earlier statement that God reconciles people in order to "present [them] holy, blameless, and without fault" (v. 22). This is the goal to which God will bring his people; it is the end for which Paul labors. To stand before God as "perfect in Christ" will be to stand before him as "holy, blameless, and without fault." "Perfect in Christ" means more than perfected in Christian faith, although it does not mean less than that; the exhortation to a steadfast and firm faith fits here with Paul's vision of Christians being brought to the end or goal of their faithful commitment, their life with God in Christ. "Perfect in Christ" implies transformation into the likeness of Christ, who is the image of God (1:15). God's perfected saints are those who have been changed by God into the glorious image of his Son (2 Cor 3:18).

The means through which the goal is attained are described here in terms of proclamation, admonition, and teaching (v. 28). Paul nurtures the Colossians in their understanding of the gospel, encouraging and exhorting them, in order to help them maintain a steadfast and firm faith (v. 23). He describes that labor using language borrowed from an athletic contest, when he speaks of the "struggle" that characterizes his work on behalf of the church (cf. 1 Cor 9:25-27; Phil 1:30; 3:10-14; 1 Tim 6:12; 2 Tim 4:7). But strikingly Paul notes that it is God's working in him, God's empowering, that enables Paul's labor and struggles. God's powerful work does not eliminate the afflictions endured for the sake of the church. Through these very afflictions God brings about his purposes, just as through the afflictions of Christ, God's purposes for reconciliation are being worked out. Paul's references to his toil and struggle likely refer to the sheer hard work of travel and the burden of care for his churches, to his wrestling in prayer for the Colossians (cf. 4:12), and to the hardships of prison life. All of this belongs to his commission as an apostle of the crucified Christ and of the gospel proclaimed about Christ. All of this anticipates the glory that will be revealed in Christ.

2:1-7

1 For I want you to know how much I am struggling for you, and for those in Laodicea, and for all who have not seen my face in the flesh. 2 I struggle so that your hearts will be encouraged by being knit together in love and that you might have all the riches of assured understanding, the knowledge of God's mystery, that is, Christ himself, 3 in whom are hidden all the treasures of wisdom and knowledge. 4 I am saying this so that no one may deceive you with specious arguments. 5 For though I am absent in the flesh, yet I am with you in spirit, rejoicing as I see the stability of your firm trust in Christ.

6 As you therefore have received Christ Jesus the Lord, walk in him, 7 rooted and built up in him and established in faith, just as you were taught, abounding in thanksgiving.

Paul has just spoken of his labors in service of the proclamation of the gospel, briefly using the metaphor of an athletic contest (1:29). Using the same metaphor, he now speaks more specifically of his labors on behalf of believers in Laodicea and others he has never met. Although Paul has apparently not visited either Laodicea or Colossae, the Christian congregations in both cities owe their existence to the efforts of coworkers in Paul's mission. The church at Laodicea is addressed in the book of Revelation (1:11; 3:14), but there is no reference to it in Acts or to a visit there in any other letters of Paul. Paul does refer later in Colossians to a letter which he apparently wrote to the Laodiceans (Col 4:13-16; see the comments there). That Paul would take it upon himself to write to the congregation at Colossae, even though he himself had not founded it, indicates his belief that his apostolic commission included pastoral care for churches within the wider orbit of his work. Elsewhere he does express his reticence to "boast in the labors of others" or to "build on someone else's foundation" (2 Cor 10:15-16; Rom 15:20-21). But he also cherishes the unity of labor for the gospel, as is attested by his statement in 1 Corinthians that while he had "planted" among them, Apollos had watered — and this was clearly all God's work (1 Cor 3:6). Paul's self-understanding as apostle to the Gentiles, and hence as an integral part of God's plan to disclose the mystery of Christ among the Gentiles, emboldened him not to limit his work only to those churches that he had actually founded.

Paul here gives expression to very particular goals that he desires for the

Christians in Colossae. Specifically, he works and prays so that their "hearts will be encouraged by being knit together in love," and that they may "have all the riches of assured understanding, the knowledge of God's mystery." Since Paul believes that in Christ God has reconciled people together into one body, now he works so that the hearts of believers will be "knit together in love." Similarly, having confessed that God's mystery has now been disclosed in Christ, Paul wants the Colossians to have a rich knowledge of God's mystery. If spirituality is "the lived experience of Christian belief,"[1] then Paul directs his efforts so that the Colossians may live out the convictions proclaimed in the gospel.

Paul speaks here of the body being "knit together in love" and, in a few verses, of it being knit together "through its joints and ligaments" (2:19). The unity of the church is the unity it has as the one body of Christ, who knits it together in love, presumably referring both to Christ's love for it and the love of believers for one another. The mutual interdependence of believers, who belong to the one body of Christ, encourages and empowers them to live within a culture whose values, morality, and religious practices regularly run counter to or undermine the commitments called for in the gospel. To persevere in their allegiance to Christ, to stand firm (1:23; 2:7), believers are dependent on Christ and each other. As a community united in love, "which penetrates to the heart and wells up from the heart,"[2] they receive encouragement from each other and from their corporate identity as believers in Christ.

Paul also labors so that the Colossians may have "the riches of assured understanding, the knowledge of God's mystery." Colossians is brimming with various synonyms for understanding, knowledge, and wisdom (e.g., 1:6, 9, 25-28; 2:23; 3:10, 16) because Paul attacks certain practices and behaviors that were supposed to grant a new and deeper knowledge of God. He does not dispute the possibility of growing in knowledge of God's ways; indeed, he labors for the maturation of Christian believers as they grow in the knowledge of their Creator (1:28; 3:10). But he does deny that the specific practices of ecstatic worship and asceticism, practices apparently advocated by certain Colossian Christians, were appropriate means of attaining such knowledge or gaining a deeper experience of God. On the contrary, since God's revelation has been made fully in Christ, Christ grants to believers the assurance of the knowledge of God. And because the mystery that is made known in Christ concerns God's reconciliation of Jew and Gentile, participation in the fellowship of believers in Christ is a lived reminder to the Colossians of what they

---

1. This is the definition offered by McGinn and Meyendorff in *Christian Spirituality*, xv.
2. Dunn, *Colossians*, 130.

have received and known in Christ. Even the existence of this small community of believers is a testimony to what the gospel has accomplished; participation in that community brings both the encouragement and the assurance of knowing, cognitively and experientially, the fullness of God's revelation.

To underscore the point, Paul introduces yet another metaphor for God's self-disclosure in Christ: in Christ "are hidden all the treasures of wisdom and knowledge." In *2 Baruch*, the "treasures of wisdom" are said to be found in the Law (44:14; 54:13). Earlier Paul has reflected the wisdom traditions which equated God's wisdom with the Torah by declaring that God's wisdom — that is, the revelation of God's ways and purposes for humankind — is fully manifested in Christ (1:25-26). Here he sweepingly asserts that "all the treasures of wisdom and knowledge are hidden in Christ." Paul does not have generic "knowledge" or "wisdom" in view but, in keeping with the emphases of the letter, the "knowledge of God's will" and "spiritual wisdom and understanding" that can lead to living in a way that is "worthy of the Lord" (1:9-10). That this treasure of wisdom is "hidden" in Christ does not mean that there are mysteries that God is currently withholding; rather, precisely the opposite: in Christ, the fullness of God is already manifest (1:19) and the "mystery" that was hidden for ages has now been revealed (1:26). Paul's assertion here, then, means that these treasures are embedded or located in Christ. If Paul's statement has the identification of wisdom with the Law as its background, then it implies that all the treasures of wisdom that are hidden in the Law are first and finally hidden in Christ. Thus the statement is comparable to the assertions regarding creation: in Colossians, the creation of the world is said to be God's work through and in Christ; similarly, the revelation of God's knowledge and wisdom is said to occur through and in Christ. Just as God creates all that is through Christ, so God fully reveals his purposes of redemption through Christ.[3]

Paul's assertion that "all the treasures of wisdom and knowledge" are "hidden in Christ" explicates further the earlier formulation "in him all the fullness of God was pleased to dwell" (1:19; cf. 2:9). That earlier statement offered an ontological predication about the identity of Christ: he is the one in whom all the fullness of God dwells. Here the accent falls on the knowledge and wisdom available in Christ. Both statements use "all" to make it clear that knowledge of God and Christ are inseparable and, more, that since the iden-

---

3. See also Bockmuehl, *Revelation and Mystery,* 188-90, especially n. 57: "Paul's concentration of hidden treasures in Christ may well be a polemical appropriation and extrapolation of Jewish views about the Torah for his purposes of expressing full revelation in Christ." Bockmuehl cites a number of rabbinic texts which argue that occupation with Torah results in revelation of secrets.

tity of God has been revealed through and in Christ, in order to understand who God is, one must acknowledge God in Christ. All the treasures of wisdom and knowledge are hidden in Christ, because all the fullness of God was pleased to dwell in him. Therefore, to seek further or deeper knowledge of God apart from Christ or in other directions leads not to further hidden treasure, but to a dead end.

Because of the fullness of God's revelation through and in Christ, Paul urges the Colossians to adhere to the teachings that they have received, to sink their roots deeply into Christ, and to remain faithful in their commitment to Christ as Lord. The acknowledgment that "Jesus is Lord" (see Rom 10:9; 1 Cor 12:3; Phil 2:11; cf. 2 Cor 4:5) was one of the earliest confessions in the church by which believers expressed their newfound allegiance to Christ. It required of Gentiles the rejection of other lords and gods (cf. 1 Thess 1:9-10), and of Jews an understanding of God that would "allow them to ascribe to the crucified and exalted Lord that which their Scriptures ascribed to God alone."[4] "Lord" is one of Paul's most frequent titles for Jesus, used some 230 times in his letters. Since "Lord" carries the nuance of superiority, mastery, or the right to command, the acknowledgment of Jesus as Lord implies the obligation to honor and obey him. Not surprisingly, then, "Lord" occurs more often especially in the latter part of Colossians, where the frequency of imperatives increases as well. Here the designation underscores the way in which Jesus, the Lord, determines the path of those who would follow him (cf. 1:10).

In urging obedience to Jesus as Lord, Paul seeks also to encourage the Colossians in the "stability" of their "firm trust in Christ," for which he has earlier commended them (2:5). Having celebrated their faithfulness, he now urges them to sink their roots even more deeply into the reality that the gospel brings to them. He does this by using a series of exhortations and images: they are to remember what they have received and been taught; they are to be rooted and built up in Christ; they are to be confirmed in their faithfulness — and all this is to lead to an abundance of thanksgiving. Whereas the false teaching apparently troubling the Colossians urged them to seek new experiences of, or probe other means of access to, the divine realm, Paul counters with an exhortation not to seek that which is new, but rather to focus on what they have known and trusted all along. Such a course inevitably seems less exciting, for nothing new is offered for consumption, nothing novel is offered for experience. But if the fullness of God is to be found in Christ, then it follows both that nothing surpasses what can be found in Christ and that there

---

4. Gorman, *Cruciformity,* 124. See also the discussion in Bauckham, *God Crucified,* and the exposition in Wright, *Climax of the Covenant,* 56-98.

are depths of wisdom and experience of God that the Colossians have scarcely begun to plumb. The "fullness of God" will not have been exhausted by the Colossians in the short years that they have been part of Christ's body!

When Paul writes that the Colossians "have received Christ Jesus the Lord," he uses a technical term ("have received") for the handing on and receiving of tradition (παρελάβετε/*parelabete*; cf. 1 Cor 11:2-3; 15:1; Gal 1:14; 2 Thess 2:15; 3:6). In 1 Cor 15:1 Paul speaks of "preaching the gospel which you received," thus emphasizing, as he does here, that the reception of the gospel marks the beginning of the Christian life and that deeper understanding of the gospel leads to growth in the Christian life. When he speaks of being rooted in Christ, Paul calls to mind imagery from the Psalms and other places in Scripture that compare the upright person to a tree that flourishes and produces fruit (Pss 1:3; 52:8; 92:12-14; Matt 7:18-19; 12:33). With a new metaphor, Paul then speaks of being "built up in him." Since the participles and verbs here are in the plural, Paul surely has as much in view the growth of the community together as he does the growth of individual believers within the community. It is the congregation that received the gospel, that was created by the preaching of the gospel, and that is to uphold it and grow in it. They are, in short, to be "established in the faith." One can construe "faith" in the subjective sense, that is, as the faith or faithfulness that an individual has; or one can understand it as "the faith," that is, the Christian faith. In the end, there will not be much difference in meaning, since Paul's hope is that the Colossians, through adherence to the gospel and commitment to each other, will continue steadfastly on the path on which they began. By being firmly rooted in the gospel, they will grow in discernment so as to be able to repel specious arguments introduced by the false teachers, who promise growth and offer a teaching that leads them along quite a different path.

2:8-15

8 Watch out so that no one takes you captive through philosophy and empty deceit according to human tradition, according to worldly ordinances, and not according to Christ. 9 For in him the whole fullness of deity dwells bodily, 10 and you have been filled in him, who is the head of all rule and authority. 11 In him also you were circumcised with a circumcision not done by human hands, putting off the fleshly "body" through Christ's circumcision of you, 12 when you were buried with him in baptism. In him you were also raised through faith in the power of God, who raised him from the dead. 13 And when you were dead in trespasses and the uncircumcision of your flesh, God made you alive together with him, by forgiving

us all our trespasses, 14 wiping away the bond of indebtedness that stood against us with its decrees. He took it from our midst, nailing it to the cross. 15 And having stripped the rulers and authorities, he displayed them publicly, triumphing over them in the cross.

Here Paul focuses on the identity of Christ and the meaning of his death, offering half a dozen images to elucidate the significance of the cross. If the present passage seems to repeat notes sounded earlier, it illustrates just how difficult it is to divide Colossians into discrete sections, as if it were written in neat chunks, with various topics systematically addressed. Furthermore, the exhortation in 2:8 ("Watch out") could just as easily be regarded as the conclusion to the previous section, rounding off Paul's urging to the Colossians to remember what they have been taught and have experienced. But the warning here against being "taken captive through philosophy and empty deceit" also anticipates Paul's new treatment of the person and work of Christ by admonishing the Colossians not to be deceived by any teaching that is "not according to Christ" and does not articulate the significance of the cross in terms of the gospel which they have heard and received. Similarly, 2:16-17 could serve as the capstone to this passage. While it is therefore impossible to treat this passage as though it were a free-standing unit, it does contain a brief but sustained treatment of the death of Jesus, presenting some of the most memorable images for what God has accomplished through it that we have in the pages of the NT.

This passage also raises the particularly knotty problem of the identification of the στοιχεῖα τοῦ κόσμου/*stoicheia tou kosmou*, translated here as "worldly ordinances" (2:8). Paul uses *stoicheia* three times, twice with the qualifying phrase "of the world" or "of the universe" (*tou kosmou*, Gal 4:3, 9 and here). *Stoicheia* occurs about half a dozen times in the NT, with several different meanings. It refers to the elements of the universe, that is, to earth, air, water, and fire (2 Pet 3:10, 12; cf. Wis 7:17; so also frequently in Philo). In Hebrews, it refers to "basic principles" or "foundational ideas," sometimes paraphrased as the "ABCs" (Heb 5:12). Outside the NT, *stoicheia* can signify the deified elements of the earth (earth, air, fire, water), hence implying a pantheistic understanding of deity immanent in the elements of the earth. The meaning of *stoicheia* as "ruling spirits" or "deities" is attested outside the NT, but not until the third century.

In Col 2:8 *stoicheia tou kosmou* is translated either as "elemental spirits of the universe" (RSV, NRSV) or "basic principles of this world" (NIV; KJV "rudiments of the world"; here "worldly ordinances").[1] On the first view, the

1. On the translation adopted here, see Bruce, *Colossians*.

stoicheia are spirits, perhaps astral deities, thought to rule this world. They are usually equated with the "principalities and powers" (1:16; 2:15), as well as with the angels referred to in 2:18. On the second view, *stoicheia* refers to the basic principles or tenets that represent the world's point of view and standards, as opposed to the norms given "according to Christ" (2:8). In spite of the trend in current interpretation of Colossians to understand the *stoicheia* in the first sense, as spirits or angelic beings or deities of some sort, the second position represents the view taken in this commentary.[2] Paul never equates the *stoicheia* with any other beings mentioned in this letter, including angels, principalities, and powers, nor does he refer to any of these beings as "demons," false deities, or evil spirits. The historical context may allow for such a meaning, but the use in the epistle counts against it, for several reasons.

First, the warning against following worldly ordinances (2:8-10) leads into the implicit admonition against taking up the practice of or following the "worldly ordinance" of circumcision (2:11-13), since in Christ one is "circumcised" by being baptized into Christ's death. Second, Paul's statement that in Christ believers have died to the *stoicheia* (2:20) provides the ground for the argument against following the self-deprecating rules and regulations rehearsed in 2:21-23. In both contexts, Paul disputes the contention that certain practices (circumcision, self-abasement) will produce some sort of spiritual experience not yet attained. Paul views adherence to such rules and rituals as nothing other than reliance on human tradition rather than on Christ.

Paul's injunctions and instructions concentrate on the growth and maturity in Christ and the faithfulness, wisdom, and unity of the body which together provide the necessary defense against deception. Paul is aware of the challenges and threats that are liable to trip up these relatively young converts; one of those threats is certain teaching which, from his vantage point, is constructed according to human precepts, according to the wisdom of the world, and not with an eye to the truth of the gospel. What makes the problem particularly delicate, but also much more dangerous, is that those who are advancing this "human wisdom" seem to have been part of the Colossian congregation. Paul is concerned that the Colossians come to a full under-

---

2. The patristic commentators took it this way as well. According to Theodoret of Cyrrhus, "elements of the world" are "the observation of cultic days." Ambrosiaster defines "of the world" as philosophy adopted by those who wish to be wise in "earthly terms" (see *ACCSNT* 9:29). Later Calvin, *Colossians*, 330, argued that "elements of the world" refers to ceremonies or ordinances, since in 2:11 Paul refers to circumcision; see also Bruce, *Colossians*, 98-100. Wall, *Colossians*, 107, takes it as a reference to earth's four basic elements; Wink, *Naming the Powers*, 74-76, suggests that here it means "basic principles or constituent elements of reality," but that in 2:20 it refers to "the elements common to religion, pagan and Jewish alike."

standing, both cognitive and experiential, of Christ and his work on their behalf, for, equipped with such discernment, believers ought to be able to withstand whatever false teaching rears its head. In canonical context, one might note the striking similarities to the admonitions in 1 John to a church torn by division and threatened with false teaching: there it is the unity of the fellowship, its faithfulness to the gospel, and love for God and each other, which will together provide the necessary equipment for the Christians to "test the spirits," to discern and to live out the truth.

Paul warns the Colossians against being taken captive "through philosophy and empty deceit, according to human tradition, according to worldly ordinances." Clearly these phrases — philosophy, human tradition, and worldly ordinances — are different ways of referring to the false teaching that Paul rejects. This teaching is empty and deceitful because it ultimately comes from human beings and not, as Paul so often insists with respect to the gospel, from God (Rom 1:1; Gal 1:15-16). Paul accepts the tradition of teaching true to the gospel that has been received by him and passed on to the Colossians (e.g., 1:5-6). It is not tradition *per se,* but tradition that falsifies the truth of the gospel, that constitutes the problem. Of course what makes the contrast between the two kinds of teaching particularly pungent is that the false teaching comes not from pagans or from detractors of the Christian faith, but apparently from those who name the name of Christ. Paul's antidote to deception is thorough saturation in the gospel of Christ.

Nor does this passage constitute a rejection either of the study of philosophy or of knowledge that is gained through scientific study of various kinds. Paul labels a "philosophy" or "tradition" hollow and deceitful if it in any way undermines trust in the adequacy of God's salvation in Christ, in whom "the whole fullness of deity dwells bodily" (2:9). Paul's statement does not simply collapse God and Christ into one, but Paul does deny that there is some remnant of deity to be found or known in another form or through means other than Christ. The addition of the adverb "bodily" drives home the point: God's presence and fullness are known through and in the particular historical figure of Jesus, leaving no room for anyone who names Jesus as Lord to seek access to God along other paths. While some philosophers of religion label (and also reject) as "exclusivist" this claim of Christian faith, others have pointed out that it is properly called "particularist." That is, the primary claim of the Christian faith is a positive one, namely, that God has become manifest in the *particular* person of Jesus of Nazareth and is therefore known in the *particular* narrative of this man's life, death, and resurrection. Therefore a Christian understanding of the identity and character of God is inseparably linked to and with this particular human being and his story.

Paul's emphasis on the "bodily" presence of God in this particular historical figure and the narrative of his earthly existence also speaks against any rejection of the material world, as though God could be found only in a "spiritual" or "higher" realm.[3] Because God's fullness dwells in Christ, the Colossians "have been filled" with knowledge of God; they do not need to look to other mediators or powers for a deeper knowledge of God and his ways.

The word *deity* (*theotētos*/θεότητος) in the phrase "fullness of deity" is unusual in the NT, as are most other Greek words meaning "divine," "divine nature," or "divinity." For where there is a firmly monotheistic faith, only one God will possess the qualities, nature, or character of "divinity." In other words, to say that God is divine or "has divinity" is tautologous. "Divinity" or "divine nature" is not, strictly speaking, something that God "possesses" so much as something that simply defines the one God. When Paul writes that the "fullness of deity" dwells in Christ, he means that the very fullness of the one true God is to be found in Christ. It is not as if Christ has a portion of deity, as if deity were a substance or characteristic that could be divided among any number of entities, so that the Colossians could or ought to look elsewhere for divine reality. If they previously believed in multiple deities or thought of divine nature as a quality shared by a number of beings, they are now exhorted to think of one true God and the embodiment of true deity in Christ. "God in Christ" defines deity.

Because the very fullness of God dwells in Christ, Christ shares in the prerogative of divine sovereignty and rule, as revealed by the description of him as "head of all rule and authority." "Head" has a variety of meanings, including "beginning, origin, source" or "preeminence, supremacy." In fact, the description of Christ as the head of the church (1:18) seems to be explicated by all these meanings: Christ is the beginning, the firstborn, and preeminent. Even as he is the agent of creation (1:15-16) and in that way its beginning (1:18), so in 2:19, Christians are told to hold fast to the head of the body, Christ, because he is the one who provides life and sustenance to the body. In the present passage (2:10) the emphasis falls on the assertion of Christ's supremacy over all rule and authority, echoing the description of Christ as preeminent (see also 1:18), but possibly also the role of Christ in creation (1:16-17). In both Jewish and early Christian thought, God's identity as Creator of the world is inseparably linked with his sovereignty as the one who governs the world.[4] Christ has supremacy over all rule and authority not because he

---

3. See Lincoln, "Colossians," 623-24.

4. See the discussion of various texts in Bauckham, *God Crucified,* and Thompson, *God of the Gospel of John,* 17-55.

has gained or usurped this authority in some way, but because it is rightfully his as the agent of God's creation of "all things visible and invisible, whether thrones or dominions or rulers or powers — all things have been created through him and for him" (1:16).

Against the background of these statements about the identity of Christ, the significance of the cross is thrown into sharp relief. Since Christ is identified as the one in whom the fullness of God dwells, the cross can scarcely be seen as anything other than God's own work, God's initiative for the forgiveness, rescue, and deliverance of humankind. Christ does not negotiate the terms of surrender with an antagonistic God. It is not as if "the Son faces the Father with his back to us," pleading for our salvation.[5] Rather, in Christ God's face is turned toward the world with forgiving grace. As the one in whom God's fullness dwells, Christ is God's own envoy of peace and reconciliation, and the forgiveness, deliverance, and life extended through Christ are God's own gifts to his creatures.

The significance of the cross is presented in a series of vivid images, including circumcision, burial and resurrection, death and life, forgiveness, the cancellation of a legal bond, and a public triumph over one's foes. In one way or another, these metaphors all signal God's reclamation of his creation through the overcoming of forces hostile to it.

Circumcision is the physical sign that marks the Jews as God's chosen people, as those who have committed themselves to following the ways and commands of God (Gen. 17:1-27). In the written sources of Second Temple Judaism it is quite clear that circumcision was viewed as one of the identity markers of the people of God, because it marked them as belonging to the covenant and as those obedient to the Law. Throughout the ancient world, the Jews were particularly known as those who practiced circumcision. The OT and the literature of Second Temple Judaism also acknowledged a spiritual circumcision of the heart (Deut 10:16; 30:6; Jer 4:4; 9:25-26; Ezek 44:7; *Jubilees* 1:23-25), while nevertheless not reaching the conclusion that physical circumcision was thereby rendered unnecessary, although it could not be seen as guaranteeing God's favor and blessing. Similarly Paul speaks of something other than physical circumcision (cf. Rom 2:28; Phil 3:3-9), and that is the sense of the circumcision of which Paul speaks here. "The circumcision of Christ" is a metaphor for what Christ accomplishes for believers through his death, to which believers are joined as they are "buried with him in baptism." This circumcision is not a mark in the flesh of believers; it is the indelible mark of death in the body of Christ that is passed on to those who are joined

---

5. Greene, "Message of the Cross," 236, 238-39.

to his body. The Gentiles who are now in Christ thus have as their definitive mark of identity not the outward, physical sign of circumcision, but the sign of Christ's death. It is the cross that marks them as God's people, now rightly related to God and in fellowship with the people of God. As Paul wrote earlier to the Colossians, though they were once estranged from God, they have been joined to the holy, chosen people of God (cf. Eph 2:11-13).

As those who were uncircumcised, outside the covenant of God, they were "dead in their trespasses" (2:13; Rom 5:12; 6:23; on the linkage of circumcision and the reception of life, see Rom 4:11-17). Christ has identified with those who were dead, joining himself to them by means of his own death so that they might also participate in his resurrection from the dead. Because he participated in death, they may participate together with him in life. The Colossians have now been initiated into God's people not through circumcision of the flesh, but through their baptism in Christ, which Paul explicates as their participation in Christ's death. As one author puts it, "baptism is a parabolic enactment of faith, a symbolic narrative. It expresses both the primary content of the faith — Jesus' death, burial, and resurrection . . . — and the nature of faith as a sharing in, not merely an affirmation of, the narrative of Jesus."[6] Identification with the narrative of Jesus' life through baptism actually generated a new form of identity.[7] The stories of those united to Christ are now to be narrated not simply in terms of their own past, but in terms of the past — and future — of Jesus Christ.

Two clauses further explain how the Colossians have been brought from death to life. First, they have received forgiveness of their sins by being joined to the one who died for their sins and was raised to life again by God. Earlier Paul wrote that they were redeemed from the power of darkness and transferred to the kingdom of God's beloved Son, in whom they received forgiveness of sins (1:13-14). This imagery has in view first forgiveness of sin, but then also deliverance from its oppressive and hostile power. As Paul put it earlier, the Colossians now live in a new kingdom, under a new power, for a new authority; here Paul speaks of receiving new life by being joined to the one who was raised to resurrection life by God. In other words, not only does God forgive all trespasses in Christ, but in doing so he vitiates the death-dealing power of sin. As Chrysostom put it, "At the cross death received his wound, having met his death stroke from a dead body."[8]

In a second and related image, Paul speaks of God "wiping away the

---

6. Gorman, *Cruciformity,* 123.

7. Johnson, *Religious Experience,* 77.

8. *ACCSNT* 9:35.

bond of indebtedness that stood against us with its decrees" (2:14). The "bond of indebtedness" was a legal document, a certificate of indebtedness, recording what one owes to another.[9] God wipes away this enormous debt, this blot on the human record, which manifested itself in estrangement from God and in evil deeds (1:21). But the graphic picture of God erasing this note and so wiping out any hint of a debt may also draw on the biblical idea of a heavenly book of life in which the names of God's faithful people are recorded (Exod 32:32-33; Ps 69:28; Dan 12:1; also Rev 3:5). In later apocalyptic literature, these books were construed as containing the good and evil deeds of humankind, and these were the books that were produced at the final judgment and served to acquit or condemn those who had done those deeds (e.g., Rev 20:12). If the "bond of indebtedness" catalogues transgression, then the image here is of God wiping the record clean, erasing the record of evil deeds, and thus removing the power of that bond to condemn. This is the beginning of that process that leads finally to Christ's presenting his people to God "holy and blameless and without fault before him" (1:22).

Paul actually takes a further step when he asserts that God "took it from our midst" by "nailing it to the cross." The bond was not merely erased; it was destroyed. It is striking that this verse does not say that Christ was nailed to the cross, but rather that the "bond of indebtedness" was put to death. The bond was destroyed, "so that no trace of it might remain. This is why he did not erase it but tore it to pieces."[10] Similarly, there is here no explicit reference to a penalty due to sin that Christ bore for sinful humanity on the cross. Rather, in an unusual and fresh image, Paul speaks of the accusing record itself being destroyed on the cross. Christ was not destroyed by the powers; rather, God's power destroyed the accusation that sin brings against humankind.

Finally, in one of the most memorable yet difficult images of Jesus' death, Paul writes that "having stripped the rulers and authorities, [Christ] made a public example of them, triumphing over them in the cross." The image is difficult because the meanings of words, the background of the image, and the implications for understanding the significance of Jesus' death are all in question. Ἀπεκδυσάμενος/*apekdysamenos*, here rendered "having stripped," is sometimes translated "he disarmed" (e.g., RSV, NRSV, NIV). The verb ἀπεκδύομαι/*apekdyomai* occurs two other times in Colossians (2:11; 3:9), both times with the sense of "removed" or "cast off," with reference to a gar-

---

9. In *Light from the Ancient East*, Deissmann argued that the *cheirograph* (here translated "bond of indebtedness") was an IOU and that the image was of crossing out a debt in writing. He describes papyri that have been "crossed" out with the "cross-shaped" Greek letter X *(chi)*; see his discussion on 332-38.

10. Chrysostom, *ACCSNT* 9:33.

ment. One might then imagine that Paul means to say Christ "divested himself" or "stripped himself" of the powers and principalities as one sheds a garment of clothing.[11] If he cast them off as one removes a garment, then the powers are pictured as clinging to or enveloping him, and in his death and resurrection Christ "cast them aside like a garment."[12] On the other hand, if the verb is taken in the active sense, with "principalities and powers" as its object, then Christ "stripped" the principalities and powers. The translation "disarmed" (NIV, RSV, NRSV) would mean that in some way Christ has taken away their weapons of destruction. Here the sense may additionally be that they have been stripped, perhaps of their armor, so that they are held up to public ridicule and humiliation.[13]

This understanding of the passage makes sense as well when the image of Christ's triumph is read against the backdrop of a triumphal procession, in which the victor in battle displays the booty won from the defeated enemy. Plutarch offers a detailed and elaborate account of one such triumphal procession, beginning with a description of the plunder taken and ending with a description of the prisoners, including the vanquished King Perseus and his children, in their humiliation (*Aemilius Paulus* 32-34). In his victories, Christ displays not weapons or treasures taken from the powers but the principalities and powers themselves in their vanquished state and in their humiliation.

Furthermore, this interpretation of the passage fits with what Paul wrote earlier about the reconciliation of the powers in Christ. The cross is the means of the reconciliation of "all things" (1:20), apparently including the powers, who were created in, through, and for Christ (1:16). Here Paul uses an image of triumph over the powers rather than pacification and reconciliation of them. But neither earlier nor here does he speak of an annihilation of the powers, although the comparison to a triumphal procession might suggest as much. But he seems to envision the restoration of the powers to their purposes in creation.[14] In its context in Colossians, the description of the powers being stripped of the garments of their dominion makes the point that they

---

11. So Dunn, *Colossians*, 167-68.

12. The second-century Gnostic *Gospel of Truth* 20:30-35 seems to reflect this understanding of the image in Colossians when it states, "Having stripped himself of the perishable rags, he put on imperishability . . . he passed through those who were stripped naked by oblivion. . . ."

13. In spite of some lexical difficulties, the majority of commentators read the verse in this way; Bruce, *Colossians*, 110-11; Harris, *Colossians*, 110; Lincoln, "Colossians," 626; O'Brien, *Colossians*, 126-28; Wink, *Naming the Powers*, 58-60. Wink notes that Athanasius understood the text in this way.

14. Green and Baker, *Scandal of the Cross*, 62.

have no autonomous power and remain subject to Christ, whose supremacy has been verified in the cross and the resurrection.[15] Because the powers were created through Christ and for him (1:16), he is their head (2:10). From this depiction of what has happened to the powers on the cross, Paul will draw the consequences for Christian behavior: Christians must not live as though they were subject to the powers or belonged to the world (2:20). Christ's supremacy has been woven into the fabric of the world in creation and is displayed in triumph in the cross and resurrection.

Gustav Aulén adduced Col 2:15 as the prime NT instance of the *Christus Victor* ("Christ is the victor") understanding of the atonement, which he identified as the "classic" (i.e., patristic) view of the atonement.[16] The point of the image, however, is not a crass display of God's superior might but a display of God's steadfast love in Christ, a love that goes to great lengths to rescue human beings from the forces to which they are unwittingly captive. As Aulén so pithily comments, "This theme is not accidental in Paul, for it recurs just in the passages where he is dwelling on the most central point of all, the love of God in Christ. It also further emphasizes the objective character of the work of redemption, and its universality; the redemption affects the whole cosmos."[17] Just as the principalities and powers proved to have no final authority over the one who is their head, so those who share in his death also share in his life and hence also his victory. They find themselves in the kingdom of God's beloved Son, subject to his rule and supremacy, not to the rule and supremacy of darkness. Because their lives have been taken up into the narrative of the death and resurrection of Christ, his power, victory, and love will now chart their destinies. What happened once for all in the past of Christ determines the future for all those in Christ.

2:16-23

16 Therefore do not let anyone sit in judgment on you in matters of food and drink or of observing festivals, new moons, or Sabbaths. 17 These are only a shadow of what is to come, but the substance belongs to Christ. 18 Do not let anyone disqual-

---

15. Hultgren, *Christ and His Benefits*, 100.

16. *Christus Victor: An Historical Study of the Three Main Types of the Idea of the Atonement* (trans. A. G. Hebert; New York: Macmillan, 1958). Aulén argued that this view reflected the dominant view among patristic writers.

17. Aulén, *Christus Victor*, 70. But Aulén's stress on the conflict between Christ and the powers is not found in this particular passage. For other readings of this passage, see Carr, *Angels and Principalities*, 168-71, 176; Gunton, *Actuality of the Atonement*, 55-56.

ify you, urging self-abasement and angelic worship, which he or she has seen upon initiation, puffed up without cause by a human way of thinking 19 and not holding fast to the head, from whom the whole body, nourished and held together by its ligaments and sinews, grows with a growth that is from God.

20 If with Christ you died to worldly principles, why do you live as if you still were bound to these worldly regulations: 21 "do not handle," "do not taste," "do not touch"? 22 All these regulations refer to things that perish with use; they are simply human commands and teachings. 23 These have indeed an appearance of wisdom in promoting a would-be religion, self-abasement, and harsh treatment of the body, but they are of no value in checking self-indulgence.

In the previous passage, Paul focused on the identity of Christ and spelled out the significance of the cross for the Colossian Gentiles who have been initiated into the full riches of God's blessings in Christ (2:12). They have been made part of God's chosen people through baptism, the "circumcision" of Christ (2:11). In being joined to Christ in death, they have also participated with him in his resurrection, thus receiving life from God (2:13). They have received forgiveness of their sins (2:13-14). Their allegiance is now to Christ (2:8), the head of all rule and authority (2:9, 15), and not to some lesser power. Nothing further can be added to the benefits of Christ's death which the Colossians have received. They have been filled with the knowledge of God through Christ, for Christ is the one in whom "the whole fullness of deity dwells bodily" (2:9), which is why those who belong to his "body" (2:19) ought not to practice "harsh treatment of the body" (2:23).

Having articulated these theological convictions about the identity of Christ and the significance of the cross, Paul now draws out their consequences with an eye toward refuting the claims and demands of the false teaching current in Colossae. Reconstruction of the false teaching depends heavily on this passage. Although the passage regularly frustrates attempts to develop a definitive portrayal, it becomes clear that the teaching focused more on certain religious practices and their validity in attaining to higher planes of spiritual knowledge and maturity than on doctrinal issues more narrowly conceived. That is to say, the issues had more to do with soteriology (how one attains salvation) and the implications for the conduct of human life than with theological understanding of various doctrinal issues. However, the distinction can scarcely be sharply maintained. For Paul, the religious practices urged on the Colossians were invalid because they did not reflect a proper understanding of Christ's identity and of the significance of the cross. Had the Colossians fully grasped the identity of Christ and the substance of the gospel, they could not have followed the injunctions that Paul here denounces.

The specious beliefs spreading in Colossae suggested that initiation into Christ and his people was not the goal or end of the process of Christian maturity. Instead, additional practices and rituals promised new growth, higher knowledge, and ultimate perfection (*teleios*/τέλειος [1:28; 4:12], *teleiotēs*/τελειότης) or fullness (the verbs *plēroun*/πληροῦν [1:9, 25] and *plērophorein*/πληροφορεῖν [4:12] and the nouns *plērōma*/πλήρωμα [1:19; 2:9] and *plērophoria*/πληροφορία [2:2]). Paul counters that the fullness of the blessings of God is to be discovered in Christ and cultivated through adherence to the gospel proclaimed about Christ, in whom "the fullness of deity dwells bodily" (2:9). Therefore, all religious practices that promise access to God and the heavenly realm through alternative avenues are dead ends.

The false teaching appears to have taken certain elements of Jewish practice, particularly observance of certain feasts and holy days, and fused these with practices of self-denial which reflected both the purity laws of the OT and Judaism and the initiation rites of certain mysteries in the region of Phrygia. Through observance of these feasts, abstention from certain foods and drinks, and fasting and practices of "harsh treatment of the body," the Colossians sought to attain higher levels of spiritual experience and knowledge. Perhaps they even thought that in some way they would enter into the heavenly realm and thus attain to a level of spirituality unavailable to those who did not devote themselves to such practices. They had entered into Christ through baptism, but that did not preclude the possibility of initiation into further religious experiences. Such experiences apparently led some to claim a superior spiritual status over against those who were content with only the "preliminary" initiation into Christ received in baptism. Circumcision, the rite of initiation of Judaism, is not mentioned, although the mention of circumcision in the previous passage (2:11) may suggest that some were seeking that as well. The observances spoken of here — festivals, new moons, and Sabbaths — when coupled with other practices such as fasting and self-denial, suggest that the false teachers were urging these practices not as means of initiation into the body of Christ but as practices to be followed after such initiation, practices designed to initiate one into another realm of spiritual experience.

An illuminating piece of literature from the ancient world at this point is the work by Apuleius known as either *Metamorphoses* or *The Golden Ass*. This long and somewhat bawdy tale recounts the adventures of Lucius, who because of greed and lust is changed into an ass, until the goddess Isis restores him to his human form. This first "metamorphosis" is recounted in chapter 11 of the book, which also tells of Lucius's subsequent initiation and "metamorphosis" into a devotee of the cult of Isis in Asia Minor. Preparation for this initiation included fasting, abstention from certain foods and strong drink, ritual washing, and the purchase of new garments — all at great expense. Although Lucius is not permitted to describe most of what he has experienced, he does describe hours spent gazing at a statue of the goddess and reports on his sense of devotion and ecstasy. Surprisingly, Lucius receives a vision telling him to undergo a second initiation — again at great expense, and requiring self-denial of various kinds — into the cult of Osiris. Although he is surprised because he thought his "full initiation had been performed long ago," he learns that "I had been initiated merely into the rites of the goddess, but had not as yet been enlightened by the sacred mysteries of that great god and highest father of the gods, the unconquered Osiris" (11.27). In other words, the successive initiations grant Lucius greater enlightenment. But no one is more troubled than Lucius to discover after his second initiation that he must undergo yet a third. The need for successive initiations indicates not his inadequacy or failure but that he has been deemed worthy by the gods to experience a blessing seldom granted to others even once (11.29).

This tale graphically illustrates what those from Gentile backgrounds, such as the Colossians, could have been acquainted with — religious practices that urged multiple initiations into higher mysteries in order for a devotee to attain higher levels of spiritual insight. But such a view may not have been limited to the mystery religions or to Gentiles. In his study of religious experience in early Christianity, Luke Johnson notes that the first-century Jewish apologist Philo of Alexandria spoke of Moses' experience in terms of a journey toward perfection and initiation into "divine mysteries" or "mysteries of the Lord."[1] Indeed, on his path to perfection, Moses eventually attained the vision of God when he entered into the darkness on Sinai.[2]

Such ideas of multiple initiations leading to higher levels of knowledge and moral perfection could easily have been fused with Christian teaching, culminating in a position that presented baptism into Jesus as an "initiation" into the "mystery" of Jesus. Colossians is replete with the language of mystery, which Paul may use to counter the assumption that faith in Jesus is yet another of the many mystery religions. Faith in Christ is open to all, indeed, to "every creature under heaven" (1:23), not just to those few devotees who can

---

1. On this whole point of multiple initiations both as part of the world of Gentile converts to Judaism and as the key to the portrayal of Moses, see Luke Johnson's discussion in *Religious Experience*, 78-103. Johnson lists a number of relevant texts in Philo. For the terminology of "mystery" in Philo, see especially *On Abraham* 122; *On Rewards and Punishments* 121; *Allegorical Interpretation* 3.71, 100, 101-3; *Sacrifices of Abel and Cain* 62.

2. For Moses as one who entered into God's presence, see, e.g., Philo, *Life of Moses* 1.158. For detailed discussion of the "mysteries" in Judaism, see further Bockmuehl, *Revelation and Mystery*.

afford the time and money to seek the higher mysteries. Paul emphasizes the unique identity of Christ and the singular character of initiation into his fellowship in order to dispel the notion that something was lacking in or available outside Christ, something which the Colossians had yet to experience.

That a Jewish element has been incorporated into this misunderstanding of the gospel is evident in Paul's warning not to let anyone sit in judgment on them with respect to "festivals, new moons, or Sabbaths." These same words appear in OT summaries of Israel's distinctive practices (1 Chr 23:31; Hos 2:11; Ezek 45:17; see *Epistle of Aristeas* 142: "[God] hedged us round on all sides by rules of purity, affecting alike what we eat, or drink, or touch, or hear, or see"). Paul's characterization of these regulations as "a shadow of what is to come" does suggest a contrast, such as is found elsewhere in his letters, between the observances and promises of the Law and their fulfillment in Christ. This might tip the balance in favor of understanding the false teaching in Colossians as an attempt to obligate Gentile converts to adopt Jewish practices. In *The Golden Ass* Lucius abstains from meat and wine in preparation for his initiation into the mysteries (11.21, 23). The "Colossian heresy" may be an inadvertent blend of Jewish laws with similar religious practices familiar to the Colossians from their pagan past.[3] The result would not be a well-articulated "false teaching" or a deliberate syncretism, but a hodge-podge of practices based on an inadequate understanding of the gospel of Christ.

A second description of the practices recommended by these false teachers is summarized in v. 18 — one of the most enigmatic passages in Colossians. Paul notes that some people are "urging self-abasement and angelic worship, which [they] have seen upon initiation." One of the striking features of this entire passage is the way in which Paul plays on the multiple meanings of certain words in order to portray the false teaching as a counterfeit religion. *Tapeinophrosynē*/ταπεινοφροσύνη occurs three times in Colossians, in 2:18, 23, where it is translated "self-abasement," and 3:12, where it has the positive sense of "humility" or "lowliness." In the Septuagint *tapeinoō*, a cognate, typically refers to fasting when this is coupled with abasement before God (e.g., Lev. 16:29, 31; 23:27, 29, 32; Ps 34:13-14). Paul will link *tapeinophrosynē* with "harsh treatment of the body" (v. 23), demonstrating that he has some sort of practice of rigorous self-mortification in view. While some may have thought of such self-denial as "humility," Paul rejects it as feigned "humiliation," because it is a humiliation that has led to being "puffed up" (v. 18). Paul will indeed urge humil-

---

3. Wink, *Naming the Powers*, 73 writes, "That [the Colossian heresy] was syncretistic is probable; that it involved ascetic practices and a rigorously Judaizing Christianity is beyond question."

ity, but not this kind of "humiliation." Genuine humility leads not to flaunting one's spiritual experiences but to dependence on each other and on Christ for growth and sustenance.

Another striking play on words occurs when Paul speaks of "angelic worship" (*thrēskeia tōn angelōn*/θρησκεία τῶν ἀγγέλων, v. 18) as a "would-be religion" (*ethelothrēskia*/ἐθελοθρησκία, v. 23). The difficult term *ethelothrēskia* (ἐθελοθρησκία), apparently coined by Paul, combines the verb *thelō*, meaning "I will" or "I want," with the noun *thrēskeia* ("worship, veneration"). This is thus a "self-manufactured" religion. In other words, this religion of self-abasement is in fact only a "would-be religion" of "humiliation" or "self-abasement," because of both its ill-conceived practices and its misdirected object: it venerates angels, rather than the God who dwells bodily in Christ (1:19; 2:9). This manufactured religion is not the gospel which has been preached to and received by the Colossians (2:6-7).

Yet another set of contrasts is found in the threefold use of *body* (vv. 17, 19, 23). Paul writes that the prohibitions being urged on the Colossians are but a shadow, "but the body (*sōma*/σῶμα) belongs to Christ." Often in Philo, in such contrasts "body" means "actuality" or "substance." The contrast, then, would be between the shadow and the reality: the rules mentioned in v. 16 are at best a shadow of the reality that is in Christ. But here it is likely that the term also refers to the body that is the church, and perhaps also to Christ's own physical body. Thus in v. 19 Paul not only implies a contrast between the shadow and the reality but further states that the "body" (or "reality") in view is the twofold body of Christ: his earthly body and the church. Thus in v. 23, "harsh treatment of the body" refers first to mistreatment of one's physical body, but by extension may well indicate that such harsh treatment constitutes an abuse of the body of Christ himself. There is a double irony here in that "harsh treatment of the body" is of no value "in checking self-indulgence," that is, more literally, it "has no value against the gratification of the flesh" ("flesh" = *sarkos*/σαρκὸς). Such self-humiliation cannot check sin or bring the Colossians before God holy, blameless, and without fault (1:22). It is a mistake to think that by punishing the fleshly body one can subdue sinful desires.

Ironically, those who make such claims end up "puffed up without cause by a human way of thinking" (v. 18) or "puffed up by the mind of flesh" (*noos tēs sarkos autou*/νοὸς τῆς σαρκὸς αὐτοῦ). Thus there is also here a double use of "flesh," which in Paul can refer to both the actual stuff of which human bodies are made and human sinfulness apart from the Spirit of God. Subduing the physical body, the "flesh," does not tame human sinfulness, the "flesh." Ironically, the contention that "humiliation" of the "flesh" leads to humility of spirit results only in being vainly puffed up. Seeking to subdue the power of the flesh, they instead became subject to it.

The contrast between humility and being "puffed up" by one's spiritual experiences echoes Paul's description of his visionary experiences in 2 Corinthians 12, where he refuses to boast in these experiences and mentions a "thorn in the flesh" that was given to him to prevent a false sense of pride and elation. His description there may also shed some light on the vexed and difficult issue of the meaning of "angelic worship" in 2:18, which could refer to either worship *given to* angels (objective genitive) or worship *offered by* angels (subjective genitive). If it refers to worship given to angels, the Colossians would be guilty either of idolatry or, as other commentators who adopt this reading think, of venerating or honoring angels,[4] invoking angels as protection against evil powers,[5] speculation on angels, or, as the church Fathers took it, of a continued practice of Judaism. Since the Law was thought to have been given by angels (Gal 3:19; Heb 2:2), adherence to its commandments would be a kind of veneration, albeit not necessarily direct worship, of angels; it might be called "angelic worship" or "angel piety."

If "worship of angels" is worship offered by angels rather than offered to angels,[6] then the phrase that follows — "which they see upon initiation" — would refer to visionary experiences of the angelic hosts as they worship in heaven. This reading takes the neuter plural pronoun (ἃ/*ha*) as referring to "angelic worship"; hence the translation, "angelic worship, which they see upon initiation." While this may be a bit awkward, the syntax of the sentence is difficult to construe on any reading. Here, "which they see" refers to the worship that the angels offer, and "upon initiation" refers, ironically for Paul, to what some Colossians claim to have experienced, namely, that they have entered into

---

4. "Veneration of angels" could refer either to rituals and practices intended to placate hostile angels or to invocation of benevolent angels for protection from the "principalities and the powers." On the whole, the church Fathers took it as honor given to angels through whom the Law was given because they saw the problem as evidence of the continued practice of Judaism (see *ACCSNT* 9:37-40). But recent interpreters have generally argued that "Judaism" is an inadequate background for or target of the polemic in Colossians (see DeMaris, *Colossian Controversy,* 62-63), and hence have suggested either that the "veneration of angels" refers to the practices of some groups of Jews who honored angels; to folk religion, either Jewish or Hellenistic, that carried over some practices of venerating angels; or to a syncretistic blend of Jewish and Hellenistic beliefs and practices. Two studies which argue that there was "veneration of angels" in Judaism are Stuckenbruck, *Angel Veneration,* and Arnold, *Colossian Syncretism;* for counterarguments, see Hurtado, *Lord Jesus Christ,* 32-42; Bauckham, *God Crucified,* 13-14.

5. This is most recently and vigorously argued by Arnold, *Colossian Syncretism,* especially 8-102.

6. Especially Francis, "Angelic Worship."

higher realms of spiritual experience in something comparable to an "initiation." This experience would be regarded as available to those who pay diligent heed to the various prohibitions and practice fasting and self-denial. The evidence for this second reading comes from various Jewish texts that refer to the possibility of worshiping *with* angels, rather than worshiping angels. Fasting was considered appropriate preparation for the reception of divine revelations and visionary experiences (Dan 10:2-9; *4 Ezra* 5:13, 20; 9:23-25; *2 Baruch* 5:7-9; 12:5-7; 43:3).[7] In the *Apocalypse of Abraham* (first-second century AD), Abraham is told to abstain from food and wine and from anointing himself with oil for forty days, is accompanied by an angel on his journey to sacrifice Isaac, and is eventually taken on a heavenly journey, where he sees angels worshiping the Eternal One (chs. 15-19). Some of the Dead Sea Scrolls, particularly the so-called "Songs of the Sabbath Sacrifices" (see also 1QSb 4.25-26) may indicate that some viewed themselves as participating in or having visions of the angels' worship of God. Already in the first century there are indications of the Jewish mystical practices which would develop later into Merkabah ("throne") mysticism, which is focused on attaining visions of God seated on his heavenly throne (the key texts are Daniel 7, Isaiah 6, and Ezekiel 1). In the NT book of Revelation, John has visions of the heavenly hosts worshiping God and the Lamb on their thrones. Through his visions, he participates in this worship.

These texts may suggest that Paul argues against a set of practices, including practices of self-denial, as if they could grant one knowledge of a higher world or deeper insights into the divine realm. But it should be noted that there were Jewish Christian writers, such as John, the seer of the Apocalypse, who thought such heavenly visions possible and even desirable. Paul himself, as noted above, refers to the abundance of his visions and to his journey to the third heaven. In other words, the idea of worshiping "with the angels" does not appear problematic in and of itself, but only if it leads to arrogance and boasting. Yet precisely in the context in which Paul speaks of his visions, he also warns of the resulting sense of elation and hints at the false sense of superiority that may accompany such visions. They may lead one to being puffed up, proud, and elitist, especially if the visions promise greater levels of spiritual knowledge or increased understanding of the mysteries of God in Christ. At every level, these promises are illusory.

Hence, when Paul enjoins the Colossians not to "let anyone sit in judgment on you" or "disqualify you" (vv. 16, 18), he means that they are not to consider themselves second-class Christians because they have not adopted these practices advocated by the false teaching. The Greek verb rendered "disqualify"

---

7. See the discussion of texts in Francis, "Angelic Worship."

has the sense of "count you out of the race" or "deprive you of a prize." The Colossians ought not to think of themselves as having lost the race or failing to attain the prize if they do not follow the novel path charted by the false teaching. Since Christ is the head of all authority, they "have been filled" in Christ (2:10), in whom the fullness of deity dwells (2:9). Since they were buried with him in baptism (2:12-13), they have been joined with him in his death; therefore, they have "died with Christ" (2:20) and are to live "according to Christ" (2:8), not according to some drummed-up prohibitions about foods and festivals.

Indeed, the *stoicheia*/στοιχεῖα or "basic principles" can also be thought of as ABCs, the rudiments of any teaching (v. 20; see the comments on v. 8). Paul's summarizing of these principles with the negative commands "do not taste, do not handle, do not touch" reflects his ironic assessment of them as commands for the immature, not the mature. They are the kinds of commands given to children to prevent them from harming themselves — not to adults striving for deeper knowledge of God and truth. The false teachers, thinking that these commands offer the way to a higher experience of the divine, are in fact pursuing a path that leads precisely in the opposite direction. Worse, they are pursuing a path that leads not to growth in Christ "the head, from whom the whole body, nourished and held together by its ligaments and sinews, grows with a growth that is from God" (v. 19) but to a stunted faith. It is not a faith deeply rooted in Christ (v. 7) and growing by means of the growth Christ gives (v. 19), but a faith that fails to flourish because it seeks fullness where there is only a void.

3:1-4

1 So if you have been raised with Christ, seek the things that are above, where Christ is, seated at the right hand of God. 2 Set your minds on things that are above, not on things that are on earth, 3 for you have died, and your life is hidden with Christ in God. 4 When Christ, who is your life, is revealed, then you also will be revealed with him in glory.

A significant portion of the first two chapters of Colossians develops a portrait of Christ and the effects of his death on the cross. Both the blessings of salvation received by those who trust in Christ and the implications of salvation for Christian conduct are touched on in these chapters. Paul scarcely writes about the one without the other, because the death and resurrection of Christ are not simply objective acts "out there" or "back then" but events in which Paul understands the believer to be so identified with Christ that what happened to

Christ also happens to the believer. Just as Christ died and was raised, so also the one who is in Christ dies and is raised to new life; just as Christ stripped the powers and principalities, so the one who is in Christ dies to them as well. From this identification with Christ in his death and resurrection certain consequences for conduct follow inevitably and necessarily. Believers live, in the present, the life which they have received through being raised with Christ. It is the integral connection between participation in Christ and the life of discipleship that stands at the heart of the present passage.

This short passage serves as something of a bridge between the previous unit, which focused on the death of Christ, and the bulk of ch. 3, which contains many specific injunctions, both negative and positive, regarding the shape of the new life in Christ. Picking up the earlier description of the believer as one who is buried and raised with Christ (2:12), Paul reasserts the fullness of this identification with Christ by describing the believer as one whose life is "hidden with Christ in God." Those who share in Christ's death and resurrection will also share in his future manifestation in glory (3:4). Paul thus sketches the believers' life in Christ with three bold strokes encompassing past, present, and future. Believers have died and have been raised with Christ; in the present their life is hidden with him; and at his coming they will be revealed in glory with him. Although the trajectory of the believers' life can be traced along that of Christ's life, believers do not imitate Christ's path, but rather participate in his death, resurrection, and parousia. They are identified with Christ in his death, resurrection, and ultimate revelation in glory. What they have, they have in him and from him, a reality which Paul summarizes in the metaphor that their lives are "hidden with Christ in God."

Earlier Paul likened what happened through Jesus' death to a circumcision not made with human hands (2:11-13). Because through baptism believers are said to be buried with Christ in his death and "raised through faith in the power of God," they have been "circumcised," or initiated into the covenant people of God. Although 3:1-4 makes no direct reference to baptism, Paul again uses the imagery of death and resurrection with Christ to explain why and how Christians have received new life. Through initiation into Christ and his community, believers participate in, but also anticipate, the benefits and reality of the life of the resurrection. In other words, believers presently participate in the fruits of salvation, but they also anticipate the consummation of that salvation — and precisely because in Christ they have a foretaste and pledge of God's future redemption.[1] If the risen Christ is the

---

1. Keck, *Paul and His Letters,* 78, notes that Paul's view of salvation can be captured in the two terms "participation" and "anticipation."

"firstborn of the dead" (1:18), then those who are joined to him in baptism and thus share in his death have also been raised with him and share in the life of the resurrection by virtue of their belonging to the resurrected Lord. Yet he alone has tasted of the resurrection life.

Consequently, then, believers are to "seek the things that are above, where Christ is, seated at the right hand of God." The description of Christ as "seated at the right hand of God" alludes to Christ's exaltation to glory through a christological reading of Psalm 110, a psalm frequently quoted in the NT to speak of the present status of glory and dignity of the risen Christ (Mark 12:36 par.; Acts 2:34-36; Rom 8:34; Heb 1:13; 5:6; 7:17; 10:13). Indeed, the reference to his presence "at God's right hand" indicates both his vindication to this position of honor and his continued sovereignty as "the head of all rule and authority" (2:10). Paul enjoins the Colossians to pursue a complete reorientation of their lives by "seeking the things that are above," which will entail bringing all of life into conformity with the sovereign Lordship of Christ. "Seek" here does not mean to hunt for something that is missing or lost, but rather to pursue what is known and available. The Colossians are not told to discover something that has not yet become theirs, but are rather urged to pursue more deeply and fully that reality in which they presently live, the reality of their Christian life.

At its simplest, the imperative enjoins the readers of the epistle to seek Christ, to cultivate the seed that has been planted in them through the gospel so that it takes root, bears fruit, and grows into maturity (1:10, 28; 2:7). But if Christ is seated above and believers are raised with Christ, then in some sense their true lives are also now lived "above" and not "below." Such a contrast in no way denies the significance of life lived below; rather, it brings to bear upon earthly realities the "pressure" of the heavenly realm. The contrast serves to counter the false teaching by denying the possibility of attaining to the heavenly realm through visions and practices of self-denial. Indeed, the attempt is superfluous and wrong-headed, for if the life of the believer is already joined to the risen Christ, then no further initiation into the heavenly realm is either required or available. Inasmuch as believers have been raised with Christ, they have access to God, the realm above; their lives are hidden with Christ in God.

There is, then, a legitimate way of seeking "the things that are above." But the way does not lead through visions and practices of humiliation or self-abasement; the way is already given to those who are joined with Christ in baptism, and it is manifested as a reorientation of the heart and mind that leads to the sort of conduct that will be specified later (especially in 3:12-17). It has to do with setting one's mind "on things that are above," where the conduct that follows appropriately from being joined to the risen Lord excludes all those grasping and self-centered practices of one's former life (3:5-11) and expresses itself now in the body of Christ in a generous, forgiving humility that seeks the good of the other. To "set one's mind on the things that are above" does not mean to "think about heaven," but to orient one's life and devotion to God rather than to the self or the world. Athanasius once described the human plight as a misdirection of the senses. Human beings "have turned their eyes no longer upward but downward"; they "were seeking about God in nature and in the world of sense, feigning gods for themselves."[2] Human beings do not seek for that which they ought to seek; they do not orient their lives toward God. That is the predicament from which human beings are delivered as they are joined to the death and resurrection of Christ.

Even as "dying and rising" involves the whole person, so the consequences that follow from them also involve the whole person. Thus Paul unpacks the implications of being identified with the risen Christ and seeking the things that are above in terms of appropriate behavior within the community of Christ. He does not view new life in Christ as withdrawal from this earth or as a turning away from concern for life here on this earth; quite the contrary. "The things above" are those values, desires, and behaviors that reflect Christ's supremacy over the cosmos, hence deriving their orientation and value from him. But they will be values and behaviors lived out *in* this world, even as the Christ who reigns above experienced life in this world unto the point of death on the cross.

It is impossible to construe the significance of the cross and the present reign of Christ as anything other than hidden, visible only to the eyes of faith. The inevitable result will be that the life of the believer, joined to Christ, can also be construed only as "hidden." In other words, because the source of the believer's life is "hidden," its contours and commitments will scarcely be understood or appreciated by those who do not share the prior commitment to a crucified and risen Lord. The "things that are above" are those realities determined by Christ; the "things below" are realities that come from "worldly principles" and powers, powers which exert no continued mastery over the Colossians who died to them and now live with Christ.

Paul enjoins the Colossians, therefore, to "set your minds on things that are above" rather than "things that are on earth" precisely because the things on earth are visible and belong to the world in which the Colossians live and because the "things that are above" are realities that are discerned by and lived in faith. But there is no dualism here between heavenly and earthly, as though to set one's mind on "the things that are above" implies a spirituality uninterested in the world created in and for Christ. The spirituality envisioned in the

2. Athanasius, *On the Incarnation of the Word* 14-15, LCC 3:69.

false teaching was based on just such a dualism. In it the body and the realm of this world needed to be left behind in order to attain to visions of God. But the spiritual life as described in Colossians consists not of attaining to visions of God, but rather of seeing the world from the perspective of Christ, seeing it through the realities demonstrated in Christ, hence, seeing with the vision that God gives in Christ. As one writer put it, what is in view here is "the sort of heavenly mindedness that transforms every part of life by seeing it in relation to the lordship of the exalted Christ."[3]

Even as the lordship of the exalted Christ is now hidden, anticipating a future revelation in glory, so the lives of believers reflect the life of their Lord. In speaking of the life of the Christian as "hidden in Christ" with God, Paul plays on the images of what is hidden and what is revealed, perhaps thus countering the false teaching. For if it taught that there were hidden treasures yet to be uncovered (see, e.g., 2:3), then Paul protests that the entire life of the Christian is in fact a life hidden in Christ. There are no secrets yet to be disclosed to the initiate; instead the initiate, having been joined to Christ, shares in the life of the risen Lord. This is not visible to the world; it is hidden, even as Christ is. But it implies a full sharing with and in Christ that leaves nothing "hidden" in terms of coming to know God.

But Paul also anticipates a future revelation of Christ in glory, where glory has the typical biblical sense of a revealed, visual, divine presence. Although some commentators deny it, this is a reference to the parousia of Christ, his second coming, to judge the world, in the sense of exercising and disclosing his rightful lordship. As Dunn points out, references to glory in Colossians (1:26-27; 3:3-4) "show more clearly than anywhere else in Paul that the second coming matches and completes the significance of the first. The revelation which for Paul in particular distinguished Christ's first appearing (the unveiling of the ages-old mystery) only achieves completion in Christ's second appearing."[4]

The description of the future revelation of Christ's glory picks up the theme sounded earlier in Colossians of the mystery of God that has been revealed in Christ, now lodging that manifestation in the future. Thus Paul plays on and overturns the meanings of "hidden" and "mystery." What was a hidden mystery has now been made known in Christ, but in such a way that there remains a hiddenness. Precisely what the false teaching advocated as being hidden — further knowledge of God — Paul asserts to be manifest in Christ. What is hidden is not knowledge of God but the destiny of the be-

---

3. Lincoln, "Colossians," 640.
4. Dunn, *Theology of Paul*, 307.

liever, and it is hidden not from the believer but from the eyes of the world. We have here an image of identity and belonging. Because the believer is identified with the crucified and risen Lord, the believer belongs to Christ and, in belonging to Christ, belongs to God. Jesus' heavenly glory and lordship over the world, his fellowship with his people, and their identity as his people are now hidden; but these will be revealed, and thus the work of calling together a people that the life, death, and resurrection of Jesus began will be consummated. Jesus' present position of honor and sovereignty at God's right hand anticipates and promises his revelation in glory.[5]

In the meantime, Paul's own apostolic ministry, marked as it is with suffering and affliction, provides a graphic instance of a life "hidden with Christ in God." In his identification with the crucified Christ, he carries out his apostolic ministry in a hidden way, for his ministry does not readily disclose the heavenly dignity and supremacy of the risen Lord. Rather it reflects the self-giving, humility, and afflictions of the crucified Christ. Just as Christ awaits a future and public disclosure of his supremacy over all powers, including the power of death, so believers await a future disclosure of themselves as those who belong to God through the one who was crucified on the cross. And yet in identification with Christ in his death, Paul also knows of the life-giving power of the God who raised Jesus up, although that life-giving power is experienced in the present as promise and hope, anticipating the future re-creation of the cosmos. Perhaps the epistle to the Colossians does not enunciate as clearly as other Pauline passages the starkness of the tension between future hope and present reality. But there is no doubt that this tension provides the fundamental framework of its conceptions about the destiny of the believer whose life is identified with Christ. And so Augustine read Colossians in light of Romans 8 when he wrote, "'When Christ appears, your life, then you also will appear with him in glory.' So now is the time for groaning, then it will be for rejoicing; now for desiring, then for embracing. What we desire now is not present; but let us not falter in desire; let long, continuous desire be our daily exercise, because the one who made the promise does not cheat us."[6]

3:5-11

5 Put to death, therefore, your earthly members: fornication, impurity, passion, evil desire, and greed (which is idolatry). 6 On account of such practices the wrath of

---

5. Bauckham and Hart, *Hope against Hope*, 120.
6. Augustine, *Sermons* 350A.4, *ACCSNT* 9:47.

God is coming on those who are disobedient. 7 These are the ways you also once followed in your former way of life. 8 But now you must put off all such things — anger, wrath, malice, slander, and abusive language from your mouth. 9 Do not lie to one another, seeing that you have cast off the old person with its practices 10 and have put on the new person, which is being renewed in knowledge according to the image of its Creator. 11 In that renewal there is no longer Greek and Jew, circumcised and uncircumcised, barbarian, Scythian, slave, and free; but Christ is all and among all!

In the previous passage, Paul described the believer as one whose life is "hidden with Christ in God." Because believers are identified with Christ as belonging to God, they are exhorted to "seek the things that are above" rather than the things that are "on the earth." The practices and attitudes named now in 3:5-9 are characteristic of the "things on earth": "fornication, impurity, passion, evil desire, and greed," "anger, wrath, malice, slander, and foul talk," and lies. This is a rather different list than the "worldly principles" of self-denial and abstention that Paul rejected because they failed to reflect adequately Christ's victory on the cross over the powers of the world (2:20-23). The practices that Paul eschews here are marked by self-indulgence and a lack of self-control. Following this catalog of prohibitions, Paul turns in 3:12-17 to speak of the values that characterize and come from a mind "set on the things above" and of a way of life characterized by humility, regard for the other, graciousness, and giving. This way of living mirrors the life, death, and resurrection of Christ and so ought properly to characterize the one who has been buried and raised with him.

This section begins with the unusually graphic and hence jarring imperative "put to death your earthly members," where "members" refers, quite literally, to parts of the body such as arms, legs, head, and so on. Here, however, Paul does not write "put to death the members of your body" but rather "put to death the members that are on earth," the "earthly members." His use of this strange phrase may well come from the false teaching at Colossae, which may have espoused practices of self-denial or "harsh treatment of the body" as a way of "putting to death the members of the body," the members that are on earth, in order that the soul might attain to the heavenly realm. Paul picks up but redefines the "members that are on earth" in terms of a list of sinful practices. It is these that are to be done away with, to be subdued, not the members of the physical body. But the deeds in view are deeds done in the body; Paul has in view the concrete embodiment of sin in human life, similar to the sentiment in Rom 7:23 that sin dwells "in my members" and that these members have thus become the instruments of sin. If, however, a person has died with Christ to the power of sin, then these "members" are released from their captivity and freed for obedience to a new master, namely, Christ himself.

The NIV's unfortunate translation — "Put to death, therefore, whatever belongs to your earthly nature" — introduces into the text the idea of an earthly *nature,* a word that does not appear in the Greek. Similarly, at 3:9 and 10, the RSV uses "nature" to translate *anthrōpon/ἄνθρωπον,* "person." But in neither case does Paul have in mind the death of some part of the human being, as if there were some aspect of human "nature" that did not need to be put to death. Nor does he think of the regeneration of *part* of the person or of only some aspect of the person's "nature." Rather, as is abundantly apparent in his use of the imagery of dying and rising with Christ in the previous passage (3:1-4) and in his earlier description of the death of the believer with and in Christ (2:12-13), Paul thinks of the death of the whole person: the whole person is identified with Christ in his crucifixion, and the whole person is raised to new life.

This identification of the person with Christ in his death both empowers and compels one to "put to death" those behaviors and actions that do not reflect a mind "set on things that are above, where Christ is" (3:1). It is typical to speak of the movement in Paul's thought from what is (dying with Christ) to what ought to be (put to death your earthly members) as a movement from "indicative" to "imperative." But here it is crucial to recognize that the indicative already includes and entails the imperative. Paul's image of identification with Christ in his death and resurrection means that the "imperative" does not obligate one as a command external or alien to the believer. Rather, the imperative reflects and grows from the reality of being joined with Christ, hidden with Christ, belonging to Christ. The impetus for conduct is not the imperative but the relationship with Christ, and the imperative describes what Christian life is to look like precisely because it is life lived in union with Christ.

Yet the imperative "put to death" is a violent image — as violent as the act of execution by which Jesus himself died. Here the violence in view is not physical, but it is no less counterintuitive to human instinct, for on the whole humans do not seek their own death and will fight, even to death, to protect themselves and their loved ones. Paul's appeal to the Colossians that they "put to death" their earthly members thus expresses the counterintuitive character of the gospel that proclaims a crucified Lord and is embodied in the life of an afflicted and suffering apostle. What is called for here is nothing less than death: death to one way of living and being in the world in order to live by a new power and for a new master.

In some ways there is nothing distinctive about the behaviors which the

Colossians are to put to death, for the vices described are typically found in both Jewish and early Christian moral literature. In Jewish thought, "fornication" tended to refer specifically to sexual relations within prohibited degrees, including marriages of brother and sister, uncle and niece, and so on, but it also referred more generally to sexual immorality, including adultery and sexual relations with prostitutes. "Impurity" can mean uncleanness, but also takes on a moral nuance so that the "uncleanness" or "impurity" is impure moral deeds, more specifically sexual impurity. "Fornication" and "impurity" are also linked elsewhere in Paul's writings (2 Cor 12:21; Gal 5:19; 1 Thess 4:3, 7). The word translated "passion" (*pathos*/πάθος) or "lust" typically carries a negative sense of dishonorable passions (cf. Rom 1:26). Although in the present context it may refer to uncontrolled sexual passion or lust, it is also quite akin to the next two terms, "evil desire" — that is, desires that both come from evil and are directed toward evil ends — and "greed."

All of these actions and attitudes characterize the grasping, unrestrained lifestyle of a person who seeks what does not properly or rightfully belong to her or him. These behaviors are contradictory to the way of living of those who have died and released their grasp on themselves; they are also opposed to the life of abundant thankfulness that Paul speaks of more than once in Colossians. For if thanksgiving grows from humility and the recognition of dependence on another and gladly receives what the other has to give, then greed, evil desire, and passion wrongly desire what the other has. As the worship of a false god, "idolatry" fails to give proper honor to the Creator of all things, who is sovereign over all, and expresses in the sphere of worship the same self-seeking impulses that are expressed as greed and lust in other spheres. Sexual immorality, greed, and anger are closely linked with idolatry because, as one commentator put it, they can be understood as worship of the gods Eros, Mammon, and Mars.[1] Therefore, all these practices, like idolatry, will be subject to God's judgment (3:6).

To these practices Paul adds "anger, wrath, malice, slander, and abusive language." If the previous vices had in common that they were concrete expressions of a grasping and self-seeking lifestyle (3:5), the practices that are condemned here are directed toward other people — but with harmful intent or results. "Anger" and "wrath" are probably synonymous, as they are for example in Prov 15:1 (LXX). In both the OT and NT, as well as in Jewish literature, anger is viewed negatively, not as a natural expression of indignation but as the improper indulgence of temper and the practice of fools (e.g., Prov 14:17, 29; 15:1, 18; 22:24; 29:22; Eccl 7:9; Sir 1:22; 27:30; Matt 5:22; Gal 5:20; Jas

---

1. Lincoln, "Colossians," 646.

1:19-20). "Malice" or "evil" (*kakia*/κακία), a cognate of the adjective "evil" in the phrase "evil desire" (3:5), is a more general term, covering any evil attitude or action intended to harm another. The last two vices named, "slander" and "foul talk," point to the high premium in both Jewish and Christian literature placed on speech as an indicator of the character of the person (e.g., Prov 10:19; Matt 12:34-37; Jas 3:10-12), for speech is so often the medium through which anger, wrath, and malice are expressed, changing relationships for the worse and wounding rather than healing.[2] Although listed separately, lying also falls under the rubric of sins of speech. Because it intends to deceive the other and because it distorts the truth, lying breeds mistrust and fails to reflect the gospel, the word of truth (1:5). All these practices give evidence of a mindset radically different from the manner of life visible in Christ. Because they do not embody in human life the character of Christ and his gospel and nurture alienation rather than reconciliation and peace, they cannot further the unity of Christ's body and have no place among those who have died and risen with Christ.

All these practices are to be "put off" (3:8). This imperative is grounded in the indicative: those who have died with Christ have died to the old sinful ways, they have "cast off" these sinful ways, and have been clothed with the new life. Taken together, the statements that believers have "cast off" the old and are to "put on" the new suggest a thoroughgoing, radical transformation, as radical as death itself. The death of the old is not the result of one's own exertion, and far less the consequence of any ascetic practices which were said to entail the "casting off" of the physical body, such as were urged by the false teaching threatening the Colossian church. There is certainly no sense that the "body" is to be cast off while the spirit or soul of the person somehow survives. Rather the metaphor of death describes what has happened by virtue of identification with Christ, in whom the "fleshly" body was "cast off" in being joined to his death (2:11), and who "cast off" the principalities and powers on the cross and in the resurrection (2:15). Believers who are joined to Christ participate in the new life in which the old has been cast off.

According to Paul, what is cast off is the "old person" and what is put on is the "new person." Awkward though this translation may be, it is better — as noted above — than translations that speak of the "old nature" being cast off. For as C. F. D. Moule put it, "these phrases do not merely mean 'one's old, bad character' and 'the new, Christian character' respectively, as though referring to an *individual's* condition; they carry deeper, wider, and *corporate* associations, inasmuch as they are part of the presentation of the Gospel in terms of

2. See Wright, *Colossians*, 137.

the two 'Adams,' the two creations."[3] What is cast off is not an old part of a new person, but the old person "as identified with the old humanity, living under the present evil age and its powers. The new person is the believer as identified with the new humanity, the new order of existence inaugurated by Christ's death and resurrection."[4]

And yet Paul speaks also of a process of renewal when he writes that the new person "is being renewed in knowledge according to the image of its Creator." As one who has "cast off the old person and has put on the new person," the believer is identified with the new age and the new humanity as one who participates in the new order of existence. Yet as the previous passage made clear, this reality is hidden, and there is yet an expectation of a coming revelation in glory, when Christ will be presented publicly as the firstborn of this new order of existence. Here Paul describes a process of renewal "according to the image of its Creator." Clearly in view here is the creation of humankind in the "image of God" (Gen 1:26-27). Because Paul has earlier identified Christ as the "image of the invisible God" (Col 1:15), Christ is the image of the renewed humanity; and, hence, the renewal of humanity according to the image of its Creator takes place in Christ, the "firstborn" of all creation. The image of casting off the old person and putting on the new does not speak of a "gradual transformation" of the person from within, as though the seeds of the new person were latent within, simply ready to grow and blossom. The "old" and "new" persons are not two facets of human personality, with one waiting to be cultivated and the other waiting to be rooted out. Rather, the new person is the image of the Creator, Christ himself, and hence comes to the believer as the risen Lord, the living one who offers transformation and renewal — not from within, and not as an accomplishment — but as a gift and by the power of God. Insofar as this new person reflects the new order of existence brought about by Christ's resurrection, the new person represents the future, the new age, the age of transformed existence. The promise of the gospel is that such transforming grace has invaded the present world and offers new life to humans. New creation is the renewal, not replacement, of this present creation. "New creation is precisely that future of the present world, of all created reality, which does not emerge from the history of this world but will be given to it by God. It requires an originating act of God, just as creation in the beginning did, but in this case it will be an act which preserves the identity of the first creation while creatively transforming it."[5]

3. Moule, *Colossians*, 119.
4. Lincoln, "Colossians," 643.
5. Bauckham and Hart, *Hope against Hope*, 128.

The inclusive character of the renewal in Christ is indicated by the naming of the opposing pairs "Greek and Jew, circumcised and uncircumcised." This formula is clearly related to the formula found in Gal 3:28, often understood, there as here, to be a baptismal formula which describes the character of the new humanity in Christ. But here the formula lacks "male and female" and includes "barbarians and Scythians." From a Jewish point of view, "Greek" (or Gentile) and "Jew" were the two categories for dividing the ancient world, and "circumcised and uncircumcised" denotes the same two categories in terms of the religious practices by which their identity was distinguished.

From a Greek point of view, however, the world was divided into "Greek and barbarian," where "barbarian" clearly conveyed contempt for inferior peoples. Aristotle, for example, argued that because of their inherent superiority, Greeks should rule barbarians.[6] Plutarch, the first-century moralist, wrote that Plato gave thanks that he was born a Greek and not a barbarian and a human rather than a creature without reason (an animal).[7] According to Diogenes Laertius (third century AD), Socrates was grateful to Fortune that "I was born a human being and not one of the brutes; next, that I was born a man and not a woman; thirdly, a Greek and not a barbarian."[8] Although one can also find quite different sentiments among ancient Greek writers, it is clear from these quotations that the Greeks regarded it by far the superior lot in life to be male, Greek, and free. Among the barbarians, the Scythians were regarded as the most contemptible of all. Josephus, for example, refers to them as "little better than wild beasts."[9] From yet another point of view, "slave and free" are the two basic social classes of ancient society. Some religious cults of the ancient world excluded slaves, while others did not.[10]

In Christ previous valuation and status based on social and religious distinctions — whether from the point of view of Jew, Greek, or any other social categories — no longer identify those who belong to Christ. Those in Christ inherit an identity which unites them to each other, and it does so by transcending the old social, religious, and ethnic barriers and divisions. That ethnic identity could serve to unite groups of people against each other is illustrated indirectly by Aristotle's advice that one should not have many slaves from the same tribe or nation since they would then be less likely to make

---

6. *Politics* 1.2 (1252b.7-10).

7. *Life of Marius* 46.1.

8. *Lives of the Eminent Philosophers, Thales* 1.33.

9. Josephus, *Against Apion* 2.269. 2 Macc 4:47 mentions the sentencing to death of men who "would have been freed uncondemned if they had pleaded even before Scythians."

10. See the discussion in Wiedemann, *Greek and Roman Slavery,* 78-79.

common cause with each other and therefore less likely to revolt.[11] But Christian identity depends not on ethnic, social, or religious factors; it depends on Christ, who "is all, and among all." Christ, rather than a humanity divided along ethnic, social or religious identities, truly reflects the image of God (1:15). As the image of God, the one through whom the world was created, and as the risen Lord, the one through whom the world is renewed, Christ unites all people in the image of their Creator.

Deriving its identity from Christ, who unifies what was previously divided, the body of believers must be characterized by practices that foster unity. In the vice lists of this passage, the practices that are to be "put off" are self-seeking, divisive, and harmful in their effects on others. The next passage offers a positive description of life in Christ, with a list of virtues that virtually describe the model of Christ's own life, virtues that are to be "put on" in order to further the unity, peace, and wholeness of the body to which these individual believers belong and from which they derive their identity.

3:12-17

12 As God's chosen ones, holy and beloved, put on heartfelt compassion, kindness, humility, meekness, and patience. 13 Bear with one another and, if anyone has a complaint against another, forgive each other; just as the Lord has forgiven you, so you also must forgive. 14 Above all, clothe yourselves with love, which binds everything together in perfect harmony. 15 And let the peace of Christ rule in your hearts, to which indeed you were called in the one body. And be thankful. 16 Let the word of Christ dwell in you richly; teach and admonish one another in all wisdom; and with thanksgiving in your hearts sing psalms, hymns, and spiritual songs to God. 17 And whatever you do, in word or deed, do everything in the name of the Lord Jesus, giving thanks to God the Father through him.

Paul has just exhorted the Colossians to "put to death" such vices as lust, greed, slander, and hatred. These are part of a way of life that has no place among those who are being renewed "according to the image of their Creator." In other words, they have no place among those who are in Christ, who are being renewed in Christ and attaining to maturity in him who is "the image of the invisible God." Paul continues to use the metaphor of clothing in the present passage with a positive exhortation to "put on" or "clothe your-

---

11. Aristotle, *Politics* 7.9.9. Livy (32.26) chronicles a slave rebellion near Rome, noting that there were large numbers of slaves "of the same national origin," namely, Carthaginian.

selves" with *compassion, kindness, humility, meekness, and patience.* While these five virtues are not direct opposites of the five vices in each of the catalogues in 3:5 and 8, they are nevertheless the fruit of a way of life that is fundamentally opposed to the way of life that those vices express. For if those vices manifest a life of self-asserting, self-seeking, and self-aggrandizing behavior, which harms others, then the virtues named in 3:12 reveal a life of self-giving, graciousness, and humility which intends the good and wholeness of the other person.

Picking up the language of his greeting (1:2), Paul now addresses the Colossians as "God's chosen ones, holy and beloved." These three ideas — that God's people are holy, chosen, and loved — come together in Deut 7:6-8, which stresses that God chose Israel not because they were a great people, but out of his love for them. That Israel was a people chosen by God marked Israel in a particular way, binding them uniquely with God's purposes for the world and identifying them as the beneficiaries of God's love. The Gentiles — which most of the Colossian Christians presumably were — are now included among the "chosen." "Chosen" is therefore close to "holy" insofar as both identify those who are set apart for and by a holy God. Paul has addressed the Colossians as "saints" (or holy) in his greeting and later asserted that the purpose of God's reconciling act was "to present you holy and blameless and without fault before him" (1:22). God accomplishes these purposes in Christ, who abolishes distinctions of race, ethnicity, and social status as the ultimate criteria of belonging to God's chosen people. God's purposes in Christ are to gather all the peoples of the world into his chosen ones.

God's incorporation of the Gentiles into the chosen, holy people of God reflects his love for them as well. Throughout the OT, Israel is often said to be the "beloved" of God or to be loved by God (e.g., 1 Kgs. 10:9; Hos 11:1). God's love for Israel is an electing love, the reason for his choosing Israel over the other nations. This theme of God's love for Israel is heightened in the Septuagint, the version of the OT used predominantly by early Christians, which often uses "beloved" (*ēgapēmenoi*/ἠγαπημένοι) — the same Greek participle as is used in Col 3:12 — in contexts where the Hebrew text has no adjective at all (e.g., Deut 32:15; 33:26; Isa 44:2) or to replace other adjectives in Hebrew.[1] Although pagans could also speak of individuals as "beloved by the gods," that Israel is loved by God is particularly stressed in the Bible, and early Christians whose native language was Greek would hear or read the same word "beloved" now applied to them as was applied to Israel in the Scriptures. They are no longer strangers to the commonwealth of Israel (Eph 2:12).

---

1. In Isa 5:7, the Hebrew "pleasant planting" becomes in the Greek "beloved planting."

The identification of the Colossians as "God's chosen ones, holy and beloved" grants them a place within the people of God, but that status also obligates them, even as it had obligated Israel, to live in a way "worthy of the Lord" (1:10). Because the Colossians follow Christ Jesus the Lord (2:6) and are identified with him in his death and resurrection, their pathway will be peculiarly marked by his teaching as well as by the pattern of his own life, death, and resurrection. Heading the list of virtues is "compassion." The English translation "heartfelt compassion" renders a phrase more literally translated "bowels of mercy" (*splanchna oiktirmou*/σπλάγχνα οἰκτιρμοῦ; cf. Phil 2:1). The *splangchna* ("inward parts, entrails") were understood to be the seat of emotions and affections. Because we assign deep emotions to the heart, the rendering "heartfelt compassion" captures the sense of the phrase. *Oiktirmos*, "pity" or "mercy," was used in the Septuagint for God's compassion (e.g., Exod 34:6). Paul also uses it for God's demeanor toward human beings (Rom 12:1; 2 Cor 1:3). Hence the implication is that in demonstrating "heartfelt compassion" for others, one follows the example of God, particularly as it is embodied in the life and death of Jesus the Lord.

"Kindness" ("generosity," "goodness": *chrēstotēta*/χρηστότητα) is likewise used by Paul of God's goodness (Rom 2:4; 11:22; Eph 2:7), as it is frequently in the Septuagint: "Taste and see that the Lord is good" (Ps 34:8 [LXX 33:9]); "you, O Lord, are good and forgiving, abounding in steadfast love to all who call on you" (Ps 86:5 [LXX 85:5]; see also Ps 25:8 [LXX 24:8]; Jer 40:11 [LXX]). Paul uses it of himself in the self-commendation of his apostolic labors and demeanor (2 Cor 6:6). In Gal 5:22, it is one of the fruits of the Spirit, hence that which the Spirit of God works in and through humans.

"Humility" (*tapeinophrosynēn*/ταπεινοφροσύνην) is similarly used by Paul to designate that which Christians are to exercise because it is what has been embodied in and modeled by their Lord, who was willing to take a lowly status. When Paul writes that Christ "humbled himself" (Phil 2:8), he uses the verbal cognate of the noun, contrasting Christ's path with "self-seeking" and "vainglory" (Phil 2:3). In Greek literature the word was used derogatorily of weakness and shame, thus underscoring the "stumbling block" that Christ's death and Christian imitation of his life posed to Christian converts or would-be converts. The noun appeared earlier in Col 2:18 and 23, where it is translated "self-abasement" or "humiliation." While the Colossian "philosophy" may have used the term positively of the humiliation of the body which they saw as requisite for attaining experiences of the heavenly realm, Paul deems their "humiliation" a false humility, because it led to being "puffed up" (2:18) and had failed to actually check the self-indulgence of human sinfulness (2:23). Paul places the term in the context of the norms incumbent upon the community of the crucified Christ in order to indicate that a genuine manifestation of "humility" leads to heartfelt compassion, kindness, meekness, and patience and neither to individualism nor to vaunting one's distinctive religious experiences.

"Meekness and patience" are also both used of Christ or God in Paul's letters, the NT, and the Septuagint, as well as of dispositions that are to characterize human beings. Paul speaks of "the meekness of Christ" (2 Cor 10:1). Christians are to restore the fallen in a "spirit of meekness" (Gal 6:1). Meekness characterizes the demeanor which Christians understand to be demonstrated by their Lord, and consequently to be exemplified by those who belong to him. It also occurred in Jesus' own teaching (Matt 5:5; 11:29). Paul characterizes God as "patient" (Rom 2:4; 9:22), where patient is the opposite of resentful or seeking vengeance; it is the willingness to put up with the exasperating conduct of others. The Greek word *makrothymia*/μακροθυμία appears in the familiar description of God's patience in Exod 34:6: "The Lord, the Lord, a God merciful and gracious, *slow to anger,* and abounding in steadfast love and faithfulness."

The attitudes and dispositions that Paul calls for in this list of five virtues stand diametrically opposed to the two lists of five vices in 3:5 and 3:8. "Heartfelt compassion, kindness, humility, meekness, and patience" are not only oriented in a decisively different direction than practices such impurity, passion, evil desire, greed, anger, malice, and abusive language, but they also embody the "mind of Christ" as he himself embodied the will of God. Although the lists are clearly different, they differ not because they are arbitrarily chosen, but because they represent fundamentally different ways of approaching others. The way of life in Christ takes as its hallmark God's own compassion and kindness and refrains from acting irritably, from self-seeking vengeance, and from the desire to hurt and harm. The way that Paul rejects takes no notice of the effects of one's behavior on others — except insofar as one deliberately intends to do harm to them. Self-giving and self-restraint stand over against self-indulgence and self-seeking.

Having laid down the fundamental contours of the new life in Christ, Paul proceeds to give a few specific examples. "Patience" (or "longsuffering") will take shape as believers "bear with one another" and "forgive each other." It comes to practical expression in the willingness to "put up with" each other, especially when others do not manifest those traits that Paul has called for and so test the resolve and love of the individual and the community. But it is not simply enough to "bear with one another," as though a gritty determination to endure the shortcomings of fellow believers were sufficient. Instead, one is to encounter fellow Christians with the same sort of forgiveness which

Christ himself showered on them. In the command "forgive each other" Paul uses not the more common word for forgive (*aphiēmi*/ἀφίημι) but *charizomai*/χαρίζομαι, a cognate of the word for "grace" (*charis*/χάρις). The gracious forgiveness one has received in Christ determines one's response to fellow believers. The one who is in Christ will demonstrate what it means to be renewed in Christ when problems and complaints arise in the body; then graciousness toward the other appears. Such a gracious stance toward the other depends on mutuality, on the recognition that at times one will also need to receive forgiveness, and on an understanding of the Christian life as an ongoing renewal with the ultimate goal of maturity in Christ. "The realistic recognition that believers as new persons are still in the process of renewal means that forgiveness is essential for the functioning of the new humanity."[2]

Paul continues to employ the metaphor of being clothed with the new life in Christ: "above all, clothe yourselves with love, which binds everything together in perfect harmony." While the general thrust of this image is clear enough, its nuance and the Greek syntax are much disputed. Paul is exhorting his readers to put on love "in addition to" all the other virtues cited, as one final garment, either "above all," perhaps as a crown on top of everything, or "over all," as a coat or belt that surrounds and binds all these virtues together. Whichever of these images he has in view, it is noteworthy that love has this place, as it does elsewhere in Paul's injunctions, not only in 1 Corinthians 13 (vv. 4, 13), but also in his statements that the Law is summed up in love (Rom 13:9, 10) and that what counts above all else is "faith working through love" (Gal 5:6). Here Paul surely reflects the teaching of Jesus, who asserted that the greatest commandments of the Law were to love God and to love one's neighbor as oneself. Hence love does not add anything to these other virtues; it is rather the distillation, the essence, the epitome of them all. As Eugene Peterson pungently paraphrases it, "If all else fails, remember love."[3] For love "binds everything together in perfect harmony." Of course, if all else has failed, then surely the love which Christ inculcates in his people as the fundamental and basic virtue has failed as well!

Paul joins two further admonitions to his previous list of virtues and injunctions regarding love and forgiveness. The Colossians are to "let the peace of Christ rule" among them and "the word of Christ dwell in them." Both acts are to be accompanied by thanksgiving; in fact, Paul summarizes this entire section with the call to "do everything in the name of the Lord Jesus, giving thanks to God the Father through him." He thus caps off a list of

2. Lincoln, "Colossians," 650.
3. Peterson, *The Message,* Col 3:14.

summons to thanksgiving in the epistle (1:3, 11-12; 2:7). Thanksgiving is the vertical correlate of the horizontal virtues found in this section. As a posture that confesses dependence on God and gratefully acknowledges the gifts God has given in Christ and through others, thanksgiving can accompany the open posture of humility and meekness, but not the closed and hostile dispositions of greed, anger, malice, or evil desire. Thanksgiving can arise from the realities of forgiveness and the experience of peace, but it does not grow naturally out of envy and wrath. And thanksgiving to God may find its proper horizontal expression in kindness and compassion to others, but it cannot be nurtured by abusive speech, lust, and fornication.

The admonitions to "let the peace of Christ rule" and "the word of Christ dwell" give a tantalizing glimpse of Paul's vision for the life of the community together. Paul appeals to each person individually, but also to the group corporately, to allow the final arbiter among them to be not individual desires or the exercise of power but Christ's peace. There is no explicit appeal to elders, deacons, or other leaders in the church; the congregation is charged with monitoring its own behavior and together carving out the path of conduct worthy of the Lord. In "let the peace of Christ rule in your hearts," the term "rule" (*brabeuō*/βραβεύω) means to act as umpire or judge, to decide or control. A cognate of it was used in 2:18, where Paul warned the Colossians not to let anyone "disqualify" (*katabrabeuō*/καταβραβεύω) them from the prize because of their lack of participation in certain practices of self-abasement and harsh treatment of the body. They are not to let others rule against them; rather, they are to let Christ rule among them. The peace that he has established through his cross (1:20), bringing Jew and Gentile, circumcised and uncircumcised together, is to serve as judge and umpire in their life together. This peace is not first a personal, subjective, inner peace, but rather the unity, the wholeness, given by Christ to the community. Since he has resolved the state of conflict and animosity that formerly existed among Jew and Gentile, they are to realize that gift concretely in the way in which they respond to and behave toward each other. Paul's use of the image of judge or umpire also implies that just as the community will need to cultivate the fruits of the peace Christ has won for them, so too will they need an arbiter outside the community. They are to look outside and beyond themselves to Christ, to seek his mind and will in their corporate life, for it is in him — and not in themselves or in what they are able to produce or conjure up — that their unity and peace are found.

There is another guide for the community, and that is "the word of Christ," which is to dwell among them. Again, the sense is not so much that "the word" somehow indwells each individual believer as that the gospel, the word from and about Christ, provided the foundation for the community in the first place (1:5-7). The Colossian believers are to allow that word to continue to guide, direct, and shape them. Paul envisions this taking place in quite specific and concrete ways, primarily as the members of the body "teach and admonish each other in all wisdom." Earlier in the epistle Paul spoke of his own tasks as "teaching" and "admonishing." His expectation that the Colossians will exercise these same responsibilities with respect to each other indicates that their own growth in the gospel and maturity in Christ expresses itself in the capacity to teach and admonish others in their growth in faith. Similarly, that they are to teach and admonish "in all wisdom" reflects the important theme in Colossians (1:9, 28; 2:3, 23) that God's wisdom is made known through and in Christ. When Christians admonish each other in wisdom, they show their understanding of God's revelation in Christ and its significance for shaping the life of discipleship.

Paul unselfishly wishes to pass on to the Colossians the responsibilities he has exercised as an apostle. But what may perhaps be the most striking feature of Paul's discussion of teaching and admonition is the means by which it happens. Since Paul began his thought by urging the Colossians to let the "word of Christ" dwell in them, one might assume that he would finish the thought with an emphasis on study, proclamation, or perhaps even obedience. But he sets his admonitions in the context of worship, and enjoins the Colossians to carry out their roles of mutual edification and instruction by singing "psalms, hymns, and spiritual songs to God." "Psalms" may refer here to the OT psalms. The only other use of "hymns" in the NT is in the similar injunction in Eph 5:19. Scholars have sometimes speculated whether the "hymns" in view might be the sort of hymn to Christ we have in Col 1:15-20; but while this is suggestive there is no definitive proof of the theory. Finally, "spiritual songs" "certainly denotes or at least includes songs sung under the immediate inspiration of the Spirit."[4]

What "psalms, hymns, and spiritual songs" share in common is that they are directed to God and sung with rather than to other members of the community. Even so, or perhaps precisely because they are sung to God, they serve to admonish the members of the community. By directing the thoughts and minds of believers to God, these acts of worship serve corrective functions in the lives of believers, reorienting them to praise and thanksgiving to God. Of course, words alone, by reminding the community of what it is in Christ and what God has done for its members through Christ or by offering praise and thanksgiving to God, can also serve to reinforce the teaching of the

---

4. Dunn, *Colossians*, 239.

letter and thus instruct the Colossians. But it is noteworthy as well that the admonition Paul speaks of is not primarily in words spoken to or about others in the community, designed to reprove or correct them; rather, as words addressed to God, these hymns and songs are songs of worship, and they instruct and admonish indirectly.

It is the worship addressed to God with grateful hearts, from a community bound together by love and shaped by Christ's peace, and not the "angelic worship" that prides itself on visions of the heavenly realm, which God desires. Paul's understanding is not so far from the prophetic call in the OT to offer up to God the true worship that flows from lives of justice and righteousness rather than empty or ostentatious displays of sacrifice and ceremony.

3:18–4:1

18 Wives, be subject to your husbands, as is fitting in the Lord. 19 Husbands, love your wives and do not become embittered against them. 20 Children, obey your parents in everything, for this is pleasing in the Lord. 21 Fathers, do not provoke your children, or they may lose heart. 22 Slaves, obey your human masters in everything, not only for the sake of external appearance but wholeheartedly, fearing the Lord. 23 Whatever your task, put yourselves into it, as done for the Lord and not for your masters, 24 since you know that you will receive the inheritance from the Lord as your reward; you are slaves of the Lord Christ. 25 For the wrongdoer will be paid back for whatever wrong has been done, and there is no partiality. 4:1 Masters, treat your slaves justly and fairly, for you know that you also have a Master in heaven.

This unit of Colossians, which treats the relationships between wives and husbands, children and their parents, and slaves and masters, has seemed to some commentators to have been dropped almost ready-made into a context which it does not fit very well and which, in turn, seems not to have affected its substance much. Indeed, a great deal of the discussion of the social context and modern application of these instructions has to do with the extent to which these codes of conduct have simply been taken over from Roman culture.[1] If these codes are simply taken over from the social and cultural context of early Christianity, then a number of questions arise: To what extent would such instructions have as their intention the goal that Christians fit into their cultural

---

1. Such lists of instructions, often referred to as "household" or "domestic codes" (German *Haustafeln*) are found also in Eph 5:21–6:9; 1 Pet 2:13–3:7.

contexts without rocking the boat? Is such an aim intrinsic to Christian morality, or have the circumstances of the Colossians or the larger cultural context of the time essentially determined Paul's injunctions regarding Christian conduct? If Paul seems not to challenge certain cultural norms or patterns — such as slavery — can such silence be taken as implicit approval? Indeed, is there anything distinctly "Christian" about the behaviors urged here, or have cultural norms simply been "baptized" in the name of conformity?

Martin Dibelius, who pioneered form-critical study of these domestic codes, argued that they were essentially borrowed from Stoicism and only lightly "Christianized." They demonstrate the church's increasing need to find its place in society as it abandoned its belief in the imminent return of the Lord, to settle in and come to terms with its apparently long(er)-term place in society.[2] It did so, at least in part, by adopting the norms advocated in both Greco-Roman (i.e., Stoic) and Jewish ethics. In other words, there is little that is revolutionary, let alone distinctly Christian, about the behavior urged in these codes. Instead, they represent something of an accommodation to accepted patterns of behavior outside the Christian community.

Dibelius's interpretation has been highly influential, although it has certainly not gone unchallenged or been left unmodified.[3] So, for example, viewing the adoption of these codes less benignly than does Dibelius, Eduard Schweizer speaks of these household codes as the "paganization" of Christianity. The codes have collapsed sole obedience to God with obedience to persons higher in class or in the social order.[4] These two allegiances in fact become one and the same.

On the other hand, Richard Hays comments, with respect to Ephesians, at least, "In all respects, then, the household code of Ephesians articulates a vision for community whose social relations are impacted by the gospel of Jesus Christ." While not egalitarian in the modern sense, nevertheless, the vision for marriage here unsettles and deconstructs the "conventional patterns" of these relationships by urging husbands to practice self-sacrificial care on analogy with the self-giving love of Christ.[5] Hays's view stands diametrically

---

2. Dibelius's commentary, *An die Kolosser, Epheser, an Philemon,* was first published in 1912 and revised in 1927 and 1953. For recent summaries of discussions of the NT household codes, see Fitzgerald, "Haustafeln," and Balch, "Household Codes," in the *Anchor Bible Dictionary.* The household codes are typically treated together because of their similarities to each other and to ancient moral exhortation.

3. See the discussion in Harink, *Paul among the Postliberals,* 133-49.

4. Schweizer, "Die Weltlichkeit des Neuen Testaments."

5. Hays, *Moral Vision,* 64-65. Hays regards Ephesians as belonging to the development of the Pauline tradition rather than written by Paul.

opposed to Schweizer's, which brands the household codes as "pagan" because they accommodate Christian ethics to pagan norms; Hays speaks of them as "impacted by the gospel" so that they in turn deconstruct conventional pagan patterns.

Although perhaps a laudable goal, it is perhaps virtually impossible to reconstruct how an early congregation would have heard the words of Col 3:18–4:1, that is, whether they would have heard them as overturning or accommodating to cultural norms. Of one thing, however, we may be certain: these words would have been heard within multiple contexts: within the Roman social order, with its traditional hierarchical ordering of relationships, within the church, with its commitment to its Lord, who gave himself sacrificially and provided the model for relationships among Christians, and within the literary context of the letter's admonitions to Christian conduct. Of particular importance, as the wording of even these fairly traditional injunctions indicates, is the location within the context of Christian conduct as modeled by Jesus, lived out in the life of the community, and commanded in the previous sections of this epistle.[6] Hence, the context within the letter merits closer attention.

Immediately preceding this passage, a list of vices that amount to ways in which people seek their own gratification while exploiting or harming others has been balanced by a set of positive injunctions regarding virtues and habits to be cultivated by those who are being renewed in the image of the Creator (3:5-17). In that renewed image, differences between Greek, Jew, and barbarian or free and slave which have previously marked people out in terms of their different status, are abolished, since the gospel of God's reconciling peace in Christ eradicates such distinctions of status or priority. In Christ, no one has an inherently superior nature or status over against another. But such a bold statement would have been directly contrary to the widespread belief in the superiority of Greeks to barbarians and in the superiority of the free to slaves. The unity which believers have in Christ reshapes the traditional view of "rules for the household." The behaviors appropriate for this household are humility, meekness, forgiveness, love, and compassion, practices and dispositions which foster unity and care for the other.

The injunctions governing Christian relationships form the backdrop for the three relationships specified here: wives and husbands, children and parents, and slaves and masters. In treating these three relationships, Paul is

---

6. Byron, *Slavery Metaphors,* argues that for Paul Jesus was the paradigmatic slave of God in living out the pattern of humiliation-obedience-exaltation that was in fact characteristic of Jewish notions of slavery to God, including Israel's enslavement and future vindication. The pattern is clear in passages such as Phil 2:6-11 and 1 Corinthians 9 but not explicitly articulated in Colossians.

no innovator. As indicated above, Martin Dibelius argued that Stoicism was the source of the injunctions in the household codes. But the more common view today argues that the background for these household codes is to be found in the stereotypical Hellenistic discussion of "household management" (*peri oikonomias*/περὶ οἰκονομίας, "concerning the household"), particularly as drawn from Aristotle's discussion of the ordering of both the household and the state.[7] Aristotle shows the ways in which Paul not only reflects cultural norms of the day but also modifies them in light of his convictions regarding Christian community.

Aristotle addresses the same three relationships. He assumes that in each pair one member is superior to the other and hence is given the obligation to rule or govern. "For that some should rule and others be ruled is a thing not only necessary, but expedient; from the hour of their birth, some are marked out for subjection, others for rule."[8] As we noted in discussion of 3:11, Aristotle assumed that Greeks, by nature superior to barbarians, ought to rule over barbarians. The same argument gives masters rule over slaves, parents over their children, and husbands over their wives. Aristotle grounds the last relationship in the intrinsic superiority of male nature. "Again, the male is by nature superior, and the female inferior; and the one rules, and the other is ruled; this principle, of necessity, extends to all mankind."[9] The right to rule is not simply assigned arbitrarily to one group, but is rather given to those who merit it on the grounds of their superior capacities and nature. Aristotle also qualifies his statements by explaining that there are fundamental differences between the rule of a father over his children and his rule over his wife. "A husband and father, we saw, rules over wife and children, both free, but the rule differs, the rule over his children being a royal, over his wife a constitutional rule. For although there may be exceptions to the order of nature, the male is by nature fitter for command than the female, just as the elder and full-grown is superior to the younger and more immature. But in most constitutional states the citizens rule and are ruled by turns, for the idea of a constitutional state implies that the natures of the citizens are equal, and do not differ at all."[10]

---

7. In dialogue with Dibelius, Yoder, *Politics of Jesus,* 178-79, argues that there is no evidence that the household codes were borrowed from Stoicism and, hence, suggests that "this kind of teaching . . . must have grown directly out of the meaning for the young church of confessing Christ as Lord." But similarities to Aristotelian ethics and to views found in Josephus and Philo (see below) make it likely that these codes were developed out of common moral exhortations of the day.

8. Aristotle, *Politics* 1.5 (1254a.23).

9. Aristotle, *Politics* 1.5 (1254b).

10. Aristotle, *Politics* 1.12 (1259a.36-39).

Very similar treatments of these themes occur in the writings of the Jewish authors Philo and Josephus, who are further concerned that conformity to the norms of Greco-Roman society should provide a testimony to Judaism's positive contribution to the good of the state. Philo uses the same three categories as Aristotle and the NT household codes, noting throughout the need for benevolence and piety to govern one's actions.[11] Similarly, Josephus writes at some length regarding the relationship of husband and wife, noting that "authority has been given by God to the husband" (*Against Apion* 2.201).[12] Later he comments on the importance of the obedience of children to their parents. In both cases, he grounds these commands in the Law itself, rather than in cultural norms of the day, but the patterns are quite similar to those found in Aristotle.

Aristotle's instructions protect the vested interests of the superior partner — husband, father, slave owner. The Roman legal code gave to the male rights over his wife, children, and slaves. In the context of such a legal code, the relationships under discussion here are conceived primarily not as relationships of covenant or mutual love, but as the proper order both within the legal code and in light of the nature of the individuals involved. Where, then, do the injunctions of Paul fit? Do they also protect the vested interests of the "superior" partner in each pair? Paul assumes that the conduct of Christians must always be guided by the norms given to them in Christ and lived out in the circumstances of this world. Within the community of fellow believers, the norm for behavior is clear: Christ's followers are to treat each other as Christ has treated them. It is clear that Paul addresses *believing* husbands, wives, parents, children, masters, and slaves, for it is highly unlikely that non-Christians would be hearing or reading the letter or that Paul intended to regulate the conduct of those outside the community.

What is less clear, however, is whether in each pair of relationships, the member not addressed is necessarily also a believer. Christians did find themselves in marriages with non-Christians (1 Cor 7:12-16), and this may have been the case more frequently for women than for men (e.g., 1 Pet 3:1-6; 2 Tim 1:5). Christian slaves also often had unbelieving masters (1 Pet 2:18-25; 1 Cor 7:21-24). Paul assumed in these cases that the legal status of these relation-

---

11. Philo, *Hypothetica* 7.1-14; *De decalogo* 165-67. In *Quod omnis probus liber sit* 79, Philo comments that slavery has annulled "the statute of Nature, who mother-like has borne and reared all men alike, and created them genuine brothers, not in mere name, but in very reality." Philo then comments that this kinship has been destroyed by "malignant covetousness," creating "estrangement instead of affinity and enmity instead of friendship." Masters are to treat their slaves with kindness and gentleness, thereby equalizing their inequality (*De decalogo* 167).

12. Josephus, *Against Apion* 2.190-219.

ships remained intact. What he sought to regulate and shape was Christian behavior in any and all circumstances of life, in the social structures and cultural contexts in which Christians found themselves and lived in obedience to their Lord. But his approach in no way grants his own tacit approval or divine authority to those structures. To "set the mind on things that are above" (Col 3:1) certainly does not imply that Christian life is somehow lived apart from or above the very real and mundane circumstances of life, nor does it imply a complete disregard for obligations that believers have taken upon themselves or for the situations in which they find themselves, even when those situations are beyond their control or influence.

There are those who are disappointed with Paul and the early church for failing to offer a more revolutionary critique of the power structures in which they found themselves. It is possible that the false teachers at Colossae held out the hope of escape from the realities of this life to an existence which allowed one a glimpse of God in heaven. In any event, Paul rejected the practices of denial and humiliation of the body as though these somehow elevated their practitioners to a higher state. It is not in being removed from the perplexing and even unpalatable circumstances of life but in persevering with grace and hope that one best models Christian conduct that is lived "in a way worthy of the Lord, pleasing to him in every way" (1:10), but simultaneously recognizes the fundamental "hiddenness" of Christian identity and anticipates the renewal of humankind in the image of its Creator.

In the present passage, believers are urged to let their relationships be lived as "in the Lord" (3:18, 20), indicating that they fear the Lord (v. 22), that their actions are done for the Lord (v. 23), that they serve the Lord (v. 24), and that they ultimately have a Lord in heaven (4:1). The genius of Colossians is that all of life, from creation to redemption, is brought under the aegis of Christ's lordship; that includes the fundamental relationships of human life, and the cosmos as it now stands — anticipating its full redemption. Those commentators who think that the household codes represent accommodation to cultural norms think also that Paul (or a later author) merely glossed the status quo with a thin veneer of Christian coloring, thereby inadvertently perpetuating institutions, such as slavery, which are fundamentally oppressive and sub-Christian. But Paul does not establish or champion either the institutions of slavery or the hierarchical ordering of the family and state. These were given to him in the culture into which he was born and lived as a citizen of the Roman Empire. Paul's concern was that Christians, whose lives are "hidden with Christ in God," should live for their Lord in whatever circumstances they find themselves. That is the paradox of Christian existence, lived *for* the "Lord in heaven" (4:1), but *under* the daily rule of human "lords" or masters who do not and cannot command the Christian's ultimate allegiance. Here, too, there is a word to those human lords and masters: they do not ultimately govern or control those under their charge and are themselves answerable to the same Lord as are those under their charge. They are not masters of their own fates, captains of their own souls — any more than they are masters and captains of the fates and souls of others.[13]

In each pair, Paul first addresses the "subordinate" partner (wives, children, slaves). Wives are told to "be subject" to their husbands; children and slaves are told to "obey" their parents and masters, respectively. Although a number of commentators point out that there is little difference between the two words, it is nevertheless striking that wives are not told to "obey." As noted above, Aristotle spoke of the rule of a husband over his wife as "constitutional" and of a father over his children as monarchic or royal; different models of government were appropriate to the different relationships. One cannot help but wonder whether Paul assumed this to be the case, even if he did not make it explicit, leading him to apply one command to wives and another to children and slaves. In any case, there is little deviation from the norms found in pagan or Jewish writers in enjoining a wife to "be subject" to her husband. This does not imply blind assent to a husband's every wish and whim. It is rather the response of Christian character spelled out in the previous section as humility, meekness, and forgiveness.

Where there is a notable deviation from societal norms, however, is in the command that husbands love their wives. One might expect, given the cultural norms of the day, that Paul would tell the husbands in the congregation to rule their wives and households, but perhaps to do so wisely, prudently, and benevolently. Paul's one command to husbands — "Husbands, love your wives and do not become embittered against them" — is taken directly from his earlier summary command to all Christians, "Above all, clothe yourselves with love, which binds everything together in perfect harmony" (3:14).[14] Paul's understanding of love as the essential virtue of the life of discipleship is carried over here into the command to husbands. By cultural con-

---

13. The allusion is to William Ernest Henley's stunningly individualistic and self-aggrandizing poem "Invictus," whose final couplet runs, "I am the master of my fate: I am the captain of my soul."

14. Marriage could also be viewed by Greek philosophers and moralists as a loving and mutually beneficial relationship. For example, the first-century Stoic philosopher Musonius Rufus wrote that "in marriage there must be above all perfect companionship and mutual love of husband and wife, both in health and in sickness and under all conditions" (*What Is the Chief End of Marriage?* 10-20). Here the language is not that of rule and superiority, but of companionship and love.

vention and by legal right men — if Roman citizens — had the superior position of rule over their wives. But "in the Lord" humility, meekness, heartfelt compassion, and forgiveness are to govern relationships. Paul thus further enjoins the husbands not to "become embittered against" their wives. They are not to harden their hearts against their wives, but to exercise the heartfelt compassion and gracious forgiveness characteristic of the Lord whom they serve. If the basic legal relationship remains intact, it is fundamentally re-ordered by its placement within the framework of the conduct expected of those who "serve the Lord Christ" (v. 24). It is simply impossible to live on the model of Jesus Christ within the structures of society and to leave the relationships within them fundamentally unchanged.

Children are told to obey their parents in "all things." Paul here reflects both Greco-Roman mores and the biblical commandment that children honor their fathers and mothers. While "all things" may at first seem to leave children vulnerable to abusive or overbearing parents, there is always an "escape clause" implicit in such apparently global commands. No one could be expected to obey any command which compelled violation of the law of God. Daniel did not break the Law when commanded by a human king to do so; the Jews did not bow to Caligula when he wished to erect standards with his image in the temple or when he ordered them to sacrifice to him; and Peter and John did not agree to stop preaching about Jesus since, as they put it, "We must obey God rather than any human authority" (Acts 5:29). These sorts of exceptions are inherently built into all commands to be subject to or to obey another.

Although some translations render v. 21 as "Parents, do not provoke your children," it is more likely that Paul is addressing fathers here, since they had particular rights over their children in Roman society. Fathers are to exercise their rights not in demanding things for themselves or in insisting on their own way, but in measuring the impact of their behavior on their children. This instruction captures in specific form the earlier injunctions against anger, malice, and abusive speech and also reiterates the positive injunctions to be gracious, forgiving, and compassionate.

The longest exhortation covers the relationship of masters and slaves. This may reflect the fact that Colossians and Philemon were apparently written at the same time, when Paul was endeavoring to reconcile Onesimus with his human master Philemon. It may simply reflect the reality that a number of the Christians in the earliest churches were slaves. There is no evidence that some of these Christian slaves were either fomenting or participating in rebellion against their masters or status and that Paul was trying to quell such movements. Just as children are told to obey their parents "in everything," so slaves are told to obey their "human masters in everything," where "human" translates the phrase "according to the flesh." The contrast is not between the slave's "flesh" and "spirit," as though the master owns a slave's body but not his soul. Rather the human master, the master "according to the flesh," is contrasted later with "the Lord Christ" (3:24), the "Master in heaven" (4:1). The Christian slave belongs wholly to his Lord Christ; he belongs "according to the flesh" to his human master.

When Paul writes that those who sincerely serve their human masters are in fact serving the Lord, he does not simply collapse the heavenly Lord and the human master; this is how Eduard Schweizer, who spoke of the "paganization" of Christianity via the adoption of the Greek household codes, read these injunctions. Jewish authors who wrote about threats of personal or national enslavement distinguished between slavery to God and to human masters, but sometimes saw the latter as part of one's obedience to God.[15] But the two forms of service or enslavement remained independent of each other, while at the same time overlapping in the person of the slave. Service of the earthly master may in fact constitute service of the Lord, but sometimes the enslavement was deemed unjustified, and there was an expectation of vindication and release. In other words, there is no constant or direct connection between being a slave of God and of a human master, since various scenarios could account for a person's enslavement in the first place.

Here the point seems to be that ultimately the slave has one master to whom he or she belongs and whom she or he serves, and that is the Lord Jesus Christ. To be sure, such an argument sounds perilously like double-talk. Of course slaves have human masters: this is what makes them slaves. The closing word to slaves, "you are slaves of the Lord," is more typically translated "you serve the Lord Christ," or, if taken as an imperative, "serve the Lord Christ." While these are possible translations, Paul may indeed mean "you are slaves of the Lord" or "you are enslaved to the Lord." In other words, a Christian slave does not belong to any human master; the Christian slave belongs to the Lord Jesus Christ. Human masters do not "own" their slaves — but neither do slaves "own" their own bodies. Indeed, they are "enslaved" to the Lord Jesus Christ. Paul's thought here can scarcely be very palatable to those for whom the right of personal self-determination constitutes an unequaled good. For Paul, it is not self-determination that constitutes genuine freedom, but rather belonging to the one who delivers from captivity to sin and death.

15. In *Slavery Metaphors*, Byron surveys different Jewish responses to slavery. While, on the one hand, Jews steadfastly understood themselves to be slaves of God, the responses to enslavement to human masters varied. Of the various responses, Philo drew the sharpest distinction between physical slavery, which was of no ultimate consequence, and slavery of the soul, which could hinder enslavement to God (see pp. 96-116).

Identity is defined in relationship to whatever or whomever one serves, and the slave who belongs to Christ is identified first and foremost as a slave of Christ. Even if the legal codes of the Roman Empire dictated that slaves belong to their human masters, in Christ all have become slaves of Christ, and slaves no less than their masters are enslaved to the Lord Christ.[16]

Paul promises slaves that they will receive "the inheritance as your reward" — a paradoxical assertion of their identity in Christ, since slaves had no rights of inheritance. Paul exploits the contrast between the right of sons and slaves to inherit in the allegory of Hagar and Sarah in Galatians 4. Here, however, he promises slaves that those who serve the Lord, who work wholeheartedly in devotion to the Lord, will surely gain the inheritance promised to them. If there is no reward in this life for hard service, nevertheless the Lord, who is an impartial judge and does not favor free masters over their slaves, will take account of the slave's service.

Finally, then, Paul turns to the masters and urges them to treat their slaves with justice and fairness. For they, too, have a Lord — or master — in heaven. Since the distinction between masters and slaves was often coupled with a view of a slave's inferiority in status, nature, and character, Paul's reminder that Christian slave owners are in fact "slaves" of Christ has turned these social conventions upside down.[17] With this assertion Paul puts slave and free, slave and master, on the same footing. Both serve the same Master; both are ultimately responsible not to a human master but to the Lord in heaven. If the master has certain legal rights in this world, he nevertheless must behave not according to what his rights may be but rather according to what his obligations are as one who serves the Lord Christ.

The household codes are worrisome because they appear to perpetuate societal patterns that lend themselves too easily to domination and abuse. But Paul stands the typical injunctions to husbands, fathers, and masters on their heads by making it very clear that those who are in power may not set the rules according to their own whims and preferences. They may seem to "rule," but the rules have in fact already been determined by Christ, who is Lord of all (cf. 3:15: "let the peace of Christ rule"). Again, the powerful may not use their power for their own ends, but must exercise it on the side of the disadvantaged, the less powerful. Their power, then, takes the form not of insisting

16. Paul would have resonated with Philo's query, "Are we not under a master, and have we not and shall we not have forever the same lord, slavery to whom gives us more joy than freedom does to any other? For of all the things that are held in honor in this world of creation slavery to God is the best" (*Dreams* 2.100).

17. For a collection of relevant primary sources, see *Greek and Roman Slavery* (ed. Thomas Wiedemann; Baltimore and London: Johns Hopkins University, 1981).

on one's legal rights or dominating the other, but rather expresses itself as humility, meekness, compassion, and love, the very traits which the Master in heaven himself displayed. Those who participate in the reality of the new humanity created in Christ live in two worlds at once: they live in the reality of the new creation, but they live in that reality in the present world order. And although it seems that the legal relationships and social conventions of slavery have been left in place, they do not finally determine the ways in which those within those relationships conduct themselves, or to whom master and slave alike ultimately belong.

4:2-6

2 Devote yourselves to prayer, keeping alert in it with thanksgiving. 3 At the same time pray for us as well that God will open to us a door for the word, that we may declare the mystery of Christ, for which I am in prison, 4 so that I may reveal it clearly, as it is necessary for me to do. 5 Conduct yourselves wisely toward outsiders, making the most of your opportunities. 6 Let your speech always be gracious, seasoned with salt, so that you may know how you ought to answer everyone.

In Paul's closing exhortations he urges the Colossians to be steadfast in prayer, particularly in prayer for him and his work of proclaiming the gospel. If Paul's task is to proclaim the word, the Colossian Christians do their part not only by praying for him but also by embodying wisdom in their relationships to unbelievers. Such wisdom is particularly revealed in the manner and content of speech with which Christians address outsiders. Earlier Paul gave instructions to the Colossian Christians regarding the sort of speech that served to further the mutuality of relationships in the body of Christ: speech was to be marked by truth and grace (3:8-9). His focus is essentially the same here: speech is to be gracious and informed with wisdom.

Paul's first injunction, that the Colossians devote themselves to prayer, recalls his earlier statement that he had "not stopped praying" for them (1:9). By placing the word for "prayer" at the beginning of the sentence, he emphasizes it; one might then translate, "Prayer — devote yourselves to it." Paul's correspondence repeatedly testifies to the importance he placed on a life permeated by prayer, as well as on the role of prayer in the life of the minister of the gospel. Prayer was not separable from his life as an apostle but was rather a crucial part of the commission given to him to preach the gospel and tend to his churches. Similarly, prayer was not an addendum to the life of the believer, but was an essential part of the Christian life.

Implicit in Paul's instructions are three characteristics of the praying Christian. First, one is to be "devoted" to prayer. The word may have the sense of persistence and perseverance, but also carries the nuance of patience; the same word is used of the devotion of the early Christians to prayer in Acts 1:14; 6:4. Early Christians appear to have engaged in prayer on regular occasions, either individually or when gathered together, as well as in times of specific need (e.g., Acts 1:14; 3:1; 6:4; 10:30, 31; 12:5; 14:23; 16:13, 16). Paul does not mean that Christians are to suspend all other activities and to devote every minute of every day praying, but that prayer is to be a regular and central feature of their lives as Christians. Neither does the call to be "devoted" to prayer mean that one should constantly repeat the same prayer, perhaps hoping thereby to gain a positive response from God by persistently asking for the same thing. Rather, the attitude of steadfastness, of patience, in prayer demonstrates one's reliance upon God.

Second, then one is to be "alert" or "watchful" in prayer. This same warning occurs in Jesus' own instructions to his disciples prior to his arrest; they were to "watch and pray" so that they might not enter into temptation (Mark 14:38). That prayer is to be marked by alertness or watchfulness indicates that it ought to engage the whole person, heart, soul, strength, and mind. Although some commentators have argued that Paul means specifically that one is to be alert for the return of Christ or the coming of the kingdom of God, it seems more likely that Paul refers, as did Jesus before his arrest, to a disposition to be alert to the challenges and temptations that threaten steadfast Christian commitment, to a realistic assessment of "the times" in which one lives and to appropriate vigilance (see v. 5).

Third, then, Paul speaks of prayer as being offered "with thanksgiving." Here he echoes an important theme of Colossians, that of thanksgiving (1:3, 12; 2:7; 3:17). He summarized his words about thanksgiving just a few verses earlier: "And whatever you do, in word or deed, do everything in the name of the Lord Jesus, giving thanks to God the Father through him" (3:17). Just as everything is to be done in the name of the Lord Jesus, so everything is to be done with thanksgiving. One prays not in a spirit of fear, anxiety, or impatience, but with thanksgiving, in acknowledgment of one's need for others and reliance upon God. Thanksgiving accompanies prayer because prayer and gratitude both manifest and grow out of the humble, open posture of trust in God which lies at the heart of the life of faith. Those who insist on a right of autonomous self-determination have not fathomed the extent to which human beings are dependent on God and live always in the world as recipients of God's goodness and grace. Similarly, those who isolate themselves from others, denying their need of other human beings, demonstrate only their failure to grasp thhat God's reconciling work in Christ has bound human beings to each other in ways that require the constant exercise of humility — the very trait which underlies both persistence in prayer and gratitude.

Paul demonstrates his own dependence on God and need for others when he asks that the Colossians pray that "God will open to us a door for the word, that we may declare the mystery of Christ" (v. 3). Paul again characterizes the content of what he preaches as the "mystery of Christ" (1:26, 27; 2:2). Beyond that, however, this image has caused some perplexity among interpreters. Luther and others, for example, thought that the "open door" referred to Paul himself and that Paul wished for the Colossians to pray that God would give him the freedom to declare the gospel, or to "reveal it clearly" (4:3). Others have thought of a veiled reference to the hearts of unbelievers, so that prayer for an open door was specifically prayer for a positive response to Paul's preaching. Paul also uses the metaphor in 2 Corinthians: "When I came to Troas to proclaim the good news of Christ, a door was opened for me in the Lord" (2 Cor 2:12). But the question there, too, is whether the "open door" refers to opportunities for Paul to preach or positive response to that preaching. It may well be that Paul connected the two. Although he was eminently realistic about the reception that his preaching would receive, he expected that declaration of the mystery of Christ would indeed bring about response. Wherever the gospel had been preached, there had been rejection, but there had also been positive response. To be sure, the response may have been relatively small by our standards. Historians of early Christianity estimate that a house church may have held somewhere between thirty-five and fifty people. Hence, when Paul writes to the Colossians that the gospel "is bearing fruit and growing in all the world" (1:6), he thinks more of the way in which the gospel has made inroads into all the world than of the size of the congregations it has produced. The proclamation of the word to "every creature under heaven" indicates the universal promise of the gospel rather than its universal reception (1:23).

But even more important was Paul's belief that it was neither his persuasive speech nor the prayers of the Colossians which opened those doors, but rather God's action. The God who opened the doors for proclamation would surely also open the hearts of those who heard. Paul understood that the gospel was sometimes "veiled" and that not all who heard it responded with gratitude. When, however, there was such a response, Paul attributed it to God's work. As he wrote elsewhere, the God who said "Let light shine out of darkness" has "shone in our hearts to give the light of the knowledge of the glory of God in the face of Jesus Christ" (2 Cor 4:6).

Paul's hope and desire to proclaim the gospel was not diminished by the fact that he wrote from prison. He may have been literally chained, restrained by shackles, but not all imprisonments were of the same severity, nor were all prisoners treated alike.[1] People were held in prisons in the Roman Empire for a variety of reasons: to await trial or sentence, for their own protection, or perhaps to await execution. A wide range of facilities were used to imprison people, including the Roman state prison for severe criminals, where conditions were notorious and chaining was a regular feature; quarries, where prisoners worked; and military barracks or camps. Sometimes people were confined to their own homes. It is less clear that prison served as a punishment for crimes or wrongdoing already committed. Prisoners of higher status were often ensured better treatment. Not all prisoners were chained, and at times Paul seems to have been confined to private rented accommodations within the vicinity of the Praetorian Guard (Acts 28:16). His movements as recorded in the various "captivity epistles" indicate that he could send individuals on errands and messages, write letters and send them, receive news, letters, and messengers, summon individuals to join him (2 Tim 4:9, 11, 13), and be attended to by local associates and coworkers. Hence while he had some degree of freedom, he was nevertheless restricted in his movements as well.

Paul is imprisoned "on account of the mystery of Christ." This does not refer to the formal charge lodged against him. Rather, he regards his life work as the proclamation of the mystery of Christ, and his imprisonment was part of God's purposes for his work of proclaiming the gospel.[2] Paul's request that he be empowered to reveal the gospel "as it is necessary" (*dei lalēsai*/δεῖ λαλῆσαι) may refer to a sense of compulsion or destiny, which Paul understands to be the compulsion of "divine necessity." Paul's commission is to "declare the mystery of Christ." Throughout the epistle, the "mystery of Christ" has summarized the unfolding of God's eschatological purposes for the reconciliation of all things to God in Christ Jesus (1:20). Paul's afflictions serve the unfolding of God's purposes and are an integral part of his commission to make the word of God fully known inasmuch as they are afflictions associated with the events of the revelation of God's eschatological salvation (see the comments on 1:24-26). In other words, Paul's afflictions and imprisonment are actually part of God's commission to him to proclaim the mystery of Christ to the Gentiles (1:27). Since the mystery of Christ was ultimately

---

1. For further discussion, see Rapske, *The Book of Acts and Paul in Roman Custody*, especially chapter 2, "The Purposes and Varieties of Custody in the Roman World."

2. Dunn, *Colossians*, 263-64.

revealed in the death and resurrection of Christ, there can scarcely be any surprise that the gospel that is preached and the apostle who proclaims it mirror the death and resurrection of Jesus.

Paul's prayer that he be granted the opportunities to declare the mysteries of Christ is matched by his exhortation that the Colossians make wise use of the time, paying particular attention to the impact of their speech on outsiders. We see here equivalence, but also difference, between Paul's understanding of his own apostolic commission and the general responsibilities of all believers. In both cases, there is to be an alertness to the opportunities for testimony to the gospel, and in both cases the spoken word plays a significant and indispensable role. Paul prays for open doors; the Colossians are to make appropriate use of the times. Paul prays for the ability to declare the mystery as he should; the Colossians are to let their speech be gracious and be wise in responding to everyone whom they meet.

It is fitting that Paul should wrap up his injunctions to the Colossians with the command "conduct yourselves wisely." The word translated "conduct" quite literally means "walk" and has been used in the epistle as Paul prayed that the Colossians would "live in a way worthy of the Lord" (1:10; see also 3:7), which will be a life lived in deep rootedness in the wisdom in Christ. Paul has prayed that the Colossians be filled with wisdom (1:9) and characterizes Christian teaching and admonition as marked by wisdom (1:28; 3:16) because these ultimately are centered in Christ, in whom all the treasures of God's wisdom are to be found (2:3). Therefore, he now exhorts the Colossian Christians to conduct themselves in ways that draw from and reveal the wisdom which they have received in Christ, particularly in relationship with those outside the fellowship of faith.

Two traits will characterize lives guided by the wisdom of Christ. First, Paul tells the Colossians to make the most of their opportunities. Quite literally, he tells them they are to "redeem" or buy back the time. The command has a fuller form in Ephesians, where we read that one is to redeem the time "because the days are evil" (5:16). There is no such qualification here, where the command is closer to the words of Galatians: "whenever we have an opportunity, let us work for the good of all, and especially for those of the family of faith" (6:10). This is the same disposition that Paul has in view when he urges the Colossians to be "alert" in prayer. Christians need not be constantly beset by apocalyptic fervor, expecting the end of the world at any time, in order to live in ways that can be characterized as watchful, alert, and sensitive to the times at hand and the opportunities that may arise in encounters with unbelievers.

A second trait that reflects a life guided by the wisdom of Christ, and that manifests one way of "making the most" of one's opportunities, has to do with the character of Christian speech. Paul urges here that speech is to be "gracious," which may mean "attractive, winsome, wholesome," something like the characterization of Jesus' "gracious words" in Luke 4:22 (cf. Ps 45:2 [LXX 44:3]: "grace is poured on your lips"). Paul may be playing on the word "grace," suggesting that Christian speech should embody God's grace, but the idea that conversation was seasoned with salt seems to have been an idiomatic expression in Greek thought. For example, Plutarch compared wit in conversation to salt on food, speaking of this wit as "graciousness."[3] Just as food without salt can be flat or insipid, so words that are not "seasoned with salt" will likewise be dull and insipid. Paul further characterizes such lively and seasoned speech by saying that Christians are to let their speech be seasoned "so that you may know how you ought to answer everyone." As salt brings out the right flavor of food, so aptly chosen words will serve when occasions arise to defend or explain one's faith.

There is a similar injunction in 1 Pet 3:15-16: Christians are to "be always prepared to give an answer to everyone who asks" and to do so with "gentleness and respect" so that they will not be guilty of maliciousness and slander. Similarly, these closing exhortations in Colossians draw on the earlier injunctions about foul talk, abuse, and slander, urging a graciousness in speech that grows out of the love, gentleness, and humility Paul described earlier as necessary for the unity of the community. These virtues are no less necessary in speech and conduct directed to outsiders. Paul underscores their testimony in his implicit comparison of them to his own apostolic preaching. If he declares the mystery of Christ, the Colossians may well be called upon "to answer everyone." If he prays for clarity, he also hopes that the Colossians will be granted a gracious word to speak to those who do not yet believe.

4:7-18

7 Tychicus will tell you all the news about me; he is a beloved brother, a faithful minister, and a fellow servant in the Lord. 8 I have sent him to you that you may know how we are and that he may encourage your hearts; 9 I have sent him with Onesimus, the faithful and beloved brother, who is one of you. They will tell you about everything here. 10 Aristarchus my fellow prisoner of war greets you, as does Mark the cousin of Barnabas (concerning whom you have received instructions); if he comes to you, welcome him. 11 And Jesus who is called Justus greets you. These

---

3. Plutarch, *Quaestiones convivales* 5.10.2.

are the only ones of the circumcision among my coworkers for the kingdom of God, and they have been a comfort to me. 12 Epaphras, who is one of you, a servant of Christ Jesus, greets you. He is always wrestling on your behalf in his prayers that you may stand mature and fully assured in everything that God wills. 13 For I testify for him that he has worked hard for you and for those in Laodicea and Hierapolis. 14 Luke the beloved physician and Demas greet you. 15 Give my greetings to the brothers and sisters in Laodicea and to Nympha and the church in her house. 16 And when this letter has been read among you, have it read also in the church of the Laodiceans; and see that you read also the letter from Laodicea. 17 And say to Archippus, "See that you complete the task that you have received in the Lord."

18 I, Paul, write this greeting with my own hand. Remember my chains. Grace be with you.

Typical of Paul's letters, Colossians closes with a list of greetings. Paul includes greetings from those who are with him in his imprisonment and asks the Colossians to pass on his greetings to a number of folks in the region of Colossae, including the church in Laodicea and a church that meets in "Nympha's house" (v. 15). The list of people mentioned betrays the social mix that comprised the early churches, for among them are a householder (v. 15), a doctor (v. 14), and a slave (v. 9). These greetings give us the most explicit information about Paul's own situation and some tantalizing clues about relationships among early Christians in the region surrounding Colossae and the character of Paul's mission and his friendships. Powerful bonds connected Paul to churches which his mission had begotten, as well as to his coworkers, who are identified with a variety of terms, including "coworkers" (v. 11), "fellow slave/servant" (vv. 7, 12), and "fellow prisoner" (v. 10). Several of the designations are compound terms, introduced with the preposition "with" (*syn-/συν-*), which is usually translated as "co-" or "fellow." When these are coupled with the personal familial terms "brothers and sisters" (vv. 7, 15), we get a glimpse of the mutuality which characterized the relationships of these early Christians and bound them together in their work for the gospel.

Among these coworkers in Paul's missionary endeavors, Tychicus is apparently carrying the letter to the Colossians, and is further charged with reporting to the Colossians on Paul's circumstances (vv. 7, 8), a task which Onesimus shares (v. 9). There was apparently no official postal system available to private citizens.[1] Although letters could be given to anyone bound for a particular destination such as merchants traveling on business, it is hardly surprising that Paul preferred to use fellow Christians and coworkers for the

---

1. See Thompson, "Holy Internet," 51.

task, as his letters seem to imply (e.g., Rom 16:1-2; Phil 2:25-29; 2 Cor 8:16-24). Moreover, his statement to the Colossians that Onesimus and Tychicus "will tell you about everything here" (4:7-9) indicates that these two messengers were to convey further information about Paul and his situation. This was apparently common practice in the ancient world as well. Cicero, for example, in writing to his wife, tells her: "Be sure to keep well, and send me letter-carriers *(tabellarios)* to let me know what is being done and how you all are."[2] Cicero does not ask for letters to let him know how everyone is but for letter carriers, as though they would be the better source of information. Other ancient letters indicate that the messenger often brought information that supplemented or interpreted the contents of the letter. One letter contains this injunction: "The rest please learn from the man who brings you the letter. For he is no stranger to us."[3] By sending letters with faithful coworkers, Paul was thus able to keep in contact with various churches when distance or circumstances made his personal presence impossible.

Tychicus not only stands in for Paul, who cannot be present among the Colossians, but he also carries out a task that Paul himself undertakes in the letter, namely, to encourage the Colossians on their pilgrimage of faith (2:2). This same Tychicus appears to be mentioned in Acts 20:4, where he is said to be from Asia, a note that would certainly fit with his activity here in the same province. He is also mentioned in the nearly identical greeting in Eph 6:21-22, in 2 Tim 4:12, where he is on his way to Ephesus, and in Tit 3:12, where he is sent to Crete. He thus figures in letters that are typically attributed to the later years of Paul's ministry and, interestingly, only in letters that are also disputed as to their authorship. Although his name is not as well known as that of Timothy or Titus, he seems to have played an important role in the Pauline mission, as the sheer number of references to him suggests.

Tychicus is further distinguished by three epithets, by no means unique to him: "beloved brother," "faithful minister," and "fellow servant in the Lord." Epaphras is earlier called "a beloved fellow servant and faithful minister" (1:7). The adjectives "beloved" and "faithful" point, first, to the ties of friendship and love which bound members of the body of Christ together (1:8; 2:2; 3:12, 14) and, second, to the trait of steadfastness or faithfulness, which Paul prized both in his coworkers (1:7; 4:7, 9) and among the Colossians (1:2, 4; 2:5, 7), as his regular and repeated use of these adjectives testifies. These three descriptions of Tychicus present him initially from the perspective of familial relations in the body of Christ, next as one who serves

---

2. *Epistulae ad Familiares* 14.1.6 (to his wife).
3. Cited in White, *Light from Ancient Letters*, 216.

Christ and his church as a "faithful minister/servant," and finally as Paul's own fellow servant or fellow slave. He is thus successively described by his relationship to Christians, to the church, and then finally to Paul. Curiously, Tychicus is not referred to in Philemon, suggesting perhaps that he did not play a role in Paul's attempts to reconcile Philemon and Onesimus.

Other coworkers include Aristarchus (v. 10), Mark (v. 10), "Jesus who is called Justus" (v. 11), and Epaphras (v. 12). Aristarchus is mentioned three times in Acts (19:29; 20:4; 27:2) as a traveling companion of Paul, particularly on the last journey to Jerusalem, and as a Macedonian from Thessalonica. In Phlm 23-24 he is listed with Mark, Demas, Luke, and Epaphras. Paul gives no further information about the character of Aristarchus's service, speaking of him only as a "fellow prisoner" or "fellow captive," or even "fellow prisoner of war." The unusual term may suggest that Aristarchus's imprisonment was not literal, that he is Paul's fellow "prisoner of war" in the battle against the powers of the present age.[4] But if Aristarchus is in prison with Paul, as he may be, it is less clear that Mark and Justus are. They are "fellow workers" with Paul and "a comfort" to him. All three are "from the circumcision," that is, Jewish believers, and it is possible that this description of them has led Paul to characterize their work as "for the kingdom of God." This language is drawn from the ministry of Jesus and characterizes Jewish hopes for redemption. Still, it also fits with Paul's earlier assertion that in Christ Christians have been saved from "the power of darkness" and transferred "to the kingdom of [God's] beloved Son" (1:13). Paul indicates that Aristarchus, Mark, and Justus are the only Jewish fellow workers left with him, insinuating that others previously with him have either deserted him or simply are no longer with him.

In this regard, the case of Mark is rather interesting, since in Acts 15:36-40 an altercation between Paul and Barnabas regarding Mark leads them to part company, a disagreement which Luke credits to Mark's desertion of Paul's party in Pamphylia (15:38). Since Mark is now with Paul and is spoken of as a "comfort" to Paul and a fellow worker in the kingdom of God, we can assume that a reconciliation has occurred and perhaps that Mark has demonstrated the sort of steadfast commitment that Paul so valued in his coworkers.[5] But unfortunately the parenthetical comment — "concerning whom you have received instructions" — gives us little further information about Mark's particular role now in Paul's mission or whether Paul harbored linger-

---

4. So Wright, *Colossians*, 191.

5. Although the different portrayals of Mark in Acts and Colossians are sometimes taken as evidence that the author of Colossians could not be Paul or that the "Mark" in question is not the same person, there is no reason to assume that some sort of reconciliation could not have taken place.

ing doubts. Suffice it to say that the cosmic reconciliation about which Paul has written so fervently in the epistle seems to have been embodied concretely in the reconciliation of Mark and Paul as well.

According to Phlm 23 Epaphras is also a prisoner, but Paul gives no indication of his imprisonment here. Earlier comments indicated that Epaphras was the one who first proclaimed the gospel to the Colossians and was regarded by Paul as "our beloved fellow servant, who faithfully serves Christ on our behalf" (1:7). Here Paul calls him a "servant" or "slave" of Christ. Although he is Paul's fellow worker in the gospel, he is ultimately Christ's — not Paul's — servant. Paul portrays Epaphras as "wrestling" or "struggling," a term that he has used of himself and his labors for the gospel (1:29; 2:1). Epaphras's hard work (4:13) corresponds to Paul's own labors in the gospel (1:29). More particularly, Paul depicts Epaphras as "wrestling in prayer." His prayers are directed to the same ends as Paul's labors: that the Colossians might be perfect (1:22, 28) and have stability and firmness in their faith (2:2). He is thus a coworker not just in theory but in fact.

Onesimus is a "faithful and beloved brother" (4:9). Hints in Phlm 11 and 13 suggest that he has rendered good service to Paul in prison, but he is never explicitly designated a coworker or fellow servant, as are Tychicus, Mark, and others. He is, however, said to be "one of you," which implies that he belongs to the church at Colossae. If, however, Onesimus has become a believer only after he left Philemon's house, then Paul introduces Onesimus by his new identity — he is now "one of you."

Paul also sends greetings to the Colossians from Luke "the beloved physician" and Demas. They are called "fellow workers" in Phlm 24, along with Mark and Aristarchus. Luke is again mentioned in the poignant statement in 2 Tim 4:11 ("Luke alone is with me"), and in that context Demas (v. 10), Mark (v. 11), and Tychicus (v. 12) are also referred to. Something of Luke's integrity comes through in his description as "beloved" physician, for elsewhere in the biblical tradition doctors are often looked upon as worthless, promising cures which they cannot deliver (e.g., 2 Chron 16:12; Job 13:4; Jer 46:11; Mark 5:26). Ancient medicine differed vastly from its modern counterpart. Physicians could treat wounds and employed various remedies to try to treat symptoms of diseases, but they could not halt or cure those diseases. In any case, the study of medicine was not nearly so formalized as today, although Luke's status will indicate that he was an educated man.[6]

In rather sharp contrast to all the other individuals named in this list of

---

6. For further information, see "Medicine" in the *Oxford Classical Dictionary* (third edition; Oxford: Oxford University Press, 1996), 947-49.

greetings, Demas appears with no epithet attesting either his role in Paul's missionary endeavors or his friendship with Paul. He is called a "fellow worker" in Phlm 24, and the reference to him in 2 Timothy implies that he had served as one of Paul's coworkers (4:10), but in none of these letters is there any praise or commendation for him; quite the contrary. In 2 Timothy we read that "Demas, because he loved this world, has deserted me and has gone to Thessalonica." We have too little evidence to speculate further on what led to Demas's disaffection either with Paul or his missionary work, but it does suggest some reason for Paul's appreciation and affection for Luke and others who had persevered with him through his imprisonments and other difficult situations and why he so prized steadfastness. His hard work, care for his churches, travels, and imprisonments would have been heavy burdens in themselves, without the further anxiety added by having coworkers desert him or the gospel.

Paul asks that the Colossians greet the Christians in Laodicea, in particular Nympha and the church in her house, which suggests that the Laodicean community consisted of more than one house church. Why Nympha and the church in her house are singled out for special greeting we do not know. She is apparently a Christian of some means, for her house is able to serve as a meeting place for a group usually estimated to consist of thirty to fifty people. Paul does not specify what her role was beyond hosting the gathering. From other letters of Paul it is clear that women served important functions of teaching and leadership. For example, Paul commends Phoebe (Rom 16:1-2), Priscilla (Rom 16:3-5; 1 Cor 16:19), Tryphaena, Tryphosa, and Persis (Rom 16:12) in glowing terms as servants of the church, fellow workers in Christ, dear friends, and a great help to him. Nympha may have aided Paul's missionary efforts in similar ways. But even offering hospitality was a great boon to the spread of the gospel and is commended as one of the Christian virtues (Rom 12:13; 1 Tim 5:10; Heb 13:2; the early Christian epistle called *1 Clement* refers to it repeatedly).

The Colossians are also to exchange letters with the Laodiceans, to whom Paul has apparently sent, or is sending, a letter as well. Paul says that the letter is to be read out to the church, that is, read aloud in public assembly. Such practices were necessary because of the limited availability of copies of each letter and because of the limitations imposed by illiteracy. Literacy rates have been estimated to have been between ten and twenty percent, though the latter is sometimes thought to be on the high end.[7]

Of Paul's relationships to the Laodicean church, the content of his letter to it, or the means by which he sent it we know nothing further. We do not

---

7. See Harris, *Ancient Literacy*; Gamble, *Books and Readers in the Early Church*, 1-41.

have the letter, although a spurious letter to the Laodiceans does exist.[8] In any case, the command to exchange letters and to greet these other Christians points to the interconnection of the earliest churches and their need and desire to maintain contact. The Roman Empire was crisscrossed by a series of well-built roads, and, although travel was by no means either easy or quick, there is ample evidence that these roads facilitated commerce and communication. The distance from Colossae to Laodicea was about ten miles. It is estimated that travelers by foot, with good traveling conditions and otherwise unimpeded, could average fifteen to twenty-five miles a day. According to Acts 10:23-24, Peter traveled from Joppa to Caesarea, a distance of about forty miles, in two days.[9]

This is the only explicit reference in Paul's letters regarding the exchange of letters, which may have been prompted by the relatively close proximity of Laodicea and Colossae. We cannot draw any further conclusions about the situation of Laodicea or speculate whether it was facing the same threat from false teaching as the church of Colossae. In any case, Paul apparently thinks that his letter to the Colossians will strengthen their commitment, just as he prays it would strengthen the Colossians. The practices of exchanging letters, reading them in public gatherings, and perhaps even copying them prior to exchange mark the beginning of the process which led eventually to regarding Paul's letters as authoritative Scripture. Though written to specific churches for specific reasons, these letters were not without wider applicability to Christians in different places. Indeed, that the New Testament consists largely of letters remains one of the most striking things about it.

Paul's last specific instruction is directed to Archippus, who is undoubtedly the person addressed in Phlm 2 as "our fellow soldier." He is sometimes taken to be the son of Philemon and Apphia (Phlm 1-2), but in any case he is a fellow Christian, a coworker of Paul's in some way, and has a specific commission or task to undertake. Whether or not Paul gave him this commission, he is aware of it and charges the church as a whole with reminding Archippus of his obligation. Although Paul does not say what the task is, he seems to assume that the church both knows that Archippus has this task and probably also knows of what it consists. While Archippus thus has a specific, personal commission, it is not a private matter but the responsibility of the church together to encourage and exhort him to complete it. Paul makes the same as-

---

8. It was known from the fourth century on. Virtually a pastiche of some of Paul's formulaic sayings, it contains nothing that suggests that it was a real letter.

9. See Thompson, "Holy Internet," 60-65.

sumption about the church's corporate responsibility for even personal matters when he writes to Philemon, urging him to take Onesimus back as a "beloved brother." Again, although personal, such matters are not private in the body of Christ.

Paul signs off by sending a greeting in his own hand (v. 18). Paul typically used an amanuensis (or secretary) to write his letters (e.g., Rom 16:22), often appending at the end a greeting written in his own hand (1 Cor 16:21-24; Gal 6:11-18; 2 Thess 3:17-18). In comparison to his other greetings, however, this one is unusually terse, which may indicate duress or fatigue. The next sentence might provide some reason for both: Paul asks that the Colossians "remember" his chains (on Paul's imprisonment, see the discussion on 4:2-6). If the allusion to "chains" is to be taken literally — Paul really was shackled — rather than figuratively as metonymy for his imprisonment, this may well account for the difficulty Paul had in doing more than penning a short greeting. By remembering his chains, the Colossians will presumably both take account of his difficult situation and remember him in prayer. But his own difficult circumstances do not impede him from offering to the Colossians the characteristic benediction "Grace be with you."

With this simple blessing, Paul ends his letter to the Colossian Christians. In his closing greetings, with its list of friends and coworkers, we catch a glimpse of the connections among early Christians and between Paul and his various churches. The letter he is sending serves as a temporary substitute for his own presence. But it gives expression to the heart of Paul's concerns for the Christians of Colossae: that they remain rooted in the gospel that has been preached to them, that they focus their hearts and minds on Christ and his work on the cross on their behalf, and that they live together in the fellowship of Christian love. His own life is ample testimony to the cultivation of these habits of heart and mind.

Theological Horizons of Colossians

The Theology of Colossians

John Barclay speaks of Colossians as offering "an integrated view of reality" and "a comprehensive vision of truth — cosmic and human, spiritual and material, divine and mundane — whose focal point is Christology." He writes further, "The theology of Colossians is at every point Christological, and it is the success of the author in disclosing Christ as the centre of all reality that integrates and energizes the letter."[1] Indeed, its christological focus is undoubtedly the distinguishing characteristic of this epistle. Colossians boldly asserts that the "mystery" or "secret" which has been revealed to the church pertains to the whole universe, to its creation and its destiny. The claims of the epistle are sweeping: "*All things* are made through [Christ] and for him" (1:16); "*all things* hold together in him" (1:17); and by his death he has reconciled *all things* (1:20). Christ is the agent of creating and sustaining the cosmos as well as of its ultimate redemption. From every angle, Christ is first: "the firstborn over creation" (1:15), the beginning of all things (1:17), the firstborn from the dead (1:18). In all things, he takes first place (1:18). He "is all and in all" (3:11).

One purpose of such christological statements is to relate Jesus to God and so to say something about the identity of both. That is to say, christological statements do not stand on their own but serve to articulate convictions about the character, purposes, and work of God in the world. Indeed, what gives potency to Paul's statements about Christ in this epistle is that they express beliefs about the revelation of God to the world. In the categories of traditional systematic theology, every *christological* statement has a

---

1. Barclay, *Colossians*, 77.

theological implication. Similarly, christological assertions have *cosmological* and *soteriological* implications. Paul's statements about Christ are in fact claims about the origins and destiny of creation, the human predicament, and God's solution to it on the cross. Finally, creation and cross together determine the shape of the life of faith, which in turn falls under the headings of *spirituality* and *ethics.*

In short, the rich significance of the christological statements in Colossians must be explored with respect to their various corollaries. As Leander Keck aptly put it,

> "Significance" is intelligible only in relation to something or someone. Accordingly, the subject-matter of christology is really the syntax of relationships or correlations. In developed christology this structure of significance is expressed in relation to God (the *theological* correlation proper), the created order (the *cosmological* correlation) and humanity (the *anthropological* correlation); each of these impinges on the others whether or not this impingement is made explicit. Consequently, from statements about God or world or humanity one can infer the appropriate christological correlates, and vice versa.[2]

Although Keck made these comments in the context of a more general discussion of NT christology, they are strikingly borne out in the vision of Colossians. "Christology" is indeed the center of the letter; but without the explication of its theological, cosmological, soteriological, and anthropological correlates, there is nothing at all to explicate. That is to say, if "christology" is the study of the person of Christ, then in Colossians this enterprise is undertaken by relating Christ to God, the world, and the life of believers and, indeed, of all humankind. One cannot discuss the center — christology — in isolation, as is shown by the most exalted christological statements. Paul's statements that Christ is "the image of the invisible God" and that "the fullness of deity dwells in him bodily" speak of the dignity of Christ in terms of his unique relationship to God. Statements such as "he is before all things" and "all things hold together in him" show Christ's exalted status with respect to the created order. And statements that speak of Christ as the "firstborn of the dead," Lord, and "your life" (3:4) describe Christ's relationship to humankind in terms of his preeminence, sovereignty, and life-giving power. Repeatedly the identity and status of Christ are articulated with reference to his relationship to God the Creator and Redeemer, the created order, and human beings who live within it.

2. Keck, "Renewal of New Testament Christology," 363.

We can put this differently. Christ stands at the center of Paul's "integrative view of reality" because his life, death, and resurrection are the primary means by which God brings new life to the cosmos. What God did for Christ in raising him from the dead to new life, God will do for all the world. As one author put it in another context, "What God has done for the body of Jesus in microcosm, God will do for the cosmos in macrocosm."[3] And what God did for Christ in raising him from the dead to new life, God will do for those who are joined to faith in him. In other words, the renewal of the world traces the narrative of Christ's death and resurrection. The powers of the world — sin, death, darkness — are put to death on the cross, so that the world may be set free and redeemed and brought to its intended purposes by its Creator. The world is renewed through Christ's death and resurrection because the death-dealing powers of the world die when he dies. Similarly, what God does for humankind traces the same narrative of Christ's death and resurrection. Those who die with Christ and are buried with him are also raised to new life. This happens not (or not only) through imitation of his death and new life, but by participation in them through faith. The believer does not simply imitate the course of Christ's life, following his path through death on the cross to new life with God. Rather, the believer becomes one with Christ and so lives in him and because of him.

In other words, we can think of three layered narratives that are in reality one narrative: God's narrative of giving life to the world, in both creation and redemption, through the agency of Christ. If, on the one hand, we think of God's dealings with the cosmos, then what happens to Christ in microcosm determines what happens to the whole world in macrocosm. The renewal of the world is the resurrection on a cosmic canvas. This is so not because Christ is part of the world, but because the world is the creation of Christ and holds together in him. Its destiny is bound up with his. If, on the other hand, we think of God's dealings with humankind, then what happens to Christ in microcosm determines what happens to all humanity and each individual. Christ's resurrection is, as it were, both writ large and writ small, but the narrative of his life, death, and resurrection is the unifying narrative that grounds the others. To say that Christ is the focal point of the integrative vision of Colossians means, more specifically, that it is the narrative of Christ's death and resurrection that provides that focal point. And in this narrative, the identity of Christ is crucial. This is the story of not just any person but of the one in whom all things were created, in whom all things hold to-

---

3. Andy Johnson, "Imagining the New Creation: On the Hermeneutical Priority of Jesus' Resurrection in Transformed Flesh" (unpublished paper).

gether, and through whom all things will be redeemed. Only because it is the story of this One can it be the story of the world and of everyone in it.

In the following section, we shall endeavor to tease out more fully the central theological themes of the epistle to the Colossians and their relationship to each other. As we pursue discussion of the theology of Colossians under the rubric of Christ as the integrating center of reality, we shall use phrases and images from Colossians to set the terms for our discussion.

"In Him All Things Were Created"

As noted above, the claims for Christ are comprehensive, and they begin with his role as God's agent in creating the world. In other words, Christ is related to the cosmos as God is, namely, as responsible for its creation. Indeed, Christ is the active agent in God's creating, sustaining, and redeeming the world. No passage in Colossians articulates as fully the view of Christ as the integrating center of reality as does the so-called "Christ hymn" of 1:15-20, as the repeated emphasis on Christ's relation to "all things" makes evident. "*All things* are made through him and for him" (1:16); "*all things* hold together in him" (1:17); and by his death he has reconciled *all things* (1:20). From creation to final reconciliation, all things are to be understood in the light of and with reference to Christ. Paul repeatedly used the Greek term πάντα (*panta,* "all things") to describe the comprehensive scope of God's work in Christ. As noted in our exegetical discussion of the "Christ hymn," Paul also rather carefully and deliberately uses a series of prepositions to underscore the agency of Christ in God's creating, sustaining, and redeeming the world. All things are created "through" (*dia*/διά), "in" (*en*/ἐν), and "for" or "to" (*eis*/εἰς) Christ (1:16). Paul thus places Christ at both the beginning and the goal of creation. In other words, creation is going somewhere: toward the goal of a perfected community, toward the transformation of the relationships of human beings to each other and to God, and toward a renewed cosmos, which provides the context of this transformed community's existence.[4]

With the repeated emphasis on *all things,* Colossians presents Christ in terms regularly confined in both biblical and later Jewish thought to Yahweh, the one God of the universe. Both the OT and a vast array of literature from Second Temple Judaism distinguished God from all other deities and powers by attributing to Yahweh, and to Yahweh alone, the creation of *all* the universe. For example, God is designated "the Creator of all things" (2 Macc 1:24-

---

4. On this point, see Watson, *Text, Church, and World,* 241-64.

25), "the cause of all things" (Philo, *De Somniis* 1.67), "the beginning and middle and end of all things," and the one who "breathes life into all creatures" (Josephus, *Against Apion* 2.190; *Antiquities* 12.22). The comprehensive sweep of God's creation of *all* things applies to Christ's agency in creation as well, so that he is related to "all things" even as God is.

Colossians consistently emphasizes the relationship of Christ to God within the monotheistic framework of first-century Jewish belief. There is one God, who created and governs the world. Within that monotheistic framework, Paul's statements about creation *in* and *through* Christ not only join the work of God and Christ, but do so by asserting that God works *through* and *in* Christ both in creation and redemption, thus rendering any sort of dualism impossible, as if redemption somehow consisted of deliverance from creation. In Paul's terms, God the Father is the ultimate source of all that is; Christ is the agent, the means, of creation and salvation.

In designating Christ as God's agent of creation, Paul also implicitly states that no other principle of coherence binds the universe together. There is no abstract "rationality" that has happened to take on an incarnate form as "Jesus of Nazareth." Rather, the one who is known through Christ's life and death is the agent of creation and, conversely, the agent of the creation of the world is known through and in the life and death of this human being, Jesus of Nazareth. In designating Christ as the one through whom the world was made, Paul gives Christ the role which was sometimes accorded to Wisdom or the Law in Jewish thought and to the *logos* of Greek philosophical speculation. As noted in the discussion of Col 1:15-20, in biblical and Jewish thought, Wisdom plays a role in the creation of the world and the instruction of God's people. It is the mediator of God's life-giving work in creating the world and revealing the ways of God to humankind. Paul writes that the fullness of wisdom, knowledge and understanding of God are made known through Christ (1:9) and that the fullness of God's mystery is hidden in Christ (2:3). Later rabbinic literature would assign this role to Torah; for example, one text speaks of the Law as "the precious instrument by which the world was created" (*Pirke Aboth* 3.15). Torah is the instrument of creation; it also serves to instruct God's people, mediating knowledge of him and his ways. In Colossians both roles are assigned to Christ. He encompasses the functions of Torah within himself. He is the greater reality, and creation and revelation take place through and in him. This does not invalidate Torah, but rather is precisely what gives it ongoing validity. For Christ is in fact the one to whom Torah alludes when it speaks of God creating the world.

Moreover, it is *for* Christ that the world was made. This may be an explicit denial of the claim found in some Jewish sources that the world was made "for the sake of Israel" (2 Esdras 6:54-59; 7:11; *2 Baruch* 14:18-19; 15:7; 21:24). It makes of Christ not just the "agent" or "mediator" of creation but also the *purpose* or *goal* for which God created the world. The creation of the world already antici-pates its ultimate goal, its perfection. This includes the perfection of human-kind, since the new humanity found in Christ is humanity as it was created to be. Even as Genesis describes the creation of humankind in the image of God as the pinnacle of God's creation of the cosmos, so Colossians describes the re-newal of humankind according to the image of God in Christ as the goal of God's creative work. While Colossians does also speak of the reconciliation of "all things," the renewal of human beings in the image of God stands at the heart and center of God's new work of creation. There is an inescapable anthropocentrism in God's creative and redemptive purposes, as the incarna-tion itself bears witness.

"All Things Hold Together in Him"

God created the world through Christ, and God also sustains the world in and through Christ (1:17). This again assigns to Christ a function peculiar to God, namely, the sovereign governance of the universe, and echoes the multi-ple assertions in the OT and Jewish literature that the God who created the world also governs it as its unique sovereign. Nothing in the created order falls outside the sovereignty of the one true God. In fact, God's creation of the world and continued sovereignty over it cannot be separated. Just as Christ is God's agent of creation, so Christ also has supremacy over all other powers, and this note is sounded boldly in Colossians in two ways: first, God's power to deliver and to restore are expressed through Christ; second, Christ has a unique status in relationship to God which renders him supreme over all other powers operative in the universe. We will examine each of these claims in greater detail.

First, Christ's power is understood to be the expression of God's own power, manifested as the power to deliver people from the usurping power of darkness and to transfer them into the realm of Christ's authority (1:13). Christ does not deliver people from creation or from God but from the power of darkness. Darkness is that realm where the various powers, visible and in-visible, human, nonhuman, and subhuman, shape the order of existence in ways that ensnare humans, leading them away from worship of the one true God (1:16). But God's power is restorative and reconciling. It is manifested in the forgiveness of sins (1:13-14; 2:13), in bringing the dead to life (2:12-13), and in the reconciliation of "all things, whether on earth or in heaven" by "making peace by the blood of [Christ's] cross" (1:20). In other words, God not only pardons what people have done, but also delivers them from the darkness that is death, establishing them in right relationship to himself and to the created order. He breaks the power of darkness through and in Christ, anticipating the ultimate renewal of the world. Because God created the world, he has not let the world run its own course. He sustains it through and in Christ, and it is in Christ that God's power of salvation is fully expressed. It follows that God's power and purposes are definitively revealed in the cross and resurrection of Christ.

Throughout Colossians, the emphasis falls on God's initiative to forgive, redeem, make peace, restore, and renew (3:10). While it is undoubtedly true that in Colossians "Christ emerges more forthrightly as a redeemer figure,"[5] nevertheless, the salvation won by Christ is always the salvation won by God through Christ. God takes the initiative to deliver humankind from a plight from which it cannot extricate itself. "God" is regularly the subject of the various verbs which refer to the salvation and deliverance of humankind. So we read that "God has rescued us from the power of darkness" (1:13), that "God was pleased to reconcile to himself all things" (1:20), and that "God made you alive together with him, by forgiving us all our trespasses" (2:13). Nowhere is God the object of the work of the cross, as though the cross did something *to* God. Nor, for that matter, did God do something *to* Jesus on the cross. Rather, on the cross, God offers salvation *through* Jesus *to* humankind. It is human beings who are reconciled, forgiven, rescued, and revivified. On the cross, God's power is disclosed not in its undeniable capacity to destroy (3:6) or as reluctant to forgive, but rather as the self-giving power to heal and renew, to bring wholeness to the world created in Christ. God's power is not grasping and manipulative, but giving and serving. God's power further empowers people to live in ways commensurate with a God who discloses power in such ways.

Second, Christ has a unique status in relationship to God which renders him supreme over all other powers at work in the universe. As already noted, Christ's exalted status is described in terms of God's work through and in him in creation and salvation. To speak of Christ's identity in terms of what God does in and through Christ is to articulate a *functional christology,* that is, to offer a portrait of Christ that describes who he is by delineating what he does

---

5. Hultgren, *Christ and His Benefits,* 91. Hultgren argues that the NT contains four main types of redemptive christology: redemption accomplished in Christ, confirmed through Christ, won by Christ, and mediated by Christ. Although he puts Colossians in the third category, redemption won by Christ, in my view it could as easily find itself in the fourth, redemption mediated by Christ, and even in the second, redemption confirmed through Christ.

or, better, what God has done through him. Unfortunately, such an approach to christology has often been rejected by those who judge that it does not do full justice to Christ's supremacy and status. But it is hard to see how, given his monotheistic commitments, Paul could have described the supremacy of Christ in more exalted terms than he does by attributing to him the definitive role in God's creation, sustenance, and redemption of the world. There is no comparable mediator figure in Jewish thought whose functions Paul simply adapts or applies to Christ. Rather, he describes the work and identity of Christ in terms reserved in Jewish thought for the one God. Obviously, such formulations ultimately did have an impact on how Christian theology, already in the New Testament, thought of the identity of both Jesus and God.[6] Hilary of Poitiers (315-67), the "Athanasius of the Western Church," inquires with respect to Paul's statement in Colossians, "If all things are through Him, and all were made out of nothing, and none otherwise than through Him, in what element of true Godhead is He defective, Who possesses both the nature and the power of God? He had at His disposal the powers of the Divine nature, to bring into being the non-existent and to create at His pleasure."[7] In other words, the One who exercises the powers of God and, specifically, the power to create and bring into being "things that are not," cannot be other than God. It is not surprising that in Colossians statements regarding the identity of Christ are so closely bound together with functionally oriented statements. It was not a leap into another universe to speak of Christ's identity in ontological categories. Rather, the articulation of the relationship of Jesus to God in ontological terms made the same judgments about his identity as did the "functional" statements of Colossians.[8]

Among the terms which assign preeminence to Christ are "firstborn of all creation" (1:15), "before all things" (1:17), "beginning" (1:18), "firstborn of the dead" (1:18), "head of the church" (1:18), and "head of every ruler and authority" (2:10). These all celebrate Christ's supreme status or rank by underscoring his priority and preeminence. In each case, the assertion of Christ's precedence in time underscores his preeminence. He has "first place in everything" (1:18, NRSV). This status, which belonged to Christ prior to creation, is confirmed through his resurrection and exaltation to a position of dignity and honor at God's right hand (3:1) and expressed in the title "Lord" (thirteen occurrences, e.g., 1:3, 10; 2:6; 3:13, 17, 18, 20), which speaks of his right to obedi-

---

6. On this point, see especially Bauckham, *God Crucified;* Wright, *Climax of the Covenant,* 99-119, especially 112-19.

7. Hilary of Poitiers, *On the Trinity* 5.4.

8. On this point see Yeago, "New Testament and the Nicene Dogma."

ence and honor. The resurrection therefore reveals who and what he is. The one through whom God created the world and gave it life is also the one through whom God re-creates the world and gives it new life.

Once again, however, it is important to emphasize that Christ does not have this status and rank independently of God, but rather precisely in relationship to God. Two passages in Colossians speak of the indwelling of God in Christ: "in him all the fullness of God was pleased to dwell" (1:19) and "in him the whole fullness of deity dwells bodily" (2:9). As we saw in exegeting those passages, both affirmations reinforce the full scope of God's revelation and salvation through Christ. But they also predicate a union of Christ with God distinguished from any other union or relationship with God. Colossians speaks of the power of God at work in the believer, but not of the *fullness* or *indwelling* of *deity* in the believer. These descriptions apply exclusively to Christ and point to the uniqueness of Christ among humans and his unique relationship to God. Such statements also illustrate how the earliest believers implicitly and explicitly formulated their beliefs within the monotheistic framework of first-century Judaism. One cannot speak of Christ independently of God. Designations of Jesus as "agent" or "mediator" of God's salvation do not give him a second-class role; rather, they seek precisely to show that the only proper way to conceive of his role and person is by speaking of the exercise of unique divine prerogatives through him. Particularly since the language of agency and mediation emphasizes the singularity of God's work in Christ, it elevates, rather than denigrates, the person of Christ.

Christ is also referred to as God's "beloved Son" (1:13), and God is described as "the Father of our Lord Jesus Christ" (1:3). Although believers also enjoy a relationship to God as Father (1:2), the relationship of Christ and God is singled out as unique. The language of "Father" and "Son" shows the mutual relationship of God and Christ by which each receives his distinctive identity, for a father is not a father without a child, and every child or son has a father. God and Christ are Father and Son in relationship to each other, and the Son mirrors the Father, is a visible representation or "image" of him, the Father's agent in creation and redemption, and participates in the divine sovereignty over the universe. Hence the statement that Christ is "the image of the invisible God" designates Christ as the particular and unique manifestation of the unseen God, the visible Son of the unseen Father.

Colossians also spells out the supremacy of Christ by speaking of him as the "mystery" of God. Because "all things" revolve around Christ as the center of the universe, he is the "mystery" of all reality (1:26-27; 2:2-3; 4:3). This "mystery," however, is not one that waits to be revealed by God or discovered by humankind, but has in fact already been made known in the person of Jesus and through the proclamation about him. Corresponding to the description of Christ as the revealed mystery of God, the epistle also uses terms such as "wisdom," "knowledge," and "understanding" and emphasizes "revealing," making known, and communication of this mystery. While not all revelation has taken verbal form, particular stress does fall on proclamation. The gospel has been preached (1:6, 28) so that the Colossians have heard and come to know the truth (1:5, 6, 7, 9, 23); the mystery has been revealed (1:26); God has made known the riches of this mystery (1:27). Christ is thus both the content and channel of God's revelation to humankind.

But all the "cognitive" terms do not point to "intellectual understanding" alone or suggest that God's revelation consists entirely of propositions about God and reality. Indeed, precisely because God's truth is revealed in and through the life, death, and resurrection of Christ, it has a personal, concrete, historical focus. The mystery is articulated and proclaimed, but it is first embodied through and in the person and life of Christ. The Colossians have come to know, then, not what is reducible to ideas about a reality, but the identity of a person — which, however, must be articulated at least in part through theological formulation. But the knowledge that is available and the response that is sought have an inevitable personal or affective dimension. When in 1:6 the Colossians are said to have "come to know the grace of God in truth," that surely includes an experience of the grace of God. The Colossians know *about* the grace of God, but they also know or experience that grace.

"Knowledge" of God's will (1:9) entails understanding, but it also involves walking worthily of the Lord and doing good deeds and requires patience and endurance (1:11). The epistle assumes that life in Christ is characterized by grace and peace (1:2), faith (1:4), love (1:4), hope (1:5), truth (1:5, 6), joy (1:11), and forgiveness (1:14). In and through these realities the truth of the gospel is both expressed and experienced. One does not only hear or respond to the gospel; one lives it. Indeed, the recurring emphasis on thanksgiving in this epistle points to the Christian life as lived in grateful and heartfelt response to God's initiative in Christ.[9] The power of God is known through creation and redemption, and it is made known and experienced through and in the lives of believers, corporately and individually. We shall return to further discussion of this aspect of Christ as the integrating center of reality in our discussion of Christian life, below.

---

9. See Meye, "Spirituality," 907, 915.

"Making Peace through the Blood of His Cross"

Colossians is brimming with metaphors for the death of Christ and with rich descriptions of its effects. It is the means of redemption and forgiveness (1:13-14; 2:14), of the pacification of those hostile to God (1:20-22), of the inclusion of all people in the family of God (1:12, 21-22; 2:11-13), and of the granting of new life (2:12-13; 3:1-3). It is the locus of Christ's triumph over the powers (2:13-15) and of the reconciliation of all the world, of the entire cosmos.

Paul thus articulates his understanding of the cross in ways that do not always square with modern sensitivities. Specifically, whereas many Christians typically understand Christ's work on the cross in terms of individual salvation and the removal of punishment, Paul speaks of the creation of a people, a new humanity, in Christ. Western Christians have a difficult time conceiving of their destinies and their predicament as somehow indicative of the situation of the entire cosmos. Paul envisions the reconciliation of "all things" — not just all people, but all things (1:20). Finally, although many Christians think of the cross as the means by which human beings get right with God, Paul thinks of the cross as the means by which God deals with the alienation of human from human, from the world in which humans live, and from God.[10] As noted earlier, Colossians manifests a three-layered narrative of God's life-giving activity, a narrative that layers the new creation of the world and of humankind with the new life given to Christ through the resurrection.

Through the cross God does not simply deal with the situation of the individual, but undertakes to bring wholeness to the whole world. The predicament of humankind and that of the cosmos are intertwined: both are in need of being rightly reordered by God, and neither will be so in isolation from each other. Sin ruptures not only the divine-human relationship but also the relationships of humans to each other and to their world, and all those relationships must be repaired.[11] But what is in view is not a return to the past, simply patching up an old piece of pottery that has been cracked. Rather, it is a remaking of the old in terms of a new model. This puts the renewal of humankind at the center of the redemption of the world, because human beings are the world's "most problematic inhabitants," the "cause and center" of the disruptive effects of sin.[12]

Through the cross God effects a change in humans' relationships to himself and to other humans and establishes Christ's supremacy over the

---

10. Green and Baker, *Recovering the Scandal of the Cross*, 29.

11. Carroll and Green, *The Death of Jesus*, 124.

12. Gunton, *Christ and Creation*, 33.

powers, whether these be understood in terms of the powers of sin and death, the political and institutional powers of human authorities, or the "cosmic" powers that surpass and pervade and vivify these other powers. In terms of classical theology, the cross atones, or mends a rift in a relationship by making to be "at one" what were formerly at odds. References to forgiveness, reconciliation, making peace, and inclusion within God's family all fit within this understanding of what the cross accomplishes. Through the cross, God restores human beings to a proper relationship to God, the relationship of wholeness intended for them in creation. Indeed, the command in Genesis to "subdue the earth" has its fulfillment only in Christ's subjection of the powers to him.

In Colossians the theme of Christ as victorious over the powers of darkness *(Christus Victor)* also figures prominently.[13] The image of victory is an image of liberation. God liberates his creation from the powers of darkness that envelop it. Through his death and resurrection, Christ has been given a position of authority and honor at God's right hand; he has triumphed over death; he has triumphed over the principalities and powers. But he has done so not by destroying them, but by firmly subjecting them to him, by reconciling and restoring them as well to their proper place in creation. Just as human beings find their proper place and role in God's creation, so too through Christ's cross does God put the powers in their place — and this is not the place of authority and domination but the place of subjugation. The so-called "transfer terminology" can be placed under the rubric of *Christus Victor* as well: God delivers people from the power of darkness and transfers them to the authority of his beloved Son. In other words, in the cross God's liberating power triumphs over the enslaving powers of darkness by setting people free and by ultimately overcoming those enslaving powers.

But it is too constricting to force all metaphors for the cross into one or the other of these categories. Other images offer different ways of conceiving of God's work through Christ. In comparing the cross to circumcision, Paul portrays the cross as the means by which Gentiles are included in the people of God (2:11-13). Through Christ's death on the cross, people belong to God and receive an inheritance from the Father (1:12). The language of family — God is Father, Jesus is the Son, and all believers are brothers and sisters — becomes a reality through the cross, which obliterates the significance of ethnic

---

13. The assertion that there are three main types of the idea of the atonement comes from Gustaf Aulén's study *Christus Victor*. He argued that "Christus Victor" was the "classic idea" of the atonement, found in the NT and revived by Luther (although subsequently obscured in Protestant orthodoxy).

and class distinctions and welcomes all into the family of God (3:10-11). The story of all the peoples of the world thus finds meaning in Christ's story. The imagery of both "transfer" and "union with Christ" converge here, for those who are transferred from one kingdom to another not only find themselves living in a new kingdom, but also find their lives emplotted in a new narrative, that of Jesus himself.

Paul also speaks of God granting life through the cross. Here he further develops the idea that people receive the benefits of Christ's death through participation in Christ's death and resurrection, so that what happens to Christ truly happens to those who are in Christ as well. He died and was raised, and those who are joined to him also die and are raised to new life — but only in and through him. Once again, the narrative of Jesus' life becomes their own. Similarly, the variety of terms used to image the death of Jesus surely also has a correspondence in what Christians experience: reconciliation, peace, the forgiveness of sins. J. D. G. Dunn puts it this way, "From the beginning . . . the doctrine of atonement was not independent of the experience of atonement. From the first Christ was known by his benefits."[14]

"You Who Were Once Estranged . . . He Has Now Reconciled"

Corresponding to every statement about the cross is an understanding of the human dilemma, the human plight for which God has provided a solution through the cross. This introduces a tension that pervades Colossians. The world was created through Christ and holds together in him. Such statements would appear to describe a world that runs smoothly and functions efficiently. Yet Colossians also speaks of the power of darkness, estrangement, and hostility, evil deeds, sins, deception, and disobedience. God's sovereign rule of the world does not, for the present, imply a perfect order of existence, but the cross does offer God's way of delivering people from the power of darkness by which their lives are shaped in ways that are inimical to God's purposes for them and for creation.

Paul speaks of the dominion of darkness (1:13), in which the situation of human beings is described as one of estrangement and hostility (1:21), and their actions are characterized as sins (1:14) and evil deeds (1:21). In Colossians, these descriptions refer first and foremost to Gentiles, whose life apart from a knowledge of God and his ways can be characterized as alienated from God and by the doing of evil deeds. Paul does not portray the situ-

---

14. Dunn, *Theology of Paul*, 232.

ation as neutral, but speaks rather of the Gentiles as living under the "dominion of darkness." He has two realities in mind: First, there are genuinely powerful forces beyond the control of human beings that shape the world in which they live. The human plight is thus characterized more by weakness and incapacity than by defiance and rebellion. Human beings do not have the power to deliver themselves from the influence of these powers, any more than creation can right itself. Both are captive and need to be rescued and redeemed from that captivity (1:13-14). They are dead and need to be brought to life (2:13). Accused by the record of their wrongdoing, they need to be freed and forgiven (1:14; 2:14-15; 3:13). Subject to the old ways of life, they need to be renewed (3:10).

Second, human beings wrongly give their allegiance to these powers, thus denying the Creator who made them and who has supremacy over all the powers. Human existence is thus also characterized by hostility to God, that is, by failure to honor and acknowledge the Creator and Sovereign of the universe and by continued disobedience manifested in practices such as fornication, impurity, passion, evil desire, and greed (3:5-6). As Paul puts it, these practices amount to idolatry: the failure in all ways to honor and acknowledge God and live in accord with God's purposes for humankind. This may be done out of ignorance, but the situation is nevertheless not viewed neutrally.

According to Paul, the cross deals with both problems. It robs the powers of their autonomy, restoring them to rightful relationship with Christ, their sovereign, thus breaking their hold on human life. Through the cross humans are transferred into a new dominion, the kingdom of God's beloved Son (1:13). Through identification with Christ in his death and resurrection, people are united with the one true Lord and empowered to live in obedience to him. The cross also delivers people from the effects of that old dominion, offering them forgiveness for sins which they have committed.

Yet clearly the cross has not effected, in the present, the final transformation of human life. According to Paul, those in Christ are in the process of "being renewed in the knowledge of the image of the Creator" (3:10), anticipating the day when they will appear "holy and blameless and without fault" (1:22) before God, perfect in Christ (1:28), the new person replacing the old (3:5-11). In the meantime, however, there is need for ongoing instruction in what it means to follow Christ, for mutual admonition within the body of Christ, and for continued forgiveness (3:12-17). United with Christ in his death and resurrection, the believer is "hidden with Christ" (3:3), not yet "revealed with him in glory" (3:4).

"Hidden with Christ in God"

Christ is not only the integrating center of reality but also the life of the believer and of the community of believers and, hence, the integrating center of individual and corporate Christian life. One is rooted and built up in Christ (2:7), buried and raised with Christ (2:11-14, 20), and "hidden with Christ" (3:3). But since Christ has been described already as the firstborn of creation and the firstborn of the dead, then being rooted in him means "being connected to the very life-centre of the universe."[15] The claim is mind-boggling: those who are united with Christ are in fact united with the one who holds the universe together, in whom it was created, and through whom it will be redeemed. Christian existence partakes of the existence of the new, restored humanity — true humanity — a claim made most evident in the characterization of Christians as raised to new life with and in Christ (2:13; 3:1-4). Believers participate in the new order of existence brought about by the resurrection of Christ. No wonder, then, that the Christian life is described as "putting off" the old person and "putting on" the new person that is being renewed or re-created in the image of its Creator. Those who are in Christ participate in a reality which affects them, but not only so, for they participate in a reality that affects the whole cosmos and all humanity.

In 2:12 this is said to happen through baptism. That is, upon baptism, the rite that marks initiation into the Christian life, people come to share first and foremost in Christ's death and resurrection. His life becomes their life. Their old way of life, described as being "dead in trespasses," is put to death (2:13), and their new life finds its purpose and takes its shape from Christ's risen life, who himself now is with God, although his presence there remains hidden to all but the eyes of faith (3:1-4). Hence, even as Christ was raised and now lives with God, so believers are raised and now live with God. Christ's life is their life; his destiny is their destiny. To put on the new person is to put on Christ and to find one's identity and life in him.

And yet there is also a promised, future disclosure of Christ's glory and supremacy (3:4). Not only will his glorious status, his universal lordship, be revealed at that time, but the identity of his people precisely as his people will also be revealed. The Christian life derives its peculiar character from the contrast between the future revelation of glory and the present hiddenness of Christ. Believers are raised to new life in this world, not in the next, and thus they anticipate but do not fully live in the life of the resurrection; they do not fully bear the renewed image of their Creator. Because the coming unveiling

---

15. Barclay, *Colossians*, 87.

of Christ in glory lies in the future, the life of the Christian must be oriented in hope to the future. Believers do not yet see the glory of Christ, who now lives in glory with his Father, publicly displayed to the world. They certainly do not experience the fullness of their own glorious transformation because they do not yet live in the glory of the resurrection life. The present earthly order is still marked by the power of darkness, and under such circumstances the Christian life can only be described as "hidden." Accordingly, the present life is lived in faith. Christian life begins with faith, the act of entrusting oneself to Christ, and is lived by faith, the continual trusting of oneself to Christ the Lord (1:4-5; 2:5-7).

Moreover, Christian life derives its shape not only from the new life lived in Christ but also from the cross of Christ. The life of the believer is "hidden" because it is lived in fellowship with the Lord who died a shameful public death on a Roman cross. His glory and his triumph are hidden. Christ's hidden victory also characterizes the life of believers, and in this way, too, his life is their life. While God genuinely effects new life, renewing believers in the image of Christ (3:11), working in them to bring them to perfection in Christ (1:28), and calling them to "put on the new person" (3:10), that newness cannot always be discerned, either by others or even by believers themselves. It is taken on faith, and the new life is lived in faith, trusting the Lord who is not seen (1:4, 23; 2:5, 7), and in hope, anticipating the Lord's manifestation in glory (1:5; 3:1-4). The need for continued forgiveness of each other (3:13) and for the admonition to "put on" the new person with its hallmark virtues of compassion, kindness, meekness, patience and humility arises because the present world finds itself this side of the final new creation, and those who live in this world are in the process of being renewed.

Because the life of faith is lived in union with the Lord of the cross, in anticipation of his manifestation in glory, the present life is marked by suffering, and this also comprises part of its hiddenness. Paul is the prime example of the hidden and suffering life in Christ. As an apostle who proclaims the gospel of the cross, Paul simply assumes that the course of his own life will reflect that of the Lord and of his death on the cross. Suffering will scarcely be a surprising part of the life of one who is an "apostle of Christ Jesus" (1:1). Paul's imprisonment while he wrote this epistle exemplifies most graphically the way in which suffering testifies to a life hidden in Christ. For although Paul speaks of his suffering as part of his apostolic commission to preach the gospel (1:24), the ambiguity of his own situation was surely apparent to him. The state which confined him to prison and the guards who watched over him undoubtedly knew him as some kind of public nuisance. But they scarcely recognized him as an apostle of a Lord, now hidden in glory, whose servants give their lives to him as he has given his life for them. It is even doubtful that the authorities and the guards had any significant understanding of "Jesus" or who he was. While Paul's suffering may have borne witness to him and to the church of his conformity to the death of Christ, it scarcely served as a triumphant public witness to the world, any more than had Jesus' cross. Part of the mystery of suffering is the lack of a clear understanding of the reasons for it and the purposes it serves. Paul had a clear sense of the larger purpose of his own suffering: it was simply part of the task of the proclamation of Christ to the Gentiles (1:25-27). But even that sense of overarching purpose must be held in faith, in anticipation of the vindication of both the crucified Lord and of those who participate in his death on the cross. Only from God's perspective, which the Colossians are called on to adopt (3:1-2), does one see the cross as the manifestation of God's salvation.

Finally, though, the image of being hidden in Christ is also an image of identity, belonging, and security. The false teaching circulating in Colossae apparently promised ways to deeper experience and understanding of God, and such a promise inevitably implies the inadequacy of one's current experience or knowledge. But Paul assures those who have responded to the call of the gospel and have experienced the grace of God that they have indeed been given that grace "in all its truth" (1:6). They may have the full assurance that they have been given knowledge of the mystery "hidden throughout the ages and generations" (1:26; 2:2), because they have come to know Christ "in whom are hidden all the treasures of wisdom and knowledge" (2:3). In other words, God's revelation through Christ is sufficient to grant true knowledge of God. In Christ, people receive God's love and election (1:2; 3:12). Therefore, being united with Christ in his death and resurrection now grants believers a sure and firm relationship with God. As a treasure is hidden and kept safe in a chest, so is the life of the believer "hidden with Christ in God."

In sum, then, the "hiddenness" of existence "with Christ in God" assures those who hold the hope of the gospel that even as they have been called by God (1:1; 3:12) they are also guarded by God as they are being renewed according to the image of their Creator (3:10). As believers participate in the new humanity re-created by God through the death and resurrection of Christ, they experience both the privileges of belonging to God's family and the ambiguity that characterizes all existence lived this side of that final revelation in glory. In addition to having a share in the inheritance granted to God's people, God's people are also called to "live in a way worthy of the Lord" (1:10). Although Colossians contains many other commands as well which call for conduct appropriate to the "new person," such conduct is not generated out of human capacity apart from God's empowering. God does not simply command a new way of life and leave its implementation to human beings. Instead, Colossians also points to the ways in which the power of God that worked through and on the cross for the salvation of humankind continues to work among his people in order to bring about that renewal that produces a life characterized by compassion, kindness, humility, meekness, patience, love, forgiveness, peace, and gratitude (3:12-15).

"As God's Chosen Ones, Holy and Beloved . . . Clothe Yourselves with Love"

In introducing concrete injunctions regarding the Christian life, Paul reminds the Colossians that they are "God's chosen ones, holy and beloved" (3:12). This is a telling juxtaposition of promise and command. It is not in order to *become* God's holy and beloved ones that Christians heed the exhortations given here, but rather precisely because they already *are* God's holy and beloved ones. God's love is not given as reward for accomplishment, but is rather the basis and power that makes obedience possible.

This is evident already in the images of salvation as a "rescue" or "deliverance" from the power of darkness and as the renewal of humanity in the image of the Creator. The first metaphor points to the weakness of humankind to deliver itself from the power that works in the world contrary to the purposes of God. The image of salvation as renewal or re-creation points to human dependence on God as well, for even as God created the world in the beginning, so now God re-creates all things. What God has begun, God will bring to completion. The work of salvation construed as the re-creation of the world promises that God works in and through Christ to accomplish his purposes from beginning to end.

God's power is therefore also disclosed as empowerment for faithful discipleship and living. The gospel grows and bears fruit among the Colossians (1:6). Growth in knowledge of God (1:10) occurs by being "greatly strengthened by his glorious power" (1:11). Paul describes his own ministry as "struggling with all the might with which [God] so mightily empowers me" (1:29). God works among and within his people so as to present them "holy, faultless, and blameless" before him (1:22). The whole body of the church is "nourished" by and "grows with a growth that is from God" (2:19). But this is the same power that effects patience and endurance (1:11) and that works in Paul as he suffers "the afflictions of Christ." It is not power that eliminates all suffering and weakness but that works in and through suffering and weakness; it is not power that exerts itself over others but expresses itself in service for others. It is not grasping but giving, because it finds its definitive expression in the fellowship of the believer with Christ in his death and resurrection. It is a power exercised in a peculiar hiddenness.

Life in Christ accordingly entails an ever-growing dependence on Christ as one is ever more deeply rooted in Christ (2:6-7). Therefore it is particularly marked by the practices of prayer and the spirit of thanksgiving. In fact Paul links prayer and thanksgiving more than once, telling the Colossians that in all his prayers he gives thanks to God for them (1:3, 9). Prayer is the appropriate setting for thanksgiving, inasmuch as both are offered to God in acknowledgment of dependence and reliance on God. Paul also links the two in exhortation: "Devote yourselves to prayer, keeping alert in it with thanksgiving" (4:2). Both prayer and thanksgiving are to be cultivated as habits. The Latin word *habitus* fits well here, for it can mean both an inclination of character, a habit, and a garment, as in a nun's habit. The new garment, the new person, given to the saints to put on (3:9-10, 14) is a gift, but it requires a reorientation and disciplined responsiveness of the entire person to God — and these are acquired in reliance upon God. Such reliance speaks the language of thanksgiving, for it arises from those who know themselves to be the recipients of God's grace in Christ. And it speaks in prayer, for while one may be grateful to others for favors rendered, the Christian life is in the final analysis a response to God for the ultimate gift of grace in Christ Jesus.

Christian life is lived in response to Christ, who is Lord. As Lord, he has the authority to command obedience. The Colossians are to live in a way "worthy of the Lord, pleasing to him in every way" (1:10), honoring him as Lord (2:6) and adhering to the gospel which was taught to them rather than to human standards and traditions that are "not according to Christ" (2:7-8). Paul characterizes both himself and Epaphras as Christ's servants (1:7, 24), who ultimately serve Christ in all that they do in their apostolic labors on behalf of the church. It is Christ, and not the church, who commands obedience. While the Colossians are to engage in mutual admonition and teaching, they are called upon to let the peace of Christ and the word of Christ govern their life together as a community. Christ has the authority to command allegiance. He exercises that authority not as an alien Lord, but as one who has identified with humankind in the shameful death of a condemned slave on a cross. It is such a Lord who calls his people to faithful discipleship. Christ is not a Lord who stands over against his people; rather he is a Lord to whom they have been joined through faith, in love and hope.

Hence the virtues held up for believers are those which reflect Christ's self-giving on the cross: lowliness, meekness, heartfelt compassion, forgiveness, love, and peace. Those brought together by God's act of reconciliation (1:20, 22) must endeavor to live together in "perfect harmony" (3:14), allowing the peace of Christ to rule among them (3:15). Those who have been called to-gether into one body (3:15), brought together into a renewed and unified humanity (3:11), are called on to "bear with one another" (3:13). They are to cease from those practices that foster division and discord, such as anger, malice, slander, and abusive language, putting on instead the virtues that make for unity, such as kindness, humility, meekness, and patience. Christians practice mutual admonition, teaching each other in all wisdom (3:16). Having received God's forgiveness for their sins (1:14; 3:13), they are to be people who forgive each other (3:13). The self-seeking, grasping ways of passion, evil desire, and greed (3:5) are to be put off, and the ways of generosity and self-giving are to be put on (3:12-15).

Such practices extend especially to relationships where there exists a power differential. Husbands, parents, and masters are to take the initiative in extending love, gentleness, and justice to those who are dependent on them. While Paul echoes many of the assumptions of his day regarding the structure of society and family, it is ultimately the reality of what God has done in Christ that shapes all Christian behavior and conduct. The way of life of those who have "put on" the new garment of Christ's renewing grace and power must be the way of those who are given the commands found in 3:18–4:1. Those in positions of authority or who have status are called on to live in ways that are particularly marked by the traits that are also said to belong to the new clothing that one puts on in Christ: loving (3:14, 19), not provoking or angering one's children (3:8, 12), and doing that which is just or righteous (4:1). Authority is thus to be characterized by that which is most characteristic of Christ the Lord, who did not exercise his authority in domination but in humility. As one writer put it, "the virtues espoused here are those gentle traits that would ease the common life of a close and intense community."[16]

This "close and intense" community is the locus of moral formation. Although modern Western society has assigned this role to the family, and sometimes to state-sponsored education, Paul located the formation of believers primarily in the sphere of the church. Many social institutions, including the household, state, and religious and civic cults could serve as normative reference groups for Christian conduct and identity. But for Paul it was clearly the church, the new household of all those who are family in Christ, which shaped the values, perceptions, and practices of his converts, for they individually and corporately derived their identity from their fellowship with Christ.

In short, the "gospel according to Colossians" begins with God's creation of the world and aims at its final re-creation. In both creation and re-

---

16. Meeks, "To Walk Worthily of the Lord," 49.

creation human beings play a central role. For while they were created for community with God and with each other, both the vertical and horizontal relationships are marred by alienation and hostility. In Christ, God purposes to heal and renew that which is wounded and dying, to perfect humankind in the image of its Creator. In the manifestation of God's life-giving purposes and power in Christ, in whom "the fullness of the deity dwelled bodily," that transforming work has begun. It awaits, however, the further final revelation of Christ in glory, which will bring to a consummation God's creating and re-creating work.

Colossians in the Context of Pauline Theology

Colossians comes to us in a collection of letters attributed to Paul with a dozen other letters and, beyond that, in the context of a collection of epistles, then within the whole New Testament and the Christian canon of the Old and New Testaments. Together these documents bear witness to God's dealings with the world, including God's creation of the world, his calling of Abraham and of the people of Israel, the deliverance of Israel from captivity in Egypt, the life, death, and resurrection of Jesus, the sending of the Holy Spirit, and the entrusting of a specific vocation to the church of Jesus Christ. Obviously, not every document in the Scriptures embodies this narrative in the same way, not only because of the different social and historical contexts that produced them, but also because the narrative is often presupposed rather than explicitly articulated. This section will suggest the ways in which Colossians invites its readers to understand themselves, their identity, and their vocation in the context of the biblical narrative of God's calling and shaping of a people. We will focus specifically on those aspects of the narrative which Colossians emphasizes in either distinct or emphatic ways within the Pauline canon. To a lesser degree we will also cast an eye on the place of Colossians within the NT and the biblical witness overall.

As one of the shorter letters in the Pauline canon, Colossians is easily overshadowed by other letters that give similar themes longer or fuller treatments or include discussions of topics, such as the Spirit, the resurrection of Christ, the plight of humankind, and the role of Israel, not covered in Colossians. Romans gives more explicit attention to the power of sin, dying and rising with Christ, eschatological hope, and the role of Israel; Corinthians, to love, the Spirit, the resurrection and the character of the church; Galatians, to law and faith; and so on. Colossians seems to introduce no topic not covered or developed more fully in other letters.

How, then, does it fit into "Pauline theology" as a whole? Two major factors immediately complicate our attempts to answer this question. First, not all scholars think that Paul is responsible for this letter as he is for Romans or Galatians, which are taken as embodying the heart of Paul's gospel. Some think that Colossians was written by a coworker of Paul during his lifetime, while others suggest that a follower of Paul penned it after Paul's death. Those who think Paul wrote the letter take Colossians as an instance of *Paul's* theology, whereas those who think that a follower or coworker wrote it might deem it more broadly *Pauline*. Whether Colossians has then adequately or accurately captured Paul's own thinking could be further debated. In what way, then, can we speak of the "contribution" of Colossians to Pauline theology? In this discussion, I will endeavor to set Colossians within the context of the canonical Pauline epistles, while noting the distinctive notes sounded by Colossians, notes that are not necessarily unique — although they may be — but notes that are sounded in different ways or come through more clearly than in the other epistles of the Pauline canon. We will see here the elasticity of Pauline theology and the ways in which Paul's theology was formulated to emphasize certain parts of a larger narrative to encourage and exhort the Colossians.

A second question is no easier to answer: How exactly does one arrive at a satisfactory delineation of "Pauline theology"?[17] Is this a reality that exists *behind* the epistles, as it were, or is it the sum of all the statements in the epistles? That is, are we trying to distill from the letters the essence of "Paul's theology," or do we simply tally up the theology of all the letters rather as a mathematical sum? The danger with either approach is that we can end up with an entity, "Pauline theology," that is only loosely attached to the actual letters of Paul or is based on prejudices about what is "Pauline." Is there some principle, or are there several key principles, that are the heart and center of "Pauline theology"?

Obviously the question of the center of Paul's thought is of importance for our discussion if we are seeking to articulate the way in which Colossians is an expression of Paul's theology. "Pauline theology" has often focused on one or two key epistles, notably the Corinthian correspondence, Galatians, Romans, and Philippians, placing any letters which do not orbit around that center in virtually a different universe. Such a procedure prejudices the description of Pauline theology against any letter that does not deal with the same problems or discuss the same topics as the so-called "pillar epistles" of Paul. How we proceed here might well predetermine our conception of the contribution of Colossians to Pauline theology.

17. For a discussion of this question, see Dunn, *Theology of Paul*, 1-26.

Over the years, these questions have been the subject of no little debate. Sometimes this debate has been cast as a quest to discover the "center" of Paul, to find that which makes Paul Paul. We may briefly examine a few proposals that have attempted to venture a judgment about the "center of Paul." Here, of course, a further question is already posed: does "Paul" speak with a different voice than, say, Matthew or Peter or John? Is the "center of Paul" likely to be unique, or something that in fact he shares in common with the entire biblical witness? In order to get at this question, we may catalogue some of the many suggestions offered about the "center of Paul."

First, following the insights of the Reformation, many scholars, and particularly those in the Lutheran and continental traditions, have located the heart of Paul's theology in justification by faith, understood particularly as the contrast between human efforts to seek right standing or "justification" before God and God's justifying grace in Jesus Christ.[18] If such a measure were used to assess Colossians, it might come off poorly indeed, for there is no overt discussion of justification, and neither the noun *dikaiosynē*— translated either as "justification" or "righteousness" — nor the verb "justify" appears in the epistle. Neither does "law" *(nomos)* nor the phrase "works of the Law." If Paul's formulation of the gospel in terms of "justification apart from the Law" is taken as the "center" of Pauline theology, Colossians merely brushes by that center in orbit. But what would be true of Colossians would be true of a number of other documents in the Pauline canon as well.

Albert Schweitzer countered that "justification by faith" was not the center of Paul's thought because it was not capable of generating other key aspects of Pauline theology, such as the role of the Spirit and the resurrection.[19] That is to say, one cannot move from the idea of "justification by faith" to a proper conception of ethical behavior, an understanding of justification by faith does not lead to a comprehension of the role of the Spirit, and so on. In fact, Schweitzer argued, Paul himself did not explicitly connect justification by faith with these other aspects of thought or with crucial matters such as baptism, the Lord's Supper, or ethics. This suggested to Schweitzer that "justification by faith" was a "subsidiary crater" and not the heart of Paul's theological thought. Schweitzer located the center of Paul's thought in what he called "the mystical doctrine of being-in-Christ." This "being-in-Christ" encompassed such aspects of Paul's thought as dying and rising with Christ, incor-

---

18. In recent years, one thinks especially of Ernst Käsemann and Peter Stuhlmacher, who have nevertheless placed "justification by faith" in the context of God's setting the whole cosmos or creation to rights. Whether or not the emphasis on "justification by faith" is "distinctly" Pauline is quite another question.

19. Schweitzer, *The Mysticism of Paul the Apostle,* 220.

poration into the body of Christ, union with Christ, and living in the Spirit. The center of Paul is to be found in such "participationist" terminology.[20] If this is an apt characterization of the center of Paul's theology, then Colossians clearly and easily belongs in this orbit. Paul's statements that the believer lives "in" Christ (2:6-7) and is circumcised in him, buried with him in baptism, and raised with him through faith (2:11-12) are but some of "participationist" images from Colossians that could be cited as evidence to place Colossians in the context of Pauline theology.

J. C. Beker argued that "the coherence of the gospel is constituted by the apocalyptic interpretation of the death and resurrection of Christ."[21] Here there is not so much a theological proposition or set of ideas at the heart of Paul as a framework or structure that makes the death and resurrection of Christ central and the ultimate victory of God the goal of God's action.[22] Since such a schema includes a turning point (the death and resurrection) and a goal (God's ultimate victory), one could speak of an essential narrative aspect of Paul's thought. This "apocalyptic interpretation" is what many scholars deem to be missing from Colossians. Gone is the overarching framework of the "already" and the "not yet," the tension of the present life as one shares in the groaning of creation for future redemption. In its place, there is a serenity of being raised with Christ already in the present, in some sense joining him as he is seated at the right hand of God (3:1). Here, it is argued, the temporal dualism characteristic of apocalyptic has been replaced by a spatial dualism, and anticipation of what is to come by participation in what already is. The contrast is no longer between what is and what will be but between what is in heaven and what is on earth. And yet Colossians also holds out the promise of the revelation of Christ in glory (3:4) and an expectation of a future judgment (3:6). Moreover, echoing the familiar Pauline triad of faith, hope, and love, Colossians emphasizes hope over the other two. Perhaps, then, its contribution would lie precisely in the formulation of Christian hope in somewhat distinctive terms.

---

20. "Participationist" is the term used by Sanders, following Schweitzer, to describe such terminology (*Paul and Palestinian Judaism,* 440). Although Sanders finds Schweitzer's insights important for understanding Paul, he does not think Colossians was written by Paul (*Paul and Palestinian Judaism,* 431).

21. Beker, "Paul's Theology," 364-77. Dunn, *Theology,* 23, cites Beker's point with approval.

22. Plevnik, "Center," 473-74, contends that several features crucial to Pauline thought argue against the adoption of Beker's proposal that apocalyptic provides the structure of Paul's thought. These features include Jesus' identity as Son of God and his filial relationship to the Father, Christ's inclusive and representative role in his death and resurrection, the believer's conformation to Christ, and the believer's (sacramental) participation in Christ.

Finally, two proposals provide ample space for Colossians to be included among the Pauline epistles. In his study of Pauline theology, Ralph P. Martin argued that its center could be found in Paul's understanding of reconciliation.[23] If that were granted, then Colossians could well serve as a chief witness to Paul's theological concerns, for the epistle speaks explicitly of the reconciling work of the cross, extending its reach to include all creation. Joseph Plevnik argues that Protestant and Roman Catholic scholars answer the question about the center of Paul rather differently, with Catholic scholars more likely to identity the center of Paul simply as "Christ."[24] That, of course, is an appealing "center." Again, here Colossians might rank as the chief witness, for, as has been said elsewhere, the genius of Colossians is to give a picture of reality that finds its integrating center in Christ. The world was made through and for him, it is sustained in him, the fullness of deity is found in him, the believer's life is hidden in him, and so on. Yet to say that "Christ" is the center of Pauline theology or of Colossians says both too much and too little. Too little because it does not deal with the contours of Paul's christology and too much because it fails to allow distinctions between the various emphases of Paul's epistles. One could say that "Christ" is the center of Colossians or of Romans, although the two letters are very different. Or, one could say that "Christ" is the center of Matthew, John, Hebrews, Revelation, 1 Peter — and Colossians. This is certainly a true statement, but it is not particularly helpful or descriptive. All these documents bear witness to Christ, but in different genres, with different images, vocabulary, and emphases, and for different purposes.

Perhaps the search for the "center" of Pauline theology may well show us that such a quest is misguided in important respects. Often that quest has proceeded as though it were an attempt to identify a single theological proposition — such as justification by faith — that served as the center of Paul's thought. But it would be a mistake to try to force Paul's thinking into a set of propositions, however true they may be, or to identify the center in one particular formulation over against others. Surely the figure of Christ, Paul's understanding of "justification by faith" and participation "in Christ," and the apocalyptic framework of Paul's thought are all inextricably connected in ways which virtually defy the isolation of any one of these from the others. But that would not mean that every item has to be present in the same way or with equal emphasis for a letter to be judged "Pauline." Indeed, the very shape of the Pauline canon — a collection of letters to churches and individuals, ad-

23. *Reconciliation: A Study of Paul's Theology.*
24. See Plevnik, "Center," especially 461-63. Fitzmyer, *Pauline Theology*, 16, identifies "christocentric soteriology" as the center of Paul's theology.

dressing specific situations at different times in Paul's life — suggests that the attempt to identify "the center" of Pauline theology will inevitably fail to do justice to the elasticity of Paul's thought. If he had thought one letter met every need, we might have a much briefer canon! But the differences of emphasis and subject matter among the epistles help us identify what is coherent or consistent in Paul's thought, as well as how it comes to expression in concrete situations.[25] Because Colossians was written to a distinctive situation to address problems which had arisen in the church at Colossae, we cannot expect that Paul will repeat all that he believes here — or in any letter. He will need to formulate what he wishes to say in ways that take into account the situation at hand.

But in trying to see how Paul — or any other author — speaks to a specific situation, we always engage in a bit of speculation as we try to reconstruct the historical and social context that gave rise to a specific letter. Thus we will want to focus on the statements of the epistle as we have them, asking whether a particular historical reconstruction would make sense in light of our explication of the letter. In other words, in engaging Paul's thought or the epistle to the Colossians, we deal first and foremost with what Paul actually wrote.

It is also helpful to think in terms of the narrative structure of Pauline theology rather than of a key proposition or key idea that forms the "center of Paul."[26] Two things are in view here. First, for Paul, the gospel is an account of what God has done. Even when Paul is summarizing the gospel in formulaic or confessional terms, it is clear that an account, with a beginning and an anticipated end, of God's gracious initiative toward humankind underlies those formulations. As noted earlier, that narrative includes God's creation of the world, his calling of Abraham and then also of the people of Israel, the sending of Jesus the Messiah, the giving of the Holy Spirit, and the empowering of the church for God's mission in the world. Second, then, Paul often retells what has happened — to Abraham, to Christ, to himself — precisely in order to include his readers within the story of Abraham, Jesus, and Paul the Jewish believer and apostle to the Gentiles. Seldom if ever does he recount the entire story. That would be unnecessary. Thus in Colossians, for example, Paul does not refer to Abraham, and only implicitly alludes to Israel. He foregrounds the inclusion of the Gentiles and his own role as apostle against the back-

25. Often adopted today is Beker's point that Paul's thought should be construed between the poles of the "coherent" and "contingent," the latter referring to the concrete or particular expressions of the Pauline gospel in different circumstances.

26. See, for example, Longenecker (ed.), *Narrative Dynamics in Paul: A Critical Assessment;* Hays, *Faith of Jesus Christ;* Gorman, *Cruciformity;* Grieb, *Story of Romans.*

ground of God's creation and ultimate redemption of all the world. In Colossians Paul endeavors to shape the imagination of his probably primarily Gentile readers so that they see their place in this grand narrative, and so live as the church of Jesus Christ anticipating God's final redemption of the cosmos. The whole narrative of redemption is presupposed; but only part of it is emphasized here. Those parts are alluded to which are most likely to serve Paul in his efforts to shape the hearts and minds of his readers, to correct their misapprehensions, and to root them more firmly in the gospel of Jesus Christ. We turn, then, to a closer look at Paul's theological narrative in order to delineate how Paul in Colossians encourages and exhorts his readers.

A Sketch of Pauline Theology

Without a doubt, the cross and resurrection are central to Paul's thought. But any one of the ways of articulating the center of Paul's thought noted above could find that statement amenable. To be more precise in coming to terms with Paul's thinking, we must place the cross and resurrection in an *eschatological framework,* which is but another way of saying that the structure of Paul's thought always has in view the *eschaton* or end of all things. Paul believed that certain eschatological hopes had begun to be fulfilled in the death and resurrection of Jesus. As he wrote in 2 Cor 1:20, "all God's promises find their 'yes' in [Christ]." He writes to the Corinthian Christians of the tradition which he had received that "Christ died for our sins in accordance with the Scriptures, that he was buried, that he was raised on the third day in accordance with the Scriptures, and that he appeared to Cephas, then to the twelve" (1 Cor 15:3-5). When Paul summarizes his "gospel" in Romans, he speaks of "the gospel of God, which he promised beforehand through his prophets in the holy Scriptures, the gospel concerning his Son, who was descended from David according to the flesh and was declared to be Son of God with power according to the spirit of holiness by resurrection from the dead, Jesus Christ our Lord" (Rom 1:1-4). In these passages we find several items of importance: (1) Jesus is the Messiah, the promised deliverer of Israel, and Lord, because he has been exalted to a position of dignity and honor by God; (2) the Scriptures promised the gospel, the coming of Christ, and his death on the cross; and (3) Christ's resurrection brought about the "turn of the ages," the era of salvation promised by God. Underlying Paul's thought, then, is the movement from promise to fulfillment, anticipating the consummation of all things. Christ's death and resurrection are pivotal events which look back toward what God has promised and anticipate the salvation that God will bring to all the world. In all his letters, Paul wants his readers, corporately and individually, to participate in the blessings of this promise while simultaneously anticipating the consummation of all things.

If we look especially at the first two points, we note that Paul often speaks of what God has done in and through Jesus in relationship to Israel and the Law given to Israel. He does so implicitly when he refers to Jesus as "Christ," or "Messiah." While it is sometimes said that in Paul's writings "Christ" has lost its significance as a messianic title for Jesus, this conclusion seems unwarranted in light of the evidence that, for Paul, Jesus' significance is to be construed first with relationship to Israel and then, through Israel, to the Gentiles. Jesus of Nazareth is the Messiah, the promised deliverer of Israel, "descended from David according to the flesh." But the gospel of God brings salvation not just to Israel but, through Israel's Messiah, to all the world (Rom 15:8-12). Through Christ, God has elected to have mercy on all (11:32). Thus in Romans, when Paul recounts God's work in the world, he begins with Abraham, in order to show the relationship of the Law, the coming of the Messiah, and the ingathering of the Gentiles to God's call to Abraham. Because in the OT the king of Israel was thought of as a son of God (2 Sam 7:12-14; Ps 2:6-8), the designation "Son of God" in the NT minimally means "Messiah," since the Messiah would be the son of David, the king, and so also the "Son of God" or "Son of the Most High." Not only had God sent his Messiah, as promised, to Israel, but the Messiah had been put to death and subsequently raised to life by God and crowned as not merely king of Israel but Lord of all. Together the events of Jesus' death, resurrection, and exaltation marked a turning point in God's purposes for the world and the fulfillment of at least the initial eschatological hopes for redemption.

Indeed, in the resurrection of Jesus, Paul sees the inbreaking of the new age promised by God, the creation of a new heaven and a new earth, and the redemption of earth and its inhabitants. Hence Paul writes to the Corinthians that they are those upon whom "the end of the ages has come" (1 Cor 10:11). Therefore, "if anyone is in Christ, that one is a new creation" (2 Cor 5:17; Gal 6:15).[27] By "age" Paul does not mean simply a period of time which gives way to another. Rather, this age is "the present evil age" (Gal 1:4), that is, the present world order which stands in stark contrast to God's "pledged redemption."[28] The turning of the ages and the arrival of "the age to come" is not a

---

27. "New creation" is taken by some to refer to the individual ("that person is a new creature"), and by others to the "new creation" itself ("then a new world has been created"). For the most recent study, see Hubbard, *New Creation in Paul's Letters and Thought*.

28. Keck, *Paul and His Letters*, 75.

matter of human progress or the gradual evolution of the world toward some inevitable goal or inherent destiny. "The age to come" is brought about only through God's intervention, by God raising Jesus to life. Jesus' resurrection event was not simply the resuscitation of a corpse, but the granting of resurrection life to him as well as to all those joined to him. Christ is "the firstfruits of those who have fallen asleep. For as by a human being came death, by a human being has come also the resurrection of the dead. For as in Adam all die, so also in Christ will all be made alive" (1 Cor 15:20-22). Christ's resurrection guarantees the future resurrection of believers and in some sense is in fact their resurrection: they are those who are made alive "in Christ." His life is indeed their life. The resurrection is the guarantee that what God has done for Christ he will do also for those who are in Christ. "For the resurrection we Christians know already has come to pass in our head, and in the members it is yet to be."[29]

Within this framework belongs Paul's understanding of the cross. As stated earlier, the cross and resurrection of Christ are central to Paul's theology, and to virtually all modern construals of that theology. Having said that, however, we must add that there is a variety of ways of conceiving the work of the cross — both in Paul and among his subsequent interpreters. He uses many metaphors for what God has done through Christ on the cross. And this itself indicates an important starting point for understanding the cross. For clearly what happens on the cross is the work of God. In many formulations, God is the subject of the salvation effected through Christ's death (Rom 3:25; 8:32; 2 Cor 5:18-21; Eph 2:4-5). One thinks, for example, of the pithy formulation that "in Christ, God was reconciling the world to himself" (2 Cor 5:19). Here God is the subject of the drama and Christ is the agent through whom salvation is offered. But there are also places where Christ is the subject of active verbs. Clearly the implication is not that Christ does one kind of work on the cross while God does another. Rather, for Paul the cross is simultaneously God's righteous act for the salvation of the world, as well as the act of the Son of God "who loved me, and gave himself for me" (Gal 2:20).

We may catalog briefly some of Paul's ways of describing the work of the cross. Most simply, "Christ died for our sins" (1 Cor 15:3; Gal 1:4; 1 Tim 1:15). What he did was "for us," and it dealt with our sin. Using images of liberation and release, Paul writes that Christ has delivered or "redeemed those under the Law" (Gal 4:5, 8; Rom 8:2) by giving himself "a ransom for all" (1 Tim 2:4-6). The course of Christ's own life, from death to resurrection, serves as one way to describe his life-giving work as the second Adam or as

---

29. Augustine, *Commentary on the Psalms* 66.1 in *ACCSNT* 9:17.

the one who undoes the act of Adam that brings death to world. By dying, Christ brings life (1 Cor 15:21-22; Rom 5:15-19; Eph 2:5; 2 Tim 1:10). Just as the disobedience of the first human brought death to all, so the obedience of Christ will bring life (Rom 5:18-19; 6:5-11, 23). Christ is the agent of God's reconciliation of the world, specifically of Jew and Gentile into one body (cf. 2 Cor 5:18-19). Through Christ, people are acquitted of their guilt before God, being justified by the grace of God (Rom 3:24; 5:9; Eph 2:8-9). They are sanctified, made holy (1 Cor 6:11). Through his blood, Christ establishes a new covenant (1 Cor 11:23-26; 2 Cor 3:5-6; Exod 24:8). These are but some of the ways that Paul explains what has happened to set the world right through God's act on the cross. In every way they show that God takes the initiative to reach out and do for the world what it cannot do for itself — redeem it from sin, death, and alienation.

God's salvific work is often understood by Western Christians in a highly individualistic way and the cross as answering the question, "How do I get right with God? How do I get saved?" But as J. Louis Martyn phrases it, "The gospel is about the divine invasion of the cosmos (theology), not about human movement into blessedness (religion)."[30] Paul not only thinks of God's gracious approach to the world but also envisions a new community created by God through the cross of Christ. In Romans, Paul speaks of this community in terms of the bringing of Gentiles into Abraham's family and the grafting of them into the olive tree. Those who were "not my people" have been called "my people," and those who were "not beloved" have been called "my beloved" by God (Rom 9:14-18, 25-26; 11:29-32). They have become heirs of the promises of God. Terms previously applied to Israel — "my people," "my beloved," "children of the living God," and "heirs" — now include Gentiles as well. Elsewhere Paul uses images of the household of God, the body of Christ, and the "new person" to characterize the results of Christ's work. That is to say, on the cross Christ has not simply "saved" individuals. Rather, the cross is God's means of setting the world right, and that includes the creation of a people who live according to God's ultimate purposes for the world.

While Paul believed that the eschatological promises of God had begun to be fulfilled in Christ, he anticipated the final consummation of those promises. Although his generation was the generation "on whom the end of the ages has come," this was not "the end of the ages." Christ has been raised to life, but all those in Christ await their own resurrection, their own renewal, as well as the renewal of all the world. What Paul awaits is the return of

---

30. Martyn, "Abrahamic Covenant," 170.

Christ, the *parousia*, which will initiate and bring about the renewal of all creation. But in the meantime the world is suspended between fulfillment and consummation, between the first and second comings of Christ for the redemption of all things. So Paul can speak of those in Christ as those who "are being changed into his likeness from one degree of glory to another" (2 Cor 3:18) and also anticipate a final transformation when all will be changed "in a moment, in the twinkling of an eye, at the last trumpet. For the trumpet will sound, and the dead will be raised imperishable, and we shall be changed" (1 Cor 15:51-52). Christ's resurrection is a sign and guarantee of the coming of the age of resurrection.

The gift of the Spirit is also an aspect and gift of the new age. Paul speaks of the Spirit as the "down payment" or "guarantee" of our future inheritance (2 Cor 1:22; 5:5; Eph. 1:13-14). In some ways the Spirit is virtually inseparable from the resurrection, since the Spirit is the Spirit of life (Rom 8:2; Gal 6:8). Paul in fact associates the Holy Spirit with Jesus' resurrection from the dead and with his being declared "Son of God in power" (Rom 1:4). Paul also associates the Spirit with adoption into the family of God, for the Spirit makes it possible for human beings to call on God as Father (Rom 8:15; Gal 4:6). That is to say, through the life-giving work of the Spirit, God adopts those who are "in Christ," his Son, as his own children. Through the Holy Spirit "the love of God is poured into our hearts" (Rom 5:5). Paul characterizes his preaching as marked by the power of the Spirit (1 Cor 2:4), and his message can be rightly understood only through the guidance of the Spirit, since otherwise it will be regarded as foolishness (1 Cor 2:12-15). The Spirit furthermore gives various gifts to the church for its ministry in the world (1 Corinthians 12–14) and enables Christians to live according to God's will rather than the flesh (Galatians 5). In short, the Spirit plays a role at the beginning, middle, and end of the life of the Christian. The Spirit adopts believers into the family of God, grants them the graces to live a life worthy of their calling, uniting them into one body, and will raise them to life in the resurrection. Christian existence is existence lived by the power of the Spirit.

But in anticipation of that time of resurrection, Paul speaks of the world and its inhabitants as in a time of struggle and travail:

> The creation waits with eager longing for the revealing of the children of God, for the creation was subjected to futility, not by its own will but by the will of the one who subjected it, in hope that the creation itself will be set free from its bondage to decay and will obtain the freedom of the glory of the children of God. We know that the whole creation has been groaning in labor pains until now, and not only the creation, but we our-

> selves, who have the firstfruits of the Spirit, groan inwardly while we wait
> for adoption, the redemption of our bodies. For in hope we were saved.
> Now hope that is seen is not hope. For who hopes for what is seen? (Rom
> 8:19-24)

Here we see clearly the tension that characterizes present human existence.
Although those in Christ have the "firstfruits of the Spirit" of life, they anticipate a life which they do not yet have in its perfection and fullness. Therefore,
they anticipate and yearn for freedom, glory, redemption, and salvation.
Moreover, the world itself is in bondage, in need of liberation. This is one of
Paul's typical characterizations of the human plight in the present moment:
humans are enslaved to powers and forces that are beyond their control and
from which they cannot liberate themselves. They need to be "transferred"
from the dominion of one master to that of another, from the realm of darkness, sin, and death to the dominion of Christ's love and life-giving power.
Paul personifies sin as a domineering master against which human beings
struggle in vain (e.g., Romans 7). Only the Spirit of life can liberate human
beings from the captivity under the sway of the powers of the world, including sin, death, and the Law when it operates through sinful human beings
(Rom 8:2-3; Gal 5:16-17). When Paul characterizes human beings as "flesh"
(sarx) he does not refer merely to their physicality (2 Cor 5:16), mortality or
frailty (1 Cor 15:50; 2 Cor 7:5), or inadequacy (Gal 2:20; Phil 1:22-23), but to the
sphere of sin's operation. The human situation is one of alienation and estrangement from God. While there are many hostile forces in the world,
forces whose purposes are inimical to God's saving ways, the ultimate enemy
of humankind is death itself. But through the death and resurrection of Jesus,
God has dealt death its final blow.

Paul conceives of his own role as God's ambassador, particularly to the
Gentiles, sent to proclaim the reconciliation realized in Christ. So important
is his understanding of his calling that it is included in his summary of the
gospel in Romans: through Christ "we have received grace and apostleship to
bring about the obedience of faith among all the Gentiles for the sake of his
name" (1:5). The grace of God brings the Gentiles into the people of God, for
God's purposes are to create one new people, who now live in "the obedience
of faith" and will eventually dwell in the renewed creation. Paul's role is not
incidental; he is God's chosen instrument to carry the gospel of reconciliation
to the Gentiles. Little wonder, then, that some scholars have argued that it is
impossible to separate Paul's "conversion" from his "call."[31] Both Acts and

---

31. Most famously, Krister Stendahl in his essay "Call Rather than Conversion."

Paul's own testimony (Gal 1:15-16) link them closely together: when he was called to follow Christ, he was also called to preach Christ.

The church of Jesus Christ is situated between fulfillment and consummation. The mission of the church is not to undertake the messianic task of bringing about that consummation, but rather to live as God's obedient people in the world in anticipation of God's final redemptive act. Those who are reconciled to God and to each other in the community of faith, the body of Christ, have Christ as Lord and example. Taking their cue from the life and death of Jesus, they are to live with each other by the power of Spirit in love, joy, peace, patience, kindness, generosity, faithfulness, gentleness, and self-control. The power of the Spirit works to bring about conformity to the mind of Christ, who did not grasp for power and prestige, but emptied himself in humble service (Phil 2:5-11). In union with their Lord, believers await the final consummation of all things, the death of death and the triumph of God's righteousness.

Colossians in the Context of Pauline and Biblical Theology

As we have seen, "the theology of Colossians is at every point Christological." Colossians offers a "comprehensive vision of truth . . . whose focal point is Christology."[32] In many ways, of course, such statements sum up not just Colossians, but Pauline theology as a whole with its emphasis on the fulfillment of eschatological hopes in the death and resurrection of Christ. In Romans, Paul speaks of Christ as the single true offspring and heir of the promises to Abraham and the goal or end of the Law. Paul summarizes his preaching in 1 Corinthians as "Jesus Christ, and him crucified" (1 Cor 2:2). In Galatians he speaks of Christ as the one who "lives in me" (Gal 2:20), and in Philippians of the "surpassing worth of knowing Christ Jesus my Lord" (Phil 3:8). Whether Paul is summarizing the work of God in the world, his own preaching, or the substance and goal of the Christian life, he does so with reference to Christ, to his death and resurrection.

All this also characterizes Colossians. But in Colossians Paul paints the christological picture more boldly on a cosmological canvas. As Andrew Lincoln puts it, "the most distinctive feature of the christology of Colossians is its sustained treatment of Christ in relation to both the creation and reconciliation of the cosmos."[33] Christ is not only the focal point of Israel's hopes or of the life

---

32. See Barclay, *Colossians*, 77.
33. Lincoln, "Colossians," 570.

of the individual believer but also the one through whom the world was made, and in whom "all things hold together" (1:17). Whereas the eschatological framework of Paul's theology so often points toward the future, anticipating God's final and decisive act of salvation, the narrative of Colossians pushes the reader back to creation. Colossians underscores the point that "all things" — all creation, all powers, all peoples — somehow have their very existence in and for Christ. The world's eschatological destiny is therefore already anticipated in its creation. Colossians takes the narrative back beyond Moses and the Law, beyond the call of Abraham to creation itself. Although Christ's role in creation is hinted at elsewhere (e.g., 1 Cor 8:6), in Colossians it is central.

With the emphasis on creation, we are taken back to the first words of Scripture: "In the beginning, God created the heavens and the earth." While other NT books reflect intentionally on God's creation of the world, the *topos* is much more common in the OT than in the NT. Besides the twin accounts of creation in Genesis, there are assertions of God's sole creation of the world (Isaiah), the mysteries of God's creativity and creation (Job), the glories of the world that God has made (Psalms), and the way in which the creation exhibits the ordered wisdom of God (Proverbs). There are places in the NT that speak of God's creation (Rom 1:20; 8:19-23), noting particularly the role of Christ in creation (John 1:1-3; 1 Cor 8:6; Heb 1:2; 2 Pet 3:5). But creation is not the subject of extensive theological reflection in the NT. Even Ephesians, which in many ways is closely linked to and most like Colossians, speaks of creation primarily with respect to the creation of human beings with an eye to the salvation that is theirs in Christ and the vocation they are to exercise (1:9-10; 2:10, "created in Christ Jesus for good works"; 4:24). It would not be overstating the case to argue that Colossians provides more raw material for continuing reflection on creation than any other book of the NT. But, like the rest of the biblical witness, creation is not an entity unto itself: it exists as the creation of God and bears witness to God's ongoing superintendence of the universe. Colossians insists that from its beginning to its end creation has been the work of God in Christ. As Revelation phrases it, Christ is "the Alpha and the Omega, the first and the last, the beginning and the end" (Rev 22:13). In Colossians the doctrine of creation functions to underwrite both Paul's assertions about the superiority of Christ to the powers of the world and Paul's moral injunctions against any abuse of the body or abstention from food or drink in an effort to gain a higher spiritual standing. The cosmological and ethical correlates of christology are explicitly drawn in Colossians.

Unlike some theories of creation that posited separate origins for matter and mind or attributed the creation of the material world to a lesser deity, the Bible affirms that God has created all that is and that this "all" is "very good." The OT bears continuing witness to God's creation of the world, noting that God's creation logically demands worship of this one God (e.g., 1 Chron 16:26, 30). In Isaiah 44–46, those who make and worship idols are taunted as worshiping artifacts that cannot save them and ignoring the God who made the world and the very wood and material from which the idols are made. As Creator of all that is, God alone is God: therefore, all the nations of the earth are to worship him. This becomes a central emphasis in biblical and later Jewish monotheistic apologetic, including the period in which our NT was written. As one author put it, "However diverse Judaism may have been in many other respects, this was common: only the God of Israel is worthy of worship because he is sole Creator of all things and sole Ruler of all things."[34] To speak of Christ, then, in terms of his role of creating the world rather than as one of God's creatures identifies him as one who exercises the prerogatives of God and so is worthy of worship as God is.

In speaking of the creation of the world "in" or "through" Christ, Colossians reflects the influence of the wisdom traditions of the OT and later Judaism, where Wisdom is a "master worker" alongside God in creation (Prov 8:27-30; 3:19; Wis 7:21-22; 8:4-6; 9:1-2, 9). Wisdom is not simply a blueprint that God uses as a plan to create the world, but is personified as an agent or helper in creation (cf. Jer 10:12; 1QH^a 9.7, 14, 19; 11QPsa^a 26.14).[35] Exactly how Jewish and NT thinkers thought of "wisdom" remains, however, a source of discussion. J. D. G. Dunn, for example, has insisted repeatedly that "wisdom" is simply an alternative way of speaking about "the effective power of God in his active relationship with his world and its inhabitants."[36] Jewish thinkers who spoke of God's "wisdom" did not think of a being distinct or separate from God. Elsewhere, God is said to have created the world by his word (Ps 33:6) or by the Torah (*Tanḥuma* Bereshit § 1 [6b]; *Genesis Rabbah* 1:1; *Pirke Aboth* 3.15). Not only is God the Creator of the world and source of its life, but God created the world through an agent — usually Wisdom or Torah (Prov 8:30; Wis 7:21-22). Often, Wisdom and word overlap to such an extent that they are nearly one and the same (Sir 24:23; Bar 4:1). But it is specifically Wisdom's role as God's agent in creation that seems to have sparked reflection on Christ's role and suggested ways of speaking about God's creation of the world through an agent, but an agent that was in fact God's own mind and

---

34. Bauckham, *God Crucified*, 11. See also Hurtado, *Lord Jesus Christ*, 36; Thompson, *God of the Gospel of John*, 54.

35. Exactly how one is to construe Wisdom — whether as a personification of divine power or a hypostatization of that power — remains a source of debate; see Thompson, *God of the Gospel of John*, 130-36.

36. Dunn, *Christology in the Making*, 219.

not a distinct being. Of course, in the NT the "agent" of God's creation is no impersonal force but Christ, the Word, the Son of God. "All things were made through him, and without him was not anything made which was made" (John 1:3). "In many and various ways God spoke of old to our fathers by the prophets; but in these last days he has spoken to us by a Son, whom he appointed the heir of all things, through whom also he created the world. He reflects the glory of God and bears the very stamp of his nature, upholding the universe by his word of power" (Heb 1:1-3).

In several of these passages, the "past tense" aspect of creation is underscored: it was, as Genesis puts it, "in the beginning" that all things "*were* created" through him. But there is also a "present tense," linked not so much with creation as with the continued "upholding" of the universe. Both Colossians, with its contention that "all things hold together in him," and Hebrews, with the statement that he "upholds the universe," indicate that Christ plays an ongoing role in the sustenance of the universe. Not only was the world created through Christ, but he is the agent of its continued governance. He will also be the agent of its renewal, when all things are redeemed and re-created through him. Colin Gunton speaks of the past, present, and future aspects of creation. These "tenses" correlate with the vision of Christ's role in creation as found in Colossians.[37]

A second feature of OT and Jewish apologetic for the uniqueness of God appeals to God's sovereignty. God is not only the sole Creator of all things, but also the sole ruler of all things; indeed, the two cannot be separated, for the God who rules over the world is the God who made the world. This is particularly celebrated in portions of Isaiah, where the God who made the world demonstrates his continued sovereignty in how the circumstances of history, such as the rise of Cyrus the Persian king, serve God's purposes. Israel's God is king or sovereign not only of his "servant Jacob, and Israel my chosen" (Isa 45:4), but indeed of all the nations. In short, to speak of God's sovereignty is to speak of the identity of God, who God is; that is, God — and no other entity or being — is the one who is sovereign. When, then, NT documents such as Colossians and Hebrews speak of Christ as the agent of God's sovereignty over the world, they include him in the unique identity of the one God of all. To say "all things were created through him and for him, he is before all things, and in him all things hold together" (Col 1:16-17), and that he is preeminent in everything (v. 18) is essentially to explicate the meaning of the statement "in him the fullness of deity dwelled bodily" (v. 19).

The NT also emphasizes the universal scope of God's sovereignty exer-

---

37. Gunton, *Christ and Creation*, 44-46.

cised through the Son. So Colossians asserts that "*all things* were made through him" and "in him *all things* hold together." Hebrews speaks of him as the "heir of *all things*"; in Matthew we read that "*all* authority has been given" to the risen Christ and in John that "the Father loves the Son and has given *all things* into his hands" (3:35; cf. also 13:3; 16:30). Elsewhere in the NT we see this kind of language used to characterize aspects of God's sovereignty. For example, in Rom 11:36 we read, "For from him and through him and to him are all things," where it appears that Paul has God in view. In 1 Corinthians 15, Paul combines the twin thoughts that all things subject to Christ are subject to God; God has put all things under subjection to Christ, until the last day, when Christ will hand over all things to the Father, so that "God may be all in all" (1 Cor 15:25-28). In the OT and in Jewish apologetic this language of "all things" points to the sweeping and all-embracing character of God's sovereignty over the world: "The earth is the Lord's and the fullness thereof" — indeed, for God made it and God governs it. All things are God's. Now the NT applies this language to Jesus as well: The Father has given "all things" into his hand. All things hold together in him. These affirmations attribute to Jesus divine activities and prerogatives, particularly those connected with the past creation and present governance of the world.

To put it differently, Christ's role in God's creating and saving purposes in the world says something not just about the identity of Jesus, but also about the identity of God. Through the Son, God's identity as Creator and Sovereign are not only known but also expressed in concrete ways for the salvation of the world. There is one God who made the world and one Lord through whom it was made, one God who governs the world and one Lord through whom God's sovereign purposes come to expression.

The repeated emphasis in Colossians on the creation of "all things," including all the physical and spiritual realities and powers of the world, serves also to unite the work of God and Christ as well as the work of creation and redemption. It is not as if some of God's work were done by Christ or some things were saved through Christ; rather, all things were created and will be redeemed through him. Yet there is some tension here in Colossians that remains unexplicated. On the one hand, the world is created through and for Christ, but on the other it is a world in which threatening powers still have influence. Though created and sustained in Christ, the world awaits its renewal in Christ. But the creation of the world by God through Christ means that it is impossible to judge the *material* world in itself as evil, or as that from which one needs to be saved. Material creation is a hindrance neither to salvation nor to Christian discipleship, although the misuse or perversion of it surely can lead one down false paths. Not surprisingly Paul decries the false teaching that promotes self-abasement and abstinence from food and drink. How can the Colossians accede to rules that dictate "Do not handle! Do not taste! Do not touch!" as though food, drink, or material objects were stumbling blocks in the path of those who sought knowledge of God, the Creator of all? Paul's insistence that God created the world in and for Christ and that in Christ the deity dwelled *bodily,* surely constitutes one of the major contributions of Colossians to biblical theology.

The statement that all thing were created "for Christ" views the very creation of the world as having not only its origin, but also its destiny, in Christ. From its beginning, creation has a goal; it is going somewhere. The purposes of God in creating the world have come to a climactic point in Christ's death and resurrection, and they will come to their consummation in the revelation of Christ in glory (3:1-4).

By emphasizing that part of the biblical narrative that speaks of God's creation, Colossians also shapes the way in which we understand salvation. Where the Law features centrally in discussion, as it does particularly in Galatians, Romans, and parts of Philippians, Christ's relationship to Israel and to Moses and the commandments, comes to the fore. Paul speaks of God's salvation in terms of continuity and discontinuity with Israel and the Law. But in Colossians Christ's relationship to Israel and the Law remains somewhat in the background, and the emphasis falls on Christ's relationship to creation, the world, and the powers within it. What God does brings the work of creation to completion; it puts the powers into their proper place; it sets the world right. The Christ of Colossians is the so-called "cosmic Christ," whose work is all-encompassing, including the creation, sustenance, redemption, and renewal of all that is in the world. Colossians thus sounds a decisive note against any view of salvation that thinks of it solely in "spiritual" terms as the liberation of the soul from this world to another, that thinks only in individual terms, or that has no place for a renewed physical cosmos.

Precisely at the point of the distinctive emphasis on the role of Christ in creation, which seems to locate his significance more in relationship to the present world order than to the coming age, some scholars have thought that Colossians is also least Pauline. Gone is the eschatological framework — the breaking in of a new age, the renewing work of the Holy Spirit, and the eager anticipation of the consummation of all things. In its place is a "cosmic Christ," supreme over the universe, with whom the believer is now seated in the heavenly places with God. But Leander Keck helpfully speaks of two modes of thinking about salvation in Paul: participation and anticipation.[38]

---

38. Keck, *Paul and His Letters,* 75.

These correspond in some ways to what is sometimes called the "already" and the "not yet" of God's act in Christ. "Participation" in Christ refers to the various ways in which the believer partakes of the benefits of Christ's death and resurrection. There is a "dying and rising with Christ"; the believer becomes joined to Christ. It is not so much that salvation is taken into the believer as that the believer is caught up into the act of Christ's death and resurrection, becoming part of Christ's life. Here also belongs so-called "transfer imagery," which sees those who are in Christ as "transferred" from one sphere of existence to another, participating in the kingdom of life and light rather than in the dominion of darkness and death. Anticipation, on the other end, fits with the eschatological structure of Paul's thought, for here salvation is thought of as that which is yet to come, that which God has yet to bring about. The guarantee of future redemption is the resurrection of Christ. Colossians emphasizes more the "already," not because it has abandoned or diluted eschatological hope but because there is simultaneously a greater emphasis on salvation as participation in Christ and in his death and resurrection.

Earlier we noted the variety of images Paul uses to explain the death of Christ: it was "for us" and it dealt with our sin; it is an act of deliverance, redemption, and ransom; as the death of the second but obedient Adam, Jesus' death and resurrection bring life to the world; it is the means of reconciliation to God and of all humankind to each other; it is the means by which people are acquitted of guilt and justified before God; it is the means of sanctification; it establishes a new covenant. Colossians also has a variety of ways of picturing what God effected on the cross. As already indicated, "transfer" terminology, which sees the cross as bringing life from death, reconciliation from alienation, and deliverance from the various powers of darkness, features prominently in Colossians. In this epistle, juridical images are not so prominent as they are in other Pauline letters. The language of wrongdoing and forgiveness is there, sometimes explicitly, but it is not prominent. Colossians pictures what happens on the cross not so much in terms of the courtroom, with God pardoning the guilty (but see 2:14), but in terms of a life-giving God rescuing those in peril of death (2:12-13), a liberating God setting people free from the oppressive powers of darkness (2:15), a reconciling God reaching out to those who are alienated and hostile (1:13, 20-22), a creator God re-creating the world, bringing it to its perfection. By placing the accent on images of freedom, life, reconciliation, and re-creation, Colossians reminds us that there is an inseparable link between creation and redemption and that the one God who created the world in Christ will also redeem it through him. Because Colossians emphasizes the role of Christ in creation, it concomitantly emphasizes the life that is in Christ.

Indeed, life and death are important images in the Pauline corpus. Human beings are subject to death because of sin, but made alive in Christ. Generally this "life" is taken to refer to what one receives at the last day, the resurrection. So Paul writes, "If we have been united with him in a death like his, we shall certainly be united with him in a resurrection like his" (Rom 6:5) and "as in Adam all die, so in Christ shall all be made alive" (1 Cor 15:22). As noted earlier, the assurance that through the resurrection those who are in Christ will participate in the resurrection to life is part of the eschatological structure of Paul's thought. In Colossians, the death and resurrection of Christ are equally central, but here the resurrection provides the power and imagery for the present Christian life and not the future promise of new life: "If you have been raised with Christ, seek the things that are above . . . for you have died" (3:1-3). This is one of the seminal instances in Colossians where the narrative of the life of the believer mirrors the narrative of the life of Christ. While such a thought is often believed to make the resurrection "present" rather than future, it is better to say that in the Christian life the reality of the resurrection is experienced but not exhausted. Elsewhere Paul holds the two together. Thus in Romans he writes, "If we have died with Christ, we believe that we shall also live with him," indicating a future reality, but also, "So you also must consider yourselves dead to sin and alive to God in Christ Jesus" (6:8, 11). In Colossians, *resurrection* itself is not present, but it becomes more clearly an image for what it means to live in Christ. To live the new life in Christ is to count oneself "dead" to the powers of evil, sin, and death that characterize this world. But it is also to reckon soberly with the reality of evil, sin, and death and, indeed, their lingering shaping influence on human life. To think of the Christian life as resurrection life also underscores the point that one has such life only by participation in Christ, by union with Christ, for he is the only one who has been raised to life and glory with God. Hence, to have been "raised with Christ" is an image of renewal and of sharing in the life that God gives in the world to come. Here we see the confluence of the narrative of Christ's resurrection, the renewal of the world, and the redemption of the individual: these reflect each other because the renewal of the world and of the individual participate in and are brought about by the resurrection of Christ.

The image of being "raised" to life with Christ can easily sound triumphalistic. Paul does not speak in Colossians in the same poignant tones as he does in Romans of the groaning of the present life and yearning for the future. But in Colossians we do find the contrast between what is hidden and what will be revealed in glory. Although the contrast is not fully developed, Colossians presumes a future revelation of a renewed state as well as a present identity that is both real and yet "hidden" to the world and perhaps to all but

God and the eyes of faith. Indeed, to live as one raised with Christ is to live by faith, not by sight.

As in the other letters of Paul, Jesus is Messiah and Lord (1 Cor 8:6; Phil 2:5-11). However, Christ now plays his role on a cosmological stage rather than primarily on the stage of Israel's history, and the effects of his death and resurrection are construed as universal in scope. To be sure, Paul elsewhere reads Israel's story as having implications for the salvation of the world. But here Paul articulates the identity of Jesus without primary reference to Israel and Torah, spelling out instead Christ's relationship to creation, the powers of the world, and pagan religion. And while, as noted earlier, Paul often sketches the human plight in terms of captivity to powers such as sin and death, here Paul also thinks of the "principalities and powers" over which Christ has triumphed.

Hence in Colossians we have a way of construing Christian faith that is not articulated with explicit reference — either positive or negative — to the Torah, Israel, Abraham and the promises given to him, and so on. Rather than comparing Christ to the wisdom embodied in Torah, Paul now explicitly spells out Christ's superiority with reference to the wisdom of the world. While Paul can speak of the sinfulness of all humankind (Rom 3:23), in Colossians he distinguishes the situations of the Gentiles and the Jews to some extent, using the language of estrangement and alienation to characterize the Colossians prior to their coming to faith in Christ (Col 1:21). The Gentiles *were* alienated from and hostile to God prior to receiving the gospel; but according to Romans the Jews have essentially *become* alienated, as branches that are cut off from the tree, in their rejection of the gospel. Either way, in Christ, both Jews and Gentiles have been made to share in the inheritance of all the saints (Col 1:12). The mystery that was hidden has now been revealed. That mystery is the plan of salvation for all the world, the gathering of Gentiles and Jews together, the revelation of the Messiah of Israel to the Gentiles, which Paul sums up in the phrase "Christ among you, the hope of glory."

What Colossians assumes, Ephesians spells out in a conjunction of descriptive phrases: you were *separated* from Christ, *alienated* from the commonwealth of Israel, *strangers* to the covenants, *without* God, and *having no hope* in the world (Eph 2:12). In other words, it is belonging to God and to God's people, to the covenants and the commonwealth of Israel, that gives people hope in this world. Through his death and resurrection, the Messiah of Israel had led the way and made a way for others through evil and death to the life of the new creation.[39] The identity given in Christ joins one to God, to Israel, and to the promises of God.

39. Bauckham, "Future of Jesus Christ," 267.

Although the human plight is portrayed differently in different letters, Colossians indirectly calls attention to the insatiability of the human appetite for gratification of its religious desires. Elsewhere Paul speaks of the human propensity to boast in one's achievements, zeal, or obedience to the Law (e.g., Phil 3:2-20; Eph 2:8-9). Boasting in the Law does not figure in Colossians, but the same mindset appears among those who through self-denial and self-abasement think that they have attained or will attain a higher level of spirituality than those who neglect such practices. Inevitably such an attitude shifts the focus from where it rightly belongs, namely, God's gracious action in Christ, to the recipient of that grace — and then virtually credits the recipient for God's action! Almost paradoxically, persistent attempts to attain a higher level of spiritual satisfaction lead one away from rather than toward the truth. Such a lifestyle is grasping and inward-looking rather than characterized by the humility, thanksgiving, and generosity that are the hallmarks of Christ's own life and should similarly be traits of those who are his people.

Corresponding to an understanding of the cosmic role of Christ and the cosmological scope of salvation, the "cosmic identity" of the church comes clearly to expression in Colossians. To be sure, elsewhere in Paul the body of Christ consists of many members, with different gifts, and these many members are drawn from Jew and Gentile alike. But Paul is not thinking in Colossians of the church as a local congregation or house-fellowship (although see 4:15-16). Rather the church is "not simply some new club or cultic association, nor merely an offshoot of Judaism, but the beginnings of a new humanity, the sign and seal of the new creation taking shape on earth, a body growing in the shape and with the energy of the renewed life of the universe."[40] No wonder, then, that Christian existence is described in terms of renewal in the image of the Creator, a "putting off" of the old humanity and "putting on" of the new humanity. Such a view of the church goes hand-in-glove with the claim that the Lord from whom the church draws its nourishment is in fact the one through whom and for whom "all things" were created. Here, then, the worldwide church is not simply the result of the worldwide preaching of the gospel; its creation is rather part of and integral to the creation of the world in and for Christ. If in Galatians or Romans Paul endeavors to encourage Gentile Christians in particular to think of the story of their own lives as having become part of the story of Israel and God's dealing with Israel, here Paul wants his readers to see their stories as part of a redeemed humanity that will live in a renewed world.

One contribution of Colossians is its emphasis on the fullness of

40. Barclay, *Colossians*, 86.

Christ for the life of discipleship. This is scarcely a unique note. In Gal 2:20 Paul writes, "It is no longer I who live, but Christ who lives in me." In Philippians he speaks of the surpassing worth of knowing Christ, of belonging to him, and of having the very righteousness of Christ working through him (Phil 3:8-12). The christological center of life is not unique in Colossians; but it receives consistent attention. Christ is the center of creation, of God's purposes for Jew and Gentile, and of the Christian life. There is movement both toward Christ, toward conformity to his example and submission to his lordship, and from Christ toward the other. To seek "the things above" one must sink one's roots more deeply into Christ, the basis of hope and faith, so that one may give oneself in love for the other. Thus the Colossians are exhorted to "live in a way worthy of the Lord" (1:10), "according to Christ" (2:8). Since in him "are hidden all the treasures of wisdom and knowledge" (2:3), their lives are "hidden with Christ." As the fullness of deity dwells in him, the Colossians are described as having been "filled in him." They live in the one who is their life (3:4).

One of the most striking features about Colossians, especially when compared to Romans, 1 and 2 Corinthians, and Galatians, is that the Spirit seems to figure so little in the letter's theology and injunctions. Paul does not assign to the Spirit the role of life and liberty or the power to "transfer" from one dominion to the other; nor does he speak of it as the potency of Christian living. Instead, the life of the Spirit, what we might call "spirituality" or Christian practice, is a matter of living according to the dominion of Jesus rather than the dominion of darkness. Two primary aspects of such spirituality are central to Colossians. First, Paul underscores the communal or corporate aspect of life in Christ, emphasizing especially those virtues and graces such as humility, forbearance, and forgiveness that foster harmony. Second, thanksgiving ought to permeate the life of the individual and the community. Thanksgiving becomes a hallmark of the "new humanity" because it demonstrates the proper relationship of the creature to the Creator. While ancient letters often included a word of thanksgiving to a god for the benefits that either the author or readers had received, such as deliverance from various sorts of calamities, Paul's letters typically include a longer and fuller paragraph of thanksgiving directed to God (e.g., Rom 1:8-10; 1 Cor 1:4-9; Phil 1:3-6). As Calvin notes, even when Paul is speaking well of his readers, "we must always notice that he uses 'thanksgiving' for 'congratulation,' by which he teaches us that in all our joys we must quickly call to remembrance the goodness of God."[41] Thanksgiving grows out of the awareness of depen-

---

41. Calvin, *Colossians*, 300.

dence, of gratitude for deliverance from the powers of darkness, and of the joy that life in communion with God in Christ and his people brings. One might almost say that Colossians contrasts two modes of worship: the proper worship of God, which is marked by humility and gratitude, and improper religion, which is characterized by boasting, self-seeking, and self-gratification. Colossians makes it clear that it is not necessarily overt idolatry that poses a genuine threat to humankind or constitutes the only improper worship of God.

The character of Christian life can also be summarized by the triad of "faith, hope, and love." This characterization occurs most famously in 1 Corinthians 13, where Paul underscores the surpassing value of love as the norm of Christian life together. Faith, hope and love are linked in 1 Thessalonians as well, where Paul writes of "the work of faith and labor of love and steadfastness of hope in our Lord Jesus Christ" (1:3; cf. 5:8). But this triad is not unique to Paul and may in fact have been a common and stable traditional way of sketching the shape of the Christian life (see also Heb 6:10-12; 10:22-24; 1 Pet 1:3-8, 21-22). But the triad nevertheless proved remarkably supple and flexible in the theological and pastoral functions to which it was put. Writing to a divided community in 1 Corinthians, Paul implicitly acknowledges the value and significance of hope and faith, but he stresses the surpassing importance of love. In Thessalonians, the emphasis falls on steadfastness and endurance, qualities necessary to a church flagging or discouraged in its commitments.

But in Colossians the dominant element of the triad is the hope that believers have in Christ. Elsewhere in Paul's letters, such as Romans, hope has the character primarily of anticipation, the expectation of future salvation. One thinks of hope within the framework of Paul's eschatology, stretched between the "already" and the "not yet," with the primary focus on the "not yet." Hope strains forward to the redemption of the cosmos. But in Colossians, hope arises from participation in Christ, and thus it has less the sense of eager anticipation of and yearning for that which is to come and more the sense of confidence arising out of present identification with Christ and thanksgiving for what is received through Christ. Because the powers of darkness have been dealt a fatal blow through Christ's death and resurrection, those whose lives are hidden in him acknowledge a different lordship in the present which will be revealed only at a future time in glory. The qualitative difference between present and future remains, but, because more emphasis falls on participation with Christ, less falls on anticipation of what is "not yet." Colossians emphasizes that hope in Christ is fully adequate, since the fullness of deity dwells in him and since in him the mysteries of the ages have been revealed.

Colossians and Constructive Theology

One of the distinctive contributions — if not the distinctive contribution — of Colossians is its comprehensive vision of reality with the focal point of christology.[42] According to Colossians, both the creative and redemptive purposes of God for the entire cosmos are expressed in and through the person and work of Christ. In other words, the account of what God has done in and for the world through Christ is the ultimate metanarrative. In the first instance, a "metanarrative" is a grand, overarching story that seeks to explain everything else, a master narrative intended to account for all events, knowledge, and experiences. Thus a metanarrative claims or seeks to give an account of reality that is unified and universal: by explaining all, it can be owned by all. As such, metanarratives are said to be characterized by comprehensiveness — they explain all things and nothing is left out. In dependence upon Jean-François Lyotard, it is often said that the postmodern world distrusts metanarratives; in fact, Lyotard defined the postmodern condition as "incredulity toward metanarrative."[43] Given the differences that characterize human experience and the intractability of the problems confronted by human beings, the idea that a single narrative comprehensively explains and unifies all human experience has seemed preposterous, even offensive. Such a narrative would threaten to overshadow all other narratives, tyrannically erasing all differences among human beings, communities, and identities. But Colossians proposes to offer just such a metanarrative, one that does indeed encompass the history of the world from creation to redemption and that bears upon the destiny of every single individual and society.

In the following discussion, we will explore both the form and the substance of the "grand narrative" of Colossians as it is centered in Christ. We shall pursue that investigation, first, by looking briefly at the very idea of "metanarratives" and current suspicions of their validity. Next, we will look at the content of the Colossian narrative, giving attention to its beginning, middle, and end and its movement from creation to cross to new creation. Finally, we will focus on the goal of this narrative, under the three headings of the knowledge of God, the identity of the people of God, and the embodied witness of the people of God in faith, hope, and love. In

---

42. Barclay, *Colossians*, 77.

43. Jean-François Lyotard's famous statement is: "Simplifying in the extreme, I define *postmodern* as incredulity toward metanarratives" (*The Postmodern Condition*, xxiv). Metanarratives are also called "grand" or "master" narratives, though they need not necessarily take the form of narrative.

many ways, this structure echoes the "three focal images" identified by Richard Hays as providing unity to the NT witness, namely, community, cross, and new creation, especially since "new creation" assumes that the God of Israel, the Creator of the world, will bring his purposes for the world, as embodied in the death and resurrection of Christ, to their great consummation.[44] Anticipating that renewal, the church of Jesus Christ is called to live in faith, hope, and love and thus to embody God's good news of redemption to the world.

Metanarrative: "All Things Hold Together in Him"

Metanarratives are, minimally, "master narratives" of the way things are. But, more specifically, according to the definition often used today, a metanarrative is something that is used to legitimate a nation, society, or individual's behavior or use of power or control. One example of a "successful" metanarrative is that which supports modern scientific endeavor. Merold Westphal argues that in order to legitimate itself, modern science "needs a story of progress from opinion and superstition to scientific truth and on to universal peace and happiness."[45] In other words, science depends on a certain construction of reality, and the construct that legitimates it is the very notion of progress. The idea of progress serves the interest of science and scientists because it supposes that investigation and experimentation chart a steady path toward a better world. Such a view of course attracts funding and undergirds continued research, but it also provides a construct within which people view the world, its destiny, and their place in it. People accept the metanarrative. Somehow we are all part of the progress of the world toward its perfection. While science and scientists have a vested, if not always acknowledged, interest in the survival of this metanarrative, its consequences are felt beyond the realm of scientific investigation. The "metanarrative of progress" has given birth to the tacit assumption that our lives are better — materially, but also morally or spiritually — than the lives of those who lived fifty, five hundred, or five thousand years before us. In other words, any metanarrative shapes how we view the world, our place in it, what we value, and how we assess the significance of persons, events, or things. Not only do we think of science as making progress, but we view the morals and behaviors of earlier people as "primitive" or worse — little rec-

44. Hays, *Moral Vision*, 193.
45. Westphal, "Postmodernism," 8.

ognizing that the very metanarrative of progress means that in ten, one hundred, or one thousand years our lives and practices will come under the same scrutiny.[46]

Because metanarratives are said to legitimate an individual, enterprise, society, or nation and are thus understood to underwrite self-interest, they are labeled oppressive and triumphalist. A metanarrative gains universal acceptance not because it is "true" but because it succeeds, through power or violence, in silencing other metanarratives. Metanarratives are thus called "totalizing" in that they work by erasing difference. If the metanarrative of one nation or society is to succeed as a universal narrative, it must do so by suppressing the difference of the other, so that this one narrative becomes everyone's narrative. But if one believes that all voices must be heard, that all stories must be told, and that all viewpoints are equally valid, then any narrative that proposes to subsume all others can do so only by suppressing those other individual stories. Finally, metanarratives are said to be based on the premise that there is such a thing as "absolute truth" and that someone — presumably someone who claims allegiance to a particular metanarrative related to that absolute truth — knows that truth. Some human beings, then, are guardians of the truth and hence have the right to act in light of it and perhaps even to impose it on others. This, it is said, is a self-serving illusion. For since all human beings are conditioned by their social locations, no one can ever attain an objective, omniscient standpoint to know the "Truth" with a capital T.

For many today, metanarratives are nothing more than lies. While metanarratives promise clarity, progress, truth, and contentment, the world has dealt up ambiguity and dissatisfaction. In a word, the metanarrative has betrayed hope.[47] A sense of purpose has given way to a profound purposelessness on both the universal and personal level. Hence, in his characterization of Generation X, Tom Beaudoin put it this way: "For Xers, both our experience and our imagination of our selves are characterized more by incoherence than coherence, more by fragmentation than unity."[48] In other words, the experience of the world is that it simply does not make sense, and that experience falsifies any claim to the contrary.

How, then, does the biblical metanarrative fare in light of these criticisms? Merold Westphal argues that "the big Christian story" both is and is

46. The extent to which the metanarrative of progress governs modern thinking can, of course, be debated.

47. For a discussion of the modern sense of betrayal, see Walsh and Keesmaat, *Colossians Remixed*, 22.

48. Beaudoin, *Virtual Faith*, 137.

not a "metanarrative."[49] As a story that begins with creation, moves through the life, death, and resurrection of Jesus, and anticipates his return, the resurrection of the dead, and the life everlasting, the biblical story is undeniably a "master narrative." But, Westphal asserts, the recital of that story does not serve an apologetic or "legitimating" purpose but rather a kerygmatic purpose: one tells the story to make it known, and not for some other purpose. Along the same lines, Middleton and Walsh argue that two dimensions of the biblical story work toward delegitimating and subverting violent and totalizing uses of the story: first, the consistent and radical *sensitivity to suffering* that pervades the narrative from the exodus to the cross; second, the rooting of the story in *God's creational intent,* which serves to delegitimate any narrow or partisan use of the story.[50] Both of these elements are central in Colossians.

In Colossians, God's creational intent for all the world is its redemption and perfection. The letter gives an account of the creation, redemption, and ultimate re-creation of the world that has its focal point in the cross, in Jesus' self-giving suffering and death. His "victory" and "triumph" are gained through the most pervasive of human experiences, suffering, and through a shameful death on the cross. Here we have a metanarrative that centers not on violence done to others but on the violence experienced by Jesus himself, whose life is given to make peace (1:20). On the cross, God's power is disclosed not in conspicuous triumph but in conspicuous weakness and self-giving love. God's purposes are accomplished not by means of conquest through violence and death inflicted on others but by absorbing violence and death so that others may have life. In this way, the death of Christ on the cross negates the death-dealing powers and principalities of this world. God characteristically moves toward the "other," toward the "enemy," and we see this in the fact that the primary effect of the cross is peacemaking and reconciliation.

Indeed, Colossians speaks of those who "were once estranged and hostile in mind" but have now been reconciled. Those who once lived as God's enemies are the recipients of the divine initiatives of peacemaking and reconciliation. Christ forgives and "makes space in himself for the enemy."[51] He does not obliterate his enemies either through violence or domination but welcomes and embraces them in such a way that they come to their created

---

49. Westphal, "Postmodernism," 9; on the same point, see Bauckham, "Coherent Story," 48, who calls the biblical story a "non-modern metanarrative," and notes, "What justifies the term metanarrative is that the biblical story is a story about the meaning of the whole of reality." This is apt also for Colossians.

50. Middleton and Walsh, *Truth,* 87; Bauckham, "Coherent Story," 51-53.

51. Volf, *Exclusion and Embrace,* 126.

identity. Through the reconciling work of the cross, the peoples of the world find a common identity in a common Lord: in the renewal that comes about through Christ, there is neither "Greek and Jew, circumcised and uncircumcised, barbarian, Scythian, slave, free man, but Christ is all, and in all" (3:11). This is a metanarrative whose primary thrust is to include rather than exclude. While Paul at times uses elements of this narrative to ground practice and exhort the Colossians, he points to it more often simply as the gospel that they have heard, the "mystery" that has been made known to them. It is the kerygma Epaphras first proclaimed to them and that Paul reiterates in this epistle. It is also an account of their lives that sets them within the grand purposes of God for all of creation.

Thus the story of the church, or the composite story of all the congregations in the world, is not simply identical with the metanarrative of which Christians understand themselves to be a part. The Christian metanarrative is the narrative of God's dealings with the world from creation to redemption; and the end of this narrative will be written by God. "Grand narratives" are totalizing and oppressive not because they attempt to account for all things, but because those who claim or retell them also too often see it as their task to manipulate the narrative for their own purposes and to bring about the end result promised in the narrative.

Here Colossians issues an important corrective when it reminds its readers that the God who created the world will also redeem it and that God is presently renewing humankind in the image of the Creator. These processes and prerogatives belong to God the Creator alone. Any human attempt to achieve the goal that God alone can bring about will be, at best, doomed to fail and, at worst, a grievous instance of blasphemy, the creature usurping the role of the Creator. The metanarrative of Colossians, and of Pauline theology generally, is profoundly disquieting because it does not promise the attainment of the end goal in this life or as a result of human effort. In fact, quite the opposite: it insists that the promise of a new world and a new humanity *cannot* be attained in the present; rather, the new world entails a remaking, a re-creation of the present world.

Colossians speaks of the reconciliation of all things in Christ. But many have sought to effect, in this world, through technology, economic programs, political actions, or other means precisely that reconciliation. That we cannot bring this goal about ought scarcely to surprise or worry those who believe that God will accomplish it and that God alone can do so. As Miroslav Volf puts it, "That messianic problem ought not to be taken out of God's hands. . . . Merely by trying to accomplish the messianic task, [many] have already done too much of the work of the antichrist." The present task, Volf continues, is not to attempt to bring about that final reconciliation but to ask "what resources we need to live in peace in the absence of the final reconciliation."[52] In other words, the biblical narrative leaves the resolution of all things in God's hands alone. Precisely this forward-looking, open-ended character of the narrative, when acknowledged and taken seriously as indicative of the lack of human control and of the proper place of the human creature in God's world, prevents the Christian narrative from being totalizing and oppressive. Meanwhile, in Colossians Paul directs his energy to "resources we need to live in peace" in the present time.

Moreover, according to Christian theology, the biblical narrative originates in revelation and legitimates only one kingdom, the kingdom of God. "In the process it delegitimates every human kingdom, including democratic capitalism and the Christian church, just to the degree that they are not the full embodiment of God's Kingdom. Modernity's metanarratives legitimate 'us,' the Christian narrative places 'us' under judgment as well."[53] The biblical story is read — and reread — not only to convert us once, but to judge us and continually convert us, so that our lives come ever more into alignment with God's kingdom, with God's redemptive purposes. It can scarcely be read as the triumphalistic story of God's people, and, if it is read in such a way, it has surely been misread! But the charge that Christianity is a "totalizing narrative" cannot be countered only by philosophical and apologetic strategies. The followers of Jesus must serve as a witness to God's intent for the wholeness of creation in the church and the world.[54] If the end of the story remains in God's hands, it does not follow that human life and effort are without significance within that story.

The contention of the biblical metanarrative is not that "Christianity is true" or the only true religion but that Christ is the truth. Since in him — and orthodox Christian theology further contends in him *alone* — "the fullness of deity dwelled bodily," his life uniquely embodies God's truth. That embodied truth was manifested not in domineering power and control, but in emptying, weakness, self-giving, laying down of himself for others.[55] It goes without saying that Christians themselves have ignored and abused their own narrative, failing to understand that the cross stands at its heart, and used it to oppress and do violence to others. We have lived as though the biblical narrative validates, rather than judges, our motives, thoughts, and behavior. We

52. Volf, *Exclusion and Embrace*, 109.
53. Westphal, "Postmodernism," 9.
54. Middleton and Walsh, *Truth*, 107.
55. Newbigin, *Gospel in a Pluralist Society*, 163.

have thus neglected the point that if the cross stands at the heart of this narrative, implicitly then so also do human failure, sin, and evil, for the cross discloses the injustice and unrighteousness of humankind. Read as a story about human sinfulness, this narrative can only with difficulty be subverted into a triumphalist narrative of human accomplishment or Christian superiority. A story whose end lies within our control or is achievable through technological advances or human efforts to bring ultimate justice is not the biblical story but a betrayal of the promise inherent in the biblical story.

It is virtually a truism today that there is no objective and omniscient standpoint available to any of us from which to pass judgments about "truth." Many have objected that this greases the slippery slope of relativism. But in many ways the contention that there is no such absolute standpoint from which to view the world actually accords well with the Christian understanding of truth. The only one who knows absolute truth absolutely is God himself. For any human being to claim to have or know "the absolute truth" is simply false; as Paul puts it elsewhere, we see through a glass dimly. Furthermore, the Christian metanarrative does not actually claim to explain everything. God has revealed himself so that he can be known and trusted, but it does not follow that God has revealed everything of himself or all that can be known about the significance of events in the world. Indeed, crucial to the theology of the great thinkers of the church is the affirmation of God's mystery, God's freedom. Not everything is made clear. As God says in Isaiah, "My thoughts are not your thoughts, neither are your ways my ways, says the LORD. For as the heavens are higher than the earth, so are my ways higher than your ways and my thoughts than your thoughts" (Isa 55:8-9). Paul himself, in wrestling with the destiny of Israel, ends not with statements of certitude but with a prayer of awe and wonder: "O the depth of the riches and wisdom and knowledge of God! How unsearchable are his judgments and how inscrutable his ways! 'For who has known the mind of the Lord, or who has been his counselor?'" (Rom 11:33-34). There are mysteries in God that God does not make known; there are mysteries in life of which understanding is not granted.

When Colossians insists that the mystery of God has been revealed in Christ, that all the treasures of wisdom are hidden in him, and that this mystery and this hidden wisdom have been revealed, it does not contradict the point about the mystery of God and God's ways. Without God's self-revelation, God would be unknowable; but as the God of Israel revealed through Jesus Christ, God is indeed knowable, and reliably knowable. There is no knowledge hidden elsewhere that grants a different or deeper revelation. But it need not and does not follow that God has revealed himself without remainder to humankind. In fact, the Christian metanarrative need have no

161

embarrassment in conceding that there are things it cannot explain such as the free workings of grace, precisely because these are lodged ultimately in the sovereign purposes of God.

While the Christian metanarrative attempts to makes sense of the world and the way human beings are to live in it, it always makes sense in a partial or fragmentary way, leaving all sorts of questions unanswered. Chief among these is the long-standing matter of the "problem of evil," or the challenge of explaining God's goodness and justice alongside the continued existence of evil, particularly the suffering of so many of the world's neediest peoples. Although many have ventured "solutions" to the problem of evil, none has proved ultimately or finally persuasive. We do not and cannot have a comprehensive explanation of the world that brings "closure" to it and ties up all the loose ends.[56] For one thing, the Bible itself does not offer any ultimate explanation of the problem of evil, but promises a future when God will deal with it ultimately and fully and wipe away every tear from every eye. But that future remains — perhaps uncomfortably but firmly so — with God. Any attempt to offer a "totalizing" solution that ties up all the loose ends and makes everything neat and tidy is bound to fail, precisely because such explanations go beyond the Bible and falsify the biblical witness that the end of the narrative lies ultimately in God's hands.

The Christian metanarrative has as its central figure a transcendent and free God. Thus whenever Christians act as though they know all that God knows and that which virtually by definition they could not know, they are guilty of the sin of presumption and of distorting the Christian metanarrative so that it justifies their ways rather than bearing witness to God's ways. God's freedom introduces an element into the metanarrative that indicates that its resolution and goal are both outside human control and human knowledge. As Richard Bauckham puts it, "Unlike the modern metanarratives the biblical story does not account for history in terms of immanent reason or human mastery, but in terms of the freedom and purpose of God and of human freedom to obey or to resist God."[57] That takes us not into the fullness of divine knowledge, but into the depths of divine mystery.

But the biblical narrative posits God as a transcendent and sovereign actor in the world and in history who has identified himself, on the cross, with the suffering of humankind. God has taken on the destiny of humankind so as to rewrite its future. Because of God's steadfast and self-giving love, the sovereignty and transcendence of God can be construed as neither tyrannical nor

56. Bauckham, "Coherent Story," 50-51.
57. Bauckham, "Coherent Story," 48.

arbitrary. Precisely in his sovereignty, God is a God who is *for us,* and this is what creation and final redemption of the world in Christ signal. Colossians proposes a metanarrative that begins with God's creation of a good world; identifies the situation of the inhabitants of the world in terms of captivity, darkness, and sin; claims that in Christ, in his identification with humankind, and in his death on a cross God has provided for the world's deliverance and healing; and anticipates the renewal of the world, which will bring all creation to its consummation. In short, creation and new creation are the two poles of God's life-giving purposes for the world. We turn, then, to a discussion of the beginning of the narrative, namely, the creation of the world in Christ, a theological affirmation that orders many other tenets about it.

"All Things Were Created in Him and for Him"

Few statements summarize the christological center of Colossians as well as the twin statements "all things were created in him and for him" and "in him all things hold together." These statements stand out because of the prominent place they assign to creation and more specifically to Christ's role in creation. They place Christ at the beginning and *telos* or end of creation and describe him as well as creation's sustaining center. In *Christ and Creation* Colin Gunton makes the same point when he speaks of the past, present, and future aspects of creation. When considered in the "past tense," the doctrine of creation asserts that the world and all that is in it come from the creative and gracious act of God. The "present tense" points to a doctrine of the preservation of the world, underscoring the world's continuing relationship of dependence upon a personal God. And the teleological orientation of creation indicates that God's creation envisions a world destined for perfection and completion.[58] According to Colossians, the past, present, and future aspects of creation are all centered in Christ. That the past, present, and future aspects happen "in" and "for" Christ means that as the agent of the world's creation, he is also God's agent for sustaining and redeeming the world and bringing it to perfection. Nothing in the world exists apart from the purposes of God in Christ.

The importance of the doctrine of creation for both theological and

---

58. Gunton, *Christ and Creation,* 44-46, who notes with approval that Basil of Caesarea spoke of the Father as the original cause of all things, the Son as the creative cause, and the Spirit as the perfecting cause, and these correspond roughly to the three "tenses of createdness." In *The Triune Creator,* 21, however, Gunton notes that tenses are "essentially problematic" when speaking of the eternal God in relationship to the temporal creation.

christological reflection is documented by the fact that in the christological controversies that dogged the early church, one of the key issues was Christ's relationship to creation. In commenting on "he is before all things" (1:17), the church Fathers took pains to note that Paul did not say "he was *made* before all things" but rather "he *is* before all things."[59] The former would imply that Christ was created like all other created things. But he is not one of the things that was created but existed prior to the creation of any thing. The Fathers also stressed the implications to be derived from the fact that Christ was the Maker of all things. As Augustine put it, "he is the creator before Adam, creator before heaven and earth, before all the angels, and the whole spiritual creation, 'thrones, dominions, principalities and powers,' creator before all things whatsoever."[60] If this is true, inquires Hilary of Poitiers, "in what way does he lack the true nature of God, since he is not lacking either in the nature or the power of God?"[61]

The force of this argument arises not from later philosophical speculation on the nature of God, but from the biblical witness that God alone is the Creator of all things.[62] This attests a strong doctrine of creation, an overtly anti-dualistic stance, since it attributes creation to one God alone. To say, then, that "all things" were created by God through Christ is to assign to Christ a distinct divine prerogative. Not without good biblical warrant did the Fathers insist that to join the Son with the Father in the work of creation implies the divine identity of the Son. When Paul writes in Colossians that "all things" were created "in him and for him," he thus places Christ in a role and assigns to him a status that elevate him far above all other powers. Indeed, this position aligns — but does not confuse — him with "God the Father Almighty, maker of heaven and earth."

While statements that the world was created *by* the Father, *through* the Son, might seem to heighten the Father's power and role in creation to the detriment of the Son, such statements rather served to underscore the *unity* of Father and Son. Ambrose argued that the distinction of prepositions does not imply an inferiority or "difference of power" between the Father and the Son because "while all things are 'of' the Father, nonetheless are they all 'through' the Son."[63] The point of such formulations was surely to *include* Christ in God's act of creating the world, rather than to *limit* the character of his power or to indicate his inferior status or role. The prepositional phrases

59. See, for example, the various citations in *ACCSNT* 9:12-17.
60. Augustine, *Sermons* 290.2, cited in *ACCSNT* 9:16.
61. Hilary of Poitiers, *On the Trinity* 5.4 (*ACCSNT* 9:16).
62. See the discussion above on Col 1:15.
63. Ambrose, *Of the Christian Faith*, 4.11.139-40 in *ACCSNT* 9:17.

— "of the Father, though the Son" — underscore the unity of the Father and Son in the work of creation, and without some such ordering monotheism would clearly have been discarded. Put differently, Paul's arguments in Colossians are not that Christ is a "being like God" who does things that are like the things that God does, but rather that the work of God the Father in creation and redemption is mediated through Christ the Son of God. This is an argument not for the subordination of the Son but the unity of the Father and the Son and their work, and it put the church on the road to trinitarianism rather than tritheism.

In a wonderful and related image, Irenaeus speaks of the Father's creation of the world with his own hands, namely, the Word and the Spirit.[64] Thus Irenaeus stresses the organic unity of Word and Spirit with the Father: the "two hands" of God are God himself in action. Word and Spirit are not alien to the Father; they are the hands of the Father himself. Therefore, the "mediator" of creation and redemption is not, properly speaking, a "mediator" at all, not someone other than God or a neutral go-between standing God and humankind. The whole of salvation history, both creation and redemption and all that lies between, is rooted in the Father, the one God revealed by Jesus. Through his "two hands" the Father creates and redeems all that is and will be.

By joining the Father and the Son together in the one work of creating the world Colossians thus decries any theology that smacks of dualism: one God created the world; and the same God will redeem it; one God created all that is in the cosmos, including humankind, which is at the center of God's re-creation of the world. In the context of Colossians, claims of the unity of Father and Son in the work of both creation and redemption provided the theological basis for refuting a philosophy that judged the spiritual superior to the material realm, which was fundamentally a hindrance to a higher grasp of divine reality. Such a view is on the road to dualism, although in terms of accepted definitions today it is properly speaking not "dualistic."

Dualism may be defined as "a doctrine that posits the existence of two fundamental causal principles underlying the existence . . . of the world."[65] There are religions and worldviews that are explicitly dualistic, positing the existence of more than one "fundamental causal principle," and worldviews that are implicitly or perhaps partially dualistic. Gnosticism, a term that refers broadly to religious and philosophical movements of the late Hellenistic and early Christian eras, was thoroughly dualistic. The Gnostics denied that

---

64. See *Adversus Haereses* 4.7.4; 4.20.1; 5.1.3; 5.6.1; 5.28.4.
65. Bianchi, "Dualism," *Encyclopedia of Religion*, 506.

the Most High God had also created the world; instead, the creation of the material universe was the work of an inferior deity, the God of the OT. The second-century church Father Irenaeus spent a good deal of energy countering the dualism of the Gnostics, insisting that the God of Israel and Father of our Lord Jesus Christ was also the God who created the world. While such a contention may seem scarcely controvertible today, subtler forms of dualistic convictions have, in fact, infected Christian beliefs. This "subtle dualism" does not espouse multiple deities, or distinguish the Creator from the one God of Israel and the Father of Jesus Christ, but it does see "matter" and "spirit" as opposed to each other, so that the former is judged to be evil and the latter good. There are far-reaching consequences for Christian belief and practice: the Christian faith is branded as solely "spiritual" in character; and salvation is construed as the salvation of the "soul" from the body. Such views have shaped how Christians conceive of the church's vocation in the world.

Both Paul in Colossians and Irenaeus in his writings against the Gnostics assumed that the God who had created the world would redeem it through Jesus Christ and that, as the Scriptures put it, the world is "very good." Human beings have a home in the earth, given to them by God. If it is not a permanent or final home, it is nevertheless the home given to them in the present by their Creator. The Gnostics, of course, denied that this earth was a home: instead, it was a prison, from which one needed release. Such "dualistic" views of salvation have permeated large sections of the Christian church, which imagine that salvation is essentially a spiritual rescue operation and that God works only to bring about "spiritual" good. Material matters such as wealth, poverty, racism, justice, and the environment are not properly "Christian" concerns, for the death of Jesus on the cross has to do with a personal, spiritual salvation. Hence, the vocation of the church is limited to the proclamation of "spiritual" salvation rather than engagement in activities that seek to reflect God's vision for the wholeness of the whole creation. Dualism undercuts the fundamental vision held out in Colossians of the creation of the world by God in Christ, in whom it is also redeemed.

Indeed, in the biblical narrative the world belongs to God, it comes from God, and all that is in it is made by God. Human beings are stewards of God's creation and have been called to fulfill a particular task. For this reason, the world might be described not only as "home" but also as "workplace." That is, it is the arena in which human beings in general and the church in particular exercise their vocation as stewards of God's creation.[66] The church

---

66. See Watson, *Text, Church and World*, 328 n. 1.

works to embody God's grace and love in the material creation, as God does, and not against it, and not somehow apart from it or to escape from it.

The salvation of human beings is always set within the redemption of the created order; the new creation is the "stage" for the redemption of humankind. To be sure, the pendulum can swing too far toward a virtual deification of creation.[67] But Colossians directs us resolutely not toward creation but toward the Creator and thus has a resolutely "Creator-centered spirituality," one that acknowledges that the world and all that is in it come from, depend on, and are destined for God in Christ. And therefore Colossians also delineates the appropriate role of the creature in relation to the Creator, that of creaturely dependence and gratitude.

But any theology, spirituality, or ethic to be derived from creation must also always consider the goal of creation, that it is itself destined to be renewed: one cannot simply read theology, or ethics, from the way the world is. Rather, theological reflection must always take into account the way God intends the world to be. Of course the assumption that the world will be renewed or re-created has been used to denigrate the value of creation or to envision salvation as a destruction of creation and the transport of souls to some sort of disembodied spiritual state. But if there is discontinuity in the movement from creation to new creation, there is also continuity: the new world is conceived more in terms of creation set right than as creation discarded.

When Irenaeus challenged the Gnostics who denied that the Supreme God was responsible for the material creation and incarnation of the Son, he insisted repeatedly and in various ways that God was the Creator. Creation is not somehow "good" in and of itself, but precisely because it is the handiwork of God. "He is the Former, He the Builder, He the Discoverer, He the Creator, He the Lord of all. . . . He is Father, He is God, He the Founder, He the Maker, He the Creator, who made those things by himself, that is, through his Word and his Wisdom."[68] For Irenaeus, as for the Apostles' and Nicene Creeds, the starting point of Christian theology was the belief that the Most High God was indeed the Creator. But Irenaeus took seriously — as did the creeds — the reality of the incarnation; and as Colossians puts it, "in him the fullness of deity dwelled *bodily*." The two beliefs reinforce each other and belong together, for if the Son of God, the agent of God's creation of the world, took to himself human flesh, it follows that nothing created or material can be deemed evil by virtue of simply being material. By insisting on God as Creator of all, Irenaeus explicitly denied that salvation entailed a negation of or

---

67. Gunton, *Christ and Creation*, 32.
68. *Adversus Haereses* 2.30.9.

deliverance from the flesh.[69] Although Irenaeus and other church Fathers could and did distinguish "body" and "soul," they did not assign salvation to the soul, or view salvation as a deliverance from the flesh. Rather, Irenaeus argues that, as, in creating Adam, God breathed the breath of life into that which he had fashioned out of the earth, so in the incarnation, "The Word of the Father and the Spirit of God, having become united with the ancient substance of Adam's formation, rendered [humankind] living and perfect. Now the soul and the spirit are certainly a *part* of the human being, but certainly not *the* human being; for the perfect human being consists in the commingling and the union of the soul receiving the spirit of the Father, and the admixture of that fleshly nature which was molded after the image of God."[70]

In its striking use of the term "body" (*sōma*/σῶμα), Colossians bears a different but commensurate witness to the unity of creation and redemption. First, the epistle notes that the "fullness of deity dwelled *bodily*" in Jesus (2:9; 1:19). In his *Confessions,* Augustine notes the distinctive character of the Christian affirmation of the incarnation. Referring to the Gospel of John, he comments that, although he read in the "books of the Platonists" of the divine nature of the Word *(Logos),* "I did not read in them that the Word was made flesh and came to dwell among us."[71] Platonism, like so much Greek philosophical thought and subsequent thinkers influenced by it, posits a dualism between the eternal or spiritual and material worlds. Gnosticism essentially radicalizes that dualism, pronouncing matter inferior and evil, attributing it to some god other than the God of Jesus Christ and envisioning salvation as deliverance from it. Hence, to imagine that in Jesus, in his "fleshly body," the "fullness of deity" dwelled, would be simply preposterous. Both Augustine and the Gnostics were aware of the scandal of such a claim. While Christian theology came to speak of the Son as of "one substance with the Father," it is also true that in his incarnation, Jesus is a human creature, and "of one substance with ourselves."[72] It is through the "fleshly body" of Jesus and his death on the cross that God brings about reconciliation, so that all those who are in Christ might be presented "holy and blameless and without fault" before God (Col 1:21-23; 2:11). This fleshly body is not devoid of deity; but it is precisely the fleshly body in which the fullness of God dwelled.

The "body" of Christ is also the church (1:18, 24; 2:19; 3:15). The one who is "before all things" and in whom "all things hold together" is also the "the head

69. *Adversus Haereses* 5.6.1.

70. *Adversus Haereses* 5.1.3; 5.6.1. Irenaeus here includes human physicality in the "image of God." On this point, see the discussion in Gunton, *Triune Creator,* 193-211.

71. Augustine, *Confessions* 7.9.

72. Gunton, *Christ and Creation,* 46.

of the body, the church." This means that the church itself is the "body" of the one who died to reconcile the entire world to God. Obviously, Paul does not simply identify the two entities as though Jesus' "fleshly" body were the church, but there is a mysterious parallel here. Just as Jesus gave his body to reconcile the world to God, so he gives his "body," the church, in the ongoing ministry of reconciliation. Paul recognizes this when he writes that even as Jesus suffered in his fleshly body, so now as an apostle he suffers in his flesh for the body, that is, the church (1:24). Paul could not have used such a metaphor had he deemed the body an inferior entity, or had he thought that somehow Jesus had effected reconciliation in his spirit as opposed to his body or his flesh. So Irenaeus can write unashamedly that the "perfect human being . . . consists in the commingling and the union of the soul receiving the spirit of the Father, and the admixture of that fleshly nature which was molded after the image of God."

Paul also uses "body" of the individual human being (2:5, 23). In one of the most important passages for determining the "Colossian heresy," Paul speaks of those who promote "harsh treatment of the body." The recommended course is not indulging the sensual appetites; in fact Paul's complaint is that such harsh treatment has no value in "checking self-indulgence." The body may be the instrument through which sin expresses itself, as Paul puts it elsewhere; but that problem is not dealt with by harsh treatment of the body. Oddly enough, Christians have often viewed the body with either embarrassment or disdain, in spite of the fact that at the heart of its faith are both the doctrine of the creation of the world through the Son and the doctrine of the incarnation, the en*flesh*ment, the em*bodi*ment of the Word of God for the salvation of the world. Numerous heresies have either denied that Jesus was truly human, with a body of flesh and blood as we have; held that the "spirit" or "deity" of Jesus departed from him on the cross, so that it was not "God incarnate" who died, but rather a merely human Jesus; or suggested that someone other than Jesus died on the cross.

In one way or another, these heresies find either the human body of Jesus or our own human bodies problematic; best to be rid of them. The epistle to the Colossians knows no such dichotomy: the fullness of deity dwelled *bodily* in Christ, whose suffering in his fleshly body gives life to those who are part of his body. And this is not the act of someone alien to that creation, but the very one through whom the creation came into being. The one who through whom the world was created becomes a creature in order to bring all that is in his creation to its perfect and final destiny. As Luke Johnson puts it:

> Since Christian life is essentially a path of response to a living God who powerfully if invisibly intrudes in the structures of human life, then spiri-

tuality also is intrinsically physical. No Christian spirituality can pretend to be adequate that stops with the cultivation of the soul. We implicitly engage God when we engage the world. Our bodies mediate the engagement of God's freedom with ours. Our bodies extend our selves into the physical world.[73]

In sum, "I believe in God the Father Almighty, Maker of heaven and earth" has far-reaching theological implications. Paul's epistle to the Colossians frames the doctrine of creation in terms of a beginning, middle, and end, positing that all God's creation happens in and for Christ. Creation is not just a past tense act: it has a purpose; it is going somewhere. Christianity "is not only a doctrine of creation. It is a doctrine of a creation whose ultimate perfecting is secured and guaranteed by the life, death, resurrection and ascension of the one who became part of the created order for the sake of its redemption."[74] In Colossians, there is no "doctrine of creation" that does not envision the future re-creation of the world. Hence, the lamp which creation shines on our knowledge of God, on the condition of humankind, or on truth or beauty will always be a partial light, for God's purposes for and through creation will be brought to their fruition only with the redemption of all things. Indeed, as Athanasius states, the purpose of the incarnation was not just to restore creation to what it once was but to prevent it from failing to achieve its perfection, its true destiny.[75] This is most clearly the case if we think of the point in Colossians that human beings are being renewed "according to the image of their Creator" and that this image is Christ himself. Since in Christ we see what human beings are to be, then the renewal of human beings in his image is not simply a restoration of what once was but a renewal according to his perfect humanity, characterized above all by obedience to God and by faith, hope, and love.

"Making Peace through the Blood of the Cross"

The cross and resurrection are central to Paul's thought. But in much Christian theology and piety, the meaning of the cross has been flattened. Usually one or perhaps two images serve to "explain" the cross, with a host of other ideas of what the cross accomplished simply left behind. And perhaps fewer people still have a rich sense of how Jesus' death on the cross impinges upon

---

73. Johnson, *Faith's Freedom*, 9-10.
74. Gunton, *Triune Creator*, 40.
75. Athanasius, *On the Incarnation of the Word* 6.

Christian life and practice today. It was something that happened "back then" to someone else, but has few practical consequences for Christian life in the present. But for Paul, Christ's death and resurrection are not simply past tense events, but present tense realities. Those who are in Christ die and rise with Christ; they live his death and resurrection. These "participationist" images of salvation, in which believers are said to be in Christ and to participate with him in his death, are central to Paul's theology of the cross, particularly in Colossians. Colossians can provide a host of images that enrich the texture of our theology of the cross.

Especially in certain pietistic traditions, the story of the cross is entirely personal and can be summarized with "Jesus died for me," or "he is my personal Lord and Savior." What Jesus did, he did for *me*. There are undeniably echoes here of Paul's statement that "the Son of God loved *me* and gave himself *for me*" (Gal 2:20). But Paul sets this personal and individual view on a bigger stage. For example, in 1 Cor 15:3 he quotes the tradition that "the Messiah died for our sins, according to the Scriptures." The references to both "the Messiah" and "the Scriptures" demand that we understand the death of Jesus in terms larger than "personal salvation." For Paul, the salvation effected by Jesus through his death is the salvation won by Israel's Messiah, as promised by God in the Scriptures. In other words, the individual finds his or her place in the drama of the redemption of God's people, Israel, as foretold in Israel's Scriptures and focused on the Messiah promised to the people of God.

But in 2 Cor 5:19 Paul moves that story onto yet another stage, the stage of the cosmic drama: "in Christ, God was reconciling the world to himself." The story of the cross is the world's story. And this is the perspective that we find in Colossians. Here the death of Jesus is construed not first with reference to the individual, to Israel, or even to all people, but with reference to the entire cosmos; on the cross, he reconciled "*all things,* whether on earth or in heaven, making peace by the blood of his cross" (Col 1:20). To be sure, the redemption of the cosmos serves as the stage for the redemption of humankind: humanity will be redeemed to live in a new heaven and new earth. Although there is some antipathy today toward thinking of salvation as "anthropocentric" or focused on the human being, at this point Colin Gunton rightly notes that the biblical doctrine of creation and redemption does manifest a decided anthropocentrism. The Word of God did not become incarnate as a human being for the sake of creation, but for the sake of those who are made in the image of God and are being remade in that image.[76]

It hardly needs to be said that Jesus' death does not obviously have this

---

76. Gunton, *Christ and Creation,* 33.

meaning. His death does not come ready-made with a self-evident interpretation — except the one apparent to all onlookers, that he was a victim of the Roman judicial system, perhaps a rebel or brigand, but on any account a pitiable specimen of a messianic figure. Many of the NT metaphors used for the cross exploit the contrast between what appeared to be and what was actually the case. For example, although Jesus was pronounced guilty by Rome, he was innocent and regarded as such by God. Moreover, this innocence belongs to all those who place their trust in him. Although the law condemned him to death, his death acquits or justifies those who have faith. Jesus' innocence is their innocence, and his acquittal by God is their acquittal. Or, if death is conceived of as a cruel tyrant, a master from whose clutches there is no escape, then the death that Jesus died, a death such as a slave might experience, becomes the means of setting the enslaved free. In still another contrast, the death of Jesus appeared to be one more victory for the powers of the world, but Paul identifies it as the means by which the powers are defeated. In one way or another, all the images for the death of Jesus clearly imply that in and through Jesus God has done for us what we could not do for ourselves: granting freedom, setting us free, overcoming the powers.

What Paul thinks God accomplished through the cross is thus always closely related to what Paul believes the human predicament to be.[77] If the powers dominate, they must be removed or subjugated; if death is the problem, then life must be given; and if sin is the besetting problem, then it must be forgiven. All these play a role in Colossians in characterizing the human condition. Perhaps the leading candidate of these for characterizing the human condition is "sin." The apparent antidote would seem to be forgiveness: where wrongs have been committed, they must be pardoned. Yet Paul appeals relatively seldom to "forgiveness" as the cure for the human condition. Although he can speak simply of the "forgiveness of sins" and of the death of Christ "for our sins," on the whole he regards "sin" not as the sum of wrongdoings ("sins"), but as a power or master to whom human beings give a false allegiance. In other words, human beings sin and need pardon, but sin is a much deeper and more insidious reality that must be dealt with more radically. It has been dealt with not simply by the offer of pardon, but by the death of the one "in whom the fullness of deity dwelled," on the cross.

Such a radical solution to the human problem reveals the radical character and power of sin. Sin is a pervasive reality, reaching into every aspect of

---

77. In *Paul and Palestinian Judaism,* 442-47, E. P. Sanders contended that Paul argued from "solution" (the death of Jesus) to "plight" (the human predicament that corresponded to the solution).

human existence and into all relationships; it is a tyrannical and insatiable master; it is a power that alienates human beings from each other and from God. The act of salvation is the act of dealing with sin, both with its power and effects. In other words, salvation is not the result of the removal of sin; rather, salvation is itself the removal of sin. In commenting on the image in Col 2:14, where God cancels the accusations against humankind by nailing those accusations to the cross, Ambrosiaster aptly put it this way: "Because death came from sin, when sin in fact was overcome, the resurrection of the dead became a reality. Indeed this could not have been done, if he had not nailed it to the cross. . . . Sin being overcome is said to be put to death; the cross is not the death of the Savior, but of sin."[78]

Of course, the Savior does die; but Ambrosiaster's point is that ultimately the Savior, having been put to death, lives, while sin has received its death sentence. But this happens for Ambrosiaster, as in Colossians and in Pauline theology overall, not simply because someone died on a cross, but because the Savior died on the cross. As the title of one recent book has it, what is of significance is "not the cross, but the crucified."[79] Death, even death on a cross, need not in and of itself have redemptive significance. What matters, rather, is *who* dies on the cross. This was a topos of ancient Christian theology, as demonstrated perhaps most famously by Anselm's thesis entitled *Cur Deus Homo?* or "Why the God-Man?" In this treatise Anselm asked why salvation had to be achieved by one who was both human and divine. In Colossians, it is the head of all rule and authority, the one through whom all the principalities and powers were made, who was subject to death on the cross. Colossians, like the Gospel of John, with which it has many affinities, presents the cross as the death of the one through whom and for whom the world itself was made. The agent of God's creation has met his death — the apparent undoing of God's creative and life-giving act — yet has through that death conquered death and the powers themselves.[80] He who had all power

---

78. From *ACCSNT* 9:34.

79. Mertens, *Not the Cross, but the Crucified: An Essay in Soteriology.*

80. In his study of the atonement, Arland Hultgren (*Christ and His Benefits,* 65-164) speaks of "four types" of redemptive christology: (1) redemption accomplished in Christ, (2) redemption confirmed through Christ, (3) redemption won by Christ, and (4) redemption mediated by Christ. While he puts most of Paul's letters under the first category, he places Colossians (and Ephesians) into the third category and the Gospel of John in the fourth category. The first and third categories are distinguished by the increasing centrality of Christ in the third, so that he is not so much the agent of God's salvation as the one who himself achieves it. But it should be pointed out that the lines between Paul's main letters and Colossians (and Ephesians) are not firmly drawn at these points.

made himself subject to the powers in order to overcome them. As Athanasius wrote, "he became what we were, in order that we might become what he is."

Hans Urs von Balthasar underscores the connection between the incarnation and the cross when he writes that God identifies with humankind precisely at that place where humankind is "at its wit's end," where it "has fallen into an abyss of grief, indigence, darkness, into the 'pit' from which he cannot escape by his own powers."[81] Von Balthasar's description of the human plight echoes the OT psalms of lament and cries for help. In the Gospel Passion narratives, Jesus' experience of suffering on the cross is described more than once with direct quotations and indirect allusions to these psalms of the righteous sufferer (especially Psalms 22, 31, and 69). Jesus' suffering and death are not portrayed as somehow of a different order or kind, but in the same terms used of human suffering, pain, and even despair. James L. Mays similarly explicates the relationship between the suffering described in the Psalms and Jesus' own sufferings. These psalms are

> the literary deposit in the scriptures that testifies to the range and depth of anguish that can and does come to those who are mortal and vulnerable and undertake to live unto God. They are the classics of life that undergoes the worst *in* faith and *for* the faith. They are the paradigms of the soul that uses afflictions, alienation, pain, and even dying as occasions to assert the reality and faithfulness of God. As such they can show us in detail the mortality that belongs to Christ in his identity with us.[82]

The one who is the head of all powers identifies with human beings not at the point of their strength, but in their weakness, becoming subject to suffering and death as they are. In this way, the one through whom the world was made identifies fully with it and becomes the one who both experiences and redeems from death. Christ's participation in human suffering and identification with human sin are not ends in themselves. Rather, Christ shares with us our situation of sin and alienation, so that we might participate in his victory and life.

God's identification with the world through and in Christ underscores the point that God is turned toward the world, and not against it, for its redemption and its healing. To borrow from Romans, the cross reveals that God is for us, and "if God is for us, who can be against us?" In spite of these words of Romans and the affirmations of Colossians that God has made peace through the blood of the cross, many Christians consciously or uncon-

81. von Balthasar, *Mysterium Paschale*, 13.
82. Mays, *The Lord Reigns*, 50-51.

sciously have adopted the viewpoint that God the Father is essentially wrathful and punitive, and Jesus, the Son of God, protects us from God's anger. Colossians provides an antidote to this misconception in its insistence that the one through whom the world was created is also the one through whom the world is redeemed. Creation and redemption cannot be torn apart, and neither can the Creator and the Redeemer. That assertion, of course, raises the question of the referent of "Creator" and "Redeemer." Indeed, both "Creator" and "Redeemer" can be applied to the Father and to the Son. As noted earlier, God the Father is the ultimate source or cause of creation and redemption, and the Son is the one through whom the world is both created and redeemed. Hence, to speak of one as "Creator" and the other as "Redeemer" has the unfortunate effect of dividing what Paul in Colossians so deliberately holds together. For there is no conflict between Father and Son with respect to the redemption of the world, for the Son is the one in whom "the fullness of deity dwelled bodily" (1:19; 2:9).

Although we noted earlier that Paul does not provide an explicit "theory" of the atonement in Colossians, there are a number of terms that might serve us well in understanding the death of Christ. One is "interchange." Without using that word, Athanasius proposed something along those lines when he wrote that "he has become what we are in order that we might become what he is." "Interchange" is close to "exchange," but the believer and Christ do not simply exchange places. The sinner remains a sinner, but receives the blessings of life in Christ; Christ remains the head of all power and authority, but also assumes the place of the lost sinner. One does not become the other, but each assumes the position of the other in an "interchange."[83] Moreover, Paul does not write that Christ died *instead of* us, so that we escape death, but that in our death we participate also in Christ's death on our behalf. The believer's life traces the course of Jesus' own life, not merely by means of imitation, but through union with him. Those who *participate* in the death of Jesus also participate in his resurrection, and so receive life in him.

Several formulations in Colossians bear witness to these basic categories of interchange and participation. Speaking primarily of the incarnation (rather than the cross *per se*), Paul writes, "In him the whole fullness of deity dwells bodily, and you have come to fullness of life in him, who is the head of all rule and authority" (2:9-10). Because the fullness of deity was found in Christ, fullness of life can be received through him. He has become what human beings are so that in him they might have the fullness of life that characterizes God's own life. In 2:12 Paul writes, "You were buried with him in

---

83. On this point, see Hooker, *Not Ashamed of the Gospel,* 20-46.

baptism, in which you were also raised with him through faith in the working of God, who raised him from the dead." Here the believer dies and is buried by means of baptism and is raised up, even as Jesus was raised up from the dead, by virtue of union with him "through faith." Paul further writes, "You, who were dead in trespasses and the uncircumcision of your flesh, God made alive together with him, having forgiven us all our trespasses" (2:13). Here again, we note that those who were dead have been made alive, because Christ participated in their death — and so they have a share in his life. These ways of explaining the cross depend on both interchange and participation. Christ participates with and identifies with us in our sin and death, so that we may through participation in his death and life receive the blessings of salvation.

Without doubt, here is one of Paul's distinctive theological contributions to our understanding of the death of Christ. Unfortunately, many of these ways of thinking about the significance of the cross have been overshadowed by an exclusive emphasis on juridical and forensic imagery. While Paul clearly does use the language of the courtroom (judgment, acquittal, and so on), he also draws on imagery from other spheres in an effort to portray the scope and breadth of God's salvation of the world through Christ. Albert Schweitzer and others have seen Paul's "participationist" view of salvation as so essential to his thinking that they have labeled it the "center" of Pauline theology. But Paul's understanding of participation in Christ is not confined to how the cross "works." Below we shall discuss the way in which "participation" in Christ's life and death provides the foundation of Paul's understanding of the Christian life. It is this all-encompassing reach of the cross into every aspect of human life that characterizes Paul's view of the cross. What happened on and through the cross is not merely past tense, it is not merely about the individual, and it does not have to do only with the "spiritual realm." Rather, the work of the cross shapes the life of the individual Christian and the church in the present world, precisely because the believer participates in the death and resurrection of the living Lord.

In our earlier discussion of the place of Colossians in Pauline and biblical theology, we noted other ways of conceiving of the work of Christ on the cross. One important set of images falls under the rubric of "transfer" terminology which overlaps with both participation and interchange. "Transfer terminology" refers to the various images in which God or Christ rescues those in peril, frees those who are captive to alien masters, or reconciles those who are alienated and hostile to God. This happens through the identification of Christ with those in captivity to sin and death; through participation in his death and life they are "transferred" to the realm of freedom and life. In this category belongs redemption from the "powers." The function of the death of Jesus with respect to the powers is twofold.

First, the cross reveals that the very structures that bring order to the world are prone to become perversely twisted against the Creator of all things. If Herod, Caiaphas, and Pilate were the powers who put Jesus to death, they did so not because they were uniquely wicked or uncomprehending, but because they were acting as agents of those perverse powers. In their proper roles, these powers would serve the ends of political and social order, but in their perversity they actually undermine justice and truth in the alleged pursuit of those goals. Jesus' death and resurrection unmask the powers as malevolent — even in their efforts to preserve God's order.[84] In other words, human attempts to do righteousness and seek justice can in fact lead to just the opposite, as the condemnation of Jesus in the name of God's law horrendously reveals.

Second, the cross provides the means of release from the powers. Although the powers thought they triumphed over Jesus, it was he who triumphed, precisely through the cross. Here is a classic example of Pauline theology where the point is scored by contrast between what is and what appears to be the case. An apparent defeat is in fact a victory. While death is powerful, it is not all-powerful; and the life that God gives through the death on a cross overcomes not only that death but the death of all those who die with the crucified one.

In all of Paul's understanding of Christ's work on the cross, there is an unflagging insistence that salvation is not in any way achieved or gained through human effort or accomplishment. Even though we "die with Christ" our salvation is not won by our deaths, but by Christ's. It is solely through union with the one "who is our life" (Col 3:4) that we have the hope of resurrection. Truly, his death is our death; his life is our life. Our death would only result in permanent death; Christ's death brings us his life as well. But the efficacy of that death derives from the fact that he is the agent of God's own creation and reconciliation of the world, the one in whom the fullness of deity dwelled bodily, who died in order to bring life to the world.

Knowledge of God and Contemporary Pluralism

"Pluralism" is a catch-all term used to characterize the situation of the world today, but it actually encompasses a number of different phenomena. Perhaps

---

84. Newbigin, *Gospel in a Pluralist Society*, 208.

most apparent in North America is the increasing cultural diversity. People from Asian, Latino, African, Middle Eastern, and European backgrounds are living side-by-side, practicing different religious, and speaking a great number of languages. This is indeed a "pluralistic" society or, perhaps better, a society marked by plurality.

Christians can gladly embrace cultural plurality. Both with respect to the vision charted for it in the Bible and its actual makeup, the Christian church is also characterized by plurality. Although individual congregations do not always mirror the diversity of the worldwide church of Jesus Christ, nevertheless, the vision throughout the NT — and one that is presupposed in Colossians as well — is that the church of Jesus Christ includes those of all classes, cultures, races, and ethnicities. Here "there is no longer Greek and Jew, circumcised and uncircumcised, barbarian, Scythian, slave, and free" (Col 3:11).

But while Christians and non-Christians alike may well want to affirm the kaleidoscopic beauty of a world of many cultures, not everything in every culture can simply be accepted as an unqualified good on the principle of "celebrating plurality." Although Scripture testifies to the diversity of the body of Christ, it also sets up guidelines for living together in a society that provide — and must provide — a way of living that does not simply equate any single set of cultural norms with God's own values and ways. We do not regard infanticide or physical abuse of women and children as value-neutral or simply attribute such practices to "cultural distinctives." But we must also grant that there are many things in our own culture that we would not want to export, including the materialism, violence, individualism, crudeness, and sexual laxity that have become so much part of the cultural fabric of twenty-first-century America. In important ways, the church always stands over against that culture of which it finds itself a part, simply because no culture — including the church itself — ever perfectly mirrors that redeemed people in the new world that God will bring about. The church must always bear witness to God's alternative vision for humankind, even as it struggles to attain to that vision.

Granted these caveats, the church can endorse both the idea and reality of cultural plurality. But the situation is quite different when it comes to religious pluralism. There are two main issues that call for attention. First, how are we to think about other religions in relationship to Christianity? Second, how are we to respond to the adherents of other religions? On these points there is a wide range of perspectives within the Christian community today.

A tripartite schema has often been used to characterize views of other religions: one is either pluralist, inclusivist, or exclusivist. These labels are generally taken to say who will be saved. An exclusivist, as the label implies, argues that there is only one true faith, Christianity, and that only those who profess faith in Christ will receive salvation. An inclusivist may well hold to the uniqueness of Christ, but does not rule out the possibility that those without explicit faith in Christ may nevertheless be saved. On this view, those who are saved are saved because of the work of Christ on their behalf, even though they do not explicitly acknowledge Christ. And a pluralist believes that no one religion provides the exclusive pathway to God. Instead, all faiths, albeit perhaps in some partial way, have some knowledge of or lead to the ultimate reality that is God. This God cannot simply be equated with the Christian God — or the "God" of any other religion for that matter.

Perhaps the best known proponent of the pluralist approach is John Hick.[85] Crucial to Hick's viewpoint is the distinction between the unknowable "Real" in Itself (i.e., God) and human experience and interpretation of "the Real." One of the main problems with Hick's distinction, as has often been pointed out, is the gap it allows between God's ultimate Being and God as known to humankind. But Hick must make a move something like this; as a pluralist, he does not want to argue that any one faith provides the norm for knowledge or experience of God. Hick must also posit that the Ultimate or Real is not simply known as or through any one conception of God and, hence, in a genuine sense God cannot be known. As Lesslie Newbigin insightfully notes, "If the Krishna of the Puranas and the Jesus of the Gospels are both revelations of God, then we must say (and this is what Hinduism in the end does say) that God is unknown and unknowable. Each of us is — in the end — shut up in his own world of ideas. He must find God in the depths of his own being because there is no action of God by which he gives himself to be known by us."[86] To say that all faiths provide knowledge of God is actually tantamount to saying that no faith does, since their accounts of God, and God's actions, are often at odds with each other. Similarly, their understandings of the human plight and of "salvation" are portrayed rather differently, hold out different hopes, and ask for rather different responses. One could argue that these differences simply establish Hick's point: there is a gap between God as God is and God as experienced by human beings. All we have access to, in the end, is the experiences of human beings — and these are widely varied.

Colossians offers itself as an interesting test case of an appropriate Christian stance toward other religions. On the one hand, there is the description of Christ in terms that are sometimes labeled "the cosmic Christ." This Christ is

---

85. See, for example, his *God and the Universe of Faiths*.
86. Newbigin, *The Light Has Come*, 43.

the agent of the creation and redemption of all that is. Even as human beings were created in the image of God, so they are being renewed in the image of their Creator. Various authors have explored the possible implications of this "cosmic christology" for thinking about the religions of the world.[87] This christology posits that all people exist "in Christ" because they are part of the creation of the cosmos "in him." Moreover, if all the world is created in, through, and for Christ, then Christ's presence permeates all creation, making Christ universally accessible to humankind. In Colossians, we also read that "all things hold together in him." If all things hold together, or are sustained, in Christ, then it follows that all people are sustained by Christ and are in relationship with him, even if they do not name his name. In other words, the vision of the creation of the world and all that is in it in and for Christ means that the human family is a fundamental cosmic unity. If all things are created and redeemed for Christ, then people of *all* religions will find their final destiny in Christ. In other words, Colossians is taken as providing the theological underpinnings for an inclusivist perspective on other faiths.

On the other hand, alongside the emphasis on the creation and reconciliation of all things in and for Christ, Colossians links the "hope of glory" with hearing the gospel, the word of truth, and standing firm in faith (1:4-6, 27). It also refers to those who have been rescued from darkness, forgiven of their sins, and transferred to the kingdom of God's beloved Son, so that they have a share of the inheritance that belongs to the saints in the light (1:12-14). Similarly, it speaks of those who have faith in God's power as those who have been raised with Christ to life (2:12). These and other words are clearly addressed to Paul's readers, the "faithful brothers and sisters in Christ" in Colossae. While they surely also refer to all those who are faithful in Christ in other congregations, Paul does not simply collapse the redeemed order into the created order. There is a renewal in Christ, a renewal in the image of the Creator, that is not identical with creation in the image of the Creator (3:10-11).

Moreover, it is hard to imagine that Paul, raised on the Jewish insistence that there is only one God, could simply have abandoned this foundational belief on coming to believe in Jesus as the Messiah and Lord. In speaking of the risen Jesus as "Lord," Paul did not sacrifice the confession of "one God."[88] The point can be reinforced by the way in which Paul uses the Shema, "Hear,

---

87. The following summary is taken from Joseph Sittler, "Called to Unity," *Ecumenical Review* 14 (1962): 177-87; and Paul Devanandan, "Called to Witness," *Ecumenical Review* 14 (1962): 155-63.

88. Numerous studies have explored the way in which early Christian faith incorporated devotion to Jesus into its framework; see especially Larry Hurtado, *Lord Jesus Christ;* Richard Bauckham, *God Crucified;* and N. T. Wright, *Climax of the Covenant.*

O Israel: The LORD is our God, the LORD alone" (Deut 6:4). Paul, writing to a church many of whose "members" had likely been recently converted out of a pluralistic, pagan context, teases apart the Shema into two affirmations, the first about God the Father and the second about Jesus Christ the Lord: "For us there is one God, the Father, from whom are all things and for whom we exist, and one Lord, Jesus Christ, through whom are all things and through whom we exist" (1 Cor 8:6). This is truly an astonishing use of this foundational biblical confession which articulates the identity of Israel in terms of its allegiance to the one God. Now Paul rereads that affirmation to include within it the confession of one God and one Lord together. What is at issue for Paul here is the identity of Jesus Christ and the necessity of formulating his beliefs about God in terms that come to him from the Scriptures. The question of religious pluralism is ultimately a question of our understanding of who God is and how God is known — as John Hick's pluralist agenda suggests in a quite different way.

Although it is often said that our world has changed and that we live in a different context than did Paul or the earliest Christians, this is an exaggerated statement. It is easy to point to the notably pluralistic pagan context in which Paul's early congregations struggled to live out their Christian commitment. Excavations in Corinth, Ephesus, Philippi, and numerous other cities show that they were replete with shrines and temples to a variety of deities, as well as to the emperors as the emperor cult increasingly exerted its influence. Ancient inscriptions attest to prayers for healing and deliverance from peril and danger offered up to these gods. People sought wisdom by consulting various oracles such as the oracle at Delphi. We have written documents that testify repeatedly to the sincere religious quests of ancient pagans, who sought to enter into experiences of the divine which offered them joy and peace. For example, in the *Metamorphoses* Apuleius describes the fate of a certain Lucius, who, after a life of moral debauchery, finds himself unhappily changed into an ass. Through an encounter with the goddess Isis, he eventually regains his human form, and he commits himself to becoming her devotee and, at great cost and great sacrifice, enters into the mysteries devoted to her. This, however, is not good enough, and eventually he undergoes two more costly and self-denying rites of initiation in order to enter the mysteries of Osiris as well. By any measure, he shows an extraordinary degree of earnestness, sincerity, and devotion. No wonder that in Acts 17 Paul speaks of the Athenians as "very religious," honoring and tending even fallen and defaced altars dedicated to gods whose names are by now long forgotten. It was in such a context that Paul penned the confession in 1 Cor 8:5-6, "indeed, there are many so-called lords and gods, but for us there is one God and one Lord."

But the confession of Jesus as Lord of all was for Paul both absolute and necessary because it articulated the relationship of Christ to God. Such a confession was necessary because it articulated who Christ is and what God has done through him. To be sure, Paul recognized the variegated human experiences of divinities, but these experiences did not lead to knowledge of the one true God of Israel, the Father of Jesus Christ. In any case, the beginning point for Paul is not the religious quest or experiences of human beings but what God has done in Christ for the ultimate redemption of his world. Paul frames his account of God's action in Christ in terms of creation and redemption, the beginning and end of all things, and therefore has little trouble in thinking of the universal significance of Christ. Jesus Christ was not just a local cult deity, but the Lord of all. To deny the universality of Jesus' lordship is also to deny God's saving purposes for all creation. The church may then become a local cult, even a cult with manifestations in various cities and countries, such as that of Isis, but it will not be the universal church of the Lord. As Lesslie Newbigin puts it: "The uniqueness and the universality are counterparts of each other. To reject both in the alleged interest of mutual tolerance among the world's religions is to deny the message at its center. If there are many different revelations, then the human family has no center for its unity."[89]

To confess that Jesus is Lord is to say, not that in him we have found a way to God, but that in him God has embodied a way to us. This means that an understanding of God and of the salvation given to us is uniquely and decisively manifested through the life, death, and resurrection of Jesus Christ. We know God, in the particular and concrete, as self-sacrificing love for the life of the world. To worship God rightly, then, is to worship the God of Israel, whose saving purposes are brought to their fulfillment in Jesus of Nazareth. This is the narrative of Scripture. Because of the connection between knowing God and the concrete manifestation of God in the particular story of Jesus of Nazareth, some writers have preferred the term "particularist" rather than exclusivist as a label for their viewpoint. In other words, the main issue is not who will be "excluded" from salvation, but rather how God is made known. Indeed, Paul's repeated emphasis in Colossians on the revelation of the mysteries of God in Christ demonstrates that his theological starting point is what God has done in and through Christ and who Christ is in relationship to God. To say there are many equally valid ways to God is not to make God more generous, but simply to make God generic. And a generic god, a god known apart from Israel's story and apart from the narrative of Jesus, is simply not the God of the Bible.

89. Newbigin, *The Light Has Come*, 43.

The paganism of Paul's day was willing to speak of many gods and many lords, enough for temples and rituals and cults aplenty in the cities of Corinth and Ephesus and Philippi and Laodicea. The paganism of our day, with its intolerance for monotheism, similarly allows many gods, and many lords. But, it should be added, not all. Most pluralists do not grant absolutely equal status to each and every religion. Buddhism, Islam, Judaism, and Christianity may be valid religious expressions — but are the Branch Davidians or Heaven's Gate or the KKK? The church in Paul's day benefited from living under the *Pax Romana,* but it could not adopt the state's tolerance for multiple deities as its own. *Pax Americana* goes further, inculcating tolerance as the highest good — but the church can no more adopt that as its slogan than could the church of Paul's day. What it is imperative for the church to articulate today if it is not simply to be assimilated into its pagan context is a theology which does not cater to the lowest common denominator of confession, but stands with Paul in affirming in the face of every possible objection and obstacle: "There is one God, and one Lord." From that starting point we may work together to bring all humankind to the point where "every knee will bow, and every tongue confess . . . that Jesus Christ is Lord."

Our context is no more pluralistic than was the context of Paul or of any of the apostles who lived, worked, and taught in the Roman Empire of the first century. Although people are fond of saying so, we do not live in unprecedented times. The world of the early church knew of claims that there were indeed "many lords and many gods." There were claims for the gods of nationalism and power such as the Caesars and Rome, for the various gods of foreign and mystery cults such as Isis and Osiris, for local and civic deities such as Athena, Artemis, and Apollo, for the gods of chance and fate, and for the generic life force of the universe. Precisely in the context of such claims, Paul affirmed that there is "one God, the Father, and one Lord, Jesus Christ." Our world, too, knows of "many lords and many gods" — and many of them take the same form as they did in Paul's own day — nationalism, imported deities, fate and fortune, and the pantheistic belief that all is God. In the ancient world, Christianity provided an alternative to the shapeless confusion of antiquity; in the modern world, it can provide the same alternative, but only if it articulates the gospel clearly.

In such a world, it is urgent that the church have the courage to speak its belief in the one Lord, for this is the content of the gospel. In making this proclamation, it must make clear that it seeks not to add another deity to the pluralistic mix but to bear witness to the Lord who is "above every name," for he is the one whom God has "set above all rule and authority, all power and dominion." In other words, the foundation of the church's confession and proclamation is who Jesus is, through God's mercy and grace, for all the world and also for us.

> To assert today that the one Creator God has revealed himself fully and finally in Jesus Christ is to risk criticism on the grounds of arrogance or intolerance. The mission of the church, however, does not commit Christians to the proposition that there is no truth to be found in other religions. All philosophies or religions which have some "fit" with the created world will thereby reflect in some ways the truth of God. [This] does not, however, imply that they are therefore, as they stand, doorways into the *new* creation. That place . . . is Christ's alone.[90]

What, then, ought to be the stance of a Christian to those of other faiths? The word "tolerance" is often used, but it asks both too much and too little. On the one hand, many use it to mean "acceptance" in the sense that to tolerate the religious views of others is to grant approval to those views. This is usually coupled with a relativism that allows that what is true for one person may not after all be true for another. On the other hand, "tolerance" says too little, because Christian faith asks for more. People of other faiths deserve respect, precisely because they are created in the image of Jesus Christ, but they also deserve the same sort of self-giving and sacrificial love that Jesus himself manifested for all people.

The Identity of the Christian Church

In speaking of the new people of God, Paul writes, "Here there cannot be Greek and Jew, circumcised and uncircumcised, barbarian, Scythian, slave, free man, but Christ is all, and in all" (Col 3:11). For all the criticism which the church receives both from its own and from those who are not part of it, it is the one true multiethnic entity in all the world. The reality of the church is far bigger than the little slice of reality any individual, congregation, or denomination knows and experiences. There is great hope in such a vision, for the church as the one body of Christ, in which all the nations of the world are gathered together to bring praise to God, is a magnificent vision. The church offers hope that human divisions, be they cultural, ethnic, or racial, need not have the final word. This may seem to threaten to erase individual or ethnic identity, dissolving either cultural distinctive or the particularity of the individual into some abstract human "essence." But the church in which there is

90. Wright, *Colossians*, 79.

neither "Jew nor Gentile" is not a church that discounts ethnic, cultural, or racial identities but rather celebrates the common identity given to us in Jesus Christ, an identity that can unite. What the diverse members of the church share is not a "common humanity," but a common human being, namely, Jesus of Nazareth, the crucified and risen Lord. It is he alone who "holds all things together," including the church, which is his body (1:17-18). As Lesslie Newbigin put it, "[at the heart of the gospel] is the denial of all imperialisms, for at its center there is the cross where all imperialisms are humbled and we are invited to find the center of human unity in the One who was made nothing so that all might be one. The very heart of the biblical vision for the unity of humankind is that its center is not an imperial power but the slain Lamb."[91]

The church's unity and identity are given to it not as some sort of disembodied Platonic ideal, but rather in identification with its crucified, self-giving Lord. This fact is important for a number of reasons, not least because it is only in recognizing and identifying with the self-giving of Jesus that the church receives its unity as a gift and can also receive the graces it needs to live out its identity. Any attempts to identify the "unity of the church" with some set of ideals, practices, or principles rather than in the church's identification with Jesus will produce at best some model that might be imitated by social groups or civic clubs, but it will not be the church of Jesus Christ, in whom the fullness of God dwelled *bodily.* Identification, therefore, with "the body," which includes the body of the Lord as distinct human being and as the corporate church, means a participation in the fully embodied reality of God. It was this reality that the Barmen Declaration insisted on when it called on the church to reject the notion that "there [are] areas of our life in which we would not belong to Jesus Christ, but to other lords," and to give allegiance only to Jesus Christ "who is the one Word of God which we have to hear and which we have to trust and obey in life and death." The "difference" between Christians and non-Christians lies primarily in the different lord to whom each gives allegiance. The members of the church find their true identity neither in denying nor reifying their cultural, racial, or ethnic heritage, but in owning Jesus Christ, the one in whom and for whom all things were created, as the head of the church. While this identity is given at baptism, the realization of what it means for personal and corporate life requires a lifetime — and more — of reflection and commitment.

But the identity of the church as drawn from multiple cultures, races, and ethnic groups forces the question of the church's relationship to any one

---

91. Newbigin, *Gospel in a Pluralist Society,* 159.

of those groups. How does a church that identifies not with a specific culture but with the Lord of all cultures relate to that specific cultural world in which it finds itself? It is not a new question. Over the years, various groups of Christians have conceived of this relationship in a variety of ways. Not surprisingly, those who acknowledged a Lord who was despised and rejected by the powers of the religious and political world saw his life's pattern mirrored in their own. But more than one conception of relationship to one's cultural and social world can grow out of identification with a crucified Lord. One can imagine the church as "faithful remnant" seeking to cling to its faith in a hostile environment, perhaps bearing its witness, perhaps simply holding on until God delivers it to a new heaven or a new earth. Or the church has seen itself as having either a prophetic voice or prophetic lifestyle, an "alternate" lifestyle over against that of its surrounding culture. Some have styled the church as God's change agent in the world, seeking to transform culture into its God-ordained patterns. But that way of putting it surely raises the question of what a "God-ordained pattern" might look like, and whether such a thing is even available.[92] In any case, these are different ways of construing the faithful behavior of the church in its context. It may well be that no one picture or model will suffice for every time and place, but that the church must always discern the shape of its obedience to the gospel.

The *Epistle to Diognetus*, an early Christian document of uncertain date, asserts that the Christian distinctive lies in neither

> country nor language nor customs. For they do not dwell in cities in some place of their own, nor do they use any strange variety of dialect, nor practice an extraordinary kind of life. . . . They dwell in their own fatherlands, but as if sojourners in them; they share all things as citizens, and suffer all things as strangers. Every foreign country is their fatherland, and every fatherland is a foreign country. (5:1-2, 5)

It is this dialectical relationship between the familiarity and foreignness, between citizenship and sojourning, that characterizes the Christian church in relationship to culture. Miroslav Volf puts it this way:

> The proper distance from a culture does not take Christians out of that culture. Christians are not the insiders who have taken flight to a new "Christian culture" and become outsiders to their own culture; rather when they have responded to the call of the Gospel they have stepped, as

92. See Mouw, *He Shines in All That's Fair*, 3-4, and the longer discussions in Volf, *Exclusion and Embrace*, 13-55.

it were, with one foot outside their own culture while with the other remaining firmly planted in it.[93]

Such a view captures the vision of Colossians, which calls its readers to "set your minds on things that are above, not on things that are on earth" and then goes on to spell out what that means in exhortations to shun fornication, impurity, passion, evil desire, greed, anger, wrath, malice, slander, abusive language, and dishonesty and instead to practice compassion, kindness, humility, meekness, patience, forgiveness, love, peace, and thanksgiving. These are the virtues needed for engagement in, rather than isolation from, social structures. While they say how a Christian is to live, they do not aim primarily at the behavior of the individual, but rather have in view the development of a community. The virtues that Paul commends — humility, patience, love — cannot be practiced in isolation; they are the foundation of harmonious human relationships and social structures. As Alasdair McIntyre presents the case in *After Virtue*, the most important ethical questions are not "What shall I do?" and "How do I decide what I should do?" Rather, the important moral questions are teleological: "What kind of person am I to become? what kind of community do I want to share in?"[94] In other words, what sorts of virtues contribute to the desired goal — and what is that goal?

Still, it is doubtful that Colossians endorses a single form of the vision of the engagement of the church in culture. It is clear, however, that the description in *Diognetus*, while theological, also describes the sociological reality of the church in its day. The church's theological identity was mirrored in its sociological mapping: Christians did not live in ghettos, and their customs and language did not distinguish them from their environs. Still, they did not merely accommodate to all social, cultural, or political realities, maintaining rather a consistently dialectical relationship to those realities. Perhaps because none of the earliest Christians lived in allegedly "Christian" nations, an unreflective nationalism or easy championing of the state was not the particular danger that threatened their allegiance to the gospel. The gospel proclaimed Jesus, not Caesar, as Lord. Colossians spells out in various ways what it means to be one who names Jesus as Lord.

According to Colossians, it is in and through the church, and in its uniting of Jew and Gentile, that God reveals his purposes for the salvation of the world. The church bears witness to a reality, to a salvation, which entails a past event but also anticipates a future realization. The church's hope is al-

93. Volf, *Exclusion and Embrace*, 49.
94. MacIntyre, *After Virtue*.

ways greater than present reality and always external to present reality. In other words, even if the church were nearly perfect in the present life, it still would not have attained to "the hope of glory" which is held forth as a promise. The glorious hope of the church cannot be brought about by human effort; but human effort and life together in the church must always take its measure by Christ. Since no individual or body has perfectly realized or perfectly sees that measure, in the present life it can only be approximated. The church struggles to discern the mind of Christ and to "walk worthily of the Lord" in all that it does. But even the life of the church together is "hidden with Christ in God" until the revelation of future glory.

"The church" is much under attack today. Cries that denominationalism or "the church as we know it" is dead are paired with dwindling membership in mainline churches, and rising membership in "seeker-sensitive" churches and "megachurches." Both are a long way from the "house churches" of Colossians and Philemon. Although we cannot simply go back to these models of the early church, the image of "house church" can serve in important ways. Understanding the church as "house church" might be taken to suggest that the church is primarily a place for fellowship, nurture, and support; in other words, the primary forces are centripetal. But the image of Christians gathered in houses may also serve to remind that the church is God's people *in* the world; the forces at work in the church are centrifugal. In different terms, the goal is not to get people into the church, but to get the church into the world or, perhaps better, since the church is already in the world, to empower the church to embody its witness to Jesus Christ in its mission. Gathering in people's homes for prayer, worship, and instruction serves as a graphic reminder that the church's business has to do with everyday life and not primarily with what goes on in the walls of a discrete building.

A Spirituality of Faith, Hope, and Love

"Spirituality" is one of today's buzzwords. Virtually everyone uses it, but without a clear and agreed upon definition, except that it is often contrasted with organized religion. But the following brief definition is useful: spirituality is "the lived experience of Christian belief."[95] Using this definition we could easily argue that Paul's letters are exercises in the nurture of spirituality: he writes his letters to mold behavior, to commend certain patterns of living, and to shape the practices of his churches. In other words, he writes so that

---

95. McGinn and Meyendorff, *Christian Spirituality: Origins to the Twelfth Century*, xv.

his congregations will mature in "the lived experience of Christian belief." Colossians is clearly such a pastoral letter.

One of the striking aspects of Colossians is the extent to which it roots the Christian life in participation in Christ, in his death and resurrection, in hidden union with him. For Paul, the daily life of a believer in Christ corresponds to the story of Christ crucified.[96] In other words, the cross and resurrection are not just something that happened "back then" to Jesus. Rather, according to Paul, believers are joined to Christ in Christ's death and resurrection. This union means that the narrative of Christ's death and resurrection becomes the narrative of Christian life. Colossians is not alone among the Pauline epistles in making this point, but it serves well to remind us of the ongoing significance of Jesus' death and resurrection in the *lived* experience of faith. One of the seminal contributions of Colossians is to reiterate the point that there is something inescapably hidden about the reality of Christian existence. As Paul writes in Colossians, our lives are *hidden* with Christ in God.

Union with Christ, participation in the narrative of his life, death, and resurrection, is ultimately the ground of Christian hope. This is not primarily because Christian hope looks backward to what was once done on the cross, but because it looks both forward and upward: forward, anticipating what God will do for the shalom of the world; and upward, participating now in the blessings of God's salvation. In this sense it is grounded in, but not focused on, the past. As Colossians reminds its readers, Christ's death is our death; his life is our life; more, "he is your life." These are present and future tense realities. So those who are united to Christ have the hope that what God did for Jesus, God will do for them *through* Christ, that the God who gives life, the God who raised Jesus, will also raise them up as well.

The hope for resurrection was a staple of first-century Jewish belief. Resurrection is both the raising of the dead to new life and the re-creation of a new world in which they will live. On the whole it refers to what happens in the future, at a single time, to all the righteous. It is corporate, global, and future. The NT belief that God raised Jesus broke this pattern, for here was the resurrection of the dead, of a single dead man, to undying and unending life, in the present. In other words, in Christ's resurrection the new age, the future reality of resurrection, has broken into the present. In the present age, believers experience the power of the new life through the Holy Spirit. They do not live in the resurrection time, but they live by the power of the Spirit, through whom God gives life. We are those "on whom the end of the ages has come."

---

96. Gorman, *Cruciformity*, 5.

Old powers — sin and death — have been defeated. The new powers of Christ's lordship, the Spirit, and righteousness, reign in place of the old. But we wait for the time when "every knee will bow and every tongue confess that Jesus Christ is Lord." We live in a time of hiddenness, not in the time of glory.

The structure of Paul's eschatology is crucial not only to understanding Pauline theology but also for a Christian perspective on human existence in the present. Without eschatology, spirituality loses its moorings. Paul clearly indicates that our hope has a future orientation, that it stands in contrast to what we see and experience in the present, and that the reality of the present does not simply extend in unbroken duration. Instead, the future brings a new heaven and new earth, transformed and redeemed by God. God will have the final word over our world and over us. Christian hope is utterly realistic. Hope sees the world as it is, but it also sees the world as God wants it to be. And precisely here is the tension of present Christian existence, for the witness of Scripture is that neither the world, the church, nor the individual will achieve God's purposes and goals in the present world. Living in this tension is not easy if both the hope for what will be and recognition of what is not are taken seriously. The temptation is to see only one part of the vision, which can lead to either triumphalism or despair. But Christian hope cannot be triumphalistic, because it looks both to the past and the death of Jesus on a cross and to the future, which lies beyond our control. What is hoped for is received as a gift, as a power operating outside ourselves, and as promise. Hope breeds trust in God. Thus hope is not despair, because it does not look to itself. It looks to God. Because hope has an object other than human potential or evolutionary progress, it need not lead to despair. To be sure, there is plenty to lead one to despair in our world. Our fragile planet is threatened by ecological crises, continued wars, despotic regimes, genocide, nuclear proliferation, poverty, economic collapse, rampant injustice and corruption, and burgeoning health crises. It is a world marked by death. But Colossians promises that these will not have the last word in God's creation.

In face of the grim realities of human life, secular hope assumes two things. First, it assumes that by rational thought or properly ordered human effort an earthly utopia can be achieved. Progress is always being made, and it is made through scientific and technological advances. Second, secular hope thus also assumes that the goal we desire is within our grasp and within our control. The failure to achieve what we desire is due either to the present incomplete state of our knowledge, to the inability of human beings to cooperate with each other, or perhaps just to lack of funding. It is said that the wars of the twentieth century brought an end to the hope of an earthly millennium, but the evolutionary myth of constant progress dies hard. It is virtually a truism, but one often ignored, that the sheer state of the world today makes a mockery of the myths of human progress. Witness the ecological disasters, including the deforestation of vast parts of the globe, famine and crop failures, all in a world where our technology for food production is at its peak and where plenty of people have far more than they need to eat. Yet in this world, thousands die of starvation, malnutrition, and disease. We have eradicated or nearly eradicated numerous diseases, yet new viruses appear and mutate faster than we can keep up with them. The proximity of multiple cultures in the shrinking global village has bred not understanding and mutual cooperation but racial strife, ethnic cleansing, tribalism, and warfare.

All this goes virtually without saying: we *know* these things to be true. Yet most of us persist in believing that we will eventually solve these problems and that after we have done so, there will be no more worlds to conquer. The metanarrative of inevitable progress has indelibly stamped itself on the modern mind. Essentially we do not believe the witness that is borne to us by the barrage of daily news. But neither have we believed the witness of Colossians that the world is captive to forces beyond its control and greater than its power — a witness borne long before media made the world a global village. We are convinced that the "powers" of Colossians are outmoded ways of labeling what we now know to be germs, institutional evil, or psychological demons. These, too, we think we can overcome. Modern disdain for the "primitive" worldview of the "powers" boils down to the belief that all things are in our control and the refusal to believe that we can ultimately be overpowered by anything, because the modern "metanarrative" is one of unfettered progress. Christian hope dispenses with the myth of progress and is thus more realistic than its secular counterpart. Christian hope need make no excuses for what some might call its pessimism about human potential, for it confesses that its hope ultimately rests in God, who alone can ultimately overcome the powers and set the world which he created to rights. Hope trusts that God will act, but in such trust there is never passivity. Rather, Christian existence in the present takes its guidance from the vision of the new world to come. In hope, the Christian believer works for healing, justice, righteousness, truth, and beauty, recognizing that these can never be achieved ultimately and perfectly in the present world and that where they are manifested, such manifestations are glimpses of the grace of God.

Introduction to Philemon

The letter to Philemon is the shortest of Paul's letters — 335 words in 25 verses in the critical Greek text — and one of a few addressed to an individual rather than a church or group of churches. Many aspects of the letter, such as its authorship and literary integrity, have never been seriously disputed. The key figures mentioned in the letter, are Paul, his Christian friend Philemon, and Philemon's slave, Onesimus, who has been with Paul for some time and whom Paul is now sending back to Philemon. Although Timothy is named as cosender or coauthor of the letter, Paul writes consistently in the first person singular, and the letter has the flavor of being written directly by Paul to Philemon. Apphia and Archippus are named in the address but, again, Paul apparently speaks primarily to Philemon, as the singular pronouns and direct address elsewhere suggest. Later the letter refers to Paul's fellow prisoner Epaphras and to fellow workers Mark, Aristarchus, Demas, and Luke (vv. 23-24). Hence, while on one level the letter is from Paul to Philemon, a host of witnesses are implicated in the events referred to and requests made in this short epistle.

The letter apparently accompanies Onesimus, whom Paul is sending back to his owner with a specific request. Beyond that simple fact, virtually every aspect of the letter's occasion and content have been debated, including its specific historical occasion, the actual substance of Paul's request to Philemon, and the ramifications of Paul's request for Christian attitudes to slavery. Indeed, these are integrally related. Has Onesimus run away from Philemon? If so, does Paul send Onesimus back, knowing that as a runaway slave Onesimus ought to be punished, but asking Philemon to spare Onesimus such a fate? Does Paul go further and ask Philemon to manumit his slave, as v. 16 ("no longer as a slave") might suggest? If so, are there implications for how Paul regards the institution of slavery generally, or is the request for manumission limited to this one occasion? If Paul does not ask Philemon to set Onesimus free, what would he have said to those slaves who sought their freedom on the Underground Railroad to the north and to those who aided them on the way? Indeed, during the struggle for the abolition of the slave trade and slavery in the eighteenth and nineteenth centuries, Paul's letter to Philemon was viewed as sanctioning slavery: after all, the great apostle returned a runaway slave to his master. But a closer look at the historical context of the letter may suggest that matters are somewhat more complicated.

The Occasion for the Letter

The "traditional" interpretation of the occasion for the letter — traditional in that it is found as early as John Chrysostom in the fourth century and has shaped most interpretation of Philemon for centuries — has Paul arguing from a position of weakness, or at least puts Paul in a delicate situation with respect to Philemon.[1] On this view, Onesimus is the slave of Philemon, a Christian probably living in Colossae and a friend of Paul's. Indeed, Philemon became a believer in Christ initially through Paul's ministry. Onesimus has run away from his master and made his way to Paul, who is in prison, although the location of Paul's imprisonment is disputed. Paul now finds himself in the delicate situation of harboring a *fugitivus,* a Latin technical term for a runaway slave (the Greek equivalent is *phygas* or *drapetēs*). Out of legal obligation, he must send Onesimus back to Philemon.[2]

Moreover, the traditional interpretation reads Paul's statement in v. 18 — "If he has wronged you in any way, or owes you anything, charge that to my account" — as suggesting that Onesimus has done something specific to compound the offense of running away, the usual suspicion being that Onesimus has stolen from his master. So Paul offers to repay what Onesimus has taken. Using some subtle rhetoric and appealing to their friendship and relationship in Christ, Paul asks that Philemon welcome Onesimus back into his household without punishment and indeed as a brother in Christ. Such a request may further imply that Paul hopes that Philemon will grant Onesimus his freedom.

There are a number of problems with this traditional interpretation.

---

1. Commentators who continue to hold this view include Stuhlmacher, *Der Brief an Philemon,* and O'Brien, *Colossians and Philemon.*

2. Justinian's *Digest* cites the third-century Roman jurist Ulpian: "Any person whatsoever who apprehends a runaway slave has an obligation to produce him in public" (*Digest* 11.4.1, from Ulpian, *On the Edict* 1; printed in Wiedemann, *Greek and Roman Slavery,* 190).

For example, if Onesimus has indeed stolen from or defrauded Philemon and then also run away, why has he deliberately sought out his master's good friend? Onesimus would have ample opportunities to hide himself from public view rather than risk capture and punishment by publicly seeking out the apostle Paul in a Roman prison. If Onesimus did not deliberately seek out Paul, then one must posit a chance meeting of the two — and in prison no less. That itself would be a great coincidence. But if Onesimus were a captured fugitive, he would in all likelihood not have been imprisoned in the same prison or under the same conditions as Paul. In short, the case that Onesimus, a fugitive slave, has sought and found Paul in prison, seems strained.

Especially since Paul was a Roman citizen, he might well have understood himself to be legally obligated to return Onesimus to Philemon, though if Philemon was not a citizen Paul might not in actuality been obligated to return Onesimus. Running away from one's master was a serious offense. As a fugitive, Onesimus could be punished by beating, being put in chains, branding, or execution; indeed, as a slave, he could be subject to these punishments by his master even if he were not a fugitive, although Roman law regulated the kind and extent of punishment that slave owners could deal out.[3] And while Paul offers to repay Philemon for any wrong that Onesimus has done, this seems to refer to something other than actually running away, which implies that running away was not Onesimus's primary offense. Notably missing from Paul's letter is any account of Onesimus's sorrow or repentance. Would Paul have sent Onesimus back, given the traditional scenario, without either eliciting or referring to Onesimus's regret?

Other scenarios which have Paul playing the role of mediator and arguing from a position of strength have been offered as alternatives. For example, it has been suggested that Onesimus has a grievance with Philemon, most likely having to do with the conditions of his service. Ancient sources attest that slaves could run to shrines for asylum, hoping perhaps to gain a new master in the person of the deity of the shrine, or perhaps to be sold to someone who would treat them more favorably. But if Philemon has mistreated Onesimus — one of the common reasons for slaves to run away — Paul makes no comment on this matter.[4] He does not ask Philemon to be less harsh in his treatment of Onesimus, a request that might be easy enough

---

3. See the texts collected in Wiedemann, *Greek and Roman Slavery*, 167-87.

4. Felder, "Philemon," 887, argues that there is greater warrant for assuming that Philemon had in some way abused his slave than for viewing Onesimus as a lazy or dishonest servant. The latter represents the "traditional view" and has a vested interest in "protecting" the master rather than the slave.

to make without offending Philemon. Elsewhere in his letters, Paul admonishes slave owners not to mistreat their slaves, as in Colossians, which is thought to have been sent at the same time as Philemon to the same church: "Masters, treat your slaves justly and fairly, for you know that you also have a Master in heaven" (4:1; similarly, Eph 6:9; cf. 1 Tim 6:1-2; Tit 2:9-10). In making such an appeal, Paul would be following the exhortations of the OT which, while not abolishing slavery, nevertheless expected slaves to be treated fairly because the Israelites had been slaves in Egypt (e.g., Exod 20:1-2; Lev 25:42-46; Deut 15:15).

But here Paul gives no such instructions to Philemon. Would he have been reticent to correct Philemon? Perhaps Paul hopes Philemon will simply "overhear" the letter to the Colossians with its instructions not to treat slaves harshly. Yet Paul wants Philemon to welcome Onesimus back, not as a slave, but as a brother beloved in Christ. Paul acknowledges that the wrong — if indeed wrong there be — lies primarily with Onesimus. Some have thought that it was not stealing, as in the traditional view, but some sort of mismanagement or error on Onesimus's part in handling some financial transaction on behalf of Philemon, thus arousing Philemon's anger. As was allowed under the laws of the time, Onesimus turns to Paul to mediate the conflict so that he can return to Philemon under more favorable conditions.[5] Often cited in this regard is a letter of Pliny the Younger to Sabinianus regarding a runaway slave:

> To Sabinianus. Your freedman, whom you lately mentioned as having displeased you, has been with me; he threw himself at my feet and clung there with as much submission as he could have done at yours. He earnestly requested me with many tears, and even with the eloquence of silent sorrow, to intercede for him; in short, he convinced me by his whole behavior that he sincerely repents of his fault.[6]

The letter goes on with a plea that Sabinianus, though rightfully angry, should forgive his freedman. Moreover, Pliny notes that he wants to request rather than compel Sabinianus to forgive the freedman. This letter affords many other striking similarities in both content and rhetorical strategy to Paul's letter to Philemon and provides a plausible parallel to the situation of Paul's letter.

Another ancient document that may argue that Onesimus was not a fugitive is found in the *Digest* of Justinian (21.1.17.4), which quotes the opinion

---

5. See, for example, the argument of Bartchy, "Philemon," 307.
6. Pliny the Younger, *Letters* 9.21.

of Proculus, a first-century Roman jurist, about a runaway slave who, while seeking an opportunity to escape, nevertheless remained hidden at home.

> Although he could not yet be seen to have run away, being still at home, he was nonetheless a fugitive; but if he had hidden only until his master's anger abated, he would not be a fugitive, just as the one who, when he realized that his master wanted to whip him, betook himself to a friend whom he induced to intercede for him.

Did Onesimus seek out Paul as a friend to "intercede for him"? If so, his goal was not to run away but to seek help in order to return to his master under better circumstances. Paul admits Onesimus's error. This may be a tactical move on Paul's part to strengthen his case with Philemon, but if in the wrong, Onesimus needed a powerful advocate, a friend to plead his case, with his master. Paul steps in to fill this role.

Both these approaches to the epistle assume that Onesimus has left his master and that Paul endeavors to reconcile the two, now on the ground of their common relationship in Christ. More difficult to determine are Onesimus's precise "status" — was he a hunted fugitive? — and whether the fault lay chiefly with Philemon or with his slave.[7] Paul comes to the defense of the vulnerable Onesimus who, as a slave who has apparently done something amiss, requires such protection. Paul follows his Lord's example of self-giving love and identification with the weak and helpless, regardless of their guilt, or perhaps precisely because of it! Who is to blame or who is at fault is not a primary concern for Paul: what matters is that the gospel can reconcile those at odds with each other, even if one has a rightful claim against the other.[8] As Cain Hope Felder states it, "the central meaning and purpose of the Letter to Philemon concern the difference the transforming power of the gospel can make in the lives and relationships of believers, regardless of class or other distinctions."[9]

---

7. Felder, "Philemon," 885-86, objects to readings that simply assume that the slave is at fault rather than the master. If the fault lies primarily with Philemon, then Paul's rhetoric is somewhat ironic: he speaks of Onesimus's wrongdoing in order to hold a mirror up to Philemon's face so that he will see the error of his own ways.

8. Allen Callahan has argued that Philemon and Onesimus were in fact blood brothers, whom Paul is seeking to reconcile; Paul wants Philemon to welcome Onesimus now as a "beloved brother," with emphasis falling on the adjective — *beloved* (v. 16). But primarily because it fails to account for the contrast in the same verse between "brother" and "slave," this view has not won wide acceptance; see Callahan's "Paul's Epistle to Philemon" and *Embassy of Onesimus: The Letter of Paul to Philemon*.

9. Felder, "Philemon," 885.

When and where did Paul write this letter? Three options have been suggested: (1) the mid-50s, during an assumed imprisonment in Ephesus (1 Cor 15:32; 2 Cor 1:8-9; 6:5; 11:23-24); (2) the late 50s, from Caesarea Maritima, as Paul was awaiting transport to Caesar (Acts 23:35; 24:26-27); or (3) the early 60s, while Paul was under house arrest in Rome (Acts 28:16, 30). The chief argument in favor of Ephesus is its proximity to Colossae, providing a realistic time frame for Onesimus's journey there and the exchange of letters. But neither Acts nor the epistles of Paul refer to an imprisonment in Ephesus. In favor of Rome is the traditional placement of the "prison epistles" (Ephesians, Colossians, and Philippians) in Rome, since Philemon and Colossians are closely connected to each other.[10] But could Onesimus really have found his way not merely to Rome but to Paul in prison in Rome? If Paul were under house arrest, then this scenario seems at least more likely than that Onesimus should have made his way to Caesarea and landed in prison there alongside Paul. In the end the issue is likely insoluble.

The Purpose of the Letter

Without doubt the most pressing theological issue raised by the epistle to Philemon for modern readers, although likely not for ancient readers, is that of the relationship of the gospel to slavery. Exactly what Paul wished to say concerning slavery, or what implications may legitimately be drawn from what he does not say, has occasioned no little debate. Paul issues no ultimatum to Philemon, or elsewhere in his epistles, regarding the evils of the institution of slavery. In fact, although Paul writes in Col 3:11 that "there is no longer Greek and Jew, circumcised and uncircumcised, barbarian, Scythian, slave, and free; but Christ is all and in all" (cf. Gal 3:28), he goes on to say, a few lines later, that slaves are to obey their earthly masters in all things (3:22). Hence, it is not surprising that Paul's approach is viewed as cautious and even reactionary: the status quo that Paul takes away with one hand he apparently gives back with the other. Thus his admonitions to slaves to obey their masters fit squarely with his counsel to slaves to "remain as they are," since "whoever was called in the Lord as a slave is a freed person belonging to the Lord" (1 Cor 7:21-24). Similarly, the "household codes" of Colossians and other later Pauline letters (Col 3:22-23; 4:1; Eph 6:5-9; cf. 1 Tim 6:1-2; Tit 2:9-10) assume

---

10. Fitzmyer, *Philemon*, 122, thinks that Colossians was written about fifteen years after this letter. Col 4:9 speaks of Onesimus as Paul's coworker, implying a different situation than that which underlies the writing of Philemon.

that slaves remain slaves. Whatever, then, it means to be united in Christ, it apparently does not change the basic social situation of master and slave. When construed in this way, at least part of the purpose of Paul's letter to Philemon is to ensure the maintenance of the social order, cementing the superior position of masters and the obedience of slaves. By implication, then, Paul can be taken as providing apostolic approval to slavery in general.

But this reading of Philemon assumes that Paul's primary purposes are to return Onesimus to Philemon and to do so in a way that preserves the status quo and does not rock the boat. Whatever Onesimus's wrong, Paul will make it good so that Onesimus can go back to his master. On this reading, Paul thus validates and sustains the hierarchical order. But Paul's purpose in writing this short epistle was not to ensure that a slave could go back to his master but that a Christian in a vulnerable position would be treated as a brother in Christ by a fellow Christian. Such treatment follows not Roman law or social convention but the demands of Christian conduct. In other words, Paul's writes primarily to effect reconciliation between Philemon and Onesimus, not as master and slave but as brothers in the Lord.[11] Indeed, Paul never speaks of Philemon as the "master" *(kyrios)* of Onesimus, using the term only for the risen Christ who is "Lord of all, of Paul, of Philemon, of Onesimus, and of all the others mentioned by name in the letter."[12] Paul did not seek to restore the relationship between Philemon and Onesimus to its previous footing but to redefine their relationship on the entirely new footing of the gospel. He does not, therefore, send Onesimus, the slave, back to Philemon, the master; he sends one brother in Christ to another so that they can acknowledge each other as such. The key words that are to shape their relationship are not master and slave but brother, fellowship (partnership), and love (vv. 16-17). Paul is not playing word games here. It is only because modern understanding of Christian community and love has been so cheapened that we fail to see the dramatically new way that Paul calls Philemon to relate to Onesimus. As is apparent from his letters, including this short epistle, Paul believes that belonging to Christ entails belonging also to all those in Christ and that such belonging radically changes how one regards and treats another, especially how the strong and those in positions of power treat the weak and powerless.

Whereas some interpreters view this epistle as a private communication seeking to urge Philemon to a particular course of conduct with respect to Onesimus, other interpreters have suggested that Paul's designs encompass

---

11. See especially Felder, "Philemon," 885-86; Wall, *Colossians*, 184; Wright, *Colossians*, 166-70.

12. Fitzmyer, *Philemon*, 38.

the Christian community as well.[13] That is, Paul is concerned not merely with the relationship between Philemon and Onesimus but also with the health of this particular Christian congregation. Derrett, for example, thinks that in light of Onesimus's conversion, Paul intends to address the question of a Christian slave's position in a Christian congregation. Wall suggests that Paul may hope to use his superior position to help Onesimus's standing in the congregation that meets in Philemon's home. Winter argues that although the letter is formally addressed to Philemon as the overseer of the congregation in Colossae, it is in fact intended for the entire church. All these studies rightly stress that for Paul Christian conduct is not a private and individualistic matter, but is lived in relationship to others, in social networks, and in conscious awareness that one belonging to Christ the Lord consequently and necessarily belongs to fellow believers in the Lord. Moreover, these studies note that certain features of the letter, such as the naming of Timothy as cosender, the multiple addressees, and the reference to other coworkers at the close, suggest that others are, minimally, "overhearing" the conversation between Paul and Philemon. As Petersen notes, when Onesimus is welcomed back to the household of Philemon, he will now also be welcomed into the fellowship of the Christian household as a brother in Christ, and this sociological fact places pressure on Philemon.[14] Petersen writes, "If Onesimus is a brother and Philemon refuses to acknowledge him as such, Philemon will be the one who is not acting like a brother. Thus the community, if it is to be consistent with its social structure and its social system, will have no choice but to expel Philemon in order to preserve the brotherhood." Petersen's speculation provocatively raises the question how the congregation would have understood and responded to Onesimus's presence among them as a "brother" and what they would expect from Philemon in responding to the return of Onesimus "no longer as a slave, but as a beloved brother."

Authorship and Canonicity

Paul's authorship of Philemon was not disputed in the early church and, consequently, neither was its canonical status, even by otherwise unorthodox thinkers such as Marcion. Tertullian, for example, notes, "The brevity of this

---

13. See, for example, Barclay, "The Dilemma of Christian Slave-Ownership"; Derrett, "Functions of Philemon"; Petersen, *Rediscovering Paul*, especially 89-109; Wall, *Colossians*, 184-86; Winter, "Paul's Letter to Philemon."

14. Petersen, *Rediscovering Paul*, 99.

Epistle is the sole cause of its escaping the falsifying hands of Marcion" (*Against Marcion* 5.21). Tertullian adds: "I wonder, however, when he received [into his *Apostolicon*] this letter which was written but to one man, that he rejected the two epistles to Timothy and the one to Titus, which all treat of ecclesiastical discipline." A similar and curious note can be found in the *Muratorian Fragment* (from Rome, ca. 150): "But he [wrote] one [letter] to Philemon and one to Titus, but two to Timothy for the sake of affection and love. In honor of the General Church, however, they have been sanctified by an ordination of the ecclesiastical discipline." If the comment regarding the acceptance of these epistles to individuals refers not merely to Titus and 1 and 2 Timothy, the so-called "pastoral" epistles among the general epistles, but also to Philemon, then Philemon was understood to have ramifications for "ecclesiastical discipline." In other words, while the letter was designed to deal initially with a specific issue, its acceptance into the canon entails and grants it a wider authority for "ecclesiastical discipline."

Still, as Paul himself attests, he wrote more letters than we have today in our canon (see 1 Cor 5:9; 2 Cor 2:4; Col 4:16). If these letters were inadvertently lost or deliberately discarded, why was Philemon spared a similar fate? Jerome's preface to his commentary on Philemon defends the epistle against charges that its relatively trivial content speaks against its inspiration and inclusion in the canon, but this does not help us understand why the letter was preserved in the first place. Some commentators, including John Knox and Peter Stuhlmacher, have argued that some personal authority beyond that of Paul's must have guaranteed the letter's inclusion in the canon, and that this was the authority of Onesimus himself.[15]

However that may be, ancient and modern discussion of Philemon's place in the canon point to its peculiar character as a personal letter to an individual recipient. The matter is resolved somewhat by arguing that the epistle is directed not to an individual — Philemon — but to the church in Philemon's house. What Paul says, he says to Philemon and to Philemon's church. But just there a problem remains, for it is not entirely clear what Paul does say regarding the manumission of Onesimus. Christians continued to have slaves. In his epistle to Polycarp, Ignatius writes, "Do not despise either male or female slaves, yet neither let them be puffed up with conceit, but rather let them submit themselves the more, for the glory of God, that they may obtain from God a better liberty. Let them not long to be set free [from

---

15. Knox, *Philemon*, 79; Stuhlmacher, *An Philemon*, pp. 18-19. Knox thinks that Onesimus is the same person as the Onesimus who was later bishop of Ephesus (Ignatius, *Ephesians* 1:3; 2:1; 6:2). Stuhlmacher allows the possibility that Christian tradition made the connection early on.

slavery] at the public expense, that they be not found slaves to their own desires" (*Polycarp* 4.3). In his *Apology* (15.4), Aristides argues that Christians treat slaves as they do all fellow Christians. In his *Plea for the Christians* Athenagoras comments in passing, "And yet we have slaves, some more and some fewer," taking for granted that Christians have slaves. If Philemon were a blanket condemnation of slavery or urged manumission for all slaves, then early Christians either ignored or rejected it. But Aristides also notes that Christian slave owners endeavored to persuade their slaves to become Christians and treated those who did convert as "brothers." If read in this light, Philemon may well have been understood to speak with apostolic authority regarding the treatment of a slave who had become a Christian. They were to be treated not just with kindness and fairness — though that too — but as Paul asks Philemon to treat Onesimus: "no longer as a slave, but as a beloved brother." What that might mean remained susceptible to various interpretations, as indeed did Philemon itself.

Slavery in the Ancient Roman World

Finally, then, we may offer a few introductory remarks about slavery in the Roman Empire.[16] Slavery was widespread, though estimates about the number of slaves are mostly speculative. Slaves were mostly foreigners, and significant numbers were prisoners of wars, although kidnapping and piracy — even though illegal — also swelled the ranks of slaves. Because of these origins, slaves often shared common ethnic or tribal backgrounds. But slave owners were advised to keep ethnic groups separated to prevent their banding together in rebellion against their masters. Slaves were widely regarded as inferior on virtually every level, and comparisons between freeborn citizens and slaves show a disdain for those unfortunately consigned to slavery.

But the economic conditions experienced by slaves could vary widely. Those who worked the mines experienced horrific conditions, and were constantly threatened by premature death. Agricultural slaves were deemed to belong to a lower stratum of slaves, whereas household slaves enjoyed much more pleasant conditions. But slaves were still slaves. In his collection of texts pertinent to slavery in the classical Greek and Roman worlds, Thomas Wiedemann writes, "At Rome in particular . . . slavery is clearly presented as a state of absolute subjection. The slave has no kin, he cannot assume the rights

---

16. A good introduction to slavery in the ancient world can be found in Bartchy, "Slavery, New Testament," in *ABD* 6:65-73.

and obligations of marriage; his very identity is imposed by the owner who gives him his name."[17] But because slaves were human, there were legal limits on the kinds of punishment and treatment that a master could give a slave. In addition, a master could be expected to exercise restraint in his behavior, controlling outbursts of anger rather than venting them on his slaves. The famous case of Vedius, who ordered his slave thrown into a pool of lampreys as punishment for breaking a cup while Vedius was entertaining Augustus, illustrates the theoretical rights of the owner. The emperor saved the man's life, ordered him freed, and exhorted Vedius against indulging his moods and anger. Although Augustus found Vedius's act horrific, in theory it seems Vedius had the authority to do as he did.[18] A master could, for example, allow a slave who was to serve as a witness to a crime to be tortured.

A slave who was regularly subject to mistreatment had little recourse, except to run away, and the evidence indicates that this occurred rather regularly. Not only does the ancient literature refer to fugitive slaves, but there were laws regarding the treatment and punishment of runaways. A repeat offender could be branded on the face, although later such a slave was instead forced to wear a metal collar identifying him as a possible fugitive. The literature also suggests that sexual abuse was rather widespread.

Manumission was possible and expected under certain circumstances. Often a master manumitted his slaves in his will upon his death, although a master could also order that a slave who was regarded as disobedient or insolent never be set free. A slave could buy his own release, although this was more feasible and common for household slaves than for agricultural slaves. Even when freed, former slaves remained in a dependent state, owing their patrons deference and obedience. In turn, former owners maintained certain rights to extracting financial benefit from their former slaves. Those who had been freed never attained to all the rights of those born free. The legal regulations for slaves, freed slaves, and freeborn persons distinguished sharply between the rights accorded to each.

There is no significant discussion in the ancient literature, however, re-

---

17. Wiedemann, *Greek and Roman Slavery,* 1. In his influential monograph *Slavery as Salvation,* Dale Martin argued that it did not matter so much that one was a slave but rather whose slave one was. He argued that managerial slaves had opportunities for upward social mobility, while nevertheless remaining slaves. Martin also argued that some voluntarily chose slavery precisely for opportunities of upward mobility. For a different construction of the evidence that challenges Martin's conclusions, see Byron, *Slavery Metaphors.* Harrill, *The Manumission of Slaves in Early Christianity,* doubts that "slave" could be considered "an honorific badge of leadership" (9, n. 11).

18. Cf. Wiedemann, *Greek and Roman Slavery,* 175-76.

garding the institution of slavery as a whole, or arguments for the manumission of all slaves. Slavery was economically advantageous to the landowners and freeborn and justified by philosophers on the basis of the supposed moral and intellectual inferiority of slaves. Exceptions tended only to prove the rule. Slavery was a staple fixture of the ancient landscape. Not surprisingly, there were slaves in the early Christian movement. Onesimus was one. Paul's letter to Philemon, however, regards Onesimus not first as a slave, but as a brother in Christ. Paul expects Philemon to regard Onesimus in the same way, thereby transforming their relationship.

Commentary on Philemon

1-3

1 Paul, a prisoner of Christ Jesus, and Timothy our brother,

To Philemon our dear friend and coworker, 2 to Apphia our sister, to Archippus our fellow soldier, and to the church in your house: 3 Grace to you and peace from God our Father and the Lord Jesus Christ.

Like their modern counterparts, ancient letters had specific forms for their salutations and closings. The greetings with which ancient letters began were often quite brief, identifying the letter's author and recipients and including a single word of greeting; for example, "Simon, to his sister Mary: Greeting." Sometimes both the authors and recipients were described, perhaps indicating the relationship of the author and recipient (e.g., "to his sister"). In the NT, these descriptions often give us further information about the author or addressees, about the author's purpose for writing, or about the theological themes of the letter.

Except in 1 and 2 Thessalonians, Paul most typically elaborates his greetings with one of two terms, either "apostle" or "slave" (*doulos,* also translated "servant") of Christ Jesus. Paul uses "apostle" most frequently when reminding his readers of his commission and authorization from the Lord to preach the gospel, as when there is a particular problem in the church or when he wishes to remind his readers of the task given him by the Lord (1 and 2 Corinthians, Galatians, Colossians, Ephesians, and 1 and 2 Timothy). In Philippians, a letter written to a church with whom he obviously has very cordial relationships, Paul identifies himself not by his commission as an apostle, but rather as a slave of Christ Jesus. In Romans he refers to himself as both slave and apostle of Christ Jesus, while in Titus he identifies himself as a slave of God and an apostle of Christ Jesus.

Philemon stands out from all these epistles, for here Paul designates himself as "a prisoner of Christ Jesus," as he does again twice in the letter, once including Epaphras in the designation (9, 23). To be sure, Paul does refer to himself in other letters in this manner (Eph 3:1; 4:1; Col 4:10; 2 Tim 1:8), but not in the initial greetings. This threefold reference to himself as a "prisoner" in such a brief letter, particularly in the opening greeting, calls attention to itself. Since in this letter Paul will make a very specific request regarding the treatment of Onesimus, Philemon's slave, one might expect Paul to refer to himself either as an apostle, thereby indicating the grounds on which he could issue his request (cf. v. 8), or as a slave, thereby identifying himself closely with Onesimus. But both descriptions are lacking in the greeting and in the rest of the letter as well. The absence of "apostle" may well reflect the fact that Paul had not personally founded the church at Colossae (Col 1:3-8) or that he does not wish to persuade Philemon by his authoritative status (v. 8).

What rhetorical effect might Paul's description of himself as a "prisoner" have? Obviously, at its simplest, the designation conveys some information regarding Paul's situation. He poignantly refers to it later, when he speaks of his longing to keep Onesimus with him while he is "in chains" (vv. 10, 13). Perhaps he is also subtly alluding to the fact that Onesimus himself might be imprisoned if Philemon does not accept his return or respond favorably to Paul's appeal on his behalf. Paul introduces a theme "on which he will play several times in the letter, no doubt because of its emotive and persuasive power."[1] In fact, in identifying himself as a prisoner, Paul underscores the vulnerable situation he is in, suggesting solidarity with the suppliant slave Onesimus. Slaves could be punished by their masters and put "in chains."[2]

Undoubtedly, then, Paul mentions his own situation in the hope of winning a sympathetic hearing for Onesimus by willingly identifying with the slave's potential predicament. Paul thus not only conveys the facts about his situation but appeals to Philemon's sympathies as a Christian brother. Paul forgoes explicit appeal to his apostolic authority. Rather, he makes his appeal by alluding to his friendship with Philemon (vv. 7-9, 14, 17, 19, 20) and to his imprisonment (vv. 1, 9, 10, 13, 23). Paul's reticence to appeal to his apostolic

---

1. Dunn, *Colossians*, 311.

2. Gaius labels such treatment a "disgrace" and notes that slaves who have suffered such a disgrace can never be come Roman citizens. Gaius, *Institutes* 1.13 (second century AD). Justinian's *Digest* quotes Ulpian (early third century) as noting that guarding runaway slaves "may even include chaining them up."

authority may indicate the delicate position in which he finds himself caught between Philemon and Onesimus. He does not want to dictate the terms of Onesimus's return. After all, reconciliation between Christian friends should not be achieved through coercion. Still, Paul may well wish to make the subtle point that in some way Philemon is a "prisoner" as well — he may not simply do what he chooses, but is bound by the compulsion of Christian love (cf. 2 Cor 5:14: "the love of Christ controls us").

Although Paul is in prison and will later refer to Epaphras as a fellow prisoner (v. 23), Timothy apparently is not in prison. Perhaps he joined Paul after Paul went to prison. In 2 Timothy, for example, Paul summons Timothy to join him, urging him to bring Mark as well (4:9-11). Depending on the circumstances of their imprisonment, prisoners were often allowed to have friends or attendants visiting or assisting them.[3] As with Colossians, then, Paul wishes this letter to be read as coming from him and Timothy as well. It may be that Timothy served as the amanuensis, the scribe who actually wrote the letter down, especially if the statement in v. 19 that Paul is writing "with his own hand" refers only to that greeting rather than to the whole letter (cf. Col 4:18). Even so, the rest of the letter uses the first person singular ("I") rather than plural ("we"), indicating the peculiarly personal character of Paul's appeal here to Philemon.

While this letter is addressed first to Philemon, several others are included in the greeting: Apphia, Archippus, and "the church in your house."[4] Philemon is further identified as a dear friend and coworker. "Dear friend," usually translated "beloved," occurs sometimes in Paul's letters as a form of address (Rom 12:19; 1 Cor 10:14; 15:58; 2 Cor 7:1) or in a phrase such as "beloved of God" (Rom 1:7), "beloved fellow servant" (Col 1:7), or "beloved brother" (Col 4:7), or as an adjective describing a person ("my beloved Epaenetus," Rom 16:5; cf. Rom 16:8, 9, 12; 1 Cor 4:14, 17; Eph 6:21, etc.). Standing alone without a possessive pronoun or noun, "beloved" is rather unusual; the translation "dear friend" tries to capture its nuance. In Colossians, Paul also uses "beloved" of

3. For details of imprisonment in Paul's day, see Brian Rapske, *The Book of Acts and Paul in Roman Custody.*

4. There is some debate regarding the intended addressees of the letter. Bruce, *Colossians,* 206-7, and O'Brien, *Colossians,* 273, argue that while others are greeted by Paul, they are in no sense included among the addressees; the letter is a private letter from Paul to Philemon. Given the sensitive nature of the matter, and the extreme tact Paul exercises in writing the letter, Bruce and O'Brien find it impossible to conceive of the epistle as intended to be read in public before the assembly of believers. Others, including Dunn, *Colossians,* 313; Lohse, *Colossians,* 190, and Fitzmyer, *Philemon,* 35, argue that the letter is indeed intended for the whole church, as the address indicates.

Epaphras (1:7), Tychicus (4:7), Luke (4:14) — and Onesimus (4:9). Paul further speaks of Philemon as a "coworker," a word used later in Philemon of Mark, Demas, Aristarchus, and Luke (v. 24), in Colossians of Justus and Mark (4:10-11), in Romans of a number of people (16:3, 9, 21), in Philippians (2:25; 4:3), and of Titus in 2 Cor 8:2-3. Many of the individuals named here were traveling companions of Paul's or served with him in his missionary endeavors in some distinctive way. Like Paul himself, however, these "coworkers" also worked at various occupations and were not what we would call "fulltime" Christian workers. Indeed, Paul can also use the term "coworkers" to designate individual Christians more broadly (2 Cor 1:24), as he considers them all to be working in the service of the gospel, whether or not they are called to specific roles like Paul, Apollos, Peter, and others.

Some scholars have speculated that Philemon was likely a rather well-to-do merchant who traveled on business ventures. He apparently had a house large enough to serve as the meeting place of a house church, usually estimated to average about thirty to fifty people. As a slave owner, he was a man of some means. That Onesimus is addressed as "one of you" in Col 4:9 means that Philemon probably lived in Colossae. But Paul had apparently never visited the church there. Paul and Philemon must then have met somewhere else, perhaps even in the course of some business ventures. During such an encounter, Paul may well have persuaded Philemon to become a Christian; and Paul is thus Philemon's "patron" (Philemon 19). Obviously, such a reconstruction is somewhat speculative, but it would fit with the data from the letters of Paul as well as with what we know of ancient travel and trading practices. It is not too fanciful to imagine Paul speaking of the good news of the gospel to various merchants with whom he came in contact on the course of his own travels or in conducting business. This scenario suggests that the gospel spread along the channels of ordinary daily commerce and communication rather than through more formalized means. Christians in their workshops, homes, and marketplace and on the road were the primary means of spreading the good news.

"Apphia" is designated "sister." She is usually assumed to be Philemon's wife, in which case "sister" refers to her status as a sister in Christ. From other Pauline letters, we know of married couples who served with Paul in various ways in the work of the gospel; most notable are Priscilla and Aquila (Rom 16:3-5; 1 Cor 16:19). If Onesimus was a household slave, then his departure from the household will also have affected her. It is also possible that Apphia is Philemon's sister, perhaps an unmarried or widowed woman living under his roof. For that matter, she could be his daughter or mother; as a "sister" she is a member of the household of faith. Although, as already indicated, some authors dispute that the letter was sent to anyone but Philemon, Theodore of Mopsuestia (fourth century) noted, "Paul makes a point of greeting Philemon and Apphia equally. He wishes to indicate thereby that in no way is there a difference of faith or strength of faith between men and women."[5]

On the assumption that Philemon and Apphia are husband and wife, Archippus is sometimes identified as their son, an assumption wryly characterized by J. L. Houlden as "an instance of legend active when history fails."[6] Other early commentators thought of Archippus as "one of the clergy" (Chrysostom, fourth century), the bishop of the church at Colossae (Jerome), and a deacon of the church (Pelagius).[7] Archippus is surely the one to whom is given the cryptic instruction "See that you complete the task that you have received in the Lord" (Col 4:17). Paul's further reference to him as "our fellow soldier," a term used for Epaphroditus in Phil 2:25, suggests a joint effort in the service of the gospel. So Archippus was apparently a coworker of Paul with some responsibility in the affairs of the house church in view here.

Because the letter is addressed to Philemon, with greetings to Apphia and Archippus, the pronoun "your" in "the church in your house" is singular. As the first-named addressee, he is the principal recipient of the letter and thus both the one most likely addressed in subsequent direct appeals in the letter and, though "Archippus" is the nearest possible antecedent, the one in whose house the church met. Moreover, if he was Apphia's husband and Archippus's father, then he was *paterfamilias,* the head of the household. A similar reference in Col 4:15 to "Nympha and the church in her house" attributes to her the same position here assigned to Philemon.

Paul's word for "church," *ekklēsia*/ἐκκλησία, can also be translated "assembly." It is one of the words used by translators of the Septuagint to translate *qāhāl,* "assembly," in the phrase "assembly of the Lord" *(qāhāl Yahweh),* along with *synagōgē* ("synagogue"), but Paul does not use *synagōgē* of the Christian assembly. His use of *ekklēsia* surely implies continuity with the "assembly of Yahweh." He does not intend to usurp the term but to place the church in direct continuity with God's people Israel. "Paul intended to depict

---

5. *ACCSNT* 9:311.

6. Houlden, *Paul's Letters from Prison,* 228. John Knox (followed more recently by Sara Winter) argued that Archippus was actually Onesimus's owner; Paul wants Philemon, a leader in the congregation in Laodicea, to support his request that Archippus take Onesimus back. Onesimus himself carries the letter to Philemon to Laodicea (the "letter from Laodicea" referred to in Col 4:16) and Colossians to Archippus in Colossae.

7. *ACCSNT* 9.311. In his letter to the Ephesians, the early Christian bishop Ignatius refers to their bishop Onesimus (1:1), but there is nothing to indicate that this is the same Onesimus.

the little assemblies of Christian believers as equally manifestations of and in direct continuity with 'the assembly of Yahweh,' 'the assembly of Israel.'"[8]

We cannot dismiss the references to Apphia, Archippus, and the church meeting in Philemon's house as mere window dressing. In several ways, Apphia, and Archippus, and the church are also implicated in Paul's appeals, Philemon's response, and the outcome of Onesimus's situation. Chrysostom, for example, wrote, "Paul has not omitted even the slaves. For he knew that often even the words of slaves have power to turn around their master. This is especially true when his request was in behalf of a slave."[9] Chrysostom thus thought likely that Paul's letter was directed to the entire church, including those who were slaves, precisely in order to give the greatest occasion for input from the community.

Paul's personal address to Philemon in the context of the larger community flies in the face of the insistence on privacy that is so great a part of the fabric of Western societies and churches. Paul assumes — and apparently thinks that Philemon will share his assumption — that the church has the right and obligation to be concerned in the personal affairs of its members. Such an assumption indirectly exhibits Paul's understanding of the unity of the body of Christ, as well as the accountability which members have to each other. Granted, the church community in question is small, likely no more than fifty persons, scarcely approximating the numbers that some churches boast today. But the point remains that Christians conduct their affairs not only in the privacy of their own homes but in the context of the community of Christ and in view of the faith which its members share. Furthermore, in a very particular way, the power and truth of the gospel are at stake in this situation. Paul wrote in Colossians of God's reconciling work in Christ, which united "Greek and Jew, circumcised and uncircumcised, barbarian, Scythian, slave, and free" (3:11). If the existence of a church composed of Jew and Gentile bore testimony to the uniting and reconciling power of the gospel, then the reconciliation of a master and his slave certainly did so as well. As noted earlier, N. T. Wright thus refers to Philemon as a "test case" for the reconciling power of the gospel.[10]

Paul's greeting ("Grace to you and peace from God our Father and the Lord Jesus Christ") is typical; it or some variation is found at the head of each of his letters. Even Galatians, where Paul includes no words of thanksgiving such as were typical of ancient letters and most of Paul's as well, has this

---

8. Dunn, *Theology of Paul*, 538.
9. *ACCSNT* 9:311.
10. Wright, *Colossians*, 166.

opening benedictory formula. A typical greeting opening in Hellenistic letters was simply "greetings" (*chairein,* as in Jas 1:2). Similarly, the typical Jewish greeting was "peace" (Luke 24:36; John 20:21, 26). By slightly altering the Hellenistic "greetings" *(chairein)* to "grace" *(charis)* and combining it with the Jewish "peace," Paul produces his characteristic "grace and peace." But similar opening greetings are found in 1 and 2 Peter and 2 John.

Paul's greeting is essentially a blessing on the readers and a prayer to God: "May God our Father and the Lord Jesus Christ send you grace and peace." In asking that God send grace and peace on the church in Philemon's house, Paul acknowledges that God alone is the source of both. He also indirectly indicates those God-given gifts that will be called upon and tested: the grace of God that has called this church into being will be needed for Philemon, for Onesimus, and for Paul; and the peace of God that is given through Christ will be needed to maintain the bonds of unity.

4-7

4 I thank my God always when I remember you in my prayers, 5 because I hear of your love and faithfulness for the Lord Jesus and for all the saints. 6 I pray that the shared experience of your faith will produce understanding of every good thing that is ours to lead us to Christ. 7 I have indeed received much joy and encouragement from your love, dear brother, because the hearts of the saints have been refreshed through you.

Following the address and opening greetings, Paul includes, as was his custom, a prayer of thanksgiving. Paul speaks here in the first person singular, as he does at this point in other letters (Rom 1:8; 1 Cor 1:4; Phil 1:3). Philemon differs from Colossians, for although both designate Paul and Timothy as their senders, in Colossians the thanksgiving is expressed in the plural: "*We* give thanks . . . for *we* have heard" (Col 1:3). In light of Paul's frequent use of the first person singular in his other letters, one ought not overstate its significance here, though it does fit with the personal character of the letter. Paul speaks here not first as apostle to coworker (v. 1) or convert (v. 19), but as fellow Christian to fellow Christian, one friend to another (vv. 7, 9, 14, 20). And later on he will appeal to his role in bringing Philemon to faith (v. 19). He also insinuates more than once that he could appeal to his apostolic authority (vv. 8-9, 21), and this would characterize him in a way that it did not characterize Timothy. Yet no other letter of Paul evidences the same sort of fraternal love as does Philemon. Perhaps the closest letter in tone — written, however, to a church rather than an individual — is Philippians, written to a congregation with whom Paul has warm bonds of friendship.

In introducing his letters with a prayer of thanksgiving, Paul is no innovator. Ancient letters often included a prayer of thanksgiving to gods or to a deity, offered up in gratitude for personal deliverance from peril, such as danger at sea or illness, or as a thanksgiving for the good health of the recipient. But just as Paul adapted the opening greeting of the ancient letter to serve his own ends, so too he regularly modified the thanksgiving and wish for good health, often by linking it with a commendation of the recipients.

A quick examination of Paul's opening thanksgivings reveals a regular pattern in their structure and content:

- I thank my God . . . because your faith is proclaimed . . . without ceasing I remember you always in my prayers. (Rom 1:8-9)
- I give thanks to my God always . . . because of the grace of God that has been given you. (1 Cor 1:4)
- I thank my God every time I remember you . . . because of your sharing in the gospel. (Phil 1:3-5)
- We always give thanks to God for all of you and mention you in our prayers, constantly remembering before our God and Father your work of faith and labor of love and steadfastness of hope in our Lord Jesus Christ. (1 Thess 1:2-3)

Paul's thanksgivings typically include a statement of his gratitude to God, a reference to his constant prayer on behalf of the recipients, and commendation of some specific aspect of the Christian faith of his addressees for which he is particularly grateful. Although Paul's pattern has become regular, it is not yet formulaic; he adapts it to the specific purposes and addressees of the letter.

In the commendation Paul often foreshadows some specific concerns that will surface in the letter or some virtue or habit for which he particularly gives thanks, so that the commendation and subsequent exhortations are often connected. For example, in Colossians Paul gives thanks for his readers' faith and love, and much of the letter is subsequently given over to exhortations to remain steadfast in faith and to a description of the shape of Christian love. To be sure, Paul's commendations tend to highlight virtues and graces such as love and faith that ought to be characteristic of all Christians, not just of those to whom he addresses the particular letter. But that in no way minimizes the sincerity or applicability of any particular commendation.

As in Colossians, Paul's thanksgiving to God for Philemon refers to his faith and love (v. 5). Translated rather literally, the Greek would read "I hear of your love and faith, which you have for the Lord Jesus and for all the saints."[1] This makes "the Lord Jesus" and "all the saints" joint objects of both love and faith (so RSV). But a number of interpreters doubt that Paul would have said this, inasmuch as it seems to make "saints" the object of "faith." Hence, they assume that what Paul did mean to say was that he had heard of Philemon's love for the saints and his faith in the Lord Jesus. Certain English translations reflect that assumption ("because I hear about your faith in the Lord Jesus and your love for all the saints," NIV; so also NRSV, TEV). Others propose that Paul was using a simple chiasm, an a-b-b-a pattern, where the first and last terms (love . . . saints) belong together, and the middle terms (faith . . . Lord Jesus) belong together.[2] Either reading may be strengthened by the fact that Paul uses different prepositions with each object, so that faith is directed *toward* the Lord Jesus, and love is intended *for* the saints. These suggestions mitigate the problem of having Paul speak of "faith" as directed toward fellow believers and bring Paul's thought more closely into line with the very similar sentiments expressed elsewhere (e.g., Col 1:4; 2 Thess 1:3).

But F. F. Bruce suggests that "faith" (*pistis*/πίστις) may have the nuance which it sometimes carries elsewhere in the letters of Paul, namely, faithfulness or "loyalty."[3] Philemon's Christian commitment includes his love for the Lord and the saints and his faithfulness to each, and it is precisely the interrelatedness of these commitments and graces which forms the basis for Paul's appeal to him. It is true, however, that when Paul offers a word of commendation to Philemon, he specifically mentions only Philemon's love, which has brought joy and encouragement to Paul and "refreshment to the saints." In writing to the Colossians, Paul also singles out the Christian grace of love as the epitome and heart of all Christian virtues (Col 1:8; 3:14), as he also does in a number of other epistles (Rom 13:9, 10; 1 Cor 13:4, 13; Gal 5:6). As Wright comments, "it is love that gives Paul the greatest encouragement, because it is the surest sign that Christ is being formed in his people."[4] In the short letter to Philemon, Paul will appeal, directly and indirectly, to the powerful bonds of Christian love as he seeks to reconcile Philemon and Onesimus.

---

1. This phrasing has suggested to some that Paul has never actually met Philemon, since his knowledge seems to come indirectly, via hearing, rather than through personal acquaintance or experience.

2. So Lohse, *Colossians,* 193; O'Brien, *Colossians,* 278; Wright, *Colossians,* 174-75.

3. Bruce, *Colossians,* 208. In fact, of the five uses of "faith" (*pistis*) in Colossians, three carry that sense (1:23; 2:5, 7). The relatively frequent characterization of the saints (Col 1:2) and of fellow workers as "faithful" (*pistos,* Col 1:7; 4:7, 9) is also noteworthy.

4. Wright, *Colossians,* 178.

Indeed, many of the themes sounded in this short opening thanksgiving are picked up in the letter, leaving the clear impression that Paul has carefully thought out what he wants to say to Philemon and knows which notes he wishes to sound most clearly. The following words or ideas in the thanksgiving are picked up in the rest of the epistle: "love" (vv. 5, 9), "fellowship" (vv. 6, 17), "good" (vv. 6, 14), "heart" (vv. 7, 12, 20), "refresh" (vv. 7, 20), and "brother" (vv. 7, 20). While the repetition of such basic words might not be noteworthy in a longer letter, it is striking in a short letter. The substance of this prayer shows that Paul's letter circles around the central theme of the Christian community bound together by mutual love and commitment. It is easy to read Paul as flattering and manipulating Philemon to get what he wants; the opening commendation borders on excess in the minds of some. But it is also clear from Paul's other letters that what he asks of Philemon is no less than what he expects of himself and all Christians — the concrete embodiment of the reconciling gospel of Christ. The situation addressed in the letter to Philemon is the practical test of Paul's vision of Christian relationships as grounded in love and mutual forgiveness (see, e.g., Col 3:12-17).

Paul's specific prayer and hope are stated in v. 6, which, unfortunately, is one of the most obscure verses in the epistle. As a result it is a bit unclear exactly what Paul is praying for. Virtually every word in this prayer can have several meanings, and every phrase is subject to different interpretations. The translation offered above, "I pray that the shared experience of your faith will produce understanding of every good thing that is ours to lead us to Christ," takes the verse to mean that the mutual participation of believers in the reality of Christian faith will lead to an understanding of all that Christians have received in Christ and that this will in turn lead believers to the goal of conformity to Jesus Christ. Although this general sense might be clear enough and, indeed, similar to sentiments expressed in other Pauline letters (e.g., Eph 4:12-13), it is of particular importance to understand the verse, if possible, because it lays a foundation for Paul's appeal to Philemon in the rest of the letter.

Perhaps the most troublesome question is the meaning of *koinōnia tēs pisteōs*/κοινωνία τῆς πίστεως, here rendered as "shared experience of your faith." One could also translate "fellowship of faith." The emphasis falls on that which is jointly and mutually shared — namely, the faith that is greater than and so unites those who share or fellowship in it. Here "faith" is not first the subjective reality of trust but that reality in which Christians participate and therefore also share or fellowship together. NIV's "sharing your faith," if taken to refer to the verbal "sharing" or communication of one's Christian commitment, misconstrues both the Greek and Paul's point. He is not speaking here of telling others about one's faith, but rather of being joined together by mutual participation in a greater reality, namely, the reality of Christ, which is appropriated through faith.[5]

Such mutual participation in the reality of Christian faith produces "understanding of every good thing that is ours." The thought is close to Paul's expansive statement urging the divided Corinthians not to cheat themselves of the rich blessings that are theirs, because "all things are yours . . . and you belong to Christ, and Christ belongs to God" (1 Cor 3:21, 23). Again, in speaking of the unity of believers in Christ, Paul writes to the Colossians that "Christ is all and in all" (Col 3:11). Participation in the blessings given in Christ leads to deeper understanding and experience of those blessings, and specifically to appreciation for the unity that belongs to those who have been reconciled in and by Christ. Such an appreciation leads to gratitude, as well as to conduct that reflects the generous and reconciling love of Christ.

Thus Paul writes that the experience and awareness of the blessings of faith are "to lead us to Christ" (literally "to Christ," *eis Christon*/εἰς Χριστόν). Christ is both the beginning and the end or goal of Christian life. Mutual participation in faith and increased awareness of the blessings one has in Christ are to lead the believer "to Christ," that is, toward full, mature life in Christ (Col 1:28; Eph 4:13). From and out of Christ and toward Christ: the movement of the Christian life always has Christ at its heart and center. In Colossians, the reality of being in Christ is spelled out in terms of participation in the cosmic reconciliation that God has effected through Christ, producing a body of believers who are being renewed in the image of Christ, where there is no Jew and Greek, no slave and free (3:11). Although there is no explicit reference in Philemon to the reconciliation effected through Christ to bring about the unity of believers in Christ, that reality underlies Paul's appeal regarding the slave Onesimus. Paul argues on the basis of Christ's reconciling work and assumes that his readers will get the point. He does not have to spell it out.

Christ's reconciliation and renewal of believers into the image of Christ also undergird Paul's prayer that participation in these realities will lead Philemon to yet fuller understanding of the blessings in Christ. This can only mean that Paul hopes and prays that Philemon will grow to appreciate ever more deeply the full unity that believers in Christ share with another. As a preface to the letter regarding the return of Philemon's slave, Onesimus, Paul prepares the way for his appeal that Philemon receive Onesimus back as a

---

5. The translation "liberality" or "generosity, which arises from your faith" offered by several commentators (Bruce, *Colossians*, 207-9; Harris, *Colossians*, 251; O'Brien, *Colossians*, 275, 280) takes *koinōnia* as that which is produced by faith rather than as the subjective participation in or experience of faith. On this point, see especially Dunn, *Colossians*, 319.

"beloved brother" (v. 16). Paul calls on Philemon to put his experience and understanding into practice by treating Onesimus as one who also shares in the reality of reconciliation and who has a share in the reconciling work of Christ. Philemon cannot deny to his slave what Christ has given to both.

8-16

8 Therefore, though I am bold enough in Christ to command you to do what you ought, 9 yet I would rather appeal to you on the basis of love. I, Paul, do this as an elderly man — and now also a prisoner of Christ. 10 I am appealing to you for my child, Onesimus, whose father I have become during my imprisonment. 11 Formerly he was useless to you, but now he is indeed useful both to you and to me. 12 I am sending him — my very heart — back to you. 13 I wanted to keep him with me, so that he might serve me on your behalf during my imprisonment for the gospel, 14 but I preferred to do nothing without your consent in order that the good you would do might be voluntary and not something forced. 15 Perhaps this is the reason he was separated from you for a while, so that you might have him back forever, 16 no longer as a slave but more than a slave, a beloved brother — especially to me but how much more to you, both in the flesh and in the Lord.

Here we have the body of Paul's letter to Philemon, in which Paul lays the groundwork for the actual appeals he will make in the closing section of the letter. Paul bases his appeal to Philemon on the bonds of love and interdependence which unite believers in the Lord. Not only does Paul draw upon the reality of this relationship in Christ in order to intercede with Philemon on behalf of Onesimus, but in making his appeal he implicitly explicates the profound character and depth of that love. He reveals what Christian love will dare to ask and the lengths to which it will go in seeking to make concrete the reconciliation which Christ effected by means of his death on the cross (see Col 1:20-23; 3:11). Paul's appeal depends on and draws on the varied relationships between Onesimus and Paul, Onesimus and Philemon, and Paul and Philemon, disclosing the common ground on which they stand in spite of the palpably different status of Philemon and Onesimus in Philemon's household. Here are master and slave, apostle and converted master, apostle and converted slave, yet all are brothers in Christ. While these various relationships overlap, Paul appeals to what these men share in Christ, not to the status that distinguishes them from each other. The mutuality and interdependence which exist among believers "in the Lord" provide the foundation for Paul's appeal and will lead to his closing requests to Philemon (vv. 17-21).

Paul's affection for Philemon is evident throughout the letter. Here, however, Paul takes particular pains to speak of his concern and love for Onesimus as well, referring to him as "my child" (v. 10) and "my very heart" (v. 12) and speaking of his reluctance to be parted from him (v. 13). This powerful and personal language is designed to win sympathy for Paul's appeal to Philemon on behalf of Onesimus. In the categories of classical rhetoric, Paul favors the appeal to *pathos*, which endeavors to put the hearer into a certain frame of mind — here, to win sympathy for Paul — rather than *ethos* (self-presentation that inspires confidence in the hearer) or *logos* (logical argumentation).[1] Paul's description of his relationship with Onesimus as that of a father to a son also indicates the particular way in which he and Onesimus have come to enjoy the connection which they now have; namely, Paul has been the means by which Onesimus has become a Christian. In several other places, Paul speaks of himself as a "father" to his converts. For example, he distinguishes his relationship to the Corinthians with the comment that "though you might have ten thousand guardians in Christ, you do not have many fathers. Indeed, in Christ Jesus I became your father through the gospel" (1 Cor 4:14-15; similarly 2 Cor 6:13; Gal 4:19; Phil 2:22). Onesimus, having left his master Philemon, found his way to his master's friend in prison and then became a Christian through Paul's ministry, even as Philemon had done before him. Although Paul does not explicitly say that he has become Philemon's "father," as he has become Onesimus's, at this point master and slave stand on common ground. Later Paul will appeal to this role in Philemon's life as part of his appeal to Philemon to welcome Onesimus into his household as a brother in Christ.

Paul next describes the service that Onesimus has rendered to him while in prison (vv. 11-13). Employing three different plays on words, Paul underscores the transformation that has occurred in Onesimus's life. First, playing on the very similar sounding terms "useless" (*achrēston*/ἄχρηστον) and "useful" (*euchrēston*/εὔχρηστον), Paul speaks of Onesimus's conversion as an event which, because it has made him a believer in Christ, has also made him "useful" with respect to both Philemon and Paul.[2] This adjective is used of Mark in

---

1. Aristotle, *Rhetoric* 1.2.3-6: "[*ethos*] depends on the personal character of the speaker; [*pathos*] on the putting the audience into a certain frame of mind; [*logos*] on the proof, or apparent proof, provided by the words of the speech itself." For discussion of the rhetorical patterns in Philemon, see Church, "Rhetorical Structure"; for a discussion of the classical categories of Aristotelian rhetoric and examples in the NT, see Kennedy, *New Testament Interpretation*.

2. In the *Shepherd*, Hermas (a former slave) makes a similar pun: when he was wealthy he was "not useful" *(achrēston)* to the Lord, but now that he has lost much of his wealth, he is "useful" *(euchrēston)* to the Lord; so also all Christians should be useful *(euchrēston)* to the Lord (*Vision* 3.6).

2 Timothy: "Get Mark and bring him with you, for he is very useful in serving me" (4:11). Here it may also denote the particular service which Onesimus has been able to offer the imprisoned Paul, making him "useful" to Paul.

Second, there is a further pun on Onesimus's name, which comes from the root of the verb *oninēmi*/ὀνίνημι, "bring profit or advantage (to someone)," that is, to be *useful* to someone. Paul will use this verb in appealing to Philemon to "let me *have some benefit* from you" (v. 20).[3] It was customary for slave owners to name or rename slaves whom they bought, so Philemon probably gave Onesimus his name. Slaves were sometimes named after their owners, the trader from whom they were purchased, after the place where they were bought, or in some other descriptive way. The prolific Roman author Varro (116-27 BC) refers to one slave named Artemas (after the trader Artemidorus), one called Ion (after Ionia), a third named Ephesius (bought at Ephesus), adding "So everyone calls his slave something different after different things, just as he likes."[4] Although Onesimus ("useful") was a typical slave's name, he has only recently begun to live up to the name, ironically only now that he is serving Paul and not his legal master.

Paul does not specify the particular way in which Onesimus has become "useful," but there is surely a twofold implication that Onesimus has become a personal solace and joy to Paul and that he has been of assistance to Paul with respect to his personal situation and also in the work of the gospel during his confinement. The slave who had departed Philemon's house and so branded himself as "useless" to Philemon had now become useful to him and to Paul by being able to offer service to Paul which Philemon himself would gladly have offered had he been in a position to do so.

But, third, in his contrast between Onesimus's former "useless" state and his currently "useful" role, Paul may also be playing on the proximity of *Chrēstos*/Χρηστός ("useful"), a common slave name, to *Christos*/Χριστός ("Christ"). Indeed, a famous text from the Roman historian Suetonius shows that these names could be confused, for Suetonius attributes Claudius's expulsion of Jews from Rome to the instigation of one named Chrestos.[5] Many historians assume that Suetonius misunderstood Christos as Chrestos, which was a

---

3. In Xenophon's *Memorabilia* 2.1.15, Socrates asks the anarchist Aristippus whether he is confident that no one would try to enslave him "because you would be thought the kind of slave who brings no master any profit."

4. Varro, *The Latin Language* 8.21. Strabo (born ca. 64 BC) writes that the Athenians named their slaves after the peoples from whom they were imported or gave them names common in those countries (*Geography*, 7, 3.12). Thus a slave's name rarely gives information about his or her own ethnicity or origin.

5. Suetonius, *Claudius* 25.4.

common name at the time, while Christos would have been unfamiliar to Latin ears.[6] It is as a Christian, a brother in the Lord, Paul's own child, that Onesimus has taken on his particular usefulness to Paul. Paul's argument reflects the traditional idea, expounded in Aristotle, that "property is a collection of . . . tools, and a slave is an animate piece of property."[7] But Paul's is not a utilitarian interest in Onesimus: he has acquired not a tool but a new son in the Lord.

If Paul has acquired a new son, then Philemon has acquired a new brother.[8] Since Paul brought both Onesimus and Philemon to faith in Christ (vv. 10, 19), he has become "father" to both and thus they have become brothers to one another. Paul does not force Philemon to obey him, but he does remind Philemon that he owes Paul no less than his slave does. Although distinguished by their status as master and slave, Philemon and Onesimus thus have in common the most significant aspect of their identity, namely, their relationship to the one Lord. It is their mutual belonging to the Lord and their relationship as brothers — not their relationship as master and slave — that must determine their interaction. The first-century Jewish apologist Philo observed that while nature had created people alike as "genuine brothers," that kinship had been destroyed by "malignant covetousness," creating "estrangement instead of affinity and enmity instead of friendship."[9] For Paul, Christ's reconciling work creates affinity and friendship in place of enmity and estrangement.

Paul makes this explicit when he writes to Philemon that Onesimus is returning to Philemon "no longer as a slave but more than a slave, a beloved brother — especially to me but how much more to you, both in the flesh and in the Lord" (v. 16). What Paul makes clear here is that while he has been a "father" to both Onesimus and Philemon, it is ultimately their relationship as brothers in the Lord Jesus Christ and their common belonging to God the Father (v. 3) that lay the basis for both their new relationship to each other and for Paul's appeal to them. Subtly emphasizing the new relationship that Philemon and Onesimus have, Paul never refers to Philemon as "master" *(kyrios)*. While it is not clear that Paul is asking that Philemon manumit Onesimus, Paul does underscore the changed situation: Onesimus must now be considered first and foremost not as a slave, but as a brother and, by virtue of being a brother in Christ, beloved. Paul has greeted Philemon as "beloved" (v. 1), and Philemon's love was the particular virtue for which Paul has commended him and given thanks to God (vv. 5, 7). Paul has made it clear to

6. Lohse, *Colossians*, 200, n. 36, cites texts from both Justin Martyr and Tertullian using similar plays on these words to defend Christian character.

7. Aristotle, *Politics* 1.4 (1253b.27-30).

8. For the significance of this language, see the discussion above of Col 1:1-2.

9. Philo, *Quod omnis probus liber sit* 79.

Philemon how much he loves Onesimus. Now, in the Lord, Philemon is to extend such love to Onesimus as well.

But while that is clear enough, the meaning of Paul's statement that Onesimus is a beloved brother "in the flesh and in the Lord" (v. 16) remains somewhat obscure. "Flesh" (*sarx*/σάρξ) typically refers in Paul to human existence in its limitation by human frailty and weakness and even sinfulness, especially as this way of life is opposed to the ways of the Spirit of God.[10] Paul might then be asserting that Onesimus has become "useful" to him and to Philemon in two spheres, that of ordinary human relations apart from the Lord and that of relationships "in the Lord," as a slave and as a Christian brother. But it is primarily Onesimus's conversion rather than some improvement in his human character or capacities —although these may be linked — that has made him useful to Paul and Philemon, his master "in the flesh."[11] It is precisely because Onesimus has become a Christian that he is Philemon's brother. Their relationship to each other as brothers exists first because of their relationship to Christ as Lord. What they are "in the Lord" determines their conduct within any relationship "in the flesh." Onesimus's new status as a brother "in the Lord" has practical consequences for the way in which Philemon is to treat him, "justly and fairly, for you know that you also have a Master in heaven" (Col 4:1). And now that Onesimus is a "brother in the Lord," how much more will Philemon be called on to exercise the Christian graces of forgiveness, meekness, compassion, and patience (Col 3:12-17)!

Paul thus lays out the new relationship between Philemon and Onesimus, the contours of which stand in marked contrast to those of typical master-slave relationships in the ancient world. Ancient Greek and Roman thinkers betray a consistently negative evaluation of slaves in terms of their moral and intellectual capacities, denying to them privileges thought worthy only of those freeborn or of higher social status.[12] Slaves are generally deemed worse than their masters in diligence, responsibility, and bravery. Their words were not to be trusted. Plutarch, for example, characterizes Spartacus, the Thracian leader of a

---

10. The NIV has Paul say that Onesimus is dear to him "as a man and as a brother in the Lord," which, while it makes good sense in English, seems to miss the sense of "in the flesh."

11. The thought is close to Col 3:22, where Paul exhorts slaves to obey their earthly *(kata sarka)* masters. For a discussion of how Jewish authors attempted to reconcile their status as "slaves of God" with enslavement to human masters, see the discussion in Byron, *Slavery Metaphors*, especially 37-143. Byron demonstrates that while Jews understood themselves to be "slaves of God," responses to enslavement to human masters varied, often depending on the reasons for the initial enslavement.

12. Numerous texts can be found in Wiedemann, *Greek and Roman Slavery*, 64-77, in the chapter appropriately titled "Moral Inferiors."

major slave revolt in 73-71 BC, as "more intelligent and more humane than one would expect of someone whom Chance had made a slave" (*Crassus* 8.2). Pliny the Elder notes that since painting was practiced by men of free birth and high status, there had "always been a ban on teaching it to slaves" (*Natural History* 35.36.77). Similarly, slaves were banned from all activities deemed appropriate to citizens, such as following in funeral processions and explicitly and notably from serving as soldiers.[13] Manumission was looked on with suspicion since it was suspected that corrupt and unclean persons were too frequently set free. Augustus therefore set minimum age limits both for those who wanted to manumit slaves and for the slaves themselves. In short, disdain for slaves is found throughout the literature of the ancient Greek and Roman world. Morally, spiritually, and intellectually inferior to freed persons, slaves were not to be trusted, but rather to be treated firmly and punished when necessary.

In sharp contrast to the expectations found in this literature, Paul urges Philemon to act in accordance with the reality that has been established in Christ and by virtue of which Philemon and Onesimus are now brothers to each other. Going beyond urging gentle and humane treatment, Paul insists that Onesimus is not to be regarded as property but as a brother; he has not simply become "useful" in his capacity as Philemon's slave, but as a brother in Christ he has also become beloved. In the Roman Empire, "Slavery is . . . a state of absolute subjection. The slave has no kin . . . his very identity is imposed by the owner who gives him his name."[14] But in Christ, the slave has gained kin: his own master is now his brother! This relationship has been created by the reconciling and renewing work of Christ, which breaks down barriers between people and groups formerly and even naturally estranged from or hostile to each other (Col 3:11).

Paul strengthens the rhetorical appeal of his letter by referring to himself as both an "elderly man"[15] and a "prisoner of Christ" (v. 9; so also v. 1). Here

---

13. When Octavian used 20,000 slaves as rowers in his fleet, he first had them manumitted (Suetonius, *Augustus* 16.1). Dio Cassius (48.34.5) refers to a runaway slave who was captured and then manumitted so that he could be executed by throwing him from the Tarpeian Rock on the Capitol; Livy describes a slave who betrayed his master and was also manumitted and executed in the same manner (see Wiedemann, *Greek and Roman Slavery*, 76). In other words, manumission hardly granted one the right of self-determination or a higher status; in this case, it was a means to serve the ends of the powerful.

14. Wiedemann, *Greek and Roman Slavery*, 1.

15. While the Greek manuscript evidence overwhelmingly supports the reading *presbytēs/* πρεσβύτης ("old man"), a number of commentators have suggested that one might understand instead the word *presbeutēs/*πρεσβευτής ("ambassador" or "emissary"). As attractive as this suggestion is, it falters on the lack of textual support; for a concise summary, see Fitzmyer, *Philemon*, 105-6.

Paul refers to his literal imprisonment (cf. v. 1; Col 4:10, 18; Eph 6:19-20), but he also alludes to his "captivity" to Christ: ultimately his obligations and servitude render him answerable not to a prison guard or magistrate but to Christ, whose "captive" he gladly is. Paul makes his request to Philemon not because Philemon is beholden to him or he to Philemon, but rather because they are both beholden to Christ. Paul notes that he is "bold enough in Christ to command you to do what you ought" (v. 8). In the role of an apostle commissioned by Christ, Paul can issue Philemon a command; one need only to consult other letters of Paul to see that he could do so when the need arose. But here he never expressly refers to himself as an apostle, not even in the opening greeting, preferring instead to appeal to Philemon on the basis of their status as brothers in Christ and coworkers in the gospel, as well as to the new relationship that Onesimus and Philemon now have in Christ. Paul's statement that he could command Philemon to "do what you ought" implies that Philemon, too, is well acquainted with the obligation of Christians to exercise the kind of compassion and forgiveness which they have received in Christ. Paul does not seek to compel Philemon to obedience, but rather to allow him to reflect on the character of the gospel and to act in accordance with it. As Eduard Lohse writes, "Love is resourceful enough to find the right way in accomplishing the good."[16]

Paul therefore writes, "I would rather appeal to you on the basis of love" (v. 9). Again, although Paul would have gladly kept his "child Onesimus" with him (vv. 10, 14), he preferred to leave the decision with Philemon "in order that the good you do might be voluntary and not something forced." Philemon's generous response to Onesimus will arise from love and forgiveness, not from an apostolic mandate to receive him. It will arise from the working of the gospel in Philemon's life, not from Paul's command.

Paul even hints that the entire course of events has been part of God's purposes to join Onesimus and Philemon in a new relationship of brotherly love (vv. 15-16). The delicacy of Paul's statement — "perhaps this is the reason he was separated from you for a while, so that you might have him back forever" — may be a use of the "divine passive." On one level, the facts are clear enough: Onesimus left Philemon. But Paul ventures that it may well be that "he was separated from you," that is to say, that God was working in order to bring Onesimus to faith so that he would not simply be returned to Philemon as his slave but presented to Philemon as his brother. And because the renewing work of Christ creates a new humanity destined for life with God in a renewed world, Philemon's relation to Onesimus as a brother will be "forever." Although not a perfect parallel, Joseph's words to his brothers, who sold him

16. Lohse, *Colossians,* 202.

into slavery, are often cited as illuminating: "You meant it for evil, but God meant it for good" (Gen 50:20).

Such is Paul's confidence in Philemon and, beyond him, in the gospel to which they both profess loyalty, that he does not simply send a letter on Onesimus's behalf, but actually sends Onesimus himself. Paul thus not only arranges a face-to-face meeting with the hopes of reconciliation, but he puts the ball in Philemon's court with respect to both Onesimus and Paul. One could think of Paul as shrewd or manipulative, leaving Philemon little choice in the matter regarding his actions. But one can also see Paul as calling upon Philemon to live up to his Christian responsibility and to the high calling of the gospel.

17-25

17 So if you consider me your partner, welcome him as you would welcome me. 18 If he has wronged you in any way or owes you anything, charge that to my account. 19 I, Paul, am writing this with my own hand: I will repay it. I say nothing about your owing me even your own self. 20 Yes, brother, let me have this benefit from you in the Lord! Refresh my heart in Christ.

21 Confident of your obedience, I am writing to you, knowing that you will do even more than I say. 22 One thing more — prepare a guest room for me, for I am hoping through your prayers to be restored to you. 23 Epaphras, my fellow prisoner in Christ Jesus, sends greetings to you, 24 and so do Mark, Aristarchus, Demas, and Luke, my fellow workers. 25 The grace of the Lord Jesus Christ be with your spirits.

Paul laid the emotive and theological foundation for his appeals. He has spoken of his own deep affection for Onesimus, appealing on his behalf to Philemon (v. 10); now he will make specific requests. Up to this point Paul has implied that the new relationship which Philemon and Onesimus enjoy in the Lord should lead Philemon to regard his slave in a new light, as a "beloved brother" (v. 16). Now Paul puts himself on the line, spelling out exactly what he hopes Philemon will do, as well as what he is prepared to do on Onesimus's behalf. If Paul expects Philemon to exercise his Christian responsibility to forgive Onesimus and welcome him into his household, Paul is prepared to take responsibility for Onesimus's wrongs and to bear the consequences on his behalf.

In his closing appeals to Philemon, Paul goes beyond expression of mere affection for Onesimus in asking Philemon to treat him as a brother for Paul's sake. Paul identifies himself with Onesimus when he urges Philemon to welcome Onesimus into his home as he would Paul. Taking matters even a step further, Paul is literally willing to put his money where his mouth is and instructs Philemon to reckon Onesimus's debts to Paul (vv. 18-19). This is usually taken as an oblique reference to the likelihood that on his departure from Philemon's household Onesimus was guilty of theft or embezzlement. Although other commentators point out that even Onesimus's departure from Philemon's house could be considered a "wrong" done to Philemon, it does seem likely that some sort of financial problem is in view. Some suggest Onesimus has somehow mishandled a financial matter that led him originally to seek a third party to intervene in a possible dispute with Philemon.[1] Paul essentially includes an IOU in the letter, binding himself to repay it by noting that he has written it in his own hand; his insistence on taking on Onesimus's debt in this manner suggests that this is likely to be a sore spot with Philemon. If Paul were not aware of a particular wrongdoing of which Onesimus was guilty, he would not have mentioned it here. The emphatic nature of Paul's statement regarding his willingness to repay Onesimus's debt suggests that he is dealing with a real and potentially tender matter.[2]

Such is the depth of Paul's love and concern as well as his identification with Onesimus. Paul not only intercedes on behalf of the estranged slave but, waiving his own rights and status, takes the lowly and tenuous position of that slave, inviting Philemon to treat slave and friend without distinction. Paul so identifies himself with Onesimus that he puts himself in his place, modeling not the boldness that he might rightly exercise in Christ (v. 8) but rather the self-giving identification with the lowly that marked Christ's own self-giving on the cross. Paul assumes the posture of his Lord, who "emptied himself, taking the form of a slave," and "humbled himself . . . to the point of death, even death on a cross" (Phil 2:7-8). Paul thus lives out the call to the cruciform existence that is to characterize those who have died and risen with Christ their Lord (Col 2:13; 3:1-3, 7-17).

As N. T. Wright aptly paraphrases Paul, "God is in Paul reconciling Philemon to Onesimus."[3] Paul effects this reconciliation not by standing apart from his friends Philemon and Onesimus as a separate third party trying to mediate or negotiate between them, but by putting himself in the place of Onesimus, appealing to Philemon to welcome his slave as though he were Paul. Taking Onesimus's vulnerable and humble status as debtor and forgo-

---

1. Bartchy, "Philemon," 308.
2. Wall, *Colossians and Philemon*, 183, contends that commentators exaggerate the peril of Onesimus's situation.
3. Wright, *Colossians*, 187.

ing his authority and rights as an apostle to command Philemon's obedience, Paul thus also models what he hopes Philemon himself will do — waive his own rights in the matter and look on Onesimus with forgiveness and love. Assuming Onesimus's status as guilty debtor, Paul pleads with Philemon to consider Onesimus as he would Paul: without guilt, without debt to Philemon.

Paul moreover actually enlists Philemon as his fellow worker in the cause of reconciliation, a role entirely appropriate for one whom Paul has designated friend and coworker (v. 1), partner (v. 17), and brother (v. 20). Paul calls on Philemon to take an active role in seeking reconciliation with his slave. As the powerful and superior member of the two, it is Philemon's responsibility to exercise his power and status in ways commensurate with the gospel of Christ, in which he is Paul's coworker. In welcoming Onesimus back into his household, he will put Paul's exhortation in Colossians into effect: "Bear with one another and, if anyone has a complaint against another, forgive each other; just as the Lord has forgiven you, so you also must forgive" (3:13).

It is exactly this reconciling work of Christ of which Paul understands himself to be the agent, not only in calling people to be reconciled to God, not only in bringing Jew and Gentile together, but also in bringing two friends, two Christian brothers, together into a new relationship within the household of God. Paul carries out his role as Christ's ambassador of reconciliation by identifying himself first with Philemon as beloved friend, coworker, partner, and brother, thus establishing their mutuality and collegiality in the Lord. Paul next identifies Onesimus as his child and his heart. By means of his identification with Philemon as a peer and fellow worker, Paul can call on Philemon to act graciously and to extend the welcome and forgiveness to Onesimus that he could command but prefers not to. By means of his identification with Onesimus, Paul puts himself in the slave's place, showing the lengths to which Christian love will go and demonstrating the full extent of Christian brotherly love. If Philemon is indeed Paul's brother, coworker, and friend, he will see Onesimus through the lens of his friendship with Paul. He will treat Onesimus as he would Paul, because he will see Onesimus as Paul and Paul as Onesimus. For Onesimus's sake, Paul assumes the role of the indebted slave in Philemon's household so that in and through Paul Onesimus may find a welcome as a dear brother into the household of faith to which he now belongs.[4] Earlier Paul wrote of Philemon's love by which the hearts of the saints have been refreshed (v. 7). When the reconciliation between

---

4. See especially the discussion in Wright, *Colossians,* 186-87.

Philemon and Onesimus occurs, Philemon's love will be the source of refreshment to Paul (v. 20).

Paul expresses his confidence in Philemon's ready assent to Paul's understanding of what the gospel requires. It is interesting, however, that Paul speaks of his confidence in Philemon's "obedience," since he earlier declined to issue a command to Philemon (v. 8). Paul's choice of words here likely indicates that he sees his previous words as more than musings on various courses of action that Philemon might take. But his willingness to speak of Philemon's obedience discloses to us more of Paul's perception of what the gospel requires than of his own right to be obeyed as an apostle. Paul, then, assumes that Philemon will extend a cordial welcome to Onesimus, even exceeding the graciousness which Paul urges.

Indeed, Paul writes, "I am writing to you, knowing that you will do even more than I say." It is not clear that Paul here requests Philemon to grant Onesimus his freedom, although the statement is often taken that way. Manumission of slaves was generally regarded as the reward for faithful service; it might therefore be unusual for Philemon to manumit Onesimus, who has apparently not demonstrated particularly faithful service. In this context, Paul's pleading on Onesimus's behalf might be seen instead as an implicit request that Philemon not delay the anticipated release of Onesimus in light of recent circumstances.[5] But even if Philemon frees Onesimus, they will still be bound both as brothers in Christ — forever, as Paul put it (vv. 15-16) — and also by virtue of the relationships that existed between masters and their former slaves. Even freed slaves could be legally bound to their former masters in continuing ways. For example, according to Greek legal traditions, slaves could be granted their freedom, but freedom was broken into four parts: freedom to represent oneself in legal matters, to hold property without fear of seizure, to earn a living as one chose, and to live where one desired. But often, on manumission some of these freedoms — most notably freedom of movement and employment — were restricted for a set period of years.[6] Paul, however, seems to envision a permanent relationship between Philemon and Onesimus governed, instead, by their status as brothers in the Lord. Here Paul expresses his confidence in Philemon's capacity to forgive and welcome Onesimus into the household.

Paul himself hopes to be released soon so that he will be able to visit

5. So Bartchy, "Slavery," in *ABD* 6:70-71. Bartchy points out that Roman law would likely not have been directly relevant to Philemon (since there is no evidence that he was a Roman citizen), but Roman practice may nevertheless cast light on the sort of request Paul was making.

6. Bartchy, "Slavery," *ABD* 6:71.

7. Wright, *Colossians*, 191.

Philemon, and he asks that Philemon make appropriate preparations (v. 22). He does not say whether he has information that might relate to an imminent release or simply expects that the term of his imprisonment will be short. Imprisonment was not a typical means of punishment in the Roman Empire, and Paul was most likely awaiting trial or sentence. But it is unlikely that we can deduce anything regarding the place or date of Paul's imprisonment from what he says here. If he is released, he says that it will be because of prayers on his behalf, but he is also well aware that as a "prisoner of Christ" his course is dictated not by his own wishes or hopes but by his Lord.

In closing Paul sends greetings from "Epaphras, my fellow prisoner in Christ Jesus," and from four coworkers, Mark, Aristarchus, Demas, and Luke. Curiously, in Colossians Aristarchus is his fellow prisoner (4:10), but not Epaphras (4:12), while here (v. 23) Epaphras is specifically named as a prisoner, using the same word, "prisoner of war," but not Aristarchus. Wright argues that in both cases the reference is not to physical chains but to a "literal" imprisonment in the battle between Christ and the powers of the present age.[7] Dunn, on the other hand, suggests that we ought to imagine some interchange between Aristarchus and Epaphras, so that Aristarchus was in prison with Paul when Colossians was written, but Epaphras has taken his place and is by Paul's side in prison when Philemon was written.[8] This implies at least some gap between the writing of the two letters, but one need not imagine that it was necessarily long. That the lists of those who send greetings in Philemon (vv. 23-24) and Colossians (4:10-14) are similar but not identical — Philemon notably leaves out Jesus Justus, and the names appear in the two books in different order — suggests that the letters were written close together in time.[9]

And so there remains only Paul's closing benediction. Just as his greetings reflect distinctive Christian content — "Grace to you and peace from God our Father and the Lord Jesus Christ" (v. 3) — so also does Paul's final thought, "The grace of the Lord Jesus Christ be with your spirits." The statement uses the plural "your," and thus may indicate that it is not merely Philemon who is being addressed, but rather the church which met in Philemon's house. Paul's closing benediction thus reinforces the perspective that the letter was written not just to Philemon but to a wider readership as well.

8. Dunn, *Colossians*, 348.

9. For further discussion of these names and their occurrence in Acts as well, see the Introduction to Colossians in this volume.

Theological Horizons of Philemon

The Theology of Philemon in the Context of Biblical Theology

It is typical to say that Paul's letters are divided into two parts. In each epistle, Paul deals first with theological issues, either correcting erroneous practice or belief on theological grounds or arguing a theological position; he then turns in the second part of the epistle to practical exhortation. If this were indeed the pattern for Paul's letters and if delineating Pauline theology depended on the presence of overt theological discussion, then it would be difficult, if not impossible, to expound "the theology of Philemon." Philemon has no discussion of — and indeed virtually no reference to — topics that might have been of theological interest in a letter that addresses a Christian slave owner on behalf of a Christian slave. Some explicit attention to matters such as the meaning of Christian freedom, relationships in the church, or the church's relationship to culture and society, might have laid a foundation for Paul to "apply" his theology to the concrete situation.

But Paul's letters move easily between practice and theology, not merely because these implicate each other, but also because Paul would not have thought of his letters in terms of the neat divisions which modern interpreters assign to them. Indeed, what are sometimes called Paul's "ethics" are simply the outworking of the gospel.[1] Although Philemon contains little explicit theology, it reflects a deep theological understanding of the renewal that God has effected in Christ and the consequences for human relationships. Three aspects of the letter support this assertion.

First, the *purpose* of this letter is to reconcile Philemon and Onesimus as

---

1. Wright, "The Letter to the Galatians," in *Between Two Horizons*, ed. Joel Green and Max Turner, 220.

Christian brothers. Paul did not write the letter to send a runaway slave back to his master or out of any convictions regarding the abiding validity of the institution of slavery and the importance of keeping this social structure intact. Rather, he wanted to bring Philemon and Onesimus together on a new footing established by the reconciling work of Christ, a topic to which Paul devotes considerable space in other epistles. The epistle to Philemon then at least implicitly raises the question how far that reconciling work extends, what shape it takes, and in what way, if at all, social institutions and structures are transformed by the work of Christ.

Second, the *familial metaphors* that recur throughout the letter testify to Paul's perception of what God has accomplished through the reconciliation that is in Christ. Paul writes that Philemon should welcome Onesimus as a brother, not as a slave. In directing this letter to Philemon, Apphia, Archippus, and "the church in your house," Paul demonstrates that he understands the church to be a *household* in which the family members are bound to each other by fraternal bonds in Christ. These family members are obligated both to the Lord and to each other. But just what Paul expects of each member of this household remains to some extent a matter of conjecture. He does not come right out and ask Philemon to set his slave free, although some commentators think that Paul insinuates as much. Similarly, although Paul addresses the letter to others alongside Philemon, it is not entirely clear exactly what he expects the church to do in this situation, since after the initial greeting Paul seems to address Philemon alone. If Paul expects the church to be "overhearing" the letter, it is not entirely clear how he thinks the household of faith will influence Philemon's actions. Still, Paul addresses Philemon not as a lone individual, but as a member of a family, a household, whose actions affect others and must reflect the reality in which they live together.

Third, behind Paul's desire to reconcile Philemon and Onesimus and behind his view of the church as a family, a household, lies his conviction that the church, the body of Christ, anticipates the eschatological *renewal of humankind* in the image of God. The epistle to the Colossians, which may well have been written about the same time as Philemon and to the same congregation, gives the theological grounding for this vision: in Christ, the purposes of God for all creation are being brought to fruition. In the redemption wrought through Christ, the purposes of God for creation and for human life in the world are renewed (Col 3:10-11). Elsewhere Paul wrote passionately about the gospel which unites Jew and Gentile, male and female, slave and free into one body in Christ Jesus (Gal 3:28; Col 3:11), about the cross as breaking down barriers between people (Eph 2:14-16), and about the new creation effected through Christ's death and resurrection (2 Cor 5:17). Paul now faces the question whether his vision of the reconciling and re-creating power of that gospel constitutes more than wishful thinking. If Paul's prestige and authority are at stake, much more so is his fundamental conviction about human relationships in Christ, the character of the church, and the way in which faith shapes Christian responsibility in this world. In other words, the situation which confronts Paul and which he subsequently addresses in this epistle tests the reconciling power of the gospel that he proclaims.[2]

In this present section, then, I want to turn to a discussion of the theology of Philemon under the rubrics of the new humanity in Christ Jesus and the familial metaphors used for the church. In the context of an epistle in which a slave and master are the key figures, the metaphors of "new humanity" and "family" force important questions: if Paul thought of the family of Christ as the new humanity, reconciled through the cross, and now belonging both to God and to each other, how did he understand these realities to affect the concrete relationship of master and slave, Philemon and Onesimus? The third part of this summary, then, will be devoted to a discussion of how Paul understood the renewing work in Christ for the relationship of master and slave and for slavery in general. But this question can be turned around as well: how does Paul's request to Philemon provide evidence to us of Paul's understanding of that reconciling work? What shape does the reconciling work of Christ take in the concrete situations of human existence?

The New Humanity in Christ Jesus

Behind the epistle to Philemon stands Paul's conviction, articulated elsewhere, that in Christ there is a new creation — a new humanity (2 Cor. 5:17), a "renewal" in which "there is no longer Greek and Jew, circumcised and uncircumcised, barbarian, Scythian, slave, and free, but Christ is all and in all" (Col 3:11). This new humanity manifests itself, first, in Christ himself, who lives in faithful obedience to God, pouring himself out in self-giving love for others, and, second, in the unified body of Christ in which there is "no slave and free." Christ's ministry, death, and resurrection call into being a new humanity — the body of Christ that is the church — who live together on the model of Christ's faithfulness and love. The model of Christ's self-giving love for the other supplies the basis for Paul's appeal to Philemon not to insist on his rights as an aggrieved slave owner but to relinquish his legal claims and

---

2. See also Wright, *Colossians,* 166.

welcome Onesimus back into the household. Philemon is to embody his faithfulness to God in his self-giving love for Onesimus, welcoming him as a brother and not a slave, looking out for the interests of Onesimus (cf. Phil 2:4). While as a slave owner Philemon has certain legal rights, as a brother in Christ he has specific moral obligations, namely, the obligations of love, and these take precedence.

While Paul writes of a new humanity, a humanity that is being renewed in the image of Christ (Rom 8:29; 1 Cor 15:49; Col 3:10-11), his letters often deal with the all too real and ordinary manifestations of human sinfulness: self-centeredness, status-seeking, anger, greed, lust, gossip, immorality, and more. To be sure, Paul does give thanks for evidence of the grace of God at work in the congregations that he has founded and in individuals whom he knows. For example, in various letters Paul commends and thanks numerous coworkers for their faithfulness to the gospel and service to him. He characterizes the Philippians as generous and steadfast in their service to him and to the gospel of Jesus Christ. Yet he speaks also of their need for unity of purpose and for humility and love. He writes to the Colossians in gratitude for their faith and love, yet encourages them toward Christian maturity in their understanding and practice of the gospel. No individual or church to whom Paul wrote had fully realized that renewed humanity promised in Christ, and sometimes one wonders whether any even came close! But Paul does not discard his deep conviction that God has done something decisive and concrete through Christ for the renewal of humankind and the world and will bring these purposes to glorious fulfillment.

And yet everywhere Paul makes it plain that these realities will not be fully and finally attained until Christ returns to complete the transformation begun in human life and in the world. In the great chapter in Romans in which Paul speaks of the hope for redemption, he writes of those who "are destined to be conformed to the image of [God's] Son" (Rom 8:29). In writing about the resurrection in 1 Corinthians, he promises that "we shall also bear the image of the man of heaven" in the resurrection of the dead (1 Cor 15:49). And in Col 3:10 Paul writes of putting on the new humanity "that is being renewed" in the image of its Creator. These passages point to the hope of a future transformation, but it is the completion of a work in progress, because the future promise of transformation is already at work in the present time. Yet there is no steady progress toward the goal, as if the promised transformation were simply the climax of the course of human life. Paul expects a transformation, an act of God in which all shall be changed, transformed. But through Christ, God's transforming grace is even now at work among the people of God. As Richard Hays rightly puts it, "The biblical story focuses on

God's design for forming a covenant *people*. Thus, the primary sphere of moral concern is not the character of the individual but the corporate obedience of the church."[3]

Paul's understanding of human beings as new creations in Christ, renewed in the image of their Creator, has typically been taken to refer to the transformation of the individual. And there is no doubt that Paul does envision such changes in the individual: the commitments, values, and practices of those who have come to be in Christ have all changed. Christian character, which manifests the virtues of love, forgiveness, forbearance, kindness, and so on, is being formed in those who are in Christ. Yet it is also clear that for Paul the "new humanity" that is in Christ refers to those who are his body, to the church. In Christ, there is one new "person" where previously there were "Greek and Jew, circumcised and uncircumcised, barbarian, Scythian, slave, and free." Even as God created humankind, male and female, in his own image, now God re-creates that humanity in the image of God.

The New Humanity as Family

In Philemon, this gospel of reconciliation comes to expression in part in the language of mutuality, love, and kinship. There is nothing uniquely Christian about the use of such terminology or the vision of human beings united as family. Israel's identity is articulated in terms drawn from the familial sphere, initially because of the tribal origins of Israel, though familial imagery became the grounds for exhortations to the people of Israel regarding their life together. Ironically and poignantly, in the later Jewish document known as the *Testaments of the Twelve Patriarchs*, the twelve sons of Jacob — some of whom had sold their dreaming and favored brother Joseph into slavery in Egypt — warn their offspring of the dangers of sibling competition, division, and rivalry. Rather, unity, mutual honoring, affection, and love were to be the guiding norms in this family. Harmony was a cherished ideal (Ps 133:1), and the children of a family were expected to love each other and look for the interests and good of the other (e.g., *Testament of Joseph* 17:1-3; *Testament of Gad* 6:1-7; 2 Macc 1:1).[4] Indeed, as one author writes, all Jews are ultimately family (Tob 2:2, "brothers"). And that did not imply that they were all to treat each other as Cain treated Abel or Joseph's older brothers treated him!

In his ministry, Jesus assumed the kinship that existed among the Jews

---

3. Hays, *Moral Vision*, 196.

4. For more details, see the discussion above of such language in Col 1:1-2.

when he spoke of a woman as a "daughter of Abraham" (Luke 13:16) and of Zacchaeus as a "son of Abraham" (Luke 19:9). The parable of the prodigal son features a father who not only is forgiving but who also endeavors to reconcile two brothers to each other (Luke 15:11-32). Jesus further spoke of his disciples as his own kin, redefining family in terms of those who were related not by blood but by the bonds of the fellowship of discipleship. Thus it is the one who does the will of God who is rightfully to be called Jesus' "mother and brothers and sisters" (Mark 3:35). Here the metaphor of family functions to define ties drawn along the lines of affiliation and community rather than blood or genealogy. This extension of the family metaphor beyond the realm of blood relatives figures prominently in Paul's letters and in early Christianity as a whole.

This family's mutual obligations to each other are underscored in Philemon by the consistent use of the language of hospitality and kin, and by the reference to God as Father (v. 3), whose character and purposes ultimately determine the shape of this family's life. While early Christian authors such as Paul would have found the ideal of God's people as a family in the pages of their Scriptures, there were also exemplars of the ideal of brotherly affection to be found among pagan authors. Aristotle, for example, wrote that "brothers love each other as being born of the same parents, for their identity with them makes them identical with each other" (*Nicomachean Ethics* 8.12.3). Similarly, in the first century the moralist Plutarch spoke of the importance of resisting the spirit of "contentiousness and jealousy among brothers," insisting that one should instead practice "the art of making mutual concessions" (*On Fraternal Affection* 17 = *Moralia* 488A). This advice was not uncommon and typifies the ideal of brotherly love. However, Plutarch and Aristotle have in mind the bonds created by birth from the same parents.

Differently but analogously, Paul speaks of the bonds created by being related to the same Father, namely, to God. This bond unites people not because of their relationship through blood or birth, but by the new life created by the Spirit who enables people to know and address God as Father. In speaking to the (predominantly) Gentile Christians in Galatians, Paul notes that the Spirit empowers them to cry to God as Father (Gal 4:6). To the Christians at Rome, both Jews and Gentiles, Paul writes similarly (Rom 8:15). In both letters, Paul takes up the language used of Israel in the OT to describe the new relationship of the Gentiles to God, and of Jew and Gentile to each other. God is a Father to Israel (e.g., Isa 63:15-16; Jer 31:9).[5] In Christ, the Gentiles have come to know Israel's God as Father, and they now know each

---

5. See the discussion in Thompson, *Promise of the Father*, 35-55.

other and the people of Israel as brothers and sisters in Christ. With this usage, Paul does not usurp the designations for Israel as God's people but rather incorporates the church, Jew and Gentile together, into the greater reality of God's people.[6]

Paul speaks of Apphia as "sister" (Phlm 2), of Philemon as "dear friend" (v. 1) and "dear brother" (vv. 7, 20), and of Onesimus as his "child" (v. 10) and urges Philemon to welcome Onesimus as a "beloved brother" (v. 16). These forms of address are part of Paul's rhetorical appeal to Philemon, but they are not simply decorative flourishes. They express Paul's convictions about the familial relationships which people share in Christ and which are to be the foundation of their identity, and on the basis of which they are to order their conduct. Paul therefore appeals to Philemon as a member of his family, entreating Philemon to treat Onesimus as a member of the family as well. As a slave in Philemon's house, Onesimus would have been a member of his household. Earliest Christianity was in many ways a movement both centered in and subsequently composed of "households." According to John 4:53, for example, the official whose son was healed came to believe in Jesus, as did his whole household. Similarly, Cornelius and his whole household came to faith (Acts 10:24, 44-48), and the same pattern is found in the conversions of Lydia (16:14-15), the Philippian jailer (vv. 31-34), and Crispus (18:8). Throughout his letters, Paul refers to various individuals and their households or families (Rom 16:10, 11; 1 Cor 1:16; 2 Tim 4:19). Apparently Philemon's conversion to Christian faith did not bring the conversion of Onesimus, his slave, along the patterns noted above. But now that Onesimus has come to faith, he is not just a member of the household of Philemon; together, they belong to the household of Christ, and its norms take precedence.[7]

The terms "brother," "sister," "son" and so on express the reality of relationships in Christ. These are not fictions Paul employs to make a point, as if he were asking Philemon to imagine something that is in fact not true.[8] These relationships are given, as real as the relationships in a biological family. The renewal of humanity in the image of Christ and the institution of the bonds of love through Christ are not what Christians are commanded to achieve, but are givens. Paul and Philemon, Onesimus, and all those in the "church in their

6. On this point, see the discussion above of Phlm 1-3 and Dunn, *Theology of Paul*, 537-38.

7. But David deSilva, *Honor, Patronage*, 228, notes the extensive overlap between the expectations of each member of a household in the dominant culture and in emerging Christian culture.

8. As Fitzmyer, *Philemon*, 85, notes, *adelphos* does not express a "fictive kinship, for Paul means it in a real sense."

house" belong to — and hence are obligated to — a common master, Jesus Christ.

In both ancient Greek and Roman society, there were numerous primarily voluntary organizations, including religious, social, and economic associations. They could be composed of people sharing occupation, nationality (for instance, foreigners in Rome seeking to preserve devotion to their native gods), or simply a desire to insure a proper funeral and burial for themselves. Membership in such groups was typically voluntary or perhaps by election, with members agreeing to perform certain obligations and adhere to certain rules.[9] The early church clearly had much in common with such organizations and could easily have been understood to be just such an association. Paul, however, grounds the identity of the church not in its members' selection of an association or club, not in some commonly shared activities or skills, but in Christ's election of Jew and Greek, slave and free, male and female, to belong to him and hence to each other.[10] This new humanity, created in the image of God and now renewed in the image of Christ, stands as a testimony — an imperfect testimony to be sure — to God's purposes for the unity of the human race, rather than the ascendancy of any single race or people.

Paul's theology of reconciliation in Christ takes shape in the way in which he appeals to Philemon on behalf of Onesimus. Philemon holds all the cards, for he is the wronged slave owner, while Onesimus, as a slave and alleged wrongdoer,[11] already has two strikes against him. But Paul identifies with Onesimus "while he was yet a sinner" (cf. Rom 5:8), taking the side of the less powerful in order to serve as an intercessor on Onesimus's behalf and a mediator between him and Philemon. In the same fashion, Paul calls upon Philemon to put aside the prerogatives of power, to treat Onesimus as a brother and friend. The mutuality of relationships in Christ places a particular obligation on those who hold power or authority in any relationship. Here the slave owner is called to treat the slave with Christian love, offering him Christian hospitality, and extending to him a generous welcome.

Paul could have referred to his own example, as he does in 1 Corinthians 9, where he points out that he has forgone his apostolic rights for the sake of the Corinthian Christians.[12] In that letter Paul also urges his readers to do the same: instead of taking each other to court, he challenges them with the ques-

---

9. For a fuller discussion, see Ferguson, *Backgrounds of Early Christianity*, 131-35.

10. On this point, see the discussion above of Col 1:1-2 on the bonds of "family" in Christ and the obligations of religious commitment over those of ordinary family ties.

11. Paul refers, even if obliquely, to Onesimus as such.

12. For reading the letter in this way, see Lampe, "Keine 'Sklavenflucht,'" 137; Fitzmyer, *Philemon*, 36.

tion, "why not rather be wronged?" (1 Cor 6:7). Jesus' own example cannot be far from Paul's mind. This is the unspoken heart of Paul's appeal to Philemon: Philemon is called on to imitate his own Master, Christ Jesus, and his humility and forgiveness. One finds the same pattern of exhortation elsewhere in Paul's letters. When discussing food offered to idols (1 Corinthians 8-10), one of Paul's concerns is that the strong not insist on their rights to the detriment of the weak. In Romans, he similarly expects the strong to forgo their rights for the sake of the weak (Rom 14:19–15:3), appealing explicitly to the example of Christ, who "did not please himself" (15:3). One might even note that Paul's desire to take a collection from the Christians of his mission churches to the Jewish saints in Jerusalem not only constitutes a symbolic act representing the unity of Jew and Gentile in Christ, but also demonstrates the kind of love with which Christ loved his church: "For you know the generous act of our Lord Jesus Christ, that though he was rich, yet for your sakes he became poor, so that by his poverty you might become rich" (2 Cor 8:9). Whether the contrast, then, lies between strong and weak, rich and poor, or powerful and powerless, Christ's generous and self-giving love becomes the model that must be brought to bear on all.

In Colossians Paul wrote of the need to "bear with one another" and forgive each other "just as the Lord has forgiven you" (3:13). Christian behavior is to be marked by compassion, kindness, patience (3:12), love (3:14), and peace (3:15). Love, writes Paul, binds all the other virtues together. In Philemon, Paul refers explicitly only to love, yet one can easily see how together these virtues provide the foundation upon which Paul builds his appeal. Precisely the sort of conduct he calls for in Colossians and summarizes in terms of loving others must guide Philemon's behavior here. We do not know what Paul told Onesimus or expected of him — and he does not report that to Philemon either. Rather, Paul simply presents his appeal to Philemon, making it clear that as the slave owner, the one with power in this relationship, he is to exercise that power as love and forgiveness. As one author puts it,

> The underlying issue, then, involves the challenge of the gospel to the status quo of relationships. Specifically, although the word 'cross' does not appear in the text, this letter expresses Paul's apostolic embodiment of the cross — by acting in love through persuasion rather than exercising his apostolic right through a command (vv. 8-9) — so that Philemon in turn will embody the cross of faith and love by voluntarily welcoming and honoring his new brother in Christ.[13]

13. Gorman, *Apostle of the Crucified Lord*, 462.

The New Humanity, Masters, and Slaves

In spite of all that Paul says regarding the new relationship that Philemon and Onesimus have in Christ, and even if Paul actually requests that Philemon grant Onesimus his freedom, one nagging question remains: why does Paul not come right out and condemn the institution of slavery as a whole? And if he does not do so where the opportunity was most obvious and available, then does the Bible implicitly grant slavery and slave holders a legitimacy that we find abhorrent? How then do the Scriptures provide any ongoing guidance for us? The issues raised by Paul's letter to Philemon are exegetical, hermeneutical, and theological and lead directly to questions about the abiding authority and use of Scripture today. Here we will focus primarily on the exegetical matters.

The exegetical question concerns what Paul wants Philemon to do and how he regards the relationship of Onesimus and Philemon now that they are brothers in Christ. If Onesimus has now become a Christian and if Paul wants Philemon to set Onesimus free, can we see any causal relationship between the two? That is, does Paul want Philemon to set Onesimus free precisely *because* they are both Christians? If Paul is requesting Onesimus's manumission, does his request betray any sort of antipathy toward slavery or conviction that the work of Christ undercuts slavery? Or does Paul rather make an immediate request that affects only one slave and one slave owner?

Obviously the hermeneutical and theological questions cannot be dealt with in isolation from the exegetical questions. But neither is it obvious to what theological conclusions the exegetical data will lead, nor are there hermeneutical guidelines that are a sure guide to the "correct" interpretation. In the debate over slavery and the slave trade in the United States in the eighteenth and nineteenth centuries, the biblical data were used on both sides. Abolitionists argued that the biblical witness was against slavery and slaveholding, while those who supported slavery adduced arguments — including Paul's silence on the evils of slavery itself — from the Bible as well.

There is no doubt that slavery was commonplace in the societies reflected in the Bible and hence is part and parcel of the tapestry of Scripture. All the patriarchs had slaves. In fact, according to Scripture, God blessed Abraham by multiplying his slaves (Gen 24:35) and told him to circumcise, but not free, them. Hagar, a slave woman, was told to return to Sarah and submit to her (16:9). This command was later interpreted to provide a parallel and precedent to Paul's returning of Onesimus to Philemon: slaves are to return to their masters. Joshua took slaves (Josh 9:23), as did David (2 Sam 8:2, 6) and Solomon (1 Kgs 9:20-21). And in the NT, slavery is part of the landscape in which Christians live (1 Cor 7:20-21; Eph 6:5-9; Col 3:22-25; 1 Tim 6:1-2; Tit 2:9-10; Phlm 10-18; 1 Pet 2:18-19).

Various scriptural injunctions regulate the treatment of slaves. The OT forbids harsh treatment of slaves on the grounds that the Israelites were once slaves in Egypt (e.g., Exod 20:1-2; Lev 25:42-45; Deut 15:15). For this reason Israelites were not to acquire other Israelites as slaves, although they were permitted to acquire foreigners as slaves (Lev 25:44-45). If they were slaves, at some point Israelites should be set free. So, for example, a male Israelite slave was to be freed after six years of servitude (Exod 21:1-6). Some injunctions seem to actually perpetuate the harsh treatment of slaves, permitting them to be beaten or struck: "When a slave owner strikes a male or female slave with a rod and the slave dies immediately, the owner shall be punished. But if the slave survives a day or two, there is no punishment; for the slave is the owner's property" (Exod 21:20-21). But it does not follow that a master can treat a slave capriciously: "When a slave owner strikes the eye of a male or female slave, destroying it, the owner shall let the slave go free to compensate for the eye" (Exod 21:26). The slave may not be wantonly or willfully abused, but neither is he or she treated as a free person. Thus, for example, if an ox gores a free person, the ox is to be killed; but if the ox gores a slave, then the owner must make compensation for that slave to his or her owner (Exod 21:28-32). In such a case, the slave is implicitly regarded as property for which payment must be made.

A curious set of injunctions regarding the treatment of slaves can be found in the book of Sirach (second century BC). Sirach recommends "bread and discipline and work for a slave." Work will keep a slave from being idle and seeking liberty; a disobedient slave needs heavy fetters, and a wicked slave deserves torture. But Sirach then adds, "Do not be overbearing toward anyone, and do nothing unjust." The master can dictate the conditions of his slave's life and the severity of his burdens, but he must act justly. Sirach also cautions his reader: "If you have but one slave, treat him like a brother, for you will need him as you need your life. If you ill-treat him, and he leaves you and runs away, which way will you go to seek him?" (33:25-31). Sirach's injunctions are directed at keeping the slave in check by treating him with a degree of severity; even his admonition to treat a slave "like a brother" aims at keeping the slave from running away.

Greek and Roman authors also discussed the treatment of slaves, urging not only moderation in punishment but also fair and humane treatment. The emperor Claudius (AD 41-54), for example, passed legislation that gave slaves their freedom if their masters did not fulfill their obligations to them.[14] While Claudius may not have been motivated by great sympathy for the plight of slaves, his edict bears testimony to the common belief that masters had certain obligations to their slaves. In a treatise on the various duties and obligations of a person, the Roman orator and writer Cicero urged that one must behave justly "even toward the lowest of people," and "the most inferior status and fate is that of slaves."[15] Seneca's *Epistle* 47 offers a sustained discussion of the treatment of slaves, condemning harsh and overbearing behavior but allowing for temperate and controlled discipline of slaves. The collection of moral maxims now known as *Pseudo-Phocylides,* possibly compiled by a Hellenistic Jew, instructs owners to provide their servants with food, not to brand them with insulting marks, and to accept their advice when it is wise. In summary, texts from the ancient world testify to a variety of ways of controlling and directing a master's treatment of his slaves. In theory the slave was the property of the master, but the master was governed by codes of reasonable conduct.

In the epistle to Philemon, Paul proposes a different norm for master-slave relationships, at least when both are Christians: they are to relate to each other as brothers. Thus he goes beyond the contemporary parallels, essentially assigning to master and slave equal status. In spite of the frequent appeals in literature of the time to treat slaves as human beings, there remains a squeamishness in the same literature about treating the slave and freeborn citizen as equals.

Against this backdrop, our understanding of the theology undergirding Philemon depends almost entirely on how we understand the purpose of the letter. If it is taken to be an exhortation to Philemon to "take back" a runaway slave, it is but a short step to understanding Paul as approving — even enforcing — slavery and the rights of the master. But Paul nowhere speaks of the right of Philemon as a slave master; he focuses solely on Philemon's obligations as a Christian brother, and these are the obligations of love. By the same token, Paul does not present Onesimus to Philemon as a slave returning to captivity, but as a brother to be welcomed because of their shared status in Christ. As Cain Hope Felder states it, "the central meaning and purpose of the Letter to Philemon concern the difference the transforming power of the gospel can make in the lives and relationships of believers, regardless of class or

14. Suetonius, *Claudius* 25.2, writes that sick and aging slaves who were abandoned by their masters were to be set free. Dio Cassius 60(61).29.7 also notes that Claudius ordered that no senator travel more than seven "markers" from the city or anyone drive through the city seated in a vehicle. In short, Claudius's rule regarding slaves may reflect less his sympathy for slaves and more a desire to extend his own power.

15. Cicero, *On Duties* 1, 13, 41.

other distinctions."[16] As head of the household and owner of slaves, Philemon had certain prerogatives and roles. Paul appeals not to Philemon's identity as owner of a household, but rather to his identity as one who belongs to the household that is the church, the body of Christ. It is the church "in his house," but it is not Philemon's church. Therefore, the commands governing the household of Christ take precedence.

Hence while Paul does not launch a full-scale attack on slavery, neither does he assume that Christian commitment has no concrete manifestation in ordinary human relationships. To the contrary, it is quite clear that for Paul conversion to Christ profoundly and significantly changes the way people relate to each other. The model for their behavior is the example of Christ himself; and the context of their relationship is the body of Christ in which they find themselves as brothers and sisters to each other. Those interpreters who have argued that Paul has in view only "spiritual" equality fail to grasp Paul's comprehensive vision of the renewal effected through the reconciling work of Christ.

Indeed, Paul makes no dualistic move in his appeal to Philemon. He could have argued that now that Onesimus had become a believer, he and Philemon shared only a "spiritual" bond in Christ, a "moral equality before God the Father," with no concrete implications for their status as master and slave. In fact, just that way of interpreting Paul shaped the thinking of those who defended the slave trade in the United States.[17] Paul, however, takes a different tack, as the list of implicit and explicit requests in the letter make clear. Paul's expectation that Philemon will welcome Onesimus as a brother in the Lord implies that he must treat Onesimus differently, but unfortunately Paul does not spell out what such changed behavior would look like. On the basis, however, of the model of "brotherly love," which even in pagan circles required putting the interests of the other first, Paul likely meant that Philemon was to look out for the interests of Onesimus, not merely his own, and "count others better than" himself (Phil 2:3-4). Although master and slave, they cannot simply continue in their relationship as though nothing has changed. The early Christian apologist Aristides of Athens defended Christianity on the basis that Christians treat slaves (as well as children and other dependents) as

---

16. Felder, "Philemon," 885.

17. Perhaps the most thorough biblical defense of the institution of slavery was provided by the influential Southern Presbyterian theologian Robert Lewis Dabney in "A Defense of Virginia, and through Her of the South," in his *Discussions Evangelical and Theological. The University of North Carolina Project Documenting the American South* has many documents available online, including a number of sermons that give the biblical justification for slavery; see http://docsouth.unc.edu.

"brothers" when they become Christians, meaning that they do not abuse them but treat them kindly (*Apology* 15.6).[18] Aristides provides a concrete example of such treatment when he says that if necessary, Christians fasted for two or three days in order to give food to the needy. Although Aristides apparently did not take the step of demanding that Christians free their Christian slaves, he did assume that Christian masters would relate to their Christian slaves with sacrificial love.[19] Paul likewise expects Philemon to look out for Onesimus's interests ahead of his own.

Paul therefore offers a third way between the Scylla of "spiritualizing the gospel" and the Charybdis of equating the gospel with "social change."[20] Christians have often wanted the Bible to speak on the side of one or the other of these options: either the gospel has to do with inner, spiritual realities or it has to do with the transformation of social structures. Although it has been said before, it bears repeating to say that Paul simply had no real options for effecting "social change" or overhauling the social structures of his day, such as slavery. The mechanisms of modern democracies and the rights of self-determination were simply not in place, including the right of universal suffrage, representatives elected to serve the interests of their constituency, and so on. Paul did not live in a participatory democracy, but in an empire. Few of the people to whom he wrote had the rights of Roman citizenship, let alone any power or prerogatives attached to those rights. As Markus Bockmuehl puts it, "The majority of early Christians would have belonged to a class whose place in society was defined predominantly by their relationships within the *household* rather than in relation to the 'public' forum of city or empire. Within the New Testament, even the spiritual or material leadership of the small Christian communities dotted around the Mediterranean would only rarely have included people in a position to persuade, influence or benefit those who, even locally, exercised power."[21] It is therefore anachronistic to imagine that Paul would have suggested that the nascent Christian movement could somehow

18. Note that Aristides' comment shows that Christians apparently continued to own slaves, as indeed do other early Christian documents; on this point see Markus Bockmuehl, *Jewish Law in Gentile Churches*, 210-11. Chrysostom argued that Gal 3:28 implied that Christ had removed the punishment which led to slavery and that Christian masters who purchased slaves should set them free (*Homily* 40.6 on 1 Corinthians).

19. There is also some evidence that communities may have purchased the freedom of slaves who lived in pagan households (Hermas, *Similitudes* 1.8; Ignatius, *Polycarp* 4.3; *1 Clement* 55:2).

20. Fitzmyer, *Philemon*, 35-36, characterizes the two views as "interiorizing" the social condition of slavery and "mildly criticizing the social structure," and cites commentators who have interpreted Philemon in both ways.

21. Bockmuehl, *Jewish Law in Gentile Churches*, 193.

be a "transforming force" in the structures of the empire or that Paul's failure to offer such a programmatic critique somehow constitutes a perennial or God-given endorsement of slavery. Although slave revolts were known in the ancient world — the most notorious being the revolt led by Spartacus in 73-71 BC — none came to a happy ending. The only options would be death or return to slavery, surely under worse conditions. Moreover, few ancient writers criticize slavery itself on moral grounds. As Dunn puts it, "Slavery had not yet come to be thought of as immoral or necessarily degrading," adding, "It took the slave trade to bring this insight home to Western 'civilization.'"[22]

Paul offers instead a vision of a transformed community in Christ whose model of mutual love, unity, and peace serves as counter-testimony to the ways and mores of the political and social structures of the world. To some extent, then, Paul envisions a Christian community separated or distinct from the world — living by different standards, guided by different expectations, and with a new web of relationships. In this sense, the church is indeed counter-cultural, living by standards and with commitments not shared by its surrounding culture and standing in direct opposition to it. In this sense, the church is to be an embodiment and foretaste of the new humanity re-created in the image of God, a template of what humankind ought to be and how it is to live. The church in Christ reveals God's ideal for humankind. Thus when Paul makes his argument to the Galatians that the Gentiles come to God on equal footing with the people of Israel, he reminds them that "they are all one in Christ Jesus" (3:28). The unity of Gentile and Jew *in Christ* anticipates the re-creation of humanity in the image of its Creator (Col 3:11) and into "one new person" (Eph 2:15).

The community that is the church offers the vision of a multinational, multiethnic body, which — at its best — lives on the model of the Lord who brought it into being through his death and resurrection. But since that Lord is the Lord of all, "is all and is in all" (Col 3:11), it follows that the way in which the Lord calls his church to live is in fact the way in which he also desires that humankind should live together. Norman Petersen describes it this way, "[Philemon] finds that 'being in Christ' makes a totalistic claim upon him from which there are no exceptions. *If he is to remain in the service of Christ the Lord, he cannot be 'in Christ' only when he is 'in church.'*"[23] All existence of the one in the service of Christ is "Christian" and is lived as such. Christian existence norms human existence. And yet there remains a tension between

---

22. Dunn, *Theology of Paul*, 698 and n. 120. Indeed, the literature produced by Christians during the nineteenth century in defense of slavery is often vitriolically and shamefully racist.

23. Petersen, *Rediscovering Paul*, 269.

the eschatological goal of unity in Christ and the present reality which often seems to negate the grand vision of the unity of all people in Christ.

Having taken all that into account, most modern readers would probably prefer Paul to have drawn a direct line from Christian commitment to a vision demanding the emancipation of slaves.[24] Some commentators do in fact read Philemon that way, interpreting the contrast between "slave" and "brother" (v. 16) as implying that one who is a brother cannot belong to another as slave: Philemon should free Onesimus because Onesimus — like Philemon himself — belongs ultimately to Christ Jesus and cannot, therefore, "belong" as well to a human master.

The Stoics argued that true freedom was not a matter of the disposition of the body but rather had to do with the freedom of the soul. For example, Seneca, the first-century Roman statesman and writer, describes all people as in some way captive — whether to the whims of fortune, to status given at birth, to wealth or prestige, or to the demands of the state or a superior.[25] It might seem, therefore, that all human beings are ultimately slaves. But if the forces of destiny (Fate, Chance, Fortune) are beyond the control of human beings, the appropriate response is not therefore despair, resignation, or even servitude, but rather discipline of one's mind and mastery of one's desires. Otherwise, one simply becomes a slave to passion. Self-control and contentment are the essence of virtue and, as the Stoic philosopher Epictetus wrote, "virtue promises good fortune and tranquility and happiness." In other words, in Stoicism it is the one who is inner-directed rather than driven by external circumstances or demands that attains to true virtue and tranquility, to genuine freedom.

There are parallels between the Stoic ideal and Paul's exhortations. Paul urges self-control (1 Cor 7:5, 9; 9:25; Gal 5:23). He notes that he does not let his external circumstances dictate his attitude, but rather comments, "I have learned in whatever state I am to be content" (Phil 4:11). This attitude seems directly reflected in his instructions to slaves in other epistles, particularly 1 Cor 7:21-24:

> Were you a slave when called? Do not be concerned about it. Even if you can gain your freedom, make use of your present condition now more

24. In *The Manumission of Slaves*, 4, Harrill defines manumission as "the formal and informal procedures and ceremonies performed by a master, legally recognized within a given society, to effect a slave's liberation." "Emancipation" means the liberation of slaves, done without observance of manumission procedures or regard for the slaveholder's interests. Abolition refers to the conviction that slavery, both in theory and in practice, is morally reprehensible.

25. Seneca, *Dialogue 9: On the Tranquility of the Mind* 10.3.

than ever. For whoever was called in the Lord as a slave is a freed person belonging to the Lord, just as whoever was free when called is a slave of Christ. You were bought with a price; do not become slaves of human masters. In whatever condition you were called, brothers and sisters, there remain with God.

There are numerous disputed points in this passage, particularly the meaning of Paul's injunction that even if one can attain freedom, one should "make use" of his or her present condition.[26] While some interpreters argue that Paul here urges slaves to accept freedom if it is offered, others contend that Paul instructs slaves *not* to seek freedom, but to remain in and "make use" of their present condition as slaves (but cf. Exod 21:3). In any case, Paul's exhortations would seem to fit nicely into the Stoic framework of moral discourse, in which external circumstances do not finally determine proper conduct or attitudes. To take it a step further, if slaves themselves ought to be indifferent to their slavery, then presumably their masters may adopt the same attitude. If Paul instructs slaves to remain slaves, then masters need scarcely overturn the apostle's injunctions by setting them free!

Paul, like the Stoics, distinguished different kinds of freedom. But for Paul, those who are "free" do not govern themselves. Freedom is not autonomy. Rather, those who are "free in Christ" are in fact "slaves of Christ." The Stoics desired freedom from all but inner determination; Paul thought human existence was to be determined by obedience to Christ. Paul would gladly endorse the sentiments of Philo of Alexandria: "Are we not under a master, and have we not and shall we not have forever the same lord, slavery to whom gives us more joy than freedom does to any other? For of all the things that are held in honor in this world of creation slavery to God is the best" (*Dreams* 2.100). While the literature of both the Greeks and Romans reveals a marked contempt for slaves, Paul — like his Jewish compatriot Philo — believes that a particular kind of slavery, namely, slavery to God, constitutes true freedom.

But it is one thing for Paul or Philo to write of his own experience and convictions; it is quite another for a powerful master to impose this view on one who is his slave, especially in the service of justifying his continued prerogatives. Similarly, for Paul to write that he has learned to be content in

---

26. Scott Bartchy, *MALLON CHRĒSAI*, argues that Paul here urges Christians to seek manumission if possible, but not all interpreters agree. Harrill, *Manumission of Slaves*, 7, calls the passage a crux whose meaning is still unresolved. The Stoic philosopher Epictetus comments that "it is the slave's prayer that he be set free immediately" (*Discourses* 4.1.33). Bartchy argues that a slave could well expect to be set free by his thirtieth birthday (*ABD* 6.71).

whatever state he is in demonstrates his own response to changing and trying circumstances, and the power of his experience of the risen Christ to grant him serenity in the midst of the vicissitudes of life.

Paul's attitude is not resignation or passivity or escapism, but a steadfast trust in and receptivity to God in the midst of his circumstances. In Philippians, for example, Paul states that the Philippians share in both the suffering of Christ and Paul's own struggle as they are "given" to do so by God (1:27-30). Paul later describes his attitude with the famous phrase "the peace of God that passes all understanding" (4:7). Paul's willingness to endure suffering and his equanimity in the face of it by no means justify or condone the abuse he may have experienced at the hands of his opponents or captors. How masters treat their slaves need not determine the slaves' response; but it does not follow that masters may do what they want. Paul essentially asks Philemon to abandon his status and rights as a slave owner and to look out for Onesimus's interests rather than his own. Had biblical interpreters more often made that request to Philemon normative, slavery might have come to an end sooner rather than later.

Philemon and Constructive Theology

Although Paul discusses few theological topics or issues in Philemon, several are implicated by or assumed in the epistle.[27] For example, an understanding of the church as the household of faith created through the reconciling work of Christ underlies the epistle, leading Paul to ask Philemon for generous and Christ-like treatment of his slave Onesimus. Since they are one in Christ, Philemon is to treat Onesimus as a brother rather than a slave. As Paul writes elsewhere, "there is no longer slave or free . . . for all of you are one in Christ Jesus" (Gal 3:28; Col 3:11). Yet such formulations raise virtually as many questions as they answer. If there is no longer slave or free in Christ, why then does Paul tell masters to treat their slaves justly (Col 4:1) rather than to set them free? Why tell slaves to submit to their masters rather than to celebrate their freedom in Christ (Gal 5:1)? Indeed, these very questions were raised by those seeking to justify the continued practice of owning slaves in the eighteenth and nineteenth centuries in the United States. Precisely because Paul did not instruct slave owners to manumit their slaves and even enjoined slaves to

---

27. Fitzmyer, *Philemon,* 37, notes a number of theological topics that touch on the main thrust of Philemon, such as the effects of the Christ-event, repentance and forgiveness, justification by grace through faith, baptism, the church, or the role of the Spirit.

obey their masters, the Bible was heard as speaking on the side of the slave owner. Scripture — or at least Scripture read with particular presuppositions — became a tool to perpetuate slavery.

In addition to a particular reading of (only!) certain scriptural precedents and commands as normative, the arguments for slavery were coupled with an increasingly virulent racism. Furthermore, theologians and biblical interpreters who endorsed slavery operated with a dualistic anthropology. A human being consisted of body and soul, and the body could be enslaved without implications for the freedom of the soul. Indeed, the freedom of the soul — that which truly mattered — was independent of one's physical state or condition. So a slave need not be regarded as "enslaved," since the slave could be truly free in the ways in which it mattered most deeply. A dualistic frame of reference was also operative in understanding salvation: since salvation pertained to an individual's soul, it followed that the primary task was "saving souls," that is, converting slaves to Christ. Rather than being released from slavery, slaves who became Christians were delivered from a far worse fate, namely, eternal condemnation. What happened to their bodies or their families was consequently irrelevant. Similarly, a dualistic understanding of the church as a spiritual entity dealing primarily if not exclusively with the inner "spiritual" human condition was operative here as well. If Paul spoke of "unity in Christ," he had in mind an invisible unity of those saved, a "spiritual" equality that did not encompass social realities and so allowed the perpetuation of slavery.

I will not rehash the arguments that were advanced for and against slavery. But the arguments on both sides are instructive in a number of ways. As hinted above, these arguments show that while ostensibly the interpretation of the Bible was alleged to be the real issue, in fact many other assumptions underlay interpretation, on both sides of the debate. Specifically, dualistic assumptions about humankind (anthropology), salvation (soteriology), and the church (ecclesiology) lay behind many of the arguments advanced for preserving slavery. Thus it was argued that slavery pertained to the body, but not the soul, even as salvation pertained to the soul, but not the body. In keeping with that view, the church dealt with matters of the soul and salvation, rather than of the body, social conditions, or political realities. These assumptions not only allowed the church, corporately and individually, to condone the continuation of slavery, but also allowed for the neglect and mistreatment of the bodies of slaves.

Many of these assumptions, or variations of them, remain with us in one form or another and call for thoughtful examination. For, as we shall see, the dualism of body and soul not only served the slave owners; at times it also enabled the slave to maintain an inner dignity and sense of freedom even when the physical conditions of life were deplorable. In the discussion that follows, we will focus briefly on three issues: dualism and anthropology, the character and significance of human freedom, and the reading of Scripture. Each topic has occupied theologians for centuries. The point here is to suggest how Philemon might contribute to the discussion and how discussions of these matters have influenced interpretation of Philemon.

Dualism

Dualism is the "doctrine that posits the existence of two fundamental causal principles underlying the existence . . . of the world."[28] Orthodox Christian theology, because it posits one Creator of all, cannot be ultimately dualistic and, indeed, has deemed heretical those mutations of Christian faith which are dualistic (such as Manicheism or Gnosticism). As a Jewish messianist, Paul believed in one God, Creator and Redeemer of the entire cosmos (1 Cor 8:6), and his thought cannot be characterized in an ultimate sense as dualistic. But Paul's thought gives evidence of some fundamental *dualities* without which it is simply impossible to articulate Pauline theology. But his dualities are not precisely the same dualisms either of his contemporaries or of later Christian thinking. Whereas ancient Greek and even early Christian dualism contrasted the physical and spiritual realms, Paul does not do so, at least not in those stark terms. To be sure, he does contrast life in the flesh with life with (the risen) Christ (Phil 1:21-23) and the earthly body with the body of the resurrection (1 Cor 15:42-54). But the duality in Paul's thought is essentially eschatological; that is to say, it contrasts what will be with what is and speaks of the transformation of the present age into the future new world by the final saving act of God. For Paul, there is a "turning of the ages," marked by the resurrection of Christ from the dead to new life, that foreshadows and points to the new creation in Christ. But both the divine action by which this "turning" has been brought about and the future consummation rest in God's hand and depend on God's initiative. Hence, the contrast or duality in Pauline thought is external to the human being rather than constitutive of the human person, and it is resolved only *extra nos,* outside of us, by God's own action.

A second duality, the contrast between human existence apart from Christ and human existence in Christ, depends on this eschatological framework. For Paul, the contrast of "flesh" and "spirit" must be lodged in the op-

28. Bianchi, "Dualism," *Encyclopedia of Religion,* 506.

position, not of two realities *within* a human being, but of flesh and spirit, the latter not a constitutive part of the person, but the Holy Spirit of God. Many ancient Greek and Roman thinkers contrasted "body" and "soul" or "flesh" and "spirit," where "body" and "flesh" referred to the material or physical realm of existence in which the soul dwelled, at least temporarily. In Pauline thought, the word usually translated "flesh" *(sarx)* has multiple meanings. It can point simply to the stuff of which bodies are made, so that life "in the flesh" refers to earthly existence (2 Cor 5:16; Phil 1:22, 24; Gal 2:20). It can indicate mortality (1 Cor 15:50; 2 Cor 7:5). But for Paul existence "in the flesh" refers more particularly to human existence viewed in terms of its sinfulness, life apart from God's revivifying Spirit. And "Spirit" pertains to existence under the aegis of God's redemptive grace (Rom 8:1-11; Gal 5:13-25).[29] The contrast, then, lies not between "body and soul" or "flesh and spirit" but between human flesh or sinfulness and God's Holy Spirit, between two modes of existence which correspond to the two "ages" whose turning point is the resurrection of Christ.

It is in this framework, then, that we must place Paul's thinking about humanity, salvation, and the church. Since the person in Christ never exists there in isolation, incorporation into Christ is necessarily incorporation into the body of Christ, the church of Christ. Hence, the duality of "flesh" and "Spirit" points not merely to the tension between human existence as shaped by this world and as shaped by God's Spirit, but to the corporate life of the body of Christ in the Spirit. The church lives by and embodies the power of the Spirit of God, the life of the resurrection, the anticipation of the new creation of the world in Christ. Yet it does so always while "groaning for the redemption of our bodies" (Rom 8:23), that is, in the present world that awaits its redemption.[30]

The dualities of Paul's thought — between future and present, between life "in Christ" and "in the flesh" — pertain also to the individual, and Paul can write of attitudes that relate to his personal experiences that suggest a duality between his physical or bodily condition and his stance of faith. In Phil

---

29. It might be noted that different theories of translation render *sarx* differently. Whereas the RSV, for example, fairly consistently renders *sarx* as "flesh," the NIV gives a variety of translations, including "human" or "human nature" (Rom 1:3), "flesh" or "physical" (2:28), "natural descent" (4:1), "mere human nature" or "sinful nature" (7:5), "unspiritual self" (v. 18), "unspiritual nature" (v. 25), "nature" or "sinful man" (8:3), and "old nature" or "sinful nature" (8:4-5). Particularly the introduction of the term "nature" suggests a dualism that does not helpfully portray Paul's thought, inasmuch as it seems to lodge "sin" in one particular, separable part of the human being.

30. See also Hays, *Moral Vision*, 198-200.

4:11-13 he bears testimony that his external circumstances do not determine his attitude toward his external circumstances. However, he also notes that his ability to transcend circumstances comes not from within but from the power that Christ gives him. That power is a foretaste and instantiation of Christ's redeeming power, by which those external circumstances will also be transformed. In other words, even the personal duality remains eschatologically oriented, since the present Christian life anticipates the life of the Spirit lived in the redeemed cosmos.

Thus when Paul speaks of the life of the individual believer, including his own, he speaks also of the eschatological tensions inherent in life in Christ through the power of the Spirit, that it is lived in a world that is awaiting redemption. It is this tension that induces the world, the church, and the individual to groan in anticipation of what is yet to be, to await God's creation of the world anew. But Paul does not locate this contrast, this tension, this struggle between two aspects of the human person, between "flesh" and "spirit" as "parts" of the human being. Indeed, the anthropological terms in Pauline thought are not easily categorized. In addition to "body" and "soul," Paul also speaks in tripartite fashion of the human being as "spirit, soul, and body" (*pneuma, psychē, sōma*, 1 Thess 5:23), heart (*kardia*, Rom 1:21, 24; 1 Cor 2:9; 4:5; 7:37), and mind (*nous*, Rom 1:28; 7:23, 25; 1 Cor 2:16; 14:14-15; Tit 1:15; Col 2:18), but there is no systematic treatment of these aspects of human life, nor is Paul's characterization of the human being uniform.

But it should be noted that for Paul it is the whole person who is either "in the flesh" or "in Christ." Similarly, it is the whole human person, not simply the soul or the spirit, that yearns for redemption. When Paul speaks of redemption, he has in mind what will happen not merely to *part* of the human being, but to the whole person. The God who created earthly bodies will transform them into "spiritual bodies," into bodies appropriate for life transformed by God's Spirit of life. And not just "bodies" will be transformed. The transformation will encompass all that a human being is, as well as the entire created order. Physical bodies are part of that order, but it is not bodies alone that require transformation. Hence, salvation encompasses all that human beings are.

To put it differently, while Paul does not simply divide the human being into "flesh" or "body" and "soul," he does indirectly testify to the fact that the human being cannot be reduced to either "body" or "soul." While Paul's thought about the human being cannot properly be called "dualistic," it nevertheless has an irreducible *duality* about it. One might say that at the most basic level, Paul's thought corresponds to the uniform testimony of Scripture and to human experience. In various ways, Scripture testifies that there is a reality about the human being that must be articulated in terms of humanity's relationship to God. Humankind is created in God's image (Gen 1:26-27). There is a longing in the human heart for transcendence, for knowledge of God, for a life that has meaning beyond the limits of physical existence. And there is testimony to some sort of perdurance of the human being beyond the grave, be it a shadowy existence in Sheol or, in later developments, resurrection (Dan 12:1-3). Hence, in discussing the question "What is a human being?" Patrick Miller comments that "there is something in the human reality that transcends the most complete analysis of the physiology and neurology of the human brain."[31] While theologians, psychologists, neurologists, and philosophers struggle to articulate the duality of the human being, the testimony of Scripture is that human beings cannot be identified without recourse to some sort of duality: created from the dust of the earth, vivified by the life-giving Spirit of God. This is the mystery of the human person. It at once characterizes the human being in its duality, as dust on the one hand and imbued with the Spirit of God on the other hand. And precisely because both aspects of human life — dust and Spirit — come from the Creator, they cannot be played off in opposition against each other.

Centuries of Christian thinking about the definition of the human being have been shaped by more sharply dualistic presuppositions that a human being consists of "body and soul," virtually always to the detriment of the body. For what this view often boils down to is that human beings are *really* soul. The body is a kind of temporary dwelling place and on death is subject to rapid decay. It disappears. Were we somehow to imagine ourselves as "bodies" our very selves would be threatened; we would disappear, cease to be. Something, however, survives death, and that is the soul. Inasmuch as the soul does not "pass away," it represents what we really are. That of course simplifies matters somewhat, but it is in fact what many people, Christian and non-Christian alike, think a human being is. "Soul" need not be the word used, but that there are two components to the human being — one temporal and material, the other enduring and immaterial — summarizes what many think about who and what they are.

The arguments that were used for the support of slavery made use of

---

31. Miller, "What Is a Human Being?" 64. Miller's essay appears in a collection of essays entitled *What About the Soul? Neuroscience and Christian Anthropology* (ed. Joel B. Green). Although not all the authors take precisely the same viewpoint, they share a commitment to bringing scientific and psychological study of the human being, along with the witness of Scripture, into dialogue, and find it necessary to speak of "duality" or "dualism" in some way, although virtually without exception to eschew traditional dualistic descriptions of the human person. For a very different take, see John Cooper, *Body, Soul, and Life Everlasting: Biblical Anthropology and the Monism-Dualism Debate*.

this dualism. Since a human being consisted of two parts, "body and spirit" or perhaps body and soul, it was common to distinguish between what was done in or to one and what was done in or to the other. True "spiritual" slavery, the kind of slavery that really mattered, was servitude to sin, and one could be freed from such servitude regardless of one's status as slave or free. Spiritual slavery had to do with inner freedom and one's eternal destiny, and was a far more serious matter than the temporal condition of slavery to another human being, which was not, in fact, determinative for one's well-being or eternal salvation. Such a dualism allows for practices that pay little or no attention to the physical body or the social conditions in which people live. What matters is the soul, and what happens to the soul. And if the "soul" and not the body is of concern to God, then it matters little what happens to the body in the present life. While certain things, such as the subjugation of some races to others, might be unfortunate or regrettable, one's social status and physical conditions in the present are outside the scope of the redemption envisioned in Christ and hence not the responsibility of those in positions of power and authority. It might be noted as well that a dualism of body and soul provided slaves a framework for resisting the master's totalizing claim to the slave's life. So, for example, here are the words of one slave for whom a dualistic framework serves to express his dual identity: "I have two masters, one on earth and one in heaven — master Jesus in heaven, and master Saunders on earth. I have a soul and a body; the body belongs to you, master Saunders, and the soul to master Jesus."[32]

There is testimony here, as Paul bears in Philippians, that external circumstances cannot erode the confidence of faith. The sense of belonging to "master Jesus in heaven" grants this slave an identity that "master Saunders" cannot touch or destroy. Similarly, in his autobiography Nelson Mandela wrote, "The human body has an enormous capacity for adjusting to trying circumstances. I have found that one can bear the unbearable if one can keep one's spirits strong even when one's body is being tested. Strong convictions are the secret of surviving deprivation; your spirit can be full even when your stomach is empty."[33] Of course in neither case does the "fullness of the Spirit" justify the deprivations experienced by the body; and in both cases the expectation and hope is for freedom where both body and spirit are filled.

These testimonies raise the question of our understanding of God's

---

32. Wm. Wells Brown, "My Southern Home: Or, the South and Its People" (accessed at http://docsouth.unc.edu/neh/brown80/brown80.html).

33. Nelson Mandela, *Long Walk to Freedom: The Autobiography of Nelson Mandela. Robben Island: The Dark Years,* Part 8, 65.

work in the world. The belief that God's work consists primarily in saving souls out of this world and for eternal life leads to a narrow focus exclusively on an individual's "spiritual" condition and to a denigration of the significance of life on this earth. In his letters, including Philemon, Paul never appeals to a distinction between "soul" and "body" when he discusses the obligations of slaves or the relationship of slaves and masters. Some of his contemporaries made such appeals, and it would not have been at all surprising had Paul followed suit. The closest is when in 1 Cor 7:22 he writes "For whoever was called in the Lord as a slave is a freed person belonging to the Lord, just as whoever was free when called is a slave of Christ." There Paul distinguishes two kinds of slavery: even the free are slaves of Christ; and even slaves are free in Christ. But he does not make these distinctions along the lines of "body" and "soul" but along the lines of identity and belonging to Christ. His point is not that freedom and slavery are equally desirable, but that for both slave and free one finds one's identity ultimately in belonging to Christ.

If the arguments of the pro-slavery authors assumed and defended a personal dualism, some also give evidence of a similarly dualistic view of the character and mission of the church. So, for example, in its defense of slavery, states' rights, and its understanding of the relationship of church and state, southern Presbyterianism depended heavily on its belief in the "spirituality of the church." On this view, the church was a purely spiritual body that did not deal with social and political matters. Robert Dabney once wrote that he had preached "the pure gospel" to countless negroes and had never once introduced the "foreign and disastrous element of politics."[34]

Slaves, of course, experienced the refusal to "contaminate" the "pure gospel" with social matters quite differently. In one of his autobiographies Frederick Douglass wrote of the Christian faith of a particular slave owner as follows: "His religion was a thing altogether apart from his worldly concerns. He knew nothing of it as a holy principle, directing and controlling his daily life, making the latter conform to the requirements of the gospel." Douglass went on to tell of the brutal treatment of slaves by this "Christian" master.[35]

---

34. From a letter written to Major General O. O. Howard, September 12, 1865, urging the North to do "more" for the Negro than the South had done; found at: http://www.crownrights .com/books/dabney_letter_howard.htm. In "The State of the Country," republished from *The Southern Presbyterian Review* (Columbia: Southern Guardian, 1861). There is much material related to slavery in the American South at the University of North Carolina website "Documenting the American South," http://docsouth.unc.edu.

35. Frederick Douglass, *My Bondage and My Freedom*, 217. Accessed at http://docsouth .unc.edu/neh/douglass55/menu.html.

Thus he contrasted in sharpest possible terms the Christian profession of those who abused their slaves with the vision of Christian faith he found in the Scriptures: "I love the pure, peaceable, and impartial Christianity of Christ: I therefore hate the corrupt, slaveholding, women-whipping, cradle-plundering, partial and hypocritical Christianity of this land. Indeed, I can see no reason, but the most deceitful one, for calling the religion of this land Christianity."[36] Few would disagree with Douglass's attack on Christian faith that condones the kinds of atrocities to which he bears witness and which he himself experienced. But the point for the present is that such a division of "Christian commitment" fit with mistreatment of slaves in part because of the dualistic anthropologies and ecclesiologies of the slave owners. Christian faith was a "spiritual" and individual commitment that did not impinge upon the treatment of the *bodies* of slaves. One could, after all, console oneself that the slaves had been brought to salvation by the preaching of the gospel.

If Paul does not make a dualistic move to separate the "spiritual" and "social" aspects of the relationship of individuals, neither does he make a dualistic move in describing the church as somehow only a "spiritual" reality, separated from the world only by an invisible commitment. The church is not merely a "spiritual" entity, if that means that its convictions do not shape the way it corporately lives out its commitments or the way it engages the world. Rather, the church embodies God's vision of the new humanity, part of God's purpose to bring peace, wholeness, and harmony, in the form of restored relationships with nature, other humans, and God. The people of God are to embody this vision of wholeness and reconciliation in their relationships, to be agents of God's reconciling power in all the world, and to bear witness to it in manifold ways. Such a calling is profoundly "spiritual" in that these purposes are the work of the Spirit of the risen Lord, who determines the church's identity. This vision of a new humanity not divided by class, race, and gender demands engagement with the lives of real people and their relationships to each other; hence, it is inevitably social and political in the sense that the church is empowered by the Spirit to live in the world — and not only within the bounds of the church — in ways that bear witness to and embody God's purposes for humankind. To imagine that unity in Christ does not assume tangible shape in the church, in relationships among people, and in the church's witness to and work in the world simply sells out the reconciling gospel of Jesus Christ.

36. Douglass, *Narrative of the Life of Frederick Douglass,* 118. Accessed at http://docsouth .unc.edu/douglass/douglass.html.

What Is Freedom?

Paul's epistle to Philemon further focuses our gaze on one particular aspect or manifestation of the issue of the identity of the human person, namely, the problem of human freedom. As one author asserts, "The most important thing to say about humans is that they are free."[37] Or, as another puts it, "That God intends his human creatures to be free is central to the Christian message."[38] But such assertions only raise a whole host of questions: What is freedom? Can the human being be free while in prison, in slavery, living under tyranny, or in poverty? In what ways are human beings "free"? Is freedom constitutive of human beings? Is "freedom" a God-given right?[39] Given the history of the use of Philemon as a tool to endorse slavery, one might ask how Paul or his epistle would answer the question of what makes for freedom. As noted above, dualistic anthropologies allow "freedom" to be conceived of under two aspects. Paul did not adopt a strict anthropological viewpoint allowing him to think of Onesimus as both "free in Christ" and yet a slave to Philemon. But the fundamental dualities of Paul's thought sketched briefly above enter into the discussion of the meaning of "freedom."

Conceivably one might reach different conclusions about the nature of freedom based on whether one thinks that Paul asks Philemon to free Onesimus or not. The dominant view has assumed that Paul returned Onesimus to Philemon without any expectation of manumission. This "traditional interpretation" served slave owners well, but they did not create it. Earlier generations of interpreters assumed that Paul set an example when he sent Onesimus back to Philemon; thus Basil the Great wrote, "All bound slaves who flee to religious communities for refuge should be admonished and sent back to their masters in better dispositions, after the example of St. Paul who . . . had convinced Onesimus that the yoke of slavery, borne in a manner pleasing to the Lord, would render him worthy of the kingdom of heaven."[40] Not only did Basil and later authors share a common understanding of Paul's instructions to Onesimus, but they likewise shared the view that

---

37. Johnson, *Faith's Freedom*, 32.

38. Jenson, *On Thinking the Human*, 32. Jenson continues, "Yet the attempt to *think* human freedom within theology, that is, to relate the proposition 'God intends us to be free' to other necessary propositions of the faith, has throughout the church's history produced mostly antinomies and conflicts, even divisions of the church" (33).

39. As Harrill, *Manumission of Slaves*, 13, notes, philosophers and intellectual historians have been trying for centuries to answer basic questions such as: What is slavery? What is a slave? What is freedom? He includes a lengthy bibliography to establish the point.

40. "The Long Rules," Q.II.R (*Fathers of the Church* 9:261-62), quoted in *ACCSNT* 9:314.

freedom was not simply to be identified with release from slavery. Clearly such a viewpoint could easily be used to justify the continuance of slavery; and yet, in spite of its potential for misuse and abuse, there is something profound and even profoundly Christian in a refusal simply to equate genuine freedom with a particular social status or condition and in acknowledging that the freedom of the Christian person may encompass, but is not determined by, the social conditions in which one lives. Here we confront again the mystery of the human person, who is not entirely determined or defined by his or her personal physical condition or state. How, then, might Philemon, in the context of the Pauline corpus, serve as a catalyst for thinking about human freedom?

There are many kinds of freedom, including political, religious, social, and psychological freedom. To a large extent, we define these separately. Given the history of the United States, for many in this country political freedom is roughly the same as either the right to vote or the freedom from state interference in religious practice and belief. If we think of freedom in psychological terms, we mean something like self-determination, a person's ability to make meaningful and thoughtful choices, rather than determination entirely by genes, upbringing, and external factors of various sorts. For many spiritual freedom would be roughly akin to the inner attitude or experience of liberation from external compulsion or oppression. Spiritual freedom need not therefore correspond to external circumstances. One might be a prisoner or live under a repressive regime and yet experience a genuine inner freedom that transcends these social conditions. For many Christians, "spiritual freedom" can be identified with "freedom from sin," that is to say, with forgiveness and hence with salvation.

It has proven difficult to bring all these varying aspects of human freedom under one Christian vision, in part because of the difficulties of defining freedom itself and in part because human beings do experience captivity of various kinds and to various degrees, whether psychological, physical, or emotional. Paul's eschatological framing of the gospel can help us here. He defines the present in terms of both slavery to the powers of sin, death, and corruption and freedom in Christ: the "freedom" for which "Christ has set us free" (Gal 5:1). This freedom anticipates "the glorious liberty of the children of God" that is yet to be attained along with the redemption of all creation (Rom 8:21). The freedom that God promises is not only freedom from bondage to death and decay, but freedom from all bondage to the powers of sin and death. Paul's vision of a redeemed creation is a vision of freedom: one in which the enslaving political, social, and spiritual powers are subjected to the ultimate sovereignty of God and, hence, people will live in that glorious liberty of God's children free from all tyrannical forces, oppression, sin and the last enemy, death.

It follows, therefore, that the full freedom of the human being entails spiritual, physical, and psychological freedom, because the powers of this world, of sin and death, no longer exert their power over human life. Instead, God's saving purposes for the world are fully realized and embodied, and life is lived not under the influence of the powers of the world, but under and for God. To be free is "to live with God, to participate in some way in God's life."[41]

But a modern assumption about the nature of freedom is that it is roughly equivalent with self-determination and that what gives meaning to human life is precisely the ability to make the choices that determine one's destiny. This may be coupled with the view that freedom is freedom from the interference, obligations, or demands of others. In the United States, such a view of freedom can be found expressed in terms of "privacy rights." Individuals are free if they may exercise their rights in the form of preventing interference — or at least undue interference — from outsiders, typically cast in terms of government authorities. Hence freedom might be construed as freedom to live where one wants, to vote according to one's preferences, to drive a car of one's choosing, to attend the school of one's choice, to worship as one pleases, to marry whom one wants, and so on. "Freedom" and "to do as one wants" are simply viewed as correlates.

Along these lines, Brian Walsh and Sylvia Keesmaat describe the modern conception of human beings "primarily as units of consumption for whom choice is the defining characteristic."[42] Choice, autonomy, and self-determination are constitutive of authentic humanness. If we apply this definition of freedom to Paul's letter to Philemon, we could conclude that unless Paul sought the manumission of Onesimus, he was complicit in the dehumanization of slaves.

Freedom and choice were of concern to ancient moralists and philosophers, but they understood the issues somewhat differently. They did not construe freedom as freedom to do whatever one wished, for such prerogatives were not given to humankind. Whereas moderns on the whole prize choice and self-determination, ancients experienced and thought of the world much more in terms of the realities that were simply given. Pagan authors spoke of Fate, Chance, or Fortune, which had determined a person's status and lot in life. Such things were not chosen, and one could not simply "determine" one's destiny.

---

41. Sachs, *Christian Vision*, 27.
42. Walsh and Keesmaat, *Colossians Remixed*, 32.

Epictetus, the first-century Stoic philosopher, put it this way: "Some things are within our power and some things are beyond our power. Those things within our power include opinions, goals, desires, and aversions, in other words, whatever affairs belong to us. Those things beyond our power include our bodies, property, reputation, and public office, that is, whatever does not properly belong to us."[43] Employing the metaphor of the drama, Epictetus also wrote: "Remember that you are an actor in a drama, of such a kind as the author pleases to make it. If short, of a short one; if long, of a long one. If it is his pleasure you should act a poor man, a cripple, a governor, or a private person, see that you act it naturally. For this is your business, to act well the character assigned you; to choose it is another's."[44] Humans live in a drama which they did not write and can do little to change, but it does not follow that they are puppets on a string without volition or the capacity for virtue and happiness. These need not be "freely chosen" — whatever that might mean — to be genuine.

The promise of freedom can be illusory and deceptive. While the modern Western tradition typically thinks of freedom as the capacity to determine one's fate, socialist thinkers have objected that freedom means little without the power to achieve what is sought or desired. The freedom to be one's own master and pursue one's own interests matters little if no work can be found and one's family is starving.[45] "Freedom" may promise more than it can deliver, since it cannot guarantee that one can pursue meaningful existence. In fact, without, for instance, the ability to provide for one's family, "freedom" leads not to self-determination, choice, or autonomy but merely to other kinds of slavery, to fear, need, struggle, poverty, or the whims and decisions of others. It used to be said that if you give someone a fish, they may eat for a day, but if you teach them to fish, they will eat for a lifetime. But what if they have no access to the water in which the fish live? If other powers control access or if access requires yet more material goods — boats, tackle, fuel, licenses — then the mere ability to fish has not in fact guaranteed a livelihood. Freedom from hunger, from poverty, from death have become elusive because other powers dictate the course one may chart.

Booker T. Washington poignantly recounted the response of slaves to the Emancipation Proclamation: "The great responsibility of being free, of having charge of themselves, of having to think and plan for themselves and

---

43. Epictetus, *Enchiridion* 1.

44. Epictetus, *Enchiridion* 17. In his treatise *On Duties*, Cicero also discusses at length the whole notion of duty and obligation.

45. Volf, *Exclusion and Embrace*, p. 102.

their children, seemed to take possession of them. . . . To some it seemed that, now that they were in actual possession of it, freedom was a more serious thing than they had expected to find it."[46] Similarly, Frederick Douglass wrote in one of his memoirs about his life in slavery as follows:

> Some apology can easily be made for the few slaves who have, after making good their escape, turned back to slavery, preferring the actual rule of their masters, to the life of loneliness, apprehension, hunger, and anxiety, which meets them on their first arrival in a free state. It is difficult for a freeman to enter into the feelings of such fugitives. He cannot see things in the same light with the slave, because he does not, and cannot, look from the same point from which the slave does. "Why do you tremble," he says to the slave — "you are in a free state"; but the difficulty is, in realizing that he is in a free state, the slave might reply. A freeman cannot understand why the slave-master's shadow is bigger, to the slave, than the might and majesty of a free state; but when he reflects that the slave knows more about the slavery of his master than he does of the might and majesty of the free state, he has the explanation. The slave has been all his life learning the power of his master.[47]

Such personal testimonies suggest that liberation from bondage or oppression, on its own, can often be a partial fulfillment of the promise of freedom, when construed as self-determination. Even in Paul's world, manumission, the ostensible granting of freedom, was often used by the powerful to their advantage and to accomplish their ends. Texts from the ancient world show that masters sometimes freed their slaves so that they could be treated as citizens — but often to the disadvantage of the slave. Needing soldiers for his wars, Octavian had 20,000 slaves manumitted (Suetonius, *Augustus* 16.1).[48] Other ancient authors give accounts of masters manumitting their slaves in order that they could be executed as freedmen. In other words, manumission did not necessarily grant one the right of self-determination.

In any case, for a Christian — or Jewish — writer, if freedom were construed as "self-determination," such freedom would have to be placed in the greater context of the purposes and will of God. The narratives of the exodus place the giving of God's commandments in the context of God's deliverance of the people from slavery: "I am the LORD your God, who brought you out of

---

46. Booker T. Washington, *Up from Slavery*, 20, 22. Accessed at http://docsouth.unc.edu/washington/washing.html.

47. Douglass, *My Bondage and My Freedom*, 339.

48. War was deemed a privilege of citizens and denied to slaves.

the land of Egypt, out of the house of bondage" (Exod 20:2). Israel was freed in order to serve God. As the Jewish apologist, Philo of Alexandria, inquired: "Are we not under a master, and have we not and shall we not have forever the same lord, slavery to whom gives us more joy than freedom does to any other? For of all the things that are held in honor in this world of creation slavery to God is the best" (*Dreams* 2.100).

Genuine freedom, therefore, consists in the capacity or right not to do as one wishes, but to belong to the Creator, to God, and to acknowledge his mastery. No doubt there is paradox here, but philosophers and theologians over the years have wrestled with precisely this paradox: genuine freedom is not freedom from constraint but freedom to live in accord with the highest good. Paul could think of freedom in terms of serving Christ, as being a slave of Christ. Later Chrysostom would note,

> Slave and free are simply names. What is a slave? It is a mere name. How many masters lie drunken upon their beds, while slaves stand by sober? Whom shall I call a slave? The one who is sober, or the one who is drunk? The one who is the slave of a man, or the one who is the captive of passion? The former has his slavery on the outside; the latter wears his captivity on the inside.[49]

The master, who has the capacity to do as he wishes — or so it seems — in this case is actually subject to his own passions.

Gustavo Gutiérrez wrote that "liberation from sin . . . attacks the deepest root of all servitude; for sin is the breaking of friendship with God and with other human beings, and therefore cannot be eradicated except by the unmerited redemptive love of the Lord whom we receive by faith and in communion with one another."[50] Gutiérrez here reflects the consistent biblical theme that God's redemptive love brings those redeemed into fellowship with each other. God delivered Israel to serve him and live corporately as a people whose lives reflected God's love for them. Jesus spoke of the dual love command as a summary of the entire law of God. And Paul likewise could write of the freedom Christians have in Christ in terms of "faith working through love." God's deliverance from bondage to freedom means that people are brought into a reality in which they may wholeheartedly serve God and their neighbors.

As David Atkinson writes, "Personal freedom means freedom of a 'heart' that is directed towards God. . . . A theological understanding of freedom concentrates not so much on the freedom from external constraints, as

---

49. "On Lazarus and the Rich Man," in *On Wealth and Poverty* 15-16.
50. Gutiérrez, *Theology of Liberation*, xxxviii.

on the freedom 'of the heart'; a freedom *for* life lived freely before that which is ultimately real — that is, God."[51] Freedom cannot simply be reduced to or equated with personal choice, autonomy, or self-determination. For the Christian, freedom is always freedom from certain powers — the power of fear, guilt, sin, and death. God in Christ delivers people from these powers so that they might love and serve their Creator and live in fellowship with each other. Paul's eschatological vision of freedom is not of humans with the power to do as they wish, but of humans living according to God's purposes for them in reconciled relationships within a restored creation. To the extent, then, that humans experience a foretaste of this future reality in the present, they experience freedom. Such freedom cannot be equated simply with freedom from external constraints of any sort, but it does surely anticipate a time when those in bondage of any sort — to crippling diseases, to poverty, to injustice and oppression, to sin and death — will enter into the fullness of the glorious liberty of the children of God.

How Do We Read Scripture?

Drawing guidelines for ethical action and moral conduct from Scripture scarcely ever boils down to simply describing "what the Bible says" and following the course it charts. There is disagreement not only on "what the Bible says," but also on *how* the Bible charts a course for its modern-day readers. Does one, for example, extrapolate general "principles" from texts and reapply them in other cultures? Does one simply carry over injunctions found in Scripture to modern society? Those who argued in support of slavery clearly believed that a simple transference of culture and context from the ancient world to the present and application of commands to slaves in the first century to slaves everywhere was the only way to honor the authority of Scripture.

Yet such an approach to biblical authority does not wrestle at all with the complexities in how Jewish thinkers of the first century read their Scriptures, or in how the Christian authors of the NT documents read the same Scriptures. Indeed, Jewish literature bears witness to discussions about the first-century meaning and applicability of Scripture and reveals that such discussions were marked by disagreements about how the ancient texts spoke to newer needs. Commands were not taken up literally or uniformly. For example, some OT laws and regulations are repeated and reinforced in the NT, some are abrogated, and some are held up as norms which determine how the

---

51. David Atkinson, in *Free to Be Different*, 59, 61-62.

rest of the Law should be read. Jesus made the commands regarding adultery more rigorous (compare Deut 24:1-4 and Matt 19:1-9). The early church concluded that the commands regarding circumcision were not binding on Gentile Christians but that, at least according to Acts 15, certain laws regarding food were binding (Acts 15:20-21).

The NT interprets the OT in a variety of ways, based on certain theological commitments rather than strictly on the literal meaning of the text. A classic example of where Christian practice has rested on theological rather than literal readings of texts is in the church's keeping of the first day of the week rather than the seventh. The Decalogue's command to honor the Sabbath clearly refers to the seventh day of the week, our Saturday. And yet early on, because of the resurrection of Jesus on "the first day," Christians apparently gathered to celebrate Sunday as "the Lord's Day" (see Rev 1:10; *Didache* 14.1; Eusebius, *Historia Ecclesiastica* 5.23-24, citing the examples of Melito, bishop of Sardis, and others). No explicit command of Scripture authorizes this change. But it was adopted early enough that Ignatius, writing about AD 110, could contrast those "who lived according to the old ways" with those who are "no longer keeping the Sabbath but living according to the Lord's day" (*Magnesians* 9.1). But why did not other church practices, such as greeting with a holy kiss, enrolling widows, having possessions in common, or sharing a meal at the celebration of the Lord's Supper become normative? The answer would touch on a multitude of factors theological, cultural, and personal; and these have always played a role in the interpretation of Scripture.

It is one of the sad facts of the history of scriptural interpretation that those with privilege and power have used the Bible to bolster their own positions and maintain their status at the expense of the underprivileged and weak. In a study of the ways in which the Spanish conquerors of Latin America portrayed Jesus to the natives there, David Batstone contends that two primary images were held up: the passive, suffering Jesus who submitted to the will of God, and the victorious and reigning Christ. Unfortunately it is not hard to guess how these two different images were used: the native peoples were to identify with the submissive Jesus, while the ruling Spanish identified with the reigning Christ.[52] So also abused women who are familiar with the Scriptures often take their cues from the portrayal of Jesus as one who patiently endured suffering and, "like a lamb before his shearers, was dumb." And their abusers simply perpetuate the injustice by allowing and encouraging the texts to be read in that way.[53]

---

52. Batstone, *From Conquest to Struggle*, 14-18.
53. See Thistlethwaite, "Every Two Minutes," 103.

But neither the submissive Jesus nor the victimized Jesus captures the Jesus of the Gospels, who was actively and willingly obedient to God, obedient "even unto death on the cross." He "set his face" to follow the path that he believed God had charted for him, and the Gospels indicate that there was a way out, although he chose not to take it. "The suffering of Jesus, as well as that of Paul and Barnabas, was grounded in their active pursuit of the mission of God, their struggle against those who oppose God's purpose."[54] Active pursuit of God's purposes may well lead to suffering, but it does not follow that suffering can automatically be assumed to be God's purposes or that those who force others to suffer have become agents of God's will. In fact, the NT consistently holds together Jesus' willingness to suffer to carry out God's purposes with the injustice done by those who betrayed and crucified Jesus. If some suffer because of their obedience to the will of God, it does not follow that those who inflict that suffering are simply demonstrating similar obedience to God's will.

It is always worth asking who will bear the brunt of the burden if a particular theology or interpretation of Scripture is adopted. When it will be those who are most vulnerable to the whims of others and least able to effect positive changes in their own circumstances, then the framework supporting such interpretation, as well as the motives of interpreters, needs to be examined. In the narratives of slave life from the American South, slaves regularly report that a favorite text preached by white preachers to them was Luke 12:47: "And that servant, which knew his lord's will, and prepared not himself, neither did according to his will, shall be beaten with many stripes." The text became not only one a warning to slaves but a justification for mistreatment of slaves by their masters. Needless to say, texts regarding the liberation of Israel from slavery and commands for masters to treat their slaves with Christian kindness disappeared from proclamation. If this is obvious to us as misuse of Scripture, it also at least testifies that it is all too easy to become selective and self-serving readers of Scripture. Modern interpreters of Scripture have endeavored to deal with the problem by intense focus on the historical, cultural, and social contexts in which our biblical texts were written and on the specific purposes for which texts were written. They have thereby sought to acknowledge the difficulty of applying any single admonition globally or universally, or at least to recognize the problems in doing so.

Augustine offered a different sort of guideline for approaching Scripture, one focused not on the mechanics of interpretation but on the spirit in which one read.

---

54. Green and Baker, *The Scandal of the Cross*, 20.

> The chief purpose of all that we have been saying in our discussion of things is to make it understood that the fulfilment and end of the law and all the divine scriptures is to love the thing [God] which must be enjoyed and the thing [one's neighbor] which together with us can enjoy that thing. . . . So anyone who thinks that he has understood the divine scriptures or any part of them, but cannot by his understanding build up this double love of God and neighbor, has not yet succeeded in understanding them.[55]

Since growing in love of God and neighbor is the goal of reading Scripture, it serves also as the central and guiding hermeneutical principle. While that principle does not guarantee faithful reading of the text, it can surely shed a probing light on readings that are self-serving rather than directed to the other.

A first guideline, then, for reading the text faithfully is to exercise a hermeneutics of suspicion toward one's own motives and interpretations. Indeed, feminist author Elisabeth Schüssler Fiorenza, who exercises a "hermeneutics of suspicion" toward a number of biblical texts, also writes that any hermeneutics of suspicion "turns its searchlight first on the reader's own reading practices and assumptions."[56] We might add that the exercise of a "hermeneutics of suspicion" toward one's own interpretations and motives is simply the outworking of a belief in human sinfulness. Since human sin leads us to self-serving actions, it follows that the readings that arise "naturally" from our "natural instincts" will not focus primarily on the good one is to do another.[57]

Many modern approaches to the biblical text have tended to assume that good interpretation of the text will lead to faithful living and that "good interpretation" is a matter of following certain methods and approaches. But in earlier centuries it was assumed that faithful Christian living undergirds good interpretation. Augustine thought that Scripture should be read in ways that fostered love for God and neighbor. Athanasius put it this way: "For the searching and right understanding of the Scriptures there is need of a good life and a pure soul, and for Christian virtue to guide the mind to grasp, so far as human nature can, the truth concerning God the Word."[58] In a similar

---

55. Augustine, *De doctrina christiana* 1.35.39–1.36.40 (CCSL 32:28-29; Green ed. p. 49).

56. Schüssler Fiorenza, *But She Said*, 53.

57. "Indeed, one might even correlate applying suspicion to oneself with the venerable Calvinist recognition of one's own (total) depravity as an essential consideration in good exegesis" (Thompson, *Writing the Wrongs*, 252).

58. Athanasius, *On the Incarnation* (Crestwood: St. Vladimir's, 1953), 96.

vein, Alasdair MacIntyre put it this way, "What the reader . . . has to learn about him or herself is that it is only the self as transformed through and by the reading of the texts which will be capable of reading the texts aright."[59] While this sounds circular, the point is clear: we are always in need of being transformed by the very texts that we seek to interpret.

Indeed, Augustine's "rule" for the interpretation of Scripture was not selected at random, but represents Jesus' own statement of the "greatest commands" of the Law, the heart of the Law as Jesus himself interprets it, and therefore has its focal point in Christ's own practice of reading Scripture. Augustine's use of a commandment intended in its original context to guide moral conduct makes it plain that for Augustine interpretation of Scripture is an inherently moral activity. Right interpretation is a matter not of properly applying scientific principles but of obedience to the central commands of Jesus and basically of faithfulness. Augustine notes that anyone who thinks he has understood Scripture but "cannot by his understanding build up this double love of God and neighbor" has actually failed in interpretation. Failure to "build up this double love" is a greater sin than exegetical inaccuracy. "Anyone who derives an idea which is useful for supporting this love but fails to say what the writer demonstrably meant in the passage has not made a fatal error, and is certainly not a liar."[60]

Augustine points us in two important directions: First, Scripture provides the norm by which we are to read Scripture. Second, it is the christocentric heart of the Scriptures that norms interpretation of the Scriptures. In referring to the "christocentric heart" of Scripture, we have in mind the movement from protology to eschatology, or from creation to the redemption of the world in Christ. Because this narrative provides the framework for Christian confession, it also provides the framework for interpreting the Christian Scriptures. Any single passage of Scripture must therefore always be read with an eye toward and within the context of the bigger picture of Scripture and of God's work in the world.

In the debates regarding slavery and the question of its ongoing validity, the anti-abolitionists tended to favor arguments from practice or precedence (the Old Testament patriarchs, Hagar), arguments from silence (neither Jesus nor the apostles condemned slavery), and arguments that tried to draw out the implications of specific verses (the commands for slaves to be obedient eliminated the option of manumission). What these arguments conspicuously lacked was any attempt to deal with the vision of the renewal of human-

---

59. MacIntyre, *Three Rival Versions of Moral Enquiry*, 82.
60. For further discussion see Thompson, *Writing the Wrongs*, 247.

ity *in Christ*. Passages that implied the erasure of social or class distinction in Christ such as Col 3:11 and Gal 3:28 were taken then — as often now — as applicable "only to the spiritual realm." Neatly splitting "spiritual" from "bodily," such interpretations were able to preserve the status quo to the benefit of those whose bodies were not bruised or abused and who did not have to take refuge in the comfort that although their bodies were enslaved, their hearts and souls were free.

Another lesson from Augustine's guidelines regarding interpretation of Scripture has to do with a proper ordering of what is more and less important. As already noted, Augustine's guidelines make central what Christ himself made central: love of God and neighbor. Throughout the Pauline corpus, love is the virtue that surpasses and unites all other graces as the greatest of all the virtues (1 Cor 13:13; cf. Gal 5:6). In Colossians, Paul commands his readers to "put on love, which binds everything together in perfect harmony" (3:14). It is of course not always so easy to discern which courses of action or readings of Scripture will build up this double love for God and neighbor. Hence, other guidelines help to provide the necessary shape and give substance to the commands to love.

Paul's epistle to Philemon makes just such an appeal to love in its consistent use of familial imagery, its appeal to relationship in Christ, and its implicit request to look out for the good of the other rather than for one's own interests. And yet modern readers might well stumble over the fact that while Paul held out these high ideals, he failed to take the next step and ask for the release of Onesimus from slavery. But it should be noted that for Paul manumission was not the highest good or goal; belonging to Christ was — and that had implications for both the master and the slave. If a Christian owned a slave, the highest duty to which that master could be called was not to set the other free but to love the slave with the self-giving love of Christ. Paul insists that those with power act as Christ did: giving it up for the sake of the other. In calling Philemon to welcome Onesimus as a brother in Christ, Paul does not think that he is compromising Christian commitment. Since Philemon belongs to Christ, then Paul calls him to the highest commitment he can imagine: to love as Christ loved.

Bibliography

Arnold, Clinton. *The Colossian Syncretism: The Interface between Christianity and Folk Belief at Colossae.* Grand Rapids: Baker, 1996.

―――. *Powers of Darkness: Principalities and Powers in Paul's Letters.* Downers Grove: InterVarsity, 1992.

Aulén, Gustaf. *Christus Victor: An Historical Study of the Three Main Types of the Idea of the Atonement.* New York: Macmillan, 1958.

Balch, David L. "Household Codes." In *ABD* 3:319-20.

Barclay, John M. G. *Colossians and Philemon.* New Testament Guides. Sheffield: Sheffield Academic, 1997.

―――. "The Dilemma of Christian Slave-Ownership." *NTS* 37 (1991): 161-86.

Bartchy, S. Scott. *MALLON CHRĒSAI. First-Century Slavery and the Interpretation of 1 Corinthians 7:21.* SBLDS 11; Missoula: Scholars, 1973.

―――. "Philemon, Epistle to." In *ABD* 5:305-10.

―――. "Slavery" (Greco-Roman)." In *ABD* 6:70-71.

Barton, Stephen C. *Discipleship and Family Ties in Mark and Matthew.* SNTSMS 80; Cambridge: Cambridge University Press, 1994.

Batstone, David. *From Conquest to Struggle: Jesus of Nazareth in Latin America.* Albany: State University of New York Press, 1991.

Bauckham, Richard. "The Future of Jesus Christ." In *The Cambridge Companion to Jesus* (ed. Markus Bockmuehl; New York: Cambridge University Press, 2001).

―――. *God Crucified: Monotheism and Christology in the New Testament.* Grand Rapids/Cambridge: Eerdmans, 1998.

―――. "Reading Scripture as a Coherent Story." In *The Art of Biblical Interpretation* (ed. Ellen F. Davis and Richard B. Hays; Grand Rapids: Eerdmans, 2003).

Bauckham, Richard, and Trevor Hart. *Hope against Hope: Christian Eschatology at the Turn of the Millennium.* Grand Rapids: Eerdmans, 1999.

Beaudoin, Tom. *Virtual Faith: The Irreverent Spiritual Quest of Generation X.* San Francisco: Jossey-Bass, 1998.

Beker, J. C. "Paul's Theology: Consistent or Inconsistent?" *NTS* 34 (1988): 364-77.

————. *Paul the Apostle: The Triumph of God in Life and Thought*. Philadelphia: Fortress, 1980.

————. *The Triumph of God: The Essence of Paul's Thought*. Philadelphia: Fortress, 1990.

Bianchi, Udo. "Dualism." In *The Encyclopedia of Religion* (ed. Mircea Eliade; New York: Macmillan, 1987).

Bockmuehl, Markus. *Jewish Law in Gentile Churches: Halakah and the Beginning of Christian Public Ethics*. Grand Rapids: Baker, 2000.

————. *Revelation and Mystery in Ancient Judaism and Pauline Christianity*. WUNT 2/36; Tübingen: Mohr, 1990.

Breytenbach, Cilliers. *Versöhnung. Eine Studie zur paulinischen Soteriologie*. WMANT 60; Neukirchen: Neukirchener, 1989.

Brown, Raymond E. *The Semitic Background of the Term "Mystery" in the New Testament*. Philadelphia: Fortress, 1968.

Bruce, F. F. *The Epistles to the Colossians, to Philemon, and to the Ephesians*. NICNT; Grand Rapids: Eerdmans, 1984.

————. *Paul, Apostle of the Heart Set Free*. Grand Rapids: Eerdmans, 1977.

Burney, C. F. "Christ as the Archē of Creation." *JTS* 27 (1925-26): 160-77.

Burtchaell, James Tunstead. *Philemon's Problem: A Theology of Grace*. Grand Rapids: Eerdmans, 1998.

Byron, John. *Slavery Metaphors in Early Judaism and Pauline Christianity: A Traditio-Historical and Exegetical Examination*. WUNT 2; Tübingen: Mohr, 2003.

Caird, G. B. *Principalities and Powers: A Study in Pauline Theology*. Oxford: Clarendon, 1956.

Callahan, Allen D. *Embassy of Onesimus: The Letter of Paul to Philemon*. Valley Forge: Trinity, 1997.

————. "Paul's Epistle to Philemon: Toward an Alternative Argumentum." *HTR* 86 (1993): 357-76.

Calvin, John. *The Epistles of Paul the Apostle to the Galatians, Ephesians, Philippians and Colossians*, tr. T. H. L. Parker. Grand Rapids: Eerdmans, 1965.

Carr, A. Wesley. *Angels and Principalities: The Background, Meaning and Development of the Pauline Phrase* hai archai kai hai exousiai. SNTSMS 42; Cambridge: Cambridge University Press, 1981.

Carroll, John T., and Joel B. Green. *The Death of Jesus in Early Christianity*. Peabody: Hendrickson, 1995.

Church, F. F. "Rhetorical Structure and Design in Paul's Letter to Philemon." *HTR* 71 (1978): 17-33.

Cooper, John. *Body, Soul, and Life Everlasting: Biblical Anthropology and the Monism-Dualism Debate*. Second ed., Grand Rapids: Eerdmans, 2000.

Dabney, Lyle. "'Justified by the Spirit': Soteriological Reflections on the Resurrection." *IJST* 3 (2001): 61-62.

Davies, W. D. *Paul and Rabbinic Judaism*. Fourth edition, Philadelphia: Fortress, 1980.

Deissmann, Adolf. *Light from the Ancient East*. Rev. ed., London: Hodder and Stoughton, 1927.

DeMaris, Richard E. *The Colossian Controversy: Wisdom in Dispute at Colossae*. JSNTSup 96; Sheffield: JSOT, 1994.

Derrett, J. D. M. "The Functions of the Epistle to Philemon." *ZNW* 79 (1988): 63-91.

deSilva, David A. *Honor, Patronage, Kinship and Purity: Unlocking New Testament Culture.* Downers Grove: InterVarsity, 2000.

Devanandan, Paul. "Called to Witness." *Ecumenical Review* 14 (1962): 155-63.

Dunn, James D. G. *Christology in the Making.* London: SCM, 1980.

————. *The Epistles to the Colossians and to Philemon.* NIGTC; Grand Rapids: Eerdmans, 1996.

————. *The Theology of Paul the Apostle.* Grand Rapids: Eerdmans, 1998.

Felder, Cain Hope. "The Letter to Philemon: Introduction, Commentary, and Reflections." In *The New Interpreter's Dictionary of the Bible* (Nashville: Abingdon, 2000), 12:881-905.

Ferguson, Everett. *Backgrounds of Early Christianity.* Third ed., Grand Rapids: Eerdmans, 2003.

Fitzgerald, John T. "Haustafeln." In *ABD* 3:80-81.

Fitzmyer, Joseph. *The Letter to Philemon.* Anchor Bible; New York: Doubleday, 2000.

————. *Pauline Theology: A Brief Sketch.* Englewood Cliffs: Prentice-Hall, 1967.

Francis, Fred O. "Humility and Angelic Worship in Col 2:18." In *Conflict at Colossae: A Problem in the Interpretation of Early Christianity Illustrated by Selected Modern Studies* (rev. ed. by Fred O. Francis and Wayne A. Meeks; Sources for Biblical Study 4; Missoula: Scholars, 1975), 163-95.

Gamble, H. Y. *Books and Readers in the Early Church: A History of Early Christian Texts.* New Haven: Yale University Press, 1995.

Gorman, Michael J. *Apostle of the Crucified Lord: A Theological Introduction to Paul and His Letters.* Grand Rapids: Eerdmans, 2004.

————. *Cruciformity: Paul's Narrative Spirituality of the Cross.* Grand Rapids: Eerdmans, 2001.

Green, Joel B., ed. *What About the Soul? Neuroscience and Christian Anthropology.* Nashville: Abingdon, 2004.

Green, Joel B., and Mark Baker. *Recovering the Scandal of the Cross: The Atonement in New Testament and Contemporary Contexts.* Downers Grove: InterVarsity, 2000.

Green, Joel B., and Max Turner, eds. *Between Two Horizons: Spanning New Testament Studies and Systematic Theology.* Grand Rapids: Eerdmans, 2000.

Greene, Colin. "Is the Message of the Cross Good News for the Twentieth Century?" In *Atonement Today: A Symposium at St. John's College, Nottingham* (ed. John Goldingay; London: SPCK, 1995), 222-39.

Grieb, A. Katherine. *The Story of Romans: A Narrative Defense of God's Righteousness.* Louisville: Westminster John Knox, 2002.

Gunton, Colin. *The Actuality of the Atonement: A Study of Metaphor, Rationality, and the Christian Tradition.* Grand Rapids: Eerdmans, 1989.

————. *Christ and Creation.* Grand Rapids: Eerdmans, 1992.

————. *The Triune Creator: A Historical and Systematic Study.* Grand Rapids: Eerdmans, 1998.

Gutiérrez, Gustavo. *A Theology of Liberation: History, Politics, and Salvation.* Second ed., Maryknoll: Orbis, 1988.

Harink, Douglas. *Paul among the Postliberals: Pauline Theology beyond Christendom and Modernity.* Grand Rapids: Brazos, 2003.

Harrill, J. Albert. *The Manumission of Slaves in Early Christianity.* HUTh 32; Tübingen: Mohr, 1995.

Harris, Murray. *Colossians and Philemon.* Exegetical Guide to the Greek New Testament; Grand Rapids: Eerdmans, 1991.

Harris, W. V. *Ancient Literacy.* Cambridge: Harvard University Press, 1989.

Hays, Richard B. *The Faith of Jesus Christ: The Narrative Substructure of Galatians 3:1-4:11.* Second ed., Grand Rapids: Eerdmans, 2001.

———. *The Moral Vision of the New Testament: Community, Cross, New Creation. A Contemporary Introduction to New Testament Ethics.* San Francisco: HarperSanFrancisco, 1996.

Hick, John. *God and the Universe of Faiths.* London: Macmillan, 1973.

Hooker, Morna. *Not Ashamed of the Gospel: New Testament Interpretations of the Death of Christ.* Grand Rapids: Eerdmans, 1994.

———. "Were There False Teachers in Colossae?" In *Christ and Spirit in the New Testament. Studies in Honour of C. F. D. Moule* (ed. B. Lindars and S. S. Smalley; Cambridge: University Press, 1973), 315-31.

Houlden, J. L. *Paul's Letters from Prison.* Pelican Commentaries; Philadelphia: Westminster, 1970.

Hubbard, Moyer. *New Creation in Paul's Letters and Thought.* SNTSMS 119; Cambridge: Cambridge University Press, 2002.

Hultgren, Arland. *Christ and His Benefits: Christology and Redemption in the New Testament.* Philadelphia: Fortress, 1987.

Hurtado, Larry. *Lord Jesus Christ: Devotion to Jesus in Earliest Christianity.* Grand Rapids: Eerdmans, 2003.

Jenson, Robert W. *On Thinking the Human: Resolutions of Difficult Notions.* Grand Rapids: Eerdmans, 2003.

Johnson, Luke T. *Faith's Freedom: A Classic Spirituality for Contemporary Christians.* Minneapolis: Fortress, 1990.

———. *Religious Experience in Earliest Christianity.* Minneapolis: Fortress, 1998.

Keck, Leander. *Paul and His Letters.* Proclamation Commentaries; second edition, Philadelphia: Fortress, 1988.

———. "Toward the Renewal of New Testament Christology." *NTS* 32 (1986): 362-77.

Kelsey, David H. "Human Being." In *Christian Theology: An Introduction to Its Traditions and Tasks* (ed. Peter C. Hodgson and Robert H. King; Philadelphia: Fortress, 1982), 141-67.

Kennedy, George. *New Testament Interpretation through Rhetorical Criticism.* Chapel Hill: University of North Carolina Press, 1984.

Knox, John. *Philemon among the Letters of Paul.* Second ed., Nashville: Abingdon, 1959.

Lampe, Peter. "Keine 'Slavenflucht' des Onesimus." *ZNW* 76 (1985): 135-37.

Lawson, John. *The Biblical Theology of St. Irenaeus.* London: Epworth, 1948.

Lightfoot, J. B. *St. Paul's Epistles to the Colossians and to Philemon.* Second ed., London: Macmillan, 1876.

Lincoln, Andrew T. "The Letter to the Colossians." In *The New Interpreter's Bible* (Nashville: Abingdon, 2000), 11:553-669.

————. "Liberation from the Powers: Supernatural Spirits or Societal Structures?" In *The Bible in Human Society* (ed. M. D. Carroll, David Clines, and Philip R. Davies; Sheffield: Sheffield Academic, 1995), 350-54.

Lohse, Eduard. *A Commentary on the Epistles to the Colossians and to Philemon.* Hermeneia; Philadelphia: Fortress, 1971.

Longenecker, Bruce, ed. *Narrative Dynamics in Paul: A Critical Assessment.* Louisville: Westminster John Knox, 2002.

Lyotard, Jean-François. *The Postmodern Condition: A Report on Knowledge, Theory, and History of Literature,* tr. Geoff Bennington and Brian Massumi. Minneapolis: University of Minnesota Press, 1984.

MacIntyre, Alasdair. *After Virtue: A Study in Moral Theory.* Notre Dame: University of Notre Dame Press, 1981; second ed., 1984.

————. *Three Rival Versions of Moral Enquiry.* Notre Dame: University of Notre Dame Press, 1990.

Mandela, Nelson. *Long Walk to Freedom.* Boston: Little, Brown, 1994.

Martin, Dale B. *Slavery as Salvation: The Metaphor of Slavery in Pauline Christianity.* New Haven: Yale University Press, 1990.

Martin, Ralph. *Reconciliation: A Study of Paul's Theology.* Rev. ed., Grand Rapids: Zondervan, 1990.

Martyn, J. Louis, "The Abrahamic Covenant, Christ, and the Church." In *Theological Issues in the Letters of Paul* (Nashville: Abingdon, 1997), 161-75.

Mays, James L. *The Lord Reigns: A Theological Handbook to the Psalms.* Louisville: Westminster John Knox, 1994.

McGinn, Bernard, and John Meyendorff, eds. *Christian Spirituality: Origins to the Twelfth Century.* World Spirituality 16; New York: Crossroad, 1985.

Meeks, Wayne A. "'To Walk Worthily of the Lord': Moral Formation in the Pauline School Exemplified by the Letter to the Colossians." In *Hermes and Athena: Biblical Exegesis and Philosophical Theology* (ed. E. Stump and T. P. Flint; Notre Dame: University of Notre Dame Press, 1993), 37-58.

Mertens, Herman-Emiel. *Not the Cross, but the Crucified: An Essay in Soteriology.* Grand Rapids: Eerdmans, 1992.

Meye, Robert P. "Pauline Spirituality." In *Dictionary of Paul and His Letters* (Downers Grove: InterVarsity, 1993), 906-16.

Middleton, J. Richard, and Brian J. Walsh. *Truth Is Stranger than It Used to Be: Biblical Faith in a Postmodern Age.* Downers Grove: InterVarsity, 1995.

Mitchell, Margaret. *Paul and the Rhetoric of Reconciliation: An Exegetical Investigation of the Language and Composition of 1 Corinthians.* Louisville: Westminster/John Knox, 1993.

Moule, C. F. D. *The Epistles of Paul the Apostle to the Colossians and to Philemon.* The Cambridge Greek Testament Commentary; Cambridge: Cambridge University Press, 1957.

Mouw, Richard J. *"He Shines in All That's Fair": Culture and Common Grace.* Grand Rapids: Eerdmans, 2001.

Newbigin, Lesslie. *The Gospel in a Pluralist Society.* Grand Rapids: Eerdmans, 1989.

————. *The Light Has Come: An Exposition of the Fourth Gospel.* Grand Rapids: Eerdmans, 1982.

Newman, C. Carey. *Paul's Glory Christology: Tradition and Rhetoric.* Supplements to *Novum Testamentum,* 69; Leiden: Brill, 1992.

O'Brien, Peter T. *Colossians, Philemon.* Word Biblical Commentary 44; Waco: Word, 1982.

Pannenberg, Wolfhart. "Can Christianity Do without an Eschatology?" In *The Christian Hope* (London: SPCK, 1970), 25-34.

Petersen, Norman. *Rediscovering Paul: Philemon and the Sociology of Paul's Narrative World.* Philadelphia: Fortress, 1985.

Peterson, Eugene H. *The Message Remix: The Bible in Contemporary Language.* Colorado Springs: NavPress, 2003.

Plevnik, Joseph. "The Center of Pauline Theology." *CBQ* 51 (1989): 461-78.

Rapske, Brian. *The Book of Acts and Paul in Roman Custody.* Grand Rapids: Eerdmans, 1994.

Ridderbos, Herman. *Paul: An Outline of His Theology.* Grand Rapids: Eerdmans, 1975.

Sachs, John Randall. *The Christian Vision of Humanity.* Collegeville: Liturgical, 1991.

Sanders, E. P. *Judaism: Practice and Belief, 63 BCE–66 CE.* London: SCM, 1992.

————. *Paul and Palestinian Judaism: A Comparison of Patterns of Religion.* Philadelphia: Fortress, 1977.

Schüssler Fiorenza, Elisabeth. *But She Said: Feminist Practices of Biblical Interpretation.* Boston: Beacon, 1993.

Schweitzer, Albert. *The Mysticism of Paul the Apostle.* New York: Macmillan, 1955.

Schweizer, Eduard. "Die Weltlichkeit des Neuen Testaments. Die Haustafeln." In *Beiträge zur alttestamentlichen Theologie* (ed. H. Donner, et al.; Göttingen: Vandenhoeck und Ruprecht, 1977), 397-413.

Scroggs, Robin. *The Last Adam: A Study in Pauline Anthropology.* Philadelphia: Fortress, 1966.

Sittler, Joseph. "Called to Unity." *Ecumenical Review* 14 (1962): 177-87.

Stendahl, Krister. "Call Rather than Conversion." In *Paul among Jews and Gentiles and Other Essays* (Philadelphia: Fortress, 1976), 7-23.

Stott, John R. W., ed. *Free to Be Different: Varieties of Human Behaviour.* Grand Rapids: Eerdmans, 1985.

Stuckenbruck, Loren. *Angel Veneration and Christology.* WUNT 2/70; Tübingen: Mohr, 1995.

Stuhlmacher, Peter. *Der Brief an Philemon.* Evangelisch-Katholischer Kommentar zum Neuen Testament; Zurich: Benziger; Neukirchen: Neukirchener, 1975.

Thistlethwaite, Susan Brooks. "Every Two Minutes: Battered Women and Feminist Interpretation." In *Feminist Interpretation of the Bible* (ed. Letty M. Russell; Philadelphia: Westminster, 1985), 96-107.

Thompson, John L. *Writing the Wrongs: Women of the Old Testament among Biblical Commentators from Philo through the Reformation.* Oxford Studies in Historical Theology; Oxford: Oxford University Press, 2001.

Thompson, Marianne Meye. *The God of the Gospel of John.* Grand Rapids: Eerdmans, 2001.

—————. *Promise of the Father: Jesus and God in the New Testament*. Louisville: Westminster John Knox, 2000.

Thompson, Michael B. "The Holy Internet: Communication between Churches in the First Christian Generation." In *The Gospels for All Christians: Rethinking the Gospel Audiences* (ed. Richard Bauckham; Grand Rapids: Eerdmans, 1998), 49-70.

Volf, Miroslav. *Exclusion and Embrace: A Theological Exploration of Identity, Otherness, and Reconciliation*. Nashville: Abingdon, 1996.

Von Balthasar, Hans Urs. *Mysterium Paschale*, tr. Aidan Nichols. Edinburgh: Clark, 1990.

Wall, Robert W. *Colossians and Philemon*. Downers Grove: InterVarsity, 1993.

Walsh, Brian, and Sylvia Keesmat. *Colossians Remixed: Subverting the Empire*. Downers Grove: InterVarsity, 2004.

Watson, Francis. *Text, Church and World: Biblical Interpretation in Theological Perspective*. Grand Rapids: Eerdmans, 1994.

Westphal, Merold. "Postmodernism and the Gospel: Onto-theology, Metanarrative, and Perspectivism." *Perspectives* 15 (2000): 6-10. Reprinted in *Christianity and the Postmodern Turn* (ed. Myron B. Penner; Grand Rapids: Brazos, 2005), 141-53.

White, John L. *Light from Ancient Letters*. Philadelphia: Fortress, 1986.

Wiedemann, Thomas, ed. *Greek and Roman Slavery*. Baltimore: Johns Hopkins University Press, 1981.

Wink, Walter. *Engaging the Powers: Discernment and Resistance in a World of Domination*. Philadelphia: Fortress, 1992.

—————. *Naming the Powers: The Language of Power in the New Testament*. Philadelphia: Fortress, 1984.

—————. *Unmaking the Powers: The Invisible Forces That Determine Human Existence*. Philadelphia: Fortress, 1986.

Winter, Sara. "Paul's Letter to Philemon." *NTS* 33 (1987): 1-15.

Wright, N. T. *The Climax of the Covenant: Christ and the Law in Pauline Theology*. Edinburgh: Clark, 1991; Minneapolis: Fortress, 1992.

—————. *The Epistles of Paul to the Colossians and to Philemon*. Tyndale New Testament Commentaries; Grand Rapids: Eerdmans, 1986.

Yeago, David. "The New Testament and the Nicene Dogma: A Contribution to the Recovery of Theological Exegesis." *Pro Ecclesia* 3 (1994): 152-64.

Yoder, John Howard. *The Politics of Jesus*. Second edition, Grand Rapids: Eerdmans, 1994.

Index of Names

Index of Scripture and Other Ancient Texts